Police

in

America

Note: The full text of the ABA Standards (see pages 291–299) are printed in 17 volumes. They may be ordered from ABA Circulation Department, 1155 E. 60th St., Chicago, Ill. 60637. Cost is $3.25 for a single volume; $38 for a set of 17 volumes; $2.25 ea. for bulk orders of 10–24 of the same title, or $1.75 ea. for 25 or more of the same title.

Police in America

edited by

JEROME H. SKOLNICK
University of California, Berkeley

THOMAS C. GRAY
Golden Gate University, San Francisco

EDUCATIONAL ASSOCIATES
a division of Little, Brown and Company   Boston

PREFACE

During the past decade the rise in crime, increasing fear of physical assault, and assertiveness and militancy of minority and student groups have resulted in greater visibility and involvement of the police in American social life, particularly in cities. Beginning early in the 1960s, when the reports of several national crime commissions made it clear that enlightened police response in strict accordance with the law was not to be taken for granted, the propriety of police response and their knowledge of the problems underlying crime, public safety, and public protest came under review and criticism. Major questions were posed regarding the structure and functions of departmental organization, the quality and direction of police training, and the proper use of police discretion. These factors were seen to bear directly on such police practices as field and station house interrogation, use of firearms, riot control, and surveillance of groups and individuals. These practices, in turn, generated public inquiry and political debate about the relationship and accountability of the police to the community.

The police were not dispassionate during this process. Police associations and unions began asserting the rights of their members for higher wages and better working conditions. Simultaneously they sought to develop and sustain distinctive interpretations of the causes and prevention of crime and public disorder, interpretations that often differed sharply from the findings and explanations of various researchers and commissions. At the same time, there developed considerable and important differences of observation, analysis, and interpretation within police circles and among researchers.

This book of readings is an attempt to reflect some of the complexity and variety of social issues and demands faced by police in the contemporary United States. To accomplish this goal, we have drawn on readings from history, scholarly research, research commissioned by government agencies and police departments, and writings of policemen themselves describing in their own words the world of the police. Just as police, researchers, and commissions do not always agree on the nature, causes, and prevention of crime, we, too, sometimes differ. Nevertheless, we both agree on the importance of the issues addressed in these readings and believe the readings themselves offer a useful basis for constructive discussion.

The readings reflect our own experience in teaching introductory college students and police recruits, advanced college students and working police, doctoral candidates and police executives, and therefore they should be of interest to both working police and police recruits, as well as to students of law enforcement and related subjects. We hope that by offering a variety of perceptions of the social reality of the policeman's world, we will elicit thoughtful discussion of subjects that are inherently controversial. To that end, each chapter is preceded by an introduction that suggests discussion topics for both students and teachers on the major issues raised by the readings.

Finally, we both believe that there is no authoritative perspective on the police or policing. We further believe that the issues presented in this book should be discussed by citizens and police. We hope these readings and questions will provide a well-rounded and stimulating introduction to the history and future of police in America.

In developing our ideas on police we have learned much from numerous students and law enforcement officials who have given us their time, their cooperation, and the challenge and stimulation of disagreement. We are especially grateful to the men and women of the Oakland Police Department, and particularly to former Chief Charles Gain, who believes in and practices research and discussion; and to the staff of the Center for the Study of Law and Society, University of California, Berkeley, in particular, Kelly Lee, Emily Knapp, and Gary Lee, for their capable assistance. Our wives, Arlene Skolnick and Donna Gray, are both professionals who know what it means to get a job done and what it takes to do it well. We appreciate their knowledge and understanding.

Jerome H. Skolnick
Berkeley, California

Thomas C. Gray
San Francisco, California

CONTENTS

INTRODUCTION: Professional Police in a Free Society

THE HISTORICAL BACKGROUND

A legislator once pointed out that in the previous seven years the population in a given area had increased only 15 percent, while crime had risen 41 percent. He also deplored the existence of an army of trained and hardened criminals who lived in the city and the sufferings they imposed on respectable members of the community. The speech sounds as though it might have been made yesterday. Actually, it was given in the English Parliament on April 15, 1829, when Sir Robert Peel introduced his "Bill for Improving the Police In and Near the Metropolis." [1]

The problems faced by England in the early nineteenth century were remarkably similar to those we face in the United States during the latter half of the twentieth. It was an age of rapid technological progress, especially in manufacturing. In addition to major economic changes, political unrest and agitation, this period witnessed the emergence of some of our democratic notions and basic institutions of freedom and equality, in particular, the rule of law.

Economic hardships following the Napoleonic wars precipitated riots and demonstrations, which led to tight restrictions upon civil liberties whenever dissent seemed likely to spread. In 1817, only twelve years before the creation of the London Metropolitan Police, the Habeas Corpus Act was suspended and other restrictive measures passed, including a tightening up of the control of public meetings. Following the "Peterloo massacre" in 1819, where hundreds of people were killed or injured during a protest against the Corn Laws and other Parliamentary abuses, the army was increased by 10,000 men, and the Six Acts known as "gag acts" were passed. According to the leading British historian of police, Charles Reith, these onerous restrictions did not solve the problems; in fact, they only created greater mistrust in the government:

> The Six Acts prohibited drilling and limited public meetings; imposed a fourpenny stamp on all periodical publications, including newspapers; authorized the seizure of anything that could be called a seditious or blasphemous libel; and allowed magistrates to search houses for arms. Their net effect was to suppress the reading of all forms of

Revised by Jerome H. Skolnick and based upon his pamphlet "Professional Police in a Free Society," *The National Conference of Christians and Jews,* 1968.

political expression and complaint of any kind of privilege of the powerful. They greatly increased the prevailing indignation against the Government, and together with the general effect of Peterloo, did much to shake faith in the principles of old-fashioned Toryism in thinking circles, especially those of the younger generations at the universities.[2]

In addition to the similarities regarding problems of order, there are startling resemblances between English laborers of the nineteenth century and black Americans of the twentieth. Like the black American, the British worker was considered by many to belong to an inferior class of people. Note the attitude of J. E. Taylor, editor of the *Manchester Guardian,* in 1838: "Let the people have a good education," he declared, "and, with the habits it would induce, the bribe of the intoxicating draught would be less powerful. Till then the elective franchise could not with safety be extended." [3] The right to vote was not given to British workers until The Second Reform Bill and was first used in 1868. John Stuart Mill, whose writings were widely influential among the educated during the 1860s and 1870s, laid the intellectual groundwork in bringing about suffrage for the English worker. He believed in complete democracy in the sense that every man and woman should take part in both national and local elections.[4]

Like the British worker, then, the black American has responded to social, economic, and political deprivation with increased militancy and the threat of revolution. The nineteenth-century British worker and the twentieth-century black American awakened the moral consciences of their nations, especially among intellectuals and the younger generation in the universities. Eventually, their demonstrations against economic hardship and political disenfranchisement came to be recognized as legitimate; at the same time, such demonstrations helped to create the need for new concepts of policing.

Long before he introduced his police bill, Sir Robert Peel, as governor of colonial Ireland, had experimented with both the legal and law enforcement systems. As a result of his experiments, he wisely recognized two fundamentals concerning police in a free society. First, he realized that police can be neither effective nor just if the laws they are required to enforce are so sweeping in their scope, and so onerous in their penalties, that they cannot receive wide public support. Peel perceived, says Charles Reith:

> ... that Police reform and Criminal Law reform were wholly inter-
> dependent; that a reformed Criminal Code required a reformed police

to enable it to function beneficially; and that a reformed police could not function effectively until the criminal and other laws which they were to enforce had been made capable of being respected by the public, and administered with simplicity and clarity. He postponed for some years his boldly announced plans for police, and concentrated his energies on reform of the law.[5]

The major thrust of Peel's reform of the criminal law was *to decriminalize,* to limit its scope and to reduce penalties drastically. For example, he abolished the death penalty for over a hundred offenses and removed numerous criminal penalties entirely.[6]

Second, both Peel and Colonel Charles Rowan, whom Peel appointed Commissioner of the New Police, were acutely aware, as a result of the Irish experience, that the support of the general public was absolutely necessary if police were to carry out their duties effectively. The Army, which formerly had been responsible for public order, was hated by the populace. Soldiers had been brought in to quell disturbances, but they had no understanding of the causes of the demonstrations and little sympathy with the demonstrators. As a result, their presence often made matters worse. They might have put out the existing fire, but instead they left greater fuel for future conflagrations. Therefore, Peel and Rowan perceived the need for a *dignified and restrained demeanor* on the part of police. Thus, as officially published in 1829, the "Instructions" to constables contained the following statement:

> . . . there is no qualification more indispensable to a Police Officer than a perfect command of temper, never suffering himself to be moved in the slightest degree, by any language or threats that may be used; if he do his duty in a quiet and determined manner, such conduct will probably induce well-disposed by-standers to assist him should he require it.[7]

Peel and Rowan also understood the centrality and significance of police understanding of community norms. Accordingly, they strategically developed *personnel recruitment policies* to select officers with whom local residents would be likely to cooperate. Critchley writes:

> Among the flood of applications which poured into Scotland Yard, those from military men of senior rank and from people with influence in Government were generally turned down. From the start, the police was to be a homogeneous and democratic body, in tune with the people, understanding the people, belonging to the people, and drawing its strength from the people.[8]

Reith comments that Rowan, who drew up the "Instructions," could not have foreseen in 1829 the full extent of the growth that was to spring from the seed he was sowing. Reith describes this as "police power which is unique in history and throughout the world because it is derived not from fear but almost exclusively from public cooperation with the police, induced by them designedly by behavior which secures and maintains for them the approval, respect and affection of the public." [9]

Statements made in 1829 are not necessarily pertinent to the problems we face today, which are even more complex and difficult. However, they do suggest that complex and difficult problems are nothing new, and that in our imperfect world we may learn something from historical analogy.

THE POLICE IN THE UNITED STATES

Today, we face a crisis of innovation in conceptions of policing every bit as crucial, and as historically significant and opportune, as the challenge posed to English authority in the early nineteenth century. The report by the President's Commission on Law Enforcement and Administration of Justice (1967) raises this challenge in examining crime in a free society. This report recognizes that "crime" is a label attaching to all sorts of human activities, ranging from political demonstrations to robbery and rape, and that no single explanation will suffice to explain these very different sorts of activities.[10] Just as the criminologist cannot afford to make the mistake of trying to explain all "crime" in the same way, neither can the modern policeman usefully take the same attitude toward all acts currently designated as criminal.

In England, for example, working people violated numerous laws to obtain suffrage and to form unions. So have Americans in the labor movement. Similarly, activism and dissent by minority groups and youth have sometimes been accompanied by unlawful acts. The police must uphold the law, so the policeman's role often involves the onerous task of protecting the interests of the "haves" against those of the "have-nots." While the police may be required to perform such services, they must also develop a new recognition of and perspective on their historical role in a free society. Fundamentally, that perspective requires penetrating examination of the nature and meaning of criminal law, civil rights and liberties, and the role of dissent and change in a constitutional democracy.

Let us proceed, then, to examine police in America today in order to see how certain concepts of policing have emerged, what these concepts mean in practice, and how we can plan for policing in the future.

Accountability

Police services in the United States have never really enjoyed the opportunity to develop in an orderly and consistent fashion. Like the growth of the country itself, the growth of police was rapid and haphazard, its most striking gains being made in the twentieth century. In many areas, especially urban ones, the development of the police reflected the quality of local government, and it cannot be said that either provided much justification for civic pride. In England, by contrast, police accountability to the rule of law has enjoyed a long and continuing acceptance. It was reaffirmed in 1885 when the English jurist and historian, Frederic W. Maitland, wrote, "It will little avail us that our law about right and remedies, crimes and punishments, is as good as may be, if the law of civil and criminal procedure is clumsy and inefficient." [11]

This same tradition of the supremacy of the rule of law in a free society was eloquently put forth by the 1962 Royal Commission on the Police to refute the argument that a national police force would lead to a "police state" in Great Britain. The Commission report stated:

> In the countries to which the term police state is applied opprobriously, police power is controlled by the government; but they are so called not because the police are nationally organized, but because the government acknowledges no accountability to a democratically elected parliament, and the citizen cannot rely on the courts to protect him. Thus in such countries the foundations upon which British liberty rests do not exist. [12]

In reading about the American police, especially through the period of the 1930s, one feels that such high-minded concerns are largely irrelevant. Not that American police conformed to the rule of law—rather, their practices seemed so far out of line with what we would today accept as responsible police conduct that a writer who summarized the 1931 Wickersham Commission Report entitled his book *Our Lawless Police*. [13] The Commission, appointed by President Hoover, found practices so appalling and sadistic as to pose no intellectual issue for civilized men. It is one thing to talk quietly to a suspect without his counsel and artfully, perhaps even deceitfully, to persuade him to incriminate himself; it is quite another to beat a confession out of him by putting a telephone book on his head and pounding the book with a blackjack so it does not

leave marks. Both techniques may be illegal, but responsible police officials would not publicly support blackjack interrogation. On the other
hand, interrogation of suspects who lack knowledge of their right to
counsel has been a standard police technique. Only relatively recently
was it declared unconstitutional by the United States Supreme Court.[14]

For many observers, the question has been, not whether the police
proceed under due process of law, but whether they operate within the
bounds of civilized conduct. In the old-fashioned police department,
riddled with political appointees and working hand in hand with the
rackets, a reformer was not concerned mainly with the niceties of constitutional rights. This is not to suggest that the old-line police departments were entirely without virtue. In many respects, they enjoyed better
relations with the community than the efficient, technologically oriented
police departments of the present day. For example, old-time ward leaders served as informal complaint bureaus. An aggrieved citizen could
talk to his precinct captain or clubhouse leader. The political machine
was effective since police officials were indebted to its influence for their
own promotions. But the country began to outgrow this system rapidly,
and the old-line police department was already on its way out by the
time the Wickersham Commission Report was published.

As the citizenry faced the arbitrary use of "club, blackjack and gun,"
the police reformer's problem was to reduce gross brutality, which seems
traditionally to have been associated with corruption. Given this situation, it is not surprising that the solution to the "police problem" in
America has been conceived as changing the qualities of people, rather
than the basic philosophies of criminal law and policing. Raymond B.
Fosdick wrote in 1920, in a characteristically American passage on police
reform: "We are concerned with facts and conditions and not with theories and labels. It is not a matter of democracy, of caste, or birth, or
position, or anything else. It is solely a matter of finding the best possible
brains to handle a most difficult public task." [15]

Seen in this light, police reform means finding a new source of police
recruits and seeking ways of having the "right" sort of people in control.
"Reform" of police means increasing the efficiency of police personnel.
It is rarely recognized that the conduct of police may be related in a
fundamental way to the character and goals of the institution itself—the
duties police are called upon to perform, associated with the assumptions
underlying the system of legal justice—and that it may not be men who
are good or bad, so much as the premises and designs of the system in
which they find themselves. For example, V. A. Leonard, a specialist in

police administration, indicates how one premise—the conception of punishment as the basis of public order—invites objectionable side effects:

> A system of legal justice based upon the thesis of punishment has exerted a tremendously negative effect upon the professionalization of police service. As a corollary, the low quality of personnel required to exercise the police power under these conditions was not conducive to good public relations, with the result that a negative public opinion had been created. The withdrawal of public interest and support, together with public apathy and indifference, has further served to retard the advance toward professionalization. No less important has been the fact that a substandard personnel became easy prey for corrupt political figures and others in the community who profit when the risks associated with vice operations are reduced.[16]

Policing as a Profession

Surely it is unrealistic to consider policing as the equivalent of such traditional "learned" professions as science, law, and medicine. Indeed, that sort of rhetorical usage of the word "profession" may alienate the working policeman because he well understands that his job does not demand the years of formal education and tested knowledge of the scientist, physician, or attorney. But if the policeman is not a *learned* professional, it does not follow that he cannot aim to be a *trained* professional, that is, a highly skilled, knowledgeable, and thoughtful craftsman. When V. A. Leonard uses the term "professional," he at least means someone who takes his job seriously, is constantly trying to improve his own ability and that of others, and is honest and capable. This is what we mean by a "professional" golfer, or a "professional" auto racer, or "professional" football coach. Respected "learned" and "trained" professionals take their work seriously.

The policeman's tasks may be more important than those performed by other "trained" or learned professionals. His job is vital to the continued functioning of society and to the personal interests of the citizens with whom he comes in daily contact, either as defendants or as those requesting help. Patrol police perform a service operation for a variety of emergencies, while the total police department—including patrol—provides an apprehension and evidence-gathering service for the criminal courts.

Given this broad, powerful, and highly responsible scope of police duties, there is a further and more fundamental issue: the lawful *authority* for police work. For example, police might be working under a totalitarian regime, where their principal responsibilities would be to provide emergency service, make arrests, and gather evidence in line with a dictatorial authority structure. But police in the United States serve under federal and state constitutional authority. For U.S. police, there is a special question: What should the concept "police professional" suggest in a society committed to constitutional democracy, which includes the notions of citizen participation in government, the accountability of public officials to the people, and legal limits upon official discretion? In the remainder of this Introduction it will be proposed that for modern American police, the idea of professionalism needs to be developed around four areas: (1) attitudes toward the rule of law, (2) accountability to the community, (3) limitations on the scope and severity of substantive criminal law, and (4) transformation of formal and informal police organization.

TOWARD A NEW PROFESSIONALISM

Professional Police and the Rule of Law

The criminal law contains a set of rules for maintaining social order. This arsenal comprises the *substantive* part of the criminal law—that is, the elements of crime, the principles under which the accused is to be held accountable for alleged crime, the principles justifying the enactment of specific prohibitions, and the crimes themselves. Sociologists usually concentrate here, asking how well this control system operates and analyzing the conditions for achieving its intended goals and the circumstances rendering it least efficient.

Another part of criminal law regulates official conduct. Involved here are such matters as the law of search, the law of arrest, the elements and degree of proof, the right to counsel, the nature of a lawful accusation of crime, and the fairness of trial. The procedures of the criminal law, therefore, stress the protection of individual liberties *within* a system of social order. Law is therefore not merely an instrument of order, but may be its adversary. Certain communities may appear disorderly, such as "bohemian" communities valuing diversity but nevertheless maintaining a substantial degree of legality. The converse may also be found: order may be maintained, but the policy and practice of legality is absent. The totalitarian social system, whether in a nation or an institution, is a situation of order without rule of law. This situation is probably best illustrated by martial rule, where military authority may claim and exercise the power of amnesty and detention without warrant. If, in addition, the writ of habeas corpus—the right to question these acts—is suspended, as it typically is under martial rule, the executive can exercise arbitrary powers.

The phrase "law and order" is misleading because it diverts attention from substantial incompatibilities existing between the two ideas. Order *under* law is concerned, not merely with achieving regularized social activity, but with the *means* used to promote peaceable behavior—certainly with procedure, but also with the substantive law itself. For example, a legislature could not lawfully designate epilepsy as a crime, even though an epileptic seizure might disturb public order. Although drug addicts may be a menace to the community, a law making it a crime to *be* an addict has been declared unconstitutional. This example, purposely selected from substantive criminal law, indicates that conceptions of legality apply to substantive law as well as to the more traditional realm of criminal procedure. In short, "law" and "order" are frequently found to be in opposition precisely because law implies considered restraint upon rules and procedures for achieving order.

In their commendable attempt to raise the standards of police conduct, leading police officials have increasingly advocated a conception of professionalism based on managerial efficiency and organizational interest. This is not surprising. The agency of enforcement cannot be expected to generate its own limitations. Administrators typically and understandably try to conceal the knowledge of their operations so that they may regulate themselves. But democratic police organizations are not merely administrative bureaucracies. They are also charged with strengthening the rule of law in society. They exercise broad discretionary powers in administering criminal *justice*. For professionalism to resolve conflicts between order and legality, it must be based upon a deeper and more thoughtful set of values than currently prevails in police literature.[17]

A new professionalism must convey a philosophy—that police should be as fully dedicated to achieving legality as to controlling misconduct. Professionalism is not merely obtaining new police cars or more sophisticated technical equipment or recruiting more highly educated applicants. Professionalism should rest on the *values of a democratic legal order,* rather than on technological proficiency.

No thoughtful person can believe that such a transformation is easy. In an article estimating the prospects for the rule of law in the Soviet Union, Leonard Schapiro has written, "It is perhaps difficult for dictators to get accustomed to the idea that the main purpose of law is, in fact, to make their task more difficult." [18] It is sometimes hard for police in a democracy to accept this idea. In the same article, Schapiro reports the case of two professors who advocated the adoption of certain principles of "bourgeois" law and criminal procedure, arguing that observance of legal norms must prevail over expediency in government legislation and administration. They were officially criticized in the Soviet Union for misinterpreting "the role of legal science in the solution of the practical tasks of government," a criticism not so different from the sort sometimes leveled by American police against professors who emphasize the importance of civil liberties.

If the police are ever to develop a conception of *legal* as opposed to *managerial* professionalism, two conditions must be met: First, police must accustom themselves to the seemingly paradoxical yet fundamental idea of the rule of law—"that the main purpose of law is, in fact, to make their task more difficult." Second, a majority of the community must reward police for observing constitutional guarantees, instead of regarding police solely as an enforcement institution. In practice, the reverse has been true.

Professional Police and the Minority Community

A posthumously published article by Professor Edmond Cahn distinguishes between "the imperial or official perspective" on law and the "consumer perspective." The "official" perspective, according to the author, is so called "because it has been largely determined by the dominant interests of rulers, governors and other officials." In contrast, the "consumer" perspective reflects the interests and opinion of those who are regulated by the law. Cahn adds, "A free and open society calls on its officials to perform their functions according to the perspective of its consumers," in this case, the accused and the accuser.[19]

Legality alone is not sufficient to bridge the gulf between police and the minority groups in our communities. Emphasis upon legality will help —it will cut down on unreasonable police interrogations, detentions, friskings, and other invasions of privacy. In addition, the idea of the police role must conform with reality. Police perform social agency activities whether they like it or not, and for this reason it would be useful for police to understand why a certain group tends toward crime.

One of the most heralded innovations in policing was the development of community relations programs. These signified recognition of a double reality. First, urban police operate in nonwhite communities, alien to the social backgrounds of most police. Second, in these communities police are often called upon to perform social services. It is instructive to examine part of the history of one of these programs to understand their problems and possibilities.

In May 1962, San Francisco Police Chief Thomas Cahill, acting on the recommendation of such civic groups as the National Association for the Advancement of Colored People and the National Conference of Christians and Jews, established a community relations bureau. It was designed to create a better understanding and closer relationship between the police department and the community and to promote greater public cooperation with the police department.

Implicit in the creation of this unit was a recognition that changing social needs required a more expansive concept of police work. The idea was that police work should also include the *prevention* of crime. More explicitly, the establishment of the bureau gave organizational meaning to the notion that police prevent crime not only by threat of punishment but also by a sympathetic understanding of residents of high-crime areas. Crime is not, in this view, simply an act of perverted will, but a product of economic disadvantage and social frustration; thus, the police reduce crime by ameliorating economic and social handicaps. In the process, community relations units were intended to reduce the social isolation of minority communities from the police. Paradoxically, their existence may have exacerbated isolation and hostility. How that can happen may be observed in the history of San Francisco's Police Community Relations Unit.

The San Francisco unit was one of the earliest and most promising. Its waning influence reflected a struggle between two opposing interpretations of the police role and its relationship to the community. The opposing interpretations created two factions. Each developed a power base to undermine the validity of the position of the opposing side. The success of the Police Community Relations Unit depended upon the sympathy of the Chief of Police. He mediated between supporters of the PCR Unit and supporters of more traditional conceptions of law enforcement. When he supported the unit, and its concepts, the unit was able to function successfully. When, with time, his enthusiasm for the unit waned, the influence of the unit diminished until it could no longer perform as it once had.

For anyone familiar with the culture of police, police resentment of a PCR unit was understandable. First, the establishment of the unit constituted acknowledgment that the Police Department had been less than successful in minority relations. Governmental agencies are usually reluctant to acknowledge failure and institute remedies. In 1962, however, the political climate encouraged innovations in the area of race relations. The Kennedy Administration was in power, and new national victories were being made in civil rights. San Francisco voters seemed receptive to innovation even if the overwhelming majority of the police were not. Thus, the unit was established despite hostility from most policemen.

Although the first battle of new against old was won, subsequent history of the unit revealed that rather than giving in, the opposition rallied increasing support—the San Francisco Police Department Community Relations Unit was both a microcosm and a barometer of what was to follow in race relations throughout the country: as national politics became more polarized, so too did the politics surrounding the unit.

Although the unit was the smallest in the Police Department, it grew to 13 men, all of whom considered themselves to be specialists in the field of community relations. What community relations meant was, in fact, ambiguous. Even within the unit, it meant different things to different officers. To two officers working with drug addicts, alcoholics, male and female prostitutes, and homosexuals, it meant informing them of their rights. It also included talking to them for hours in a Central City Economic Opportunity Office and trying to get them jobs. To another the program meant bringing the Negro into "focus." To others it meant spending time with the youth of the area, in groups such as Citizens Alert and Youth for Service, trying to sound out the problems of those dwelling in the Hunters Point area, an economically depressed minority section of San Francisco.

The initial problem of the unit persisted: how to maintain its identity as a police organization and at the same time to win the confidence of the minority group population—which included not only Negroes but Mexican Americans, Filipinos, and Orientals and marginal groups such as prostitutes, homosexuals, and hippies, each considered a police problem. As the duties and responsibilities of the men in the PCR Unit increased, so too did the hostility of the rest of the police force.

The PCR Unit suffered from the stigma of deviating from standard police practices. The role of the PCR man was often described as a "social work" role by other police. Many members of the police force mistakenly equated social worker with socialist and communist. At a session of the 8th Annual National Conference of Christians and Jews

Institute, one of the captains present referred to the PCR Unit as the "Commie Relations Unit," a term that became the usual derisive one used by most San Francisco police.

Police resentment may be, however, attributed to a more fundamental concern. The idea of social work activities for police undercuts the basic conception of the policeman's role. Police like to see themselves as strong, aggressive, masculine hunters protecting the weak. In oversimplified terms, they are the good guys who beat up the bad guys who threaten the littler people. But the social worker role requires that police reconceptualize their role and consequently their identities. They must be understanding as well as tough, sensitive as well as courageous. One policeman, commenting on the unit, stated: "If I had wanted to be a social worker, I would have gone to social work school. I wanted to be a cop and sociologists can't come around and tell me about being a social worker. I'm a cop, that's all I'm going to be."

Probably the greatest barrier to acceptance within the department was the informal complaint procedure developed by the PCR Unit. Because it was responsive to the concerns of minority-group members, in fact, the PCR Unit became an informal complaint bureau, not only for complaints directed against the police but also for complaints directed against other public agencies such as the Fire Department, the Welfare Department, and the schools. As it gained the confidence of the minority group community, the San Francisco PCR Unit became the informal "ombudsman" of the City of San Francisco. The police outside the unit tended to regard the PCR Unit as an internal security force. This notion, coupled with the fact that PCR men had so little contact with the rest of the force, caused the PCR Unit to be regarded as a suspicious, aloof, mysterious, and probably subversive branch of the Police Department.

In fact, PCR units are always in a dilemma—they cannot function smoothly. If they are in complete harmony with their departments, they cannot reflect community antagonisms. The purpose of police-community relations is not simply "public relations" in the sense of advertising the police department or of improving the police "image." Nor is it simply an emergency device to be used in time of trouble, to "cool off" an angry neighborhood. To be useful, a police-community relations program should serve as a means for opening up the police service to suggestions and criticism from those they police. By permitting the citizens who come into the most frequent contact with police to criticize that service, and by requiring the police to be accountable to the communities that are policed, these programs should ultimately strengthen the department.

But in the short run, they make life uncomfortable. In this regard, the words of the President's Commission on Law Enforcement and Administration of Justice are as relevant for the 1970s as they were for the 1960s:

> Improving community relations involves not only instituting programs and changing procedures and practices, but re-examining fundamental attitudes. The police will have to learn to listen patiently and understandingly to people who are openly critical of them or hostile to them, since those people are precisely the ones with whom relations need to be improved. Quite evidently, it is not easy for a man who was brought up to obey the law and to respect law enforcement officers to maintain his poise and equanimity when he is denounced, sneered at, or threatened. However, policemen must do just that if police-citizen relationships on the street are to become person-to-person encounters rather than the black-versus-white, oppressed-versus-oppressor confrontations they too often are.
>
> The police must adapt themselves to the rapid changes in patterns of behavior that are taking place in America. This is a time when traditional ideas and institutions are being challenged with increasing insistence. The poor want an equal opportunity to earn a share of America's wealth. Minority groups want a final end to the discrimination they have been subject to for centuries. Young people, the fastest growing segment of the population, have more freedom than they have ever had. The police must be willing and able to deal understandingly and constructively with these often unsettling, even threatening, changes.[20]

Police Professionalism and Overcriminalization

Most criminal court cases involve violations of moral norms—prostitution, gambling, drunkenness, drug use—or instances of annoying behavior under the "disturbing the peace" catchall. The enforcement of conventional morality typically produces two closely related consequences. One is a more threatening environment for the policeman. The other is the development of organized crime for selling forbidden goods and services. We have already noted that the problem of maintaining order through law is complicated by the fact that different people may have different ideas of proper social order. Some believe that proper social order is achieved when people dress alike, think alike, actively participate in programs of self-improvement, and refrain from activities that may be harmful to them. According to that conception, many "social problems" could be included in the category of criminal behavior, including drinking alcoholic beverages, using drugs or marihuana, smoking cigarettes, eating cholesterol, or dealing in foreign currency. The question ultimately rests on the extent of the social contract, the point at which individual liberty prevails over societal needs as these are defined by authorities.

In a totalitarian society there is little focus on individuality and much on general social requirements. As a result, the *potential* criminal population rises, and with it, increased contact by the populace with those officials charged with reducing criminality. By contrast, in nontotalitarian societies most citizens have few contacts with public officials. "Their private lives," writes a student of citizenship, "are mainly outside the ken of government, and ready compliance with laws or rules further minimizes the occasions for legal and administrative actions." [21] If we could assume that we actually live in a society whose citizens subscribe overwhelmingly to a similar morality, *conventional* morality would indeed be, as the term suggests, *customary* morality. All evidence, however, is to the contrary. The United States is a nation of diversity—of ethnic, regional, and generational differences. We cannot through *legal moralism* coerce an entire nation to virtue as virtue is defined by those holding political power at a given time.

One of the consequences of *legal moralism* is to make the policeman's job more difficult. The extension of criminal sanctions beyond the area of assaults against persons and property into the area of so-called conventional morality increased the "production quotas" for police. As a representative of the FBI stated to the President's Commission on Law Enforcement and Administration of Justice:

> The criminal code of any jurisdiction tends to make a crime of everything that people are against, without regard to enforceability, changing social concepts, etc. . . . The result is that the criminal code becomes society's trash bin. The police have to rummage around in this material and are expected to prevent everything that is unlawful. They cannot do so because many of the things prohibited are simply beyond enforcement, both because of human inability to enforce the law and because, as in the case of prohibition, society legislates one way and acts another way. If we would restrict our definition of criminal offenses in many areas, we would get the criminal codes back to the point where they prohibit specific, carefully defined, and

serious conduct, and the police could then concentrate on enforcing the law in that context and would not waste its officers by trying to enforce the unenforceable, as is done now.[22]

Such an increase in jurisdiction not only makes the police the guardian of public morality but also increases the danger of police work. The actually assaultive must be guarded against, but a population of the potentially assaultive is also created—those who will attack others to continue their illegal activities. Consequently, by enlarging police jurisdiction, society alters the police environment. It is seen as, and actually becomes, more threatening. Furthermore, if the policeman's job is to observe deviations from "normality," a more rigid definition of normality will make him more watchful and suspicious.

Legal moralism also feeds organized crime. This has been the American experience following the prohibition of alcohol, opiates, and gambling. Forbidding an activity offers a "protective tariff" to those engaged in the sale of illicit goods and services, thereby increasing the profits of their activities. The late Professor Herbert Packer of the Stanford Law School has described the operation of this tariff in narcotics as follows:

> As we know from current experience . . . people go on buying narcotics even if they have to steal money to pay the price. Economic theory explains this phenomenon by introducing the concept of elasticity of demand. It is only when the demand is quite elastic that increases in price will reduce the amount demanded. People who are willing to pay two thousand dollars for a car will not ordinarily want the same car if its price is suddenly doubled. But when the demand is inelastic, when the commodity is something that people want so badly that they will pay almost any price to get it, if its sale is illegal, the crime tariff goes into operation. Regardless of what we think we are trying to do, if we make it illegal to traffic in commodities for which there is an inelastic demand, the actual effect is to secure a kind of monopoly profit to the entrepreneur who is willing to break the law.[23]

An additional consequence of legal moralism is police corruption. As New York's Knapp Commission Report made clear, such corruption is not attributable to the presence of isolated "rotten apples" in the police force. Rather, corruption is based on a combination of illicit connections with organized criminals and a widespread system of payoff and cover-up. But for such corruption to prevail, an underlying condition must be operative—a profitable system of illicit enterprise subsidized by the protective tariff of the criminal law.

Finally, legal moralism may undermine the moral authority of the criminal law. For example, whatever may be the negative effects of marihuana use, there is no evidence to substantiate the purportedly violent and destructive behavior that brings heavy penalties. The penalties associated with marihuana use and sale have approximated and sometimes exceeded penalties for committing such serious assaultive crimes as strong-arm robbery and forcible rape. Excessive zeal in setting penalties cannot help but undermine the moral authority of the criminal law.

Professional Police and Police Organization

Police organization is highly complicated, more complicated than is usually realized because of the multitude of functions performed by police. The increasing complexity of police services led the President's Commission on Law Enforcement and Administration of Justice to envisage the day when all personnel with general enforcement powers would have bachelor's degrees and to urge police departments to take immediate steps to establish a minimum requirement of a bachelor's degree for all supervisory and executive positions. Whether or not advanced education will solve the problems besetting the police departments, there is no question that the trend in American policing is toward higher educational requirements and rationalization of police services.

As police departments develop in this direction, there will be a concomitant development in ideas concerning the relation of policemen to the organizations in which they are employed, especially to the military character of such organizations. For example, a student of police, Michael Banton, distinguishes between officers who tend to be in a largely punitive or inquisitorial role and those who are in an emergency service or assistance role.[24] This distinction suggests that the day may come when specialization becomes an integral feature of police organization. For example, the Federal Bureau of Investigation accepts candidates up to the age of forty-one, which is about six years higher than the typical maximum age of acceptability for new members found in most police departments, although the age of investigators in police departments is probably comparable to the age of investigators in the FBI. Recognition that police departments perform various tasks suggests, first, that police departments and civil service commissions should reconsider and possibly modify presently rigid recruitment standards concerning age, height, weight, and visual acuity. Furthermore, height standards frequently discriminate against otherwise capable members of certain minority groups, who might be particularly effective in policing minority areas of cities, as well as the general population.

A second and more complicated issue revolves around the question of prior local residence as a requirement for acceptance in many police departments. Residence requirements typically demand that an applicant have lived in a community for six months before becoming eligible for police work. Thus, young men from rural communities may automatically be rendered ineligible for urban police work. Similarly, young men who have put in a period of service in the military police may be disqualified for police work in civilian life. Possibly of greater consequence is the limitation such a requirement places upon the available pool of manpower. Nonetheless, although this requirement may appear irrational on its surface, there may be an underlying rationality to it. Minority community spokesmen increasingly complain that police working in their areas operate as an army of occupation isolated from the citizenry. Absentee residence tends to contribute to that isolation. Police, and other municipal workers, are seen as exploiters, people who earn their living from the local community but whose interest is casual and minimal. At the same time, rigid residence requirements may result in a variety of inequities, some of which have been mentioned. In addition, where municipalities are contiguous, local residence requirements intended to heighten police interest may exclude minority policemen who cannot afford to reside in the area where the police station is actually located, or who prefer to live in communities they grew up in. As is the case with many other issues regarding the police, there is no simple solution.

To improve the quality of police recruitment, we not only need to raise salaries in an era of increasing educational requirements; we also need to re-examine the prerequisites of the officer. In the past, police organization has been paramilitary with encompassing obligations of obedience. For many working policemen, the military model of organization stifled initiative and rewarded conformity. As educational requirements become more important for police recruitment and advancement, consideration will have to be given to how to permit the individual policeman to take more initiative and to assert more independent judgment.

Police typically find themselves in a position where opportunities to change employers are highly restricted, except at the highest executive levels. While a professor, for example, can move to another college or university at original or higher rank, most police departments require entrance at the lowest rank. In effect, each municipality has a separate "army," and every recruit has to start from scratch.

Such a system contains obvious disadvantages for developing professional police. It limits employment opportunities. It encourages parochialism by demanding responsiveness to local organizational needs and conditions. It restricts freedom to disagree with or challenge superiors. It limits appreciation of the assertion of rights by others, since under such a system police themselves are forbidden to dissent from the opinions of superiors. It reduces police salaries, since municipalities are not required to compete for the services of already trained, middle-level police officials, such as experienced patrolmen, sergeants, and lieutenants. Finally, it lays a structural foundation for corruption by suppressing income.

Once we begin to probe basic assumptions of the paramilitary organizational model, other questions naturally come to mind. Do all police have to carry guns at all times? Is it necessary to have a "roll call" for all patrolmen? To what extent does possession of a gun at home interfere with a man's capacity to enjoy the company of his family, friends, and neighbors? Why can't off-duty police simply share the same responsibilities of citizenship as all other citizens? Why must patrolmen always wear uniforms? Would a badge or armband do as well under some circumstances, yet symbolize a closeness to the citizenry? Given the increasingly social services that police are asked to provide and the problem of police isolation, why not have a police training curriculum that not only emphasizes such subjects as social welfare, psychology, sociology, anthropology, and legal philosophy but also establishes contact with *nonpolice* training facilities—such as universities—so as to reduce isolation?

At the same time, we must also recognize that policing as a profession must develop on a model different from those of the traditional "free" professions, such as law and medicine. Policing does require a more highly developed authority structure and organizational capacity to meet challenges to public safety. But these challenges too easily come to dominate—out of all proportion to reality—the culture and organization of the entire police department. Furthermore, it may not be the military model itself that is undesirable, but rather accretions upon it that are essentially unrelated to the nature of police work, for example, the notion that a policeman must be "on duty" 24 hours a day, even where no crisis exists. The important point is this: Contemporary police are more than an alternative to an army, as they were in the early nine-teenth century. The community increasingly demands more of the police in the way of public services. These demands require a professionalism that goes beyond technology, efficiency, and obedience.

The developing professionalism of police must pattern itself upon a *legal model* and take seriously the idea that policemen are *law* enforce-ment officers. Legal values of constitutional authority, consistency, and fairness must become part of the policeman's approach to the world, and police organizations must develop a tradition of inquiry into their own underlying assumptions and organizational mechanics. Police isola-tion too often leads to defensiveness, rather than critical self-inquiry, to rigidity rather than experimentation and honest consideration of alter-natives. Police professionalism is an aspiration that may become a reality. Such an achievement can only be realized through major changes in attitude, toward openness and away from defensiveness, toward a com-mitment to competence, and toward critical inquiry to achieve that competence.

NOTES

1   A. A. W. Ramsay, *Sir Robert Peel* (New York: Dodd, Mead, 1938), p. 250.
2   Charles Reith, *The Police Idea: Its History and Evolution in England in the Eighteenth Century and After* (London: Oxford University Press, 1938), pp. 203–204.
3   *Manchester Times,* Sept. 29, 1838. Cited in Donald Read, "Chartism in Man-chester" in Briggs, ed., *Chartist Studies* (London: Macmillan, 1960).
4   G. M. Trevelyan, *A Shortened History of England* (Baltimore: Penguin, 1959), pp. 511–513.
5   Reith, *The Police Idea,* p. 236.
6   Ramsay, *Sir Robert Peel,* p. 69.
7   Reith says that the only copies that appear to be in existence are with The Chadwick Papers in University College Library, London, and at Scotland Yard. The portion quoted is from Charles Reith, *A New Study of Police History* (London: Oliver and Boyd, 1956), p. 140.
8   T. A. Critchley, *A History of Police in England and Wales, 900–1966* (Lon-don: Constable and Company Ltd., 1967), p. 52.
9   Reith, *New Study,* p. 140.
10 The President's Commission on Law Enforcement and Administration of Justice, *The Challenge of Crime in a Free Society* (Washington, D.C.: U.S. Government Printing Office, Feb. 1967).
11 Frederic W. Maitland, *Justice and Police* (London: Macmillan, 1885), pp. 1–2.
12 *Royal Commission on the Police Cmnd. 1728.* (London: Her Majesty's Sta-tionery Office, 1962), p. 45.

13 Ernest Jerome Hopkins, *Our Lawless Police* (New York: Viking, 1931).

14 See, for example, *Miranda* v. *Arizona,* 384 U.S. 436 (1966).

15 Raymond Fosdick, *American Police Systems* (New York: The Century Company, 1920), p. 221.

16 V. A. Leonard, *Police Organization and Management* (Brooklyn, N.Y.: The Foundation Press, 1951), p. 6.

17 See Jerome H. Skolnick, *Justice Without Trial: Law Enforcement in Democratic Society* (New York: Wiley, 1966), pp. 235–239.

18 Leonard Schapiro, "Prospects for the Rule of Law," *Problems of Communism* **14** (March–April 1965).

19 Edmond Cahn, "Law in the Consumer Perspective," *University of Pennsylvania Law Review* **112** (November 1963): 1–21.

20 The President's Commission on Law Enforcement and Administration of Justice, *The Challenge of Crime,* p. 10.

21 Reinhard Bendix, *Nation-Building and Citizenship* (New York: Wiley, 1964), p. 20.

22 The President's Commission on Law Enforcement and Administration of Justice, *Task Force Report: The Courts* (Washington, D.C.: U.S. Government Printing Office, 1967), p. 107.

23 Herbert L. Packer, "The Crime Tariff," *The American Scholar* **33** (1964): 551–557.

24 Michael Banton, *The Policeman in the Community* (London: Tavistock Publications, 1964).

The line-up appears serious and intent as these policemen take their oath of office.

I

Behind the Police

ORIGINS AND DEVELOPMENT OF THE POLICE

19th-century sketch depicting daily roll call at the Boston Police Department Headquarters.

Change has always been a major interest of scholars and laymen alike. From 19th-century writers on revolution to 20th-century writers on society, we see a repeated emphasis on the question of how societies change, how institutions change, and how organizations change.

Changes in society, in institutions, and in organizations are all discussed in the readings in this chapter on the origins and development of the police. One generalization seems valid. These readings suggest that major social dislocations will be followed by major responses in institutions and organizations. During the early 19th century, in response to the major social dislocations created by the industrial revolution, by war, and by poverty, a variety of new institutions was created. The London Metropolitan Police was established as a rational response to problems of public order. The Parliamentary response in England, in creating the new police, was a radical innovation for its day because police were widely feared. As E. P. Thompson writes:

> The Parliamentary Committee of 1818 saw, in Bentham's proposals for a Ministry of Police "a plan which would make every servant of every house a spy on the actions of his master, and all classes of society spies on each other." Tories feared the over-ruling of parochial and chartered rights, and of the powers of the local J.P.s; Whigs feared an increase in the powers of Crown or of Government; Radicals like Burdett and Cartwright preferred the notion of voluntary associations of citizens or rotas of householders; the radical populace until Chartist times saw in any police an engine of oppression. A quite surprising consensus of opinion resisted the establishment of "one supreme and resistless tribunal, such as is denominated in other countries the "High Police"—an engine—invented by despotism. . . .[1]

Accordingly, Peel incorporated two central ideas as the basis for The New Police: (1) that the criminal law needs to be restricted in order for the police to operate, and (2) that the police must have the confidence of the community. Thus, police were disarmed in their public duties, and special uniforms were designed to make them appear very tall (which led to the designation "Bobbies," after Sir Robert Peel). Third, recruitment policies that favored men who would be acceptable to the communities being policed were encouraged.

The British police developed, not merely on a short-term responsive basis, but according to a well-thought-out plan. By contrast, the American police, although spurred to development by the British innovation, did not develop according to a carefully considered plan. In particular, the New York City police force, as described by Richardson, never freed itself from political control, and throughout the 19th century its policies and personnel were strongly subject to political influence.

The British police, the New York police, and the Boston police all were begun in an era of protest and rioting. Indeed, the mandate for the Boston police came about specifically as a result of riots, particularly those between people of English background and the immigrant Irish. For example, during the Broad Street riot of June 11, 1837, the residents of Irish tenements along the street were driven out and beaten by a mob that was eventually estimated at 15,000, which was more than one-sixth of the whole population of Boston at that time. Lane writes, ". . . the problem of mob violence, which had already troubled Mayor Quincey, soon compelled the municipality to take a more significant step, to create a new class of permanent police officers, with new standards of performance." [2] Although ostensibly modeled on the London police, the Boston police changed its function throughout the 19th century on a very pragmatic basis. As new public agencies to deal with such matters as public health developed, the police were gradually eliminated from those concerns and became more narrowly responsible for what we now regard as the central police concerns of patrol, investigation, and crime prevention.

We have included these readings on the history of the London police not only because the organization developed there but also because it influenced the creation of police forces in the United States. Therefore any student trying to understand contemporary American policing should consider it in the light of its historical antecedents, both British and American.

We have also included these readings because they raise a number of fundamental issues about law enforcement in a democratic society. These include: What is an appropriate scope for criminal law, particularly in light of the consequences for police activities and attitudes? A related issue is, What should be the scope of police duties? Should police, for example, be engaged in the arresting of drunks as criminals? Should police carry out such emergency service activities as carrying injured citizens to hospitals or finding means of entry for persons who have locked themselves out of their own homes? Should the police or the military forces handle major civil disturbances? If the police should handle these disturbances, in what ways should their methods differ from those of the military? And, ultimately, What principles of organization would be appropriate for police development today in light of these readings?

NOTES

1 E. P. Thompson, *The Making of the English Working Class* (New York: Random House, 1966), p. 82.
2 Roger Lane, *Policing the City* (Cambridge, Mass.: Harvard University Press, 1967), p. 26.

The New Police in London, 1750–1830

T. A. CRITCHLEY

POLICING AS A NEW SCIENCE

One of the successful applicants for a post as magistrate in the new offices established by the Middlesex Justices Act, 1792, was a Glasgow merchant named Patrick Colquhoun. A self-made man who had been appointed Lord Provost of Glasgow at the early age of thirty-seven, he turned his immense energy selectively to a wide variety of social problems; but his dominating interest, throughout twenty-five years as a Metropolitan magistrate, was in the reform of the police. In 1797 he published *A Treatise on the Police of the Metropolis,* which was widely acclaimed and went through no fewer than seven editions in the course of ten years. Its language was revolutionary: "Police is an improved state of Society. . . . Next to the blessings which a Nation derives from an excellent Constitution and System of general Laws, are those advantages which result from a well-regulated and energetic plan of Police, conducted and enforced with purity, activity, vigilance, and discretion."

The treatise broke new ground. In the painstaking manner in which he marshalled statistics relating to crime and criminals, and

From *A History of Police in England and Wales,* 2nd edition, as it appeared in the Patterson Smith Series in Criminology, Law Enforcement and Social Problems, No. 201 (Montclair, N.J.) by T. A. Critchley, pp. 38–50. Copyright © 1967, 1972 by T. A. Critchley. Reprinted by permission of Constable and Co., Ltd. and Patterson Smith Publishing Corp.

in relying on this systematic evidence as a basis for drawing up wide-ranging plans, Colquhoun adopted a technique which is commonplace in our own times, but was then virtually unknown. He threw down a challenge to the traditionalists in declaring that a well-regulated police, whose primary aim should be the prevention of crime, was "perfectly congenial to the principle of the British constitution," and proceeded to develop sweeping proposals embracing the reform of the criminal law and the magistracy, projects for the moral reformation of society, and a system of preventive police which owed much to an acknowledged admiration of the French—which had reached "the greatest degree of perfection"—a fact which so delighted them that at the height of the Napoleonic War Colquhoun's treatise was translated and published in France. Fascinated by the novelty of his subject, Colquhoun wrote in the Preface to the sixth edition of his *Treatise* (published in 1800) that "police in this country may be considered as a new science; the properties of which consist not in the judicial powers which lead to punishment and which belong to the magistrates alone; but in the prevention and detection of crimes; and in those other functions which relate to internal regulations for the well order and comfort of civil society." This science "was not yet perfectly understood."

Colquhoun followed the abortive proposals of 1785 in insisting on the complete separation of judicial and police powers. He proposed the creation of a central police board, consisting of five commissioners, who were to be "able, intelligent, prudent and indefatigable" men. The Home Office itself had too many other tasks to enable it to give the "strength, vigour, and energy" to a police system, but the board should be under the general control of the Home Secretary. A nucleus of professional police should be established in every parish, at the head of which should be a "high constable of the division," who would be assisted by a parochial chief constable. These officers would be paid and controlled by the central police board, and they would take charge of the local constables elected by the court leet or the magistrates without the option of employing deputies. To reap the full benefit of centralization, Colquhoun carried forward three ideas borrowed from the Fielding brothers, to whose pioneer work he justly paid tribute: the central police board should organize an intelligence service; it should maintain a register of known offenders, with classified information about particular groups; and it should publish a *Police Gazette,* not only for the purpose of aiding in the detection of crime but also as a vehicle of moral education—"with commentaries suited to the comprehension of the vulgar, tending to operate as warnings, and to excite a dread of crimes," with "occasional observations on the horrors of a goal; on punishments—whipping, the pillory, the hulks, transportation and public execution."

Colquhoun's proposals thus represent an important link between the old and the new ideas. In essence, his plan was put forward as a means of revitalizing the parish constabulary and superimposing over it a meed of professional direction and co-ordination deriving authority from the Home Secretary. This balance was nicely adjusted to the spirit of the times. Colquhoun's ideas were enthusiastically received by the Press and in Parliament, but not in the City, where the proposed police board was seen as "a new Engine of Power and Authority so enormous and extensive as to threaten a species of despotism and inquisition hitherto without a parallel in this country." [1] In the same year that he published his treatise, Colquhoun was one of only three witnesses (another of whom was his close friend and associate, Jeremy Bentham) to be called before a Select Committee on Finance, etc., appointed to consider particularly police, including convict establishments. For a time Colquhoun carried all before him. In a closely reasoned and well-documented report, this committee, in its *Twenty-eighth Report,* published in 1798, substantially endorsed his plans. The Government prepared a Bill, and the moment seemed ripe at last for the establishment of a modern police system in London. Then, for reasons which remain a mystery, the whole project was abandoned. For the next ten years interest in general police reform died away, until a shock to public confidence even greater than that caused by the Gordon Riots of 1780 allowed the voice of reform to be heard once again.

In December 1811, two whole families in the East End of London were silently exterminated in macabre circumstances which created a wave of public panic. One, consisting of a linen-draper named Marr, his wife, child and shop assistant, was savagely butchered with a ripping chisel and maul. The sense of horror had not abated when, a week later, a man named Williamson and his wife and servant were found with their skulls fractured and their throats cut; a bloodstained iron crowbar and maul lay beside the bodies. De Quincey later treated the "Wapping murders" with light irony in his essay, *Murder considered as One of the Fine Arts,* but no one treated them lightly at the time. Complacency about the need for reforming the police vanished overnight. The watchmen in the area were instantly discharged. Special armed patrols were appointed, and several neighboring parishes volunteered to supply additional men for night patrolling. Public concern mounted throughout the whole country, and just as after the Gordon Riots, so again a welter of suggestions poured into the Home Office from all over the country. Some even favored radical reform of the parish constable system, but most seem to have looked no further than an improvement in the quality of the parish police and the nightly watch. Even Colquhoun now contented himself with a series of minor suggestions designed to improve the quality of watchmen.

The Home Secretary acted in two ways. The murderer, a man named Williams, was at length caught; but he evaded justice by hanging himself from a beam so low that, as the *Morning Post* commented, he must have been obliged "to sit down as it were to accomplish his purpose." The Home Secretary accordingly satisfied public opinion by authorizing the body to be displayed, along with the ripping chisel and maul, in a high, open cart which, driven slowly along the crowded streets, at length paused outside the Marrs' house and then drove on to where a hole had been dug in the ground. The body was flung in and a stake driven through it. Second, the Home Secretary moved Parliament to set up a committee of enquiry into the state of the nightly watch and the effectiveness of the various local Acts within the Metropolitan area, but made it clear that he did not expect or desire any radical recommendations from the committee. Pitt's abortive Bill of 1785 seems to have been entirely forgotten, although the report of 1798 embodying Colquhoun's proposals was specially reprinted for the use of the new enquiry. The committee, however, disregarded it. They produced a hasty, ill-informed, and disappointing report, the principal recommendation of which was to introduce arrangements by which the state of the watch should be regularly inspected by officers paid to make rounds during the night. By these means it was thought that elderly and unfit watchmen could be weeded out. The committee proposed better arrangements for supplying information to the eight "police offices," as the magistrates' offices were now generally called, and the office of the Chief Magistrate of Bow Street was to be recognized as a clearing-house for crime under the direct authority of the Home Secretary. A Bill embodying these recommendations was introduced into Parliament in July 1812, but by then the shock of the Wapping murders had faded. The Bill was quietly dropped. In the calm light of reason, men argued that no police system, however perfect, could ever prevent murders from being committed. The most that could be hoped for was to prevent a murderer's escape or to detect him more speedily, and these considerations pointed to the need to strengthen the nightly watch. With such agreeable and stoical reflections, taxpayers were relieved at being spared the burden of a costly police system which nobody wanted, and the zealots for personal liberty achieved a further triumph. Colquhoun's "new science of police" was not merely imperfectly understood. Nobody wanted to understand it.

RIVER POLICE AND
BOW STREET RUNNERS

In the meantime, the stagnancy of the long debate about the theory of policing had not held up some useful reforms that were gradually providing London with a nucleus of professional police—offensive to constitutional principles as they might be.

In two chapters of his *Treatise,* Colquhoun called attention to the extent to which the vast wealth which poured into the Port of London was a prey to thieves, and he later dilated on this in a *Treatise on the Commerce and Police of the River Thames,* published in 1800. With characteristic precision, he estimated that there were no fewer than 10,000 thieves, footpads, prostitutes, and pilferers at work on the jetties and quays that lined the riverside, and that the plunder and pillage represented an annual loss of over half a million pounds. This argument for the establishment of a preventive police for the river appealed instantly to the shipping interests, and a Marine Police Establishment was set up in June 1798 (four-fifths of the cost being borne by West Indian merchants), consisting of some sixty salaried officers—considerably more full-time men than in all the police offices put together. The men were given careful instructions to "spurn with indignation" any attempt to corrupt them and at all times to display "the utmost zeal, vigilance, prudence, discretion, and sobriety." Colquhoun had associated himself with a man of buccaneering propensities named John Harriot in recommending the scheme to the Government, and the new force was placed under Harriot's immediate command, with Colquhoun as its superintending magistrate. The experiment met with striking success; and two years later, in July 1800, the Thames River Police Act, which owed much to the joint efforts of Colquhoun and Bentham, converted the private venture into a public concern. A ninth police office was created on the lines of that of Bow Street and the seven set up by the Middlesex Justices Act, 1792, and the justices of the new Thames Police Office were

empowered to appoint and dismiss constables. The Thames magistrates acted directly on the detailed instructions of the Home Secretary; and the Thames river police thus became the first regular professional police force in London.

It was followed, before long, by a rapid expansion of the Bow Street foot and horse patrols founded half a century earlier by the Fielding brothers. The seven police offices created by the Middlesex Justices Act had been authorized to employ not more than six constables each, but this limit was increased in 1811 to twelve. The magistrates office at Bow Street, however, which had existed from much earlier times, enjoyed a prestige and a freedom from statutory regulation which provided the Chief Magistrate, with the Home Secretary's support, unlimited scope for experiment. The holder of the office in the early years of the nineteenth century, Sir Richard Ford, was an enterprising man. Dividing his time equally between the Home Office and Bow Street, he was ever ready to act on the Home Secretary's directions in appointing his constables as spies and informers to deal with enemy aliens during the Napoleonic Wars. He also took vigorous steps to combat crime. In 1805 he revived John Fielding's idea of a horse patrol and stationed some sixty men on the principal roads within twenty miles of London. They were carefully selected, preference being given to applicants who had served in a cavalry regiment. This roisterous body of men, some of whom made substantial fortunes out of their shady business in trafficking in crime, undoubtedly formed something of a *corps d'élite,* creating in their own lifetime the myth of the Bow Street Runners, described as "a closely knit caste of speculators in the detection of crime, self-seeking and unscrupulous, but also daring and efficient when daring and efficiency coincided with their private interest." [2] They undertook missions all over the country and even abroad but also contrived to clear such notorious places as Hounslow Heath of highwaymen. Their routine duty was to patrol the main roads as far out as Enfield, Epsom, Windsor and Romford, giving confidence to travelers with their greeting, "Bow Street Patrol."

In 1821 a second echelon, 100 strong, was established. This, curiously known as the "Unmounted Horse Patrol," served to train men for promotion to the mounted branch and operated in the suburban areas within a radius of five or six miles from London. Elaborate arrangements for conference points between the two branches of the horse patrol were worked out. The men were sworn in by the Chief Magistrate of Bow Street to act as constables throughout Middlesex, Surrey, Essex, and Kent, and they acted under the direct authority of the Home Secretary: both branches of the Horse Patrol were commanded by a Home Office official named William Day, who, as Keeper of the Criminal Registers in the Department, had helped to organize the first patrol in 1805; he later set up office in Cannon Row. These patrols became the first uniformed police force in the country (the river police had no distinguishing uniform). They wore blue coats with yellow metal buttons, a scarlet waistcoat, blue trousers, Wellington boots, and black hats. To the scarlet waistcoats they owed the nickname "Robin Redbreasts."

The foot patrol, in the meantime, had been considerably strengthened. Like the horse patrol, it also split into two branches. The first in point of time was a night patrol, about 100 strong, which came to be organized in an increasingly sophisticated manner. By 1818 one body, known as the "country party," would start their beats between four and five miles from London, patrolling inwards along the main roads leading into the capital, while a "town party" would set out from the center to meet them. In 1821, however, the increase of crime in central London led to the withdrawal of the "country party" into the inner area, their place in the outer suburbs being taken by the unmounted horse patrol mentioned earlier. The foot patrols were given a measure of local discretion, generally starting off at about dusk and remaining out until one o'clock in the morning. They wore no uniform but carried a truncheon, a cutlass, and occasionally a pistol. They were heartily detested by watchmen, who regarded them as spies set on themselves, but they co-operated with the horse patrols.

The fourth and last of these special Bow Street patrols was an outcome of a recommendation by a Parliamentary committee of 1822 under Peel's chairmanship. This was a special foot patrol by day, consisting of 27 men, designed as a preventive force against daylight robbery, and instructed to watch for suspicious activities which might suggest plans for night burglaries. The men, mostly old soldiers, appeared in the streets for the first time in August 1822, wearing uniforms (in contrast to the plain-clothes night patrol) which consisted of a blue coat and trousers and a red waistcoat, which, Peel thought, would make them "proud of their establishment."

Hence by 1828, on the eve of the formation of the Metropolitan Police, a substantial corps of professional full-time officers already existed in London: the constables employed by the seven police offices, the various Bow Street patrols, and the Thames river police, totaling some 450 men directly under the control of the Home Secretary. It was a meager force to serve a population of nearly one and a half million, and at the best it could do little more than attempt to catch a few criminals and bring them to justice. As a preventive force it was negligible. In addition, there were upwards of 4,500 watchmen employed by the City of London or, in the Metropolitan district, by various parishes, often under Improvement Act powers. The total cost to London of the old police during its last years amounted to the not inconsiderable sum of about a quarter of a million pounds.

THE UTILITARIANS

By the 1820s the agonizing struggle to avoid introducing a police system into London was entering its concluding stages, though few could have suspected it, for the currents of fresh thinking that helped to bring matters to a head flowed deeply below the surface of public affairs.

Sixty years earlier, when the Fieldings were striving to educate public opinion, they had ranged indiscriminately over the whole field of criminal law reform and police reform; but as the century advanced the two movements followed divergent paths, each attracting its own, largely separate, protagonists. Most of the early thinkers in this field —Blackstone (1723–1780), Adam Smith (1723–1790), and Paley (1743–1805)— were hostile to the idea of a preventive police, holding, to put it in Utilitarian terms, that the greatest happiness for the greatest number was unlikely to be advanced by an elaborate system calculated to interfere with individual liberty: an admittedly imperfect police system was part of the price of freedom. Thus they assumed a position directly contrary to that of the police reformers, who held that without an efficient police the happiness of both State and individual was constantly at risk. The argument, therefore, involved one of the greatest of all human issues—namely, the responsibility of the State in relation to

the rights of the individual. To this argument there could (and can) be no finality, but an escape from the logical dilemma was available to those who saw in the reform of the criminal law a preferable alternative to the creation of a civil force of police. Hence the cause of penal reform drew support from that of police reform, for it faced none of the obstacles that stood in the way of the latter: its objects were attainable without significant public expense, and it offered no threat to personal liberty. It thus became possible to argue that the more dangerous ideas should be shelved until the effect on society of such humanitarian measures as the abolition of public executions and the amelioration of prison life had been evaluated. While, therefore, for many years the police reformers supported the reform of the criminal code, the law reformers were generally hostile to the cause of police reform.

After the turn of the eighteenth century, however, under the influence of Jeremy Bentham (1748–1832), the two movements began to draw together once more. A man of catholic learning, liberal principles, and incalculable influence in many branches of public affairs, Bentham had early been impressed by the work of the Italian Marquis Beccaria, whose *Essay on Crime and Punishments,* with a commentary by Voltaire, had been published in an English translation in 1767. Beccaria wrote: "It is better to prevent crimes than to punish them. This is the chief aim of every good system of legislation, which is the art of leading men to the greatest possible happiness or to the least possible misery, according to calculation of all the goods and evils of life." [3] Beccaria pleaded for the revision of traditional attitudes toward crime and punishment but was himself lukewarm toward the French idea of policing. Bentham, working out his vast and labyrinthine philosophies of Utilitarianism over a period of many years, espoused both causes and attracted disciples to further each— Romilly, the criminal law reformer, whose influence did much to purify the criminal code from its medieval barbarity; and Colquhoun, the pioneer police reformer, whose work has already been mentioned. And then, toward the end of his long life, Bentham proposed in his *Constitutional Code* the creation of a completely centralized preventive police system under the control of the Government. These views came to the attention of a young lawyer, Edwin Chadwick, who was to play a notable part in gathering up the thinking of three-quarters of a century and complete the Utilitarians' theoretical study of the "science of police," without which Peel's political skill could have achieved little.

But these powerful currents of thinking caused few surface ripples. Parliament continued to regard the police idea with disfavor. Three more Parliamentary committees, in 1816, 1818, and 1822, rejected it as incompatible with British liberty. The first published copius evidence but made no proposals. The second at last recognized the weakness of a system of parish constables and watchmen and proposed to rescue the office of high constable from oblivion by attaching a salary to it and giving the high constable effective control over the parish constables, who themselves should be more carefully selected; a reliable certificate of character should be required from the deputies, and a limit put to their period of service. On one point, however, this committee was emphatic: a system of police on the Continental model would be "odious and repulsive, and one which no government could be able to carry into execution. . . . It would be a plan which would make every servant of every house a spy on the actions of his master, and all classes of society spies on each

other." The third committee, of 1822, set up on the motion of the newly appointed Home Secretary, Peel, similarly contented itself with proposals for minor reform designed to strengthen the traditional system, recommended the formation of the Bow Street day patrol, and took the conventional line (warmly endorsed by *The Times*) about the dangers of any new-fangled system of police. In a much-quoted passage they declared:

> It is difficult to reconcile an effective system of police, with that perfect freedom of action and exemption from interference, which are the great privileges and blessings of society in this country; and Your Committee think that the forfeiture or curtailment of such advantages would be too great a sacrifice for improvements in police, or facilities in detection of crime, however desirable in themselves if abstractedly considered.

THE METROPOLITAN POLICE ACT, 1829

The Chairman of this thoroughly reactionary committee was, of all men, the Home Secretary, Robert Peel, who nevertheless in the same year was speaking in Parliament of a project for "a vigorous preventive police, consistent with the free principles of our free constitution." [4] A politician of exceptional genius, Peel was clearly not prepared to commit his reputation too swiftly or too deeply to so controversial a public issue as police reform, although there is no doubt that he had set his heart upon it from the beginning of his term at the Home Office. Instead, he devoted his early years as Home Secretary to the cause of the reform of criminal law. So passed several years, during which Peel seems to have been preparing himself, by discussion with authorities abroad as well as at home, to re-enter the struggle for police reform when he judged the moment ripe. By 1826 he had drawn up a plan for setting up a single police system within a radius of ten miles of St. Paul's with the exception of the City, "with which," he told a correspondent, "I should be afraid to meddle." [5] Then in the following year, 1827, he found himself a fellow member with Lord John Russell of yet another Parliamentary committee on criminal matters. The second report of this committee, published in July 1828, struck a modern note in asserting that "the art of crime, if it may be so called, has increased faster than the art of detection." For the counties, the committee rather lamely saw a means of salvation once again in the office of high constable, but significantly commented that there was ground "for instituting inquiry into the management of the Police of all our great towns."

The recommendation came too late, for six months earlier the stage had been set for the last of this wearisome procession of Parliamentary inquiries. In February 1828, Peel moved for the appointment of an inquiry with disarming terms of reference: "to enquire into the cause of the increase of the number of commitments and convictions in London and Middlesex for the year 1827; and into the state of the police of the Metropolis and the district adjoining thereto." Having thus adjusted priorities to a realistic assessment of the state of public opinion, he proceeded in all that followed to display consummate Parliamentary skill. His latest biographer has suggested that he was deliberately dull and unemotional. He delivered some unexciting statistics about crime and, playing the whole matter down, declared, "I must confess that I am not very sanguine with respect to the benefits to be derived from this committee." He despaired of persuading the City of London to co-operate in any general system of policing. He described the defects of the existing arrangements but did not "believe that any effectual remedy can be devised by which the evil can be cured." Nevertheless, he did not wish to disguise the fact that "the time is come, when, from the increase in its population, the enlargement of its resources, and the multiplying development of its energies, we may fairly pronounce that the country has outgrown her police institutions and that the cheapest and safest course will be found to be the introduction of a new mode of protection." Addressing himself now to "those who live in agricultural districts," he demanded: "Why, I ask, should we entrust a grocer, or any other tradesman, however respectable, with the direction and management of a police for 5,000 or 6,000 inhabitants? Why should such a person, unpaid and unrewarded, be taken from his usual avocations and called upon to perform the laborious duties of a night constable?" He apologized for speaking for so long, observing that, although the select committee would be concerned only with London, "the subject matter of the inquiry is connected with objects of such deep importance, not merely as they regard the security of individual property, but also as they regard the morals and habits of the entire population." There is little doubt that Peel saw as his ultimate objective the creation of a police system throughout the country.

The committee reported within six months, in July 1828. Among the witnesses was Edwin Chadwick, who, with Bentham and Colquhoun made up the trinity of Utilitarians whose school of thought finally reconciled the English ideal of liberty with the French idea of police. Chadwick, "the heir of Bentham's doctrine of police," and his devoted friend and admirer during the last years of the philosopher's life, played a valuable part in representing to the committee the Utilitarians' insistence on the primary importance of the preventive nature of police work. The report of the committee[6] gave Peel all he wanted. It noted that the existing police system in London had been almost uniformly condemned by all previous inquiries and recommended the creation of an Office of Police under the direction of the Home Secretary, who should have unified control over the whole police in the Metropolitan area, including the nightly watch. Specially appointed justices should be in charge of the Police Office, but the committee abstained from advising on the detailed management of the force. The cost should be met partly from public funds and partly by a special rate levied on the Metropolitan parishes. Probably in fulfillment of a bargain struck behind the scenes, the committee recommended that the City should be excluded from the arrangement but refrained from offering convincing reasons for doing so.

In April of the following year, 1829, Peel introduced his "Bill for Improving the Police in and near the Metropolis." The circumstances could not have been more favorable. In the Duke of Wellington he now had a Prime Minister who, ever since the shock of Peterloo, had preferred to entrust the maintenance of law and order to professional police rather than soldiers; influential public opinion had been educated by the work of Bentham and Colquhoun; confidence in parish constables and watchmen had largely disappeared; and political opposition had been bought off or conciliated. The Bill largely followed the recommendations of the committee, defining the area for which the new Police Office was to be responsible as the "Metropolitan police district," a district extending over roughly a seven-mile radius from central London. The "two fit persons" who as justices were to take charge of the

Police Office were authorized to create and administer a police force composed of "a sufficient number of fit and able men." The men were to be sworn in by one of the justices as constables and to have the powers and privileges of a constable at common law. The justices (or commissioners, as they were called later) were to exercise their powers to direct and control the force under the authority of the Home Secretary, and their power to frame orders for the government of the force was likewise subject to his approbation. A Receiver was to be appointed by the Crown with a duty to control the revenue required for the force and manage its property and legal business, and power was given to levy a police rate throughout the Metropolitan police district. Thus the Bill provided for a complete separation of police administration in London from its centuries-old link with the magistracy and the parishes. In introducing the Bill, Peel declared that "the chief perquisites of an efficient police were unity of design and responsibility of its agents." He intended to proceed slowly in establishing a police force, with a "cautious feeling of his way and deriving aid from experience, essential to the ultimate success of all reforms." He would apply the Bill to a few districts in the vicinity of the Metropolis at first and then gradually extend it to the others as "its advantages unfolded themselves." [7]

It is one of the most remarkable facts about the history of police in England that, after three-quarters of a century of wrangling, suspicion, and hostility toward the whole idea of professional police, the Metropolitan Police Act, 1829, was passed without opposition and with scarcely any debate. Part of the explanation no doubt lies in the adroitness Peel showed in excluding the City from his plans, in return for which it seems probable that the Whigs undertook to give the Bill an easy passage. "Pray pass the bill through this session," Peel wrote to the Duke of Wellington when it was to go up to the House of Lords, "for you cannot think what trouble it has given me." [8] Another remarkable fact is that Peel's Act remains the governing statute of the Metropolitan Police to this day. Recognition of Peel's genius ought not, however, to obscure his own want of

originality of thinking about police reform. Regrettably, in harvesting the corn, he failed to acknowledge his debt to those who had long prepared the way: Henry and John Fielding, who sowed the seed three-quarters of a century earlier, Patrick Colquhoun, who raised the crop, and Bentham, who tilled the soil in which it grew.

NOTES

1 G. M. Trevelyan, *English Social History* (1942), p. 527.
2 *First Report of the Constabulary Commissioners* (1839), p. 1080, para. 122.
3 Quoted in Jenifer Hart, "Reform of the Borough Police, 1835–1856," *English Historical Review* (July 1955).
4 Ibid.

5 See S. E. Finer, *The Life and Times of Sir Edwin Chadwick* (1952), pp. 126–127; also Chadwick's Evidence to the Select Committee on Police, 1853.
6 Hart, "Reform."
7 G. M. Trevelyan, *History of England* (1956 ed.), p. 642.
8 Thomas Carlyle, *Chartism* (1839).

The Early Years of the New York Police Department

JAMES F. RICHARDSON

In police as in other matters, New York followed the lead of London. The Gordon Riots of 1780, which broke out because of the possibility of ending Catholic political disabilities, had shown the helplessness of the civil authorities of London in the face of a rampaging mob; but it was almost fifty years before the English capital acquired an effec-

From *The New York Police: Colonial Times to 1901* by James F. Richardson, pp. 23–29, 48–50, 284–289. Copyright © 1970 by Oxford University Press, Inc. Reprinted by permission.

tive police force. Corruption and inefficiency were the norm during this interval. English police officers, the counterparts of New York's constables and marshals, also earned their living by fees and rewards. A parliamentary inquiry of 1828 turned up much evidence of illicit co-operation between police officers and criminals. Officers received £40 for arresting perpetrators of the most serious crimes and often let youthful offenders alone until they committed a £40 crime. The night watch in London was organized by parishes, which led the parochial officials to appoint as watchmen aged and infirm men who thus would not have to be supported by the parish poor rate. London watchmen were often drunk or asleep on duty and generally were objects of derision and crude practical jokes.

As was later the case in New York, police reform in London came only after a long series of exposures of the evils of the existing system and cries for reform. Patrick Colquhoun, a London police magistrate, with the help of Jeremy Bentham, published a persuasive argument on the necessity for an improved police system for London in the 1790s. His *Treatise on the Police of the Metropolis* went through seven editions. Peel made use of Colquhoun's work in drawing up his police bill, but it was only after twenty years of discussion and parliamentary investigations in 1812, 1816, 1818, 1822, and 1828 that Peel was able to establish a centralized police force administered by the Home Office and staffed by men with specialized training. In 1812 one writer agreed on the necessity of a stronger night watch while regarding any centralized police as "a system of tyranny; an organized army of spies and informers, for the destruction of all public liberty, and the disturbance of all private happiness. Every other system of police is the curse of despotism. . . ." In 1818 a parliamentary committee feared that the proposed police plan "would make every servant of every house a spy on the actions of his master, and all classes of society spies on each other."

The new police force was given the responsibility for the prevention as well as detection of crime, and "blood money" rewards for apprehending criminals were abolished. The first commissioners of the new force were Charles Rowan and Richard Mayne, both respected magistrates. The "Peelers" met furious opposition from many groups, especially the Radicals, who expressed the traditional English aversion to a standing army. They and others were concerned about interference with civil liberties and the possible use of the police as an instrument of government repression. The government did use the police as labor spies in 1833, but the new force gradually won the support of the politically dominant upper- and middle-class groups who enjoyed its protection.[1]

Between 1830 and 1845 the existence of this model plus a marked upsurge in crime, vice, and disorder spurred efforts to provide a similar police force for New York City. The 1830s and 1840s were decades of rapid population growth with sharp increases in immigration, heightened distinctions between class, ethnic, and religious groups with consequent social strain, and a dizzying economic cycle of boom and bust. These social changes greatly complicated the city's police problem. No longer was the city a homogeneous community with a common culture and a shared system of values and moral standards. Rather the city was becoming a mosaic of subcommunities, separated from one another by barriers of class and culture and by attitudes and behavior derived from different traditions or, in the case of many immigrants, by the destruction of tradition.

In such a situation it was not always easy to determine what was normal and what was deviant, what was acceptable behavior and what was antisocial. The old patterns of deference to one's betters and social control by informal mechanisms such as gossip no longer prevailed. There was no longer a single set of leaders who could claim with some legitimacy to set the tone for the whole society. Of course, in the past many had refused to follow the prescribed standards, but in an essentially deferential society they had not challenged the existence and the rightness of those standards. Now each group established its own set of values and its own leadership and resented any intrusion or imposition by other leaders. Old stock and some immigrant middle-class Protestants still claimed universal validity for their values of Sabbatarianism and the combined pursuit of piety and profit. Many immigrants and those of lower status rejected these values and behaved in ways thought immoral and degraded by the elite. Increasingly, the Protestant middle class modified its behavior to distinguish itself from the Irish. A case in point is the use of alcohol. More and more, those who thought of themselves, and wanted to be considered by others, as "respectable" opposed the use of alcohol. The Irish did not go along.[2]

Crime and disorder became more prevalent and more worrisome. Between 1814 and 1834 the city's population increased by about 63 percent per decade, while the number of complaints entered at the police courts had risen more than four times. Between 1834 and 1835 alone, the number rose from 8719 to 10,168. The *Weekly Herald* of February 15, 1840, noted that in the previous ten months there had been nineteen riots and twenty-three murders. In August 1840 the *Commercial Advertiser* asserted, "It is notorious that the New York police is wretchedly inadequate to the arrest of offenders and the punishment of crime; as to *prevention* of crime, we might almost as well be without the name of a police, as we are all but without the substance." The city's streets were pathways of danger.

> Destructive rascality stalks at large in our streets and public places, at all times of the day and night, with none to make it afraid; mobs assemble deliberately. . . . In a word, lawless violence and fury have full dominion over us whenever it pleases them to rage, and it is more owing to the forebearance of the riotous and viciously inclined, than to any preventive or repressive means employed, or ready to be employed, that we are indebted even for the degree of security and tranquility with which men possess their property or their lives.[3]

In 1842 a joint special committee of the council made melodramatic reference to the constant increase in crime and the inability of the police to deal with it.

> The property of the citizen is pilfered, almost before his eyes. Dwellings and warehouses are entered with an ease and apparent coolness and carelessness of detection which shows that none are safe. Thronged as our city is, men are robbed in the street. Thousands, that are arrested, go unpunished, and the defenseless and the beautiful are ravished and murdered in the day time, and no trace of the criminals is found. The man of business, in his lawful calling, at the most public corner of our city, is slaughtered in the sunshine and packed up and sent away, by the most public and known channels of trade, and suspicion is hardly excited.[4]

Moralists continuously complained about alcohol causing poverty and crime; they did not often reverse the proposition and speculate on the impact of poverty upon alcoholism. Yet there was substance to their charges. In 1835 there were almost three thousand licensed drinking places in New York City, a ratio of one for every fifty persons in the city over the age of fifteen. And many of those arrested for petty thievery and prostitution as well as for being drunk and disorderly were heavy drinkers. Of course cause and effect here would not be easy to determine. In 1844 a committee of the Board of Aldermen estimated that there were ten thousand practicing prostitutes in the city. Some of them were very young, not even into the teens. In general, by the early 1840s prostitution was open, public, and widespread. Opponents hoped that an improved police force, if it could not eliminate prostitution, would at least make it less visible. Much the same was true of gambling, which was extensive, lucrative, and enjoyed practical legal immunity.[5]

As much as moralists objected to commercialized vice, except perhaps when they profited from it or wished a clandestine respite from respectability, their most serious fears arose from the threat riots posed to property and public order. And riots were frequent in the 1830s; there were so many in 1834 alone that it was long remembered in New York history as the year of riots. Most of the rioters of the period came from the Five Points and the Bowery. The Five Points, located on the site of the present Columbus Park and given its name by the fact that five streets intersected there, was the city's most noisome slum by the 1820s. Before 1820 the area's working-class amusement places had been relatively respectable in character. By 1828 the grand jury condemned the Five Points "as a rendezvous for thieves and prostitutes." One building, the infamous "Old Brewery," was the home of some one thousand people, about evenly divided between Irish and blacks. This establishment was supposed to have averaged a homicide a night for fifteen years. In 1830 Jacob Hays and other police officers raided the Five Points and found some young men of "respectable appearance" in hovels "rioting and associating with the blacks in the most shameful manner." In the great cholera epidemic of 1832, the area had the highest death rate in the city. Ignorant of the germ theory of disease and the relationship between overcrowding, fouled water, and epidemic, the comfortable could attribute the sufferings of the poor to their vicious and dissolute ways. The thought of the era made

man the maker of his own destiny; wealth or poverty, morality or vice was the individual's own choice, the result of conscious decision based on character. Therefore the poor had no one to blame but themselves for their plight, and stern repression was the agreed-upon response to any violent outbreaks.[6]

Yet the civil authorities often lacked the means to repress rioters. The first riot of 1834 accompanied the municipal elections. The voting period was three days at this time, and elections for city officials were held in the spring, while state and national elections were held in the fall. Giving special interest to the spring election of 1834 was the fact that the legislature had recently made the mayoralty an elective office. The three days of the election were three days of hard fighting between Whigs and Democrats, particularly in the Sixth Ward. Political feeling had been exacerbated by Jackson's veto of the bill to recharter the national bank and by his removal of the government deposits from the Bank of the United States, while the political struggle became intertwined with an ethnic one between the Irish and the native Americans. The scope of fighting proved too much for the police officers and the watch to contain, so the militia had to be called out to restore order.[7]

Regarded with distaste and even loathing by native Protestants, the newly arrived Irish Catholics, to give themselves some feeling of social superiority, were extremely antiblack and antiabolitionist. These feelings flared into violence in July 1834. The riot began with a disturbance at the Bowery Theater because of the time-worn excuse that an English actor had made disparaging remarks about Americans. Edwin Forrest was able to quiet the crowd, which then left the theater and proceeded to the house of a prominent abolitionist, Lewis Tappan. There the rioters broke into the house, carried the furniture into the street and made a bonfire of it. In the next two days the mob badly damaged the Episcopal African Church and pulled down and looted the houses of many blacks and abolitionists. Two or three thousand uniformed militia with a large body of citizens organized as special constables eventually restored order. The authorities resorted, belatedly, to these strong measures when it became clear that the spread of the riots would endanger whites as well as blacks. Also, as Gustave de Beaumont put it, "there was a general spirit of reaction, not in favor of the Negroes, but against their oppressors." Hunger riots and disturbances between immigrants and nativists, and strikers and strike breakers, required the use of the militia and "well-affected citizenry" to supplement the police officers and the watch. During the great fire of 1835, which destroyed much of the Pearl Street textile district, looting was so widespread that the mayor again had to call in troops.

These outbreaks dramatically highlighted the weakness of the police of the city; there was also increasing evidence of its inability to deal with more routine police matters. The police and the watch could not stop the activity of thieves at fires nor the brawls between the volunteer fire companies, who sometimes spent more time and energy fighting each other than they did the fires. Yet it was not easy to make significant improvements in the existing system, let alone adopt a completely new one.[8]

*   *   *

The question of police reform played a significant role in the city election of 1845, but it was not the most important issue. Both Whigs and Democrats concentrated their attacks upon the antiforeign and anti-Catholic activities and beliefs of the Native Americans. Also at issue were the high taxes and the blue laws prevailing under Mayor Harper. Democratic journals such as the *Morning News* did castigate the Native Americans for not adopting the state-sponsored police law of May 7, 1844, which the paper referred to as "the excellent law of police reform passed . . . after being well matured by the wise deliberation of many of our oldest, most intelligent and respectable citizens." The paper therefore called upon the voters to elect the Democratic candidates for mayor and the Common Council so that the police law of 1844 would be put into effect.[9]

The Democrats won the election of 1845, and in his annual message Mayor William F. Havemeyer called for the adoption of the state law. The council bill was signed into law on May 23, 1845, and New York at last achieved a police force akin to London's.[10]

Even though New York's force was established only sixteen years after London's, it was not to be so effective or so highly regarded. Poverty was no stranger to mid-nineteenth-century London, but the population of the English city was not nearly so ethnically and culturally heterogeneous as that of New York. Such heterogeneity made the police problem more acute by increasing group tensions. Nor were the police of London obliged to enforce laws at variance with the habits and inclinations of a large part of the population. In New York, on the other hand, the police were charged with keeping the saloons closed on Sunday.[11]

Administrative direction and personnel policy also differed significantly in New York and London. In New York, policemen of all ranks were appointed for limited tenure by elected officials. It is not surprising that to secure reappointment policemen had to be politically active for the officials who appointed them. Furthermore they could not enforce the law too strenuously against the supporters of those responsible for their appointments. In London, on the other hand, policemen were appointed and dismissed by commissioners who were free from any kind of local control and responsible only to the Home Secretary. The commissioners of the metropolitan police attempted to recruit prospective policemen from areas outside London, direct from the farm whenever possible, to avoid the problem of excessive familiarity between police and people and to provide the commissioners with an opportunity to mold their recruits as they saw fit. In New York, policemen had to be residents not only of the city but also of the ward in which they were appointed and served. This arrangement, along with the process of appointment, ensured that the police would be enmeshed in local politics.[12] On the other hand, a local resident might have an easier time keeping the peace if he could establish good relationships with his neighbors, and there might be less tendency to regard the police as an army of occupation imposed from outside the locality.

Finally, the group tensions and antagonisms which required an improved police system for New York made the creation of such a system more difficult. There was not a broadly based consensus in New York on what laws should be enforced, who should enforce them, and how. Those who provided such sought-after but illegal services as gambling, prostitution, and saloons that opened on Sunday wished to limit police activity in these areas. Those who were morally opposed to such services pressed the police to be as energetic as possible in suppressing them. Each group exerted whatever political influence it possessed to bring about its view of "proper" police procedure. Elected officials were naturally concerned about their constituents' relationships with the police; they also had more direct interests. How

policemen acted toward repeaters and ballot-box stuffers on Election Day was of great moment to them, and appointing supporters as policemen provided politicians with an opportunity to secure and enlarge their personal political followings, an opportunity they were loath to lose. The police arrangements of New York cannot be considered apart from the social and political structure of the city, and if tension and antagonism marked this structure, it is not surprising that inefficiency and instability characterized the police force of the 1840s and early 1850s.

*   *   *

Although the department grew considerably over the next fifty years, by the end of the century it had by no means achieved professional status. The police did not function according to the criteria of managerial efficiency and productivity and freedom from political interference put forth by such recent experts in police administration as the late William Parker and O. W. Wilson. The department was subservient to the reigning political machine rather than independent of it. Politicians, whose primary concern was to advance their own power and influence, made the key decisions on police. The department's administrative structure maximized the politicians' leverage over police commanders and individual members of the force. From the beginning of a policeman's career, he was made to realize that the terms of his working life depended upon his satisfying the needs of the district leaders, and that the impartial administration of justice was the last thing these men wanted. Rather, their interests were best served by a system open to personal intervention and manipulation at every stage, from initial police action to final disposition.

Nor did the department have any conception of a legal professionalism which would put a higher premium on the rule of law in a democratic society than on attempts to create social control through the use of force or bureaucratic methods. The police often acted on the assumption of guilt rather than the assumption of innocence, while their concern for the civil liberties of the poor and the politically powerless was minimal. In the political culture of the late nineteenth century such a concern would have been highly unlikely in any event. The respectable elements of society drew a sharp line between themselves and the undeserving poor; the police were to treat the former with respect and the latter with whatever methods kept them in line. It was not what the police did that mattered, but to whom they did it. The police did not willingly seek out procedural limitations on their mode of operation, nor did society insist that they treat everyone with due regard to his dignity as a human being and his constitutional rights.

The attempt to impose morality by law increased the conflicting pressures on the department as well as its vulnerability to political takeover. The more statute law on moral behavior, the more individuals there were who would make every effort to capture and control the regulators, the police. The fact that the laws which created crimes without victims were written by the legislature in Albany made it easier for those regulated by the laws to achieve their ends. They could point to outside interference by "hayseeds" as justification for molding and modifying police behavior to offset the formal requirements of the law. Those who used the law to validate their values as the accepted ones of the society tried to force the department to make the formal code into the operative one. They were unsuccessful because of their minority position in the city, and because gambling and Sunday drinking were not violations of the moral codes of most policemen.

The police could effectively enforce only those moral principles that both they and the majority of the community agreed upon.

The men who set departmental policy, the captains and the inspectors, were those most likely to view their action or inaction as negotiable. If the essence of corruption in government is the use of public office for private gain, police commanders like Timothy Creeden who had to pay for their positions had little choice but to be corrupt.

One may ask, however, if corruption was an entirely negative phenomenon. It helped modify official behavior to meet widespread private demands; it helped reward the politician for his public services; and it provided flexibility to allow people of widely varying backgrounds to live together without undue violence, if not necessarily in peace and harmony. Yet corruption contradicted the official morality. In a capitalistic society each man supposedly followed his self-interest, and the system's functioning assumed the rationality of economic man. Only the public servant was forbidden to pattern his behavior according to this model. He was to pursue the public interest in a coolly disinterested manner and to accept society's low valuation of his worth without question. But many of those who sought political office and power did so as a means of upward mobility. For ambitious young men of the slums, without capital or formal education, public office was a way to escape poverty and insecurity and to attain power. Many of the participants in the political and administrative structure did not share the conception of disinterested public service that the middle-class ethos presupposed, and the police acted according to the operative values rather than the official ones.

Although corruption may have been functional in providing for the adjustments necessary to a heterogeneous community, it still was often dysfunctional for police-community relations in that it made law officers into lawbreakers. The department had the legal responsibility to prevent behavior many people thought harmless, and any attempt to live up to that responsibility brought charges of "rigid" and "harsh" conduct. When the police ignored the law for a price, however, they violated public trust and represented lawless law enforcement. Community hostility to the force increased the sense of separation from the community among policemen and made them defend each other against outside attack, no matter how justified. They committed perjury for each other as a matter of course, which in turn intensified public suspicion. The greater the degree of separation, or the apprehension of it, the less likely were police and civilians to interact in an atmosphere of mutual trust and respect.

Police brutality and abuse of authority flourished in such a climate of distrust. If civilians did not respond to the uniform as a legitimate symbol of moral authority and the patrolman had not established a network of relationships with the people on his beat to keep the peace peacefully, the alternative was the use of gun and club. The constant complaints and well-documented instances of brutality indicate that this was too often the case, although the surviving evidence does not allow any precise generalizations about the nature of the relations between individual policemen and their usual constituency.

Hostile confrontations between police and civilians were most likely to occur when a number of them without previous relationships came together, such as in a fire or parade or in the adversary situation of a strike. In a parade or fire, policemen might be dealing with people they had never seen before, and who were acting in ways quite different from their normal behavior pattern. In a strike the department was charged with

the protection of life and property, which in practice meant getting strikebreakers past picket lines. The police made up for the numerical imbalance in these confrontations by the free use of the club. Desiring order and respect, and aware of their low status in the eyes of the public, they responded by trying to impose these values through physical coercion.

The discretionary authority of the police was awesome. Their decision to shoot or not, or to make an arrest or let someone go with a warning and a box on the ears, determined whether a man or boy kept or lost his most precious possessions, his life and his liberty. The wider the gap between the department and the community, the more likely it was that this discretionary authority would be regarded as illegitimate and even tyrannous. In the 1860s and 1870s, most of those arrested by the police as well as most of the force itself were Irish. The takers and the taken shared the same ethnic and social origins, although the police often did not let this influence them, as in the draft riots. In the last two decades of the century, when many Italians and East European Jews came to New York, there were greater divergences between the police and the poor, since the Irish retained, and even increased, their dominance in the department. The recent immigrants and the blacks often found that the Irish police regarded them with contempt and treated them accordingly.

In 1874 Mayor William Havemeyer gave the New York Police Department the sobriquet by which it has since been known, "the finest." There is a long record of heroism to justify this term, from those killed and disabled in the line of duty to those who put their lives and health in danger as a matter of routine to rescue people from drowning or burning buildings or to stop runaway horses. It would be easy to fill many pages with accounts of the heroic exploits of individual policemen; what would be more difficult is assessing the impact of these exploits upon the public's view of the department and the police conception of their role in society. If prestige and rewards came primarily for the "good collar," the spectacular arrest, this is what most policemen would strive for, rather than for keeping the peace peacefully. If the public image of the "good cop" was that of a gun-toting hero or the club-swinging suppressor of the "dangerous classes," police-

men would not be prone to conceive of their role as mediators of domestic and social controversy, as harmonizers whose function was to minimize urban conflict and violence rather than to contribute to its existence.

As long as society could not agree on what the police were to be and do, or if it demanded contradictory things from the force, it could hardly expect consistency, honesty, efficiency, and respect for civil liberties to be the dominant characteristics of police performance.

NOTES

1   A. A. W. Ramsay, *Sir Robert Peel* (London: 1928), pp. 87–89; W. L. M. Lee, *A History of Police in England* (London: 1901), pp. 192–93, 201, 219–23; the quotations are taken from E. P. Thompson, *The Making of the English Working Class* (New York: 1964), pp. 81–82.

2   *Cf.* Joseph R. Gusfield, *Symbolic Crusade: Status Politics and the American Temperance Movement* (Urbana: 1963), pp. 37–60.

3   *Commercial Advertiser,* August 20, 1840.

4   *Bd. of Ass't Ald. Procs. and Docs.,* vol. 19, no. 56, p. 188.

5   *Bd. of Ald. Docs.,* Vol. 3, no. 88, pp. 563–64, Vol. 10, pt. 1, no. 53, p. 104.

6   *M.C.C.,* XVIII, p. 421; Herbert Asbury, *Gangs of New York* (New York: 1938), pp. 2–16; *Commercial Advertiser,* June 5, 1830; *Evening Post,* July 18, 1832; Charles Rosenberg, *The Cholera Years* (Chicago: 1962); Sigmund Diamond, *The Reputation of the American Businessman* (New York: 1966), pp. 5–7. This attitude was not universal. For a sensitive contemporary appreciation of the relationship between living conditions and riots, see John H. Griscom, M.D., *The Sanitary Condition of the Laboring Population of New York* (New York: 1845), pp. 23–24. Other vivid accounts are in Collyer, *Lights and Shadows,* pp. 6–7, and Charles Dickens, *American Notes for*

General Circulation, 2 vols., (London: 1892), I, pp. 213–16.

7   Naturally, each side blamed the other for causing the riots. For the Whig viewpoint see Philip Hone, *The Diary of Philip Hone, 1828–1851,* 2 vols., Allan Nevins, ed. (New York: 1927), I, pp. 122–23; the Democratic case is given in *Evening Post,* April 17, 1834.

8   Gustave de Beaumont, *Marie, or Slavery in the United States,* trans. Barbara Chapman (Stamford: 1958), pp. 245–49; Hone, *Diary,* I, pp. 134–35; *Bd. of Ald. Docs.,* vol. 1, no. 17, pp. 145–50, vol. 3, no. 1, pp. 12–13.

9   Louis D. Scisco, *Political Nativism in New York State* (New York: 1901), pp. 53–54; *Morning News,* April 4, 7, 8, 1845.

10   *Bd. of Ald. Procs.,* XXIX, pp. 24–25; *Procs. Approved by the Mayor,* XIII, p. 36.

11   Just before the First World War an American investigator found universal agreement among British and Continental police officials that any attempt to legislate moral standards that were unacceptable to a large portion of the population would be disastrous to the morale and efficiency of the local police force (Raymond Fosdick, *European Police Systems* [New York: 1915], pp. 379–82).

12   Fosdick, *European Police Systems,* pp. 40, 48, 200–204; *Bd. of Ald. Procs.,* XXIX, 24–27.

Policing the City: Boston, 1822–1885

ROGER LANE

In 1820 the Boston city government's concept of police involved duties inherited from the selectmen and other town officers. The city marshal, who assumed these functions in 1823, was principally concerned with municipal administration. His office, before and after its incorporation with other agents of police, provided an expedient means of dealing with a variety of urban problems. The widespread duties, reaching into many areas of local government, made it inconceivable that any outside authority should be involved. The enforcement of criminal law, in the early nineteenth century, was still the responsibility of aggrieved citizens, or of the sheriffs, courts, and constables created by the commonwealth. Much of it was in fact ignored, and an attempt to apply it could be politically disruptive as well as physically dangerous.

But the employment of police in municipal administration was governed not by theory but by convenience. Boston was a conservative city, rarely innovating bold projects or new techniques. But it was always well managed, with an unusually high tax rate and proportionally superior services. The police were valued especially for the flexibility that made them adaptable to new demands. But when better machinery was developed the government did not hesitate to transfer their responsibilities. The creation of

the sewer, health, street, and building departments all diminished the role of the police in local administration.

The lessening of such uses coincided with an increase in their use to "maintain order." The local authorities never denied their responsibility in this matter. Marshals and watchmen were always charged, in some degree, with keeping the streets clear of human as well as material disorder and obstruction, a task that necessarily called for the invocation of law and force and which became more aggressive as the concept of order itself expanded.

In contrast to the business of municipal administration, in which other agencies progressively assumed the functions of police, the business of maintaining order was one in which the police progressively assumed the functions of the citizens. As long as the community was small there were sanctions more powerful than law, and when the law was invoked, the sheriffs, constables, and courts relied in practice on the initiative of the inhabitants in making complaints and swearing out warrants. Boston was physically compact, with settled traditions, comparatively easy to govern and to police. But as the city developed, problems arose which the community was unable to meet in traditional fashion. The creation of a professional, preventive police was both a result and a cause of the inability of citizens to deal with these matters by themselves.

Riot, one of the first problems recognized as beyond control, dramatized the need for force. The leaders of government were firmly set against popular violence as a means of political and social protest, except in the explosive case of slavery. After the creation of the new police in 1838 only the great Draft Riot of 1863 proved impossible to contain.

The issue of felonious criminality was more complex. Those mad or desperate offenses which accounted for most serious crime were not proportionately on the increase during the nineteenth century. But the citizens were progressively worse equipped to protect themselves from, or to punish, criminals; and there was a rise in sophisticated crimes for profit, with which only a few were able to deal privately. Both conditions contributed to the demand for an aggressive police. So did the growing concept that the state itself had an interest in preventing criminality, greater than that of injured individuals.

A third general social problem was continuously demanding. It is impossible to assess accurately the changing incidence of the disorderly behavior of which drunkenness was the center and symbol. But it is clear that such behavior became ever less tolerable. The demands of an interdependent urban economy made drunkenness more disruptive than it had been under the town. Tighter standards of middle-class behavior, coupled with the reform movements that began in the 1830s, made it more easily condemned. As Boston became a city of strangers, the ineffectiveness of the older sanctions was widely recognized.

A continuing conflict over the proper enforcement of the laws complicated the use of police to arrest for these misdemeanors. Whether drunkenness was regarded as a sin, or later as a disease, reformers never doubted that it was a basic social evil or that morality was properly the concern of legal authority. Before the 1830s the law in many matters was regarded as the expression of an ideal. But the creation of a strong police raised the

exciting possibility that the ideal might be realized, that morality could be enforced and the state made an instrument of social regeneration. Local authorities briefly tried and then rejected the experiment. But even after 1850; with conservatives in almost continuous control of Boston, reformers continued to press the issue and to focus their hopes on the legislature. For a brief period in the 1860s the commonwealth repeated the experiment and then discovered that prohibition was tolerable only when evaded.

Conflict over the liquor laws never stopped, but it eased significantly after the Civil War. However they differed with reformers over the existence of vice, the men who governed Boston were always concerned with its social effects. As dominant opinion in the city became more disapproving of public misbehavior, the effort to control disorder involved an increasing intolerance of moral offenses. With the demands of law eased, the city accepted the duty of execution. By 1885 the police were primarily agents of law enforcement, and disputes centered around matters of degree rather than of principle.[1]

Apart from the issue of vice control, and more briefly the reclamation of fugitive slaves, the development of police authority was not usually in controversy. The acts of policemen might be resented individually and specifically, and the marshal or chief was not usually popular: no head of the department from 1822 to 1878 ever held any other office after leaving it. But there was agreement on the need for strength and no resentment of the general exercise of power.

The agreement resulted in part from the fact that the growth of police was not in itself responsible for any major change in the conception of what the state could do. The criminal and administrative codes expanded enormously; Governor Butler, in 1883, charged with some reason that the manufacture of offenses had become "a state industry." But this multiplication reflected a growth in complexity rather than in severity; the state in the eighteenth century was theoretically more restrictive than in the nineteenth. The real change was in practice and attitudes. The increase of police simply made feasible the expectation that most codes would be enforced, and not indirectly by the citizens but directly by agents of authority.[2]

Furthermore, the development of the department did not add to the powers of peace officers as individuals. There was a notable increase in the number of statutory cases in which the police could make arrests without written warrant. But in some ways these laws limited personal discretion. The old statutes defining the powers of the watch and various other officers were broad enough to fit most cases, at least under the section dealing with "suspicious persons." The judiciary held the key to the exercise of legal force, and it maintained that the discretion given peace officers was broad and ancient under the common law. The arming of patrolmen, together with increased numbers and improved communications, did give the officers a decided physical advantage. But at the same time the democratization of politics and the press opened channels of protest against abuses.

Above all, the police were never a group apart. Only in a few matters, notably detective corruption, did they have a distinct and separate interest. The fee system, which had created resentments earlier, was controlled once the department was professionalized. The police in Boston, unlike those in other countries, and the constables, did not serve directly as agents of the courts, and their efforts as individuals often softened the formal demands of justice. The variety of their functions, most of which were innocuous and some humane, kept them from being identified exclusively with force. And it was the conscious policy of both state and city, through formal requirements of residence and such informal requirements as fatherhood, to keep the officers close to the citizens.

The change from municipal to state control in 1885 made some difference. The new commissioners abandoned such locally popular functions as the distribution of free soup and assumed such unpopular ones as the protection of property during strikes. They also broke the political deadlock over such expensive improvements as the signal system. But fundamentally the force remained unchanged, charged with the same duties, recruited from the same classes, subject to the same pressures. There was no diminution in the purely municipal functions, already in essence reduced to two: the department continued to serve as the "eyes and ears" of others, reporting problems when found, and it remained responsible for traffic control, directly and through the licensing power.[3]

Nor was there any important addition to the business of law enforcement. The city had already accepted its responsibility for controlling vice through license and had succeeded in licensing the great majority of liquor dealers. There was no immediate drop in the number of permits granted and no change in the more general policy of arrest. The police were still concerned only with the regulation of public behavior, and not with any more fundamental reform.[4]

The experience of state control merely demonstrated in Boston what other cities had already learned, that political change at the top was not enough either to solve problems built into the structure of American law or to upset the complex relations between police and the public. The legislature had intended no such revolution. The officers, and the commissioners, were still citizens of Boston. The city retained formal and informal controls over their actions, and the state, while more remote, was neither oppressive nor unresponsive. The police department was in fact what it was designed to be, simply a useful tool of government. So long as government itself was still regarded as a tool of the people, the citizens remained confident of their ultimate ability to use both as desired.

NOTES

1 The Boston police were brought under state control later than in most other major cities where the experiment was tried; see Raymond B. Fosdick, *American Police Systems* (New York, 1920), p. 95. The fact that the transition was made only after most outstanding issues had been settled accounts for the relatively quiet way in which it was accepted; in New York City, in contrast, the municipal police, encouraged by the local authorities, conducted an armed battle with the metropolitan force which replaced them in 1857; see Augustine E. Costello, *Our Police Protectors: History of the New York Police from the Earliest Period to the Present Time* (New York, 1885), p. 102. In general, state control proved satisfactory enough that the acknowledged authority, in 1920, noted that for thirty years the force had "stood well in the lead of police organizations throughout the nation" (Fosdick, *American Police Systems,* p. 122). The lack of any deeply rooted differences contributed also to the long continuance of state control; the department was given back to the city only recently, by st. 1962, ch. 322.

2 Butler quoted in Senate Doc. no. 1 (1883), *Address of His Excellency Benjamin F. Butler,* p. 45.

3 Last soup distribution in *Annual Police Report* (1890), p. 17; strike protection in *City Council Minutes,* February 17, 1887, pp. 179–180; signals in *Annual Police Report* (1886), p. 26.

4 Licenses in *Annual Police Report* (1886), p. 23. The men appointed by the state were subject, also, to the same temptations which had beset their predecessors. In 1888 the new head of detectives was fired for moral turpitude. In 1891, the commissioners were investigated for misconduct in the enforcement of the vice laws and other offenses, and the superintendent resigned after revelations of an unsavory association. See Boston *Herald,* July 6, 1888, February 8, 1891, and October 7, 1891.

2

PERSONALITY AND SOCIALIZATION

A Maine policeman elects to spend his off-duty hours with his Cub Scouts
— a special troop of retarded or handicapped children.

Police evoke powerful feelings. Even cursory observation suggests that police are overrepresented as the subjects of television programs, plays, and popular literature. There is a wide audience for an occupation that combines elements of danger and authority. Some people regard police as larger-than-life, heroic figures, protectors of the weak and innocent against evil individuals and rampant hordes. Others see the police as brutal sadists who enjoy cornering and physically overpowering adversaries. In fact, as the articles in this section suggest, the policeman is usually neither a heroic figure nor a sadistic beast. He is a man who is called upon to do a certain kind of job. The elements of the job, the legal system, the police administration, and the subculture of police all combine to socialize and develop a working personality that is seen by the citizens with whom police come in contact.

The articles in this section explore the bases and outcome of the personality and socialization of police. They raise certain questions that are useful for students of police to discuss: Are certain "types" of people principally drawn to police work? Do certain personality characteristics lend themselves especially well to carrying out the policeman's role? Does the policeman's view of the world develop principally before or after a person becomes a policeman? Is there an authoritarian personality? And are police especially likely to possess it?

Two of the quotes in the Skolnick article, those of Colin McInnes and Thomas Brooks, suggest that police are very conventional people. Radano's article, based upon his experience as a policeman, portrays police as something other than observers of conventional morality. Are the views expressed by Skolnick and the picture offered by Radano inconsistent? Can they be reconciled, and if so, how? Gray offers yet another explanation of police personality based upon the subculture's understanding of the requirements of the job. Is Gray's explanation consistent with those offered by Skolnick, Radano, and Niederhoffer?

As we will see later, when the topic of police discretion is discussed, it is usually in the context of policemen enforcing the law against citizens. Radano's article makes clear that the policeman is often faced with discretionary decisions regarding the conduct of his fellow patrolmen. Suppose a young policeman is invited to a "coop"? What should his response be? What should the response of police administrators be? Ultimately, the answers to these questions suggest a broader issue that is essential to any discussion of police role: On the factual side, who is more responsible for the growth and development of the individual policeman—the man himself, his colleagues, or the police administrator? On the moral level, who should be?

So we see that the issue of police personality and socialization is not merely an abstract, academic one but one that goes to the heart of organization and the conceptions of the propriety of police behavior held by police administrators, the working police, and recruits. We cannot decide the question of propriety without understanding the reality of personality and socialization. At the same time, we cannot understand the attitudes and personality of police without some discussion of what is *lawful* and *moral*. Ultimately, we want to arrive at some idea of what society should realistically demand as *proper* conduct by police in light of the requirements of the job and how individual police and police departments can contribute to that goal.

(

Why Police Behave the Way They Do

JEROME H. SKOLNICK

A recurrent theme of the sociology of occupations is the effect of a man's work on his outlook on the world. Doctors, janitors, lawyers, and industrial workers develop distinctive ways of perceiving and responding to their environment. Here I will concentrate on analyzing certain outstanding elements in the police milieu: danger, authority, and efficiency, as they combine to generate distinctive cognitive and behavioral responses in police—"a working personality." There are distinctive recognizable tendencies in police as an occupational grouping. Some of these may be found in other occupations sharing similar problems. So far as exposure to danger is concerned, the policeman may be likened to the soldier. His problems as an authority bear a certain similarity to those of the schoolteacher, and the pressures he feels to prove himself efficient are not unlike those felt by the industrial worker. The combination of these elements, however, is unique to the policeman. Thus, the police, as a résult of their social situation, tend to develop ways of looking at the world distinctive to themselves, cognitive lenses through which to see situations and events.

The policeman's "working personality" is most highly developed in his constabulary role of the man on the beat. For analytical purposes that role is sometimes regarded as an enforcement speciality, but in this general discussion of policemen as they comport themselves while working, the uniformed "cop" is seen as the foundation for the po-

From *New York/World Journal Tribune* (October 23, 1966), pp. 12–14. Reprinted by permission.

liceman's working personality. The police, unlike the military, draw no caste distinction in socialization. Every officer of rank must serve an apprenticeship as a patrolman. This feature of police organization means that the constabulary role is the primary one for all police officers, and that whatever the special requirements of roles in enforcement specialities, they are carried out with a common background of constabulary experience.

The process by which this "personality" is developed may be summarized: the policeman's role contains two principal variables, danger and authority, which should be interpreted in the light of a "constant" pressure to appear efficient. The element of danger seems to make the policeman especially attentive to signs indicating a potential for violence and lawbreaking. As a result, the policeman is generally a "suspicious" person. Furthermore, the character of the policeman's work makes him less desirable as a friend, since norms of friendship implicate others in his work. Accordingly, the element of danger isolates the policeman socially from that segment of the citizenry which he regards as symbolically dangerous and also from the conventional citizenry with whom he identifies.

The element of authority reinforces the element of danger in isolating the policeman. Typically, the policeman is required to enforce laws representing puritanical morality, such as those prohibiting drunkenness, and also laws regulating the flow of public activity, such as traffic laws. In these situations the policeman directs the citizenry, whose typical response denies recognition of his authority, and stresses his obligation to respond to danger. The kind of man who responds well to danger, however, does not normally subscribe to codes or puritanical morality. As a result, the policeman is unusually liable to the charge of hypocrisy. That the whole civilian world is an audience for the policeman further promotes police isolation and, in consequence, solidarity. Finally, danger undermines the judicious use of authority.

In attempting to understand the policeman's view of the world, it is useful to raise a more general question: What are the conditions under which police, as authorities, may be threatened? To answer this, we must look at the situation of the policeman in the community. One attribute of many characterizing the policeman's role stands out: The policeman is required to respond to assaults against persons and property. When a radio call reports an armed robbery and gives a description of the man involved, every policeman, regardless of assignment, is responsible for the criminal's apprehension. The *raison d'être* of the policeman and the criminal law, the underlying collectively held moral sentiments which justify penal sanctions, arises ultimately and most clearly from the threat of violence and the possibility of danger to the community. Police who "lobby" for severe narcotics laws, for instance, justify their position on grounds that the addict is a harbinger of danger since, it is maintained, he requires $100 a day to support his habit, and he must steal to get it. Although the addict is not usually a violent criminal, criminal penalties for addiction are supported on grounds that he may become one.

The policeman, because his work requires him to be occupied continually with potential violence, develops a perceptual

shorthand to identify certain kinds of people as symbolic assailants, that is, as persons who use gesture, language, and attire that the policeman has come to recognize as a prelude to violence. This does not mean that violence by the symbolic assailant is necessarily predictable. On the contrary, the policeman responds to the vague indication of danger suggested by appearance. Like the animals of the experimental psychologist, the policeman finds the threat of random damage more compelling than a predetermined and inevitable punishment.

Nor, to qualify for the status of symbolic assailant, need an individual ever have used violence. A man backing out of a jewelry store with a gun in one hand and jewelry in the other would qualify even if the gun were a toy and he had never in his life fired a real pistol. To the policeman in the situation, the man's personal history is momentarily immaterial. There is only one relevant sign: a gun signifying danger. Similarly, a young man may suggest the threat of violence to the policeman by his manner of walking or "strutting," the insolence in the demeanor being registered by the policeman as a possible preamble to later attack.[1]

However, the policeman may well, as a personality, enjoy the possibility of danger, especially its associated excitement, even though he may at the same time be fearful of it. Such "inconsistency" is easily understood. Freud has by now made it an axiom of personality theory that logical and emotional consistency are by no means the same phenomenon.

However complex the motives aroused by the element of danger, its consequences for sustaining police culture are unambiguous. This element requires him, like the combat soldier, the European Jew, the South African (white or black), to live in a world straining toward duality and suggesting danger when "they" are perceived. Consequently, it is in the nature of the policeman's situation that his conception of order emphasize regularity and predictability. It is, therefore, a conception shaped by persistent *suspicion*. The English "copper," often portrayed as a courteous, easygoing, rather jolly sort of chap, on the one hand, or as a devil-may-care adventurer, on the other, is differently described by Colin MacInnes, the British suspense writer:

> The true copper's dominant characteristic, if the truth be known, is neither those daring nor vicious qualities that are sometimes attributed to him by friend or enemy, but an ingrained conservatism, an almost desperate love of the conventional. It is untidiness, disorder, the unusual, that a copper disapproves of most of all: far more, even, than of crime which is merely a professional matter. Hence his profound dislike of people loitering in streets, dressing extravagantly, speaking with exotic accents, being strange, weak, eccentric, or simply any rare minority—of their doing, in fact, anything that cannot be safely predicted.[2]

Policemen are indeed specifically *trained* to be suspicious, to perceive events or changes in the physical surroundings that indicate the occurrence or probability of disorder. A former student who worked as a patrolman in a suburban New York police department describes this aspect of the policeman's assessment of the unusual:

> The time spent cruising one's sector or walking one's beat is not wasted time, though it can become quite routine. During this time, the most important thing for the officer to do is notice the *normal*. He must come to know the people in his area, their habits, their automobiles and their friends. He must learn what time the various shops close, how much money is kept

on hand on different nights, what lights are usually left on, which houses are vacant. . . . Only then can he decide what persons or cars under what circumstances warrant the appellation "suspicious."

The patrolman in one community I studied closely, and probably in most communities, has come to identify the black man with danger. James Baldwin vividly expresses the isolation of the ghetto policeman:

> . . . The only way to police a ghetto is to be oppressive. None of the police commissioner's men, even with the best will in the world, have any way of understanding the lives led by the people they swagger about in twos and threes controlling. Their very presence is an insult, and it would be, even if they spent their entire day feeding gumdrops to children. They represent the force of the white world, and that world's criminal profit and ease, to keep the black man corraled up here, in his place. The badge, the gun in the holster and the swinging club make vivid what will happen should his rebellion become overt. . . .
>
> It is hard, on the other hand, to blame the policeman, blank, good-natured, thoughtless and insuperably innocent, for being such a perfect representative of the people he serves. He, too, believes in good intentions and is astounded and offended when they are not taken for the deed. He has never, himself, done anything for which to be hated—which of us has?—and yet he is facing, daily and nightly, people who would gladly see him dead, and he knows it. There is no way for him not to know it: there are few things under heaven more unnerving than the silent, accumulating contempt and hatred of a people. He moves through Harlem, therefore, like an occupying soldier in a bitterly hostile country, which is precisely what and where he is, and is the reason he walks in twos and threes.[3]

While Baldwin's observations on police-

Negro relations cannot be disputed seriously, there is greater social distance between police and "civilians" in general regardless of their color than Baldwin considers. Thus, Colin MacInnes has his English hero, Mr. Justice, explaining:

> ... The story is all coppers are just civilians like anyone else, living among them not in barracks like on the Continent, but you and I know that's just a legend for mugs. We *are* cut off: we're *not* like everyone else. Some civilians fear us and play up to us, some dislike us and keep out of our way, but no one—well, very few indeed—accepts us as just ordinary like them. In one sense, dear, we're just like hostile troops occupying an enemy country. And say what you like, at times it makes us lonely.[4]

MacInnes' observation suggests that by not introducing a white control group, Baldwin has failed to see that the policeman may not get on well with anybody regardless (to use the hackneyed phrase) of race, creed, or national origin. Policemen whom one knows well often express their sense of isolation from the public as a whole, not just from those who fail to share their color. The police I studied were asked, for example, to rank the most serious problems police have. The category most frequently selected was not racial problems but some form of public relations: lack of respect for the police, lack of co-operation in enforcement of law, lack of understanding of the requirements of police work. One respondent answered: "As a policeman my most serious problem is impressing on the general public just how difficult and necessary police service is to all. There seems to be an attitude of 'law is important, but it applies to my neighbor—not to me.' "

One policeman related the following incident:

Several months after I joined the force, my wife and I used to be socially active with a crowd of young people, mostly married, who gave a lot of parties where there was drinking and dancing, and we enjoyed it. I've never forgotten, though, an incident that happened on one Fourth of July party. Everybody had been drinking, there was a lot of talking, people were feeling boisterous, and some kid there—he must have been 20 or 22—threw a firecracker that hit my wife in the leg and burned her. I didn't know exactly what to do—punch the guy in the nose, bawl him out, just forget it. Anyway, I couldn't let it pass, so I walked over to him and told him he ought to be careful. He began to rise up at me, and when he did, somebody yelled, "Better watch out, he's a cop." I saw everybody standing there, and I could feel they were all against me and for the kid, even though he had thrown the firecracker at my wife. I went over to the host and said that it was probably better if my wife and I left because a fight would put a damper on the party. Actually, I'd hoped he would ask the kid to leave, since the kid had thrown the firecracker. But he didn't, so we left. After that incident, my wife and I stopped going around with that crowd, and decided that if we were going to go to parties where there was to be drinking and boisterousness, we weren't going to be the only police people there.

All occupational groups share a measure of inclusiveness and identification. People are brought together simply by doing the same work and having similar career and salary problems. As several writers have noted, however, police show an unusually high degree of occupational solidarity. It is true that the police have a common employer and wear a uniform at work, but so do doctors, milkmen, and bus drivers. Yet it is doubtful that these workers have so close-knit an occupation or so similar an outlook on the world as do police. Set apart from the conventional world, the policeman experiences an exceptionally strong tendency to find his social identity within his occupational milieu.

When considering how authority influences rejection, the policeman typically singles out his responsibility for enforcement of traffic violations. Resentment, even hostility, is generated in those receiving citations, in part because such contact is often the only one citizens have with police, and in part because municipal administrations and courts have been known to utilize police authority primarily to meet budgetary requirements rather than those of public order. When a municipality engages in "speed trapping" by changing limits so quickly that drivers cannot realistically slow down to the prescribed speed or, while keeping the limits reasonable, charging high fines primarily to generate revenue, the policeman carries the brunt of public resentment.

While traffic patrol plays a major role in separating the policemen from the respectable community, other of his tasks also have this consequence. Traffic patrol is only the most obvious illustration of the policeman's general responsibility for maintaining public order, which also includes keeping order among onlookers at public accidents, sporting events and political rallies. These activities share one feature: the policeman is called upon to *direct* ordinary citizens and therefore to restrain their freedom of action. Resenting the restraint, the average citizen in such a situation typically thinks something along the lines of "He is supposed to catch crooks; why is he bothering me?" Thus, the citizen stresses the "dangerous" portion of the policeman's role while belittling his authority.

Closely related to the policeman's au-

thority-based problems as *director* of the citizenry are difficulties associated with his injunction to *regulate public morality*. For instance, the policeman is obliged to investigate "lovers' lanes" and to enforce laws pertaining to gambling, prostitution, and drunkenness. His responsibility in these matters allows him much administrative discretion, since he may not actually enforce the law by making an arrest but instead merely interfere with continuation of the objectionable activity. Thus, he may put the drunk in a taxi, tell the lovers to remove themselves from the back seat, and advise a man soliciting a prostitute to leave the area. But the policeman is apt to cause resentment because of the suspicion that policemen do not themselves strictly conform to the moral norms they are enforcing. Thus, the policeman, faced with enforcing a law against fornication, drunkenness, or gambling, is easily liable to a charge of hypocrisy.

The policeman, as a result of the unique combination of the elements of danger and authority, experiences a special predicament. It is difficult to develop qualities enabling him to stand up to danger and to conform to standards of puritanical morality. The element of danger demands that the policeman be able to carry out efforts that are in their nature overtly masculine. Police work, like soldiering, requires an exceptional caliber of physical fitness, agility, toughness, and the like. The man who ranks high on these masculine characteristics is, again like the soldier, not usually disposed to be puritanical about sex, drinking, and gambling.

On the basis of observations, policemen do not subscribe to moralistic standards for conduct. For example, the morals squad of the police department, when questioned, was unanimously against the statutory rape age limit, on grounds that as late teenagers they themselves might not have refused an offer from a 17-year-old girl. Neither, from observations, are policemen by any means total abstainers from the use of alcoholic beverages. The policeman who is arresting a drunk has probably been drunk himself; he knows it and the drunk knows it.

Finally, to round out the sketch, policemen are notably conservative, emotionally and politically. If the element of danger in the policeman's role tends to make the policeman suspicious, and therefore emotionally attached to the status quo, a similar consequence may be attributed to the element of authority. The fact that a man is engaged in enforcing a set of rules implies that he also becomes implicated in *affirming* them. Labor disputes provide the commonest example of conditions inclining the policeman to support the status quo. In these situations, the police are necessarily pushed on the side of the defense of property. Their responsibilities thus lead them to see the striking and sometimes angry workers as their enemy and, therefore, to be cool, if not antagonistic, toward the whole conception of labor militancy. If a policeman did not believe in the system of laws he was responsible for enforcing, he would have to go on living in a state of conflicting cognitions, a condition which a number of social psychologists agree is painful.

This hypothetical issue of not believing in the laws they are enforcing simply does not arise for most policemen. In the course of the research, however, there was one example. A black civil rights advocate (member of CORE) became a policeman with the conviction that by so doing he would be aiding the cause of impartial administration of law for blacks. For him, however, this outside rationale was not enough to sustain him in administering a system of laws that depends for its impartiality upon a reasonable

measure of social and economic equality among the citizenry. Because this recruit identified so much with the black community as to be unable to meet the enforcement requirements of the police department, his efficiency was impaired, and he resigned in his rookie year.

Police are understandably reluctant to appear to be anything but impartial politically. The police are forbidden from publicly campaigning for political candidates. The London police are similarly prohibited and before 1887 were not allowed to vote in parliamentary elections, or in local ones until 1893. It was not surprising that one chief of police forbade questions on the questionnaire that would have measured political attitudes. One policeman, however, explained the chief's refusal on grounds that "a couple of jerks here would probably cut up, and come out looking like Commies."

During the course of administering the questionnaire over a three-day period, I talked with approximately 15 officers and sergeants in one police department, discussing political attitudes of police. In addition, during the course of research itself, approximately 50 were interviewed for varying periods of time. Of these, at least 20 were interviewed more than once, some over time periods of several weeks. Furthermore, a number of police were interviewed for periods ranging from several hours to several days. Most of the time was *not* spent on investigating political attitudes, but I made a point of raising the question, if possible making it part of a discussion centered around the contents of a right-wing newsletter to which one of the detectives subscribed. One discussion included a group of eight detectives. From these observations, interviews, and discussions, it was clear that a Goldwater type of conservatism was the dominant political and emotional persuasion of the police. I encountered only three policemen who claimed to be politically "liberal," at the same time asserting that they were decidedly exceptional.

Writing about the New York police force, Thomas R. Brooks suggests a similar interpretation. He writes: "Cops are conventional people. . . . All a cop can swing in a milieu of marijuana smokers, interracial dates and homosexuals is the nightstick. A policeman who passed a Lower East Side art gallery filled with paintings of what appeared to be female genitalia could think of doing only one thing—step in and make an arrest." [5]

NOTES

1 Something of the flavor of the policeman's attitude toward the symbolic assailant comes across in a recent article by a police expert. In discussing the problem of selecting subjects for field interrogation, the author writes:
A. Be suspicious. This is a healthy police attitude, but it should be controlled and not too obvious.
B. Look for the unusual.
1. Persons who do not "belong" where they are observed.
2. Automobiles which do not "look right."
3. Businesses opened at odd hours, or not according to routine or custom.
C. Subjects who should be subjected to field interrogations.
1. Suspicious persons known to the officer from previous arrests, field interrogations and observations.
2. Emaciated appearing alcoholics and narcotics users who invariably turn to crime to pay for cost of habit.
3. Person who fits description of wanted suspect as described by radio, teletype, daily bulletins.
4. Any person observed in the immediate vicinity of a crime very recently committed or reported as "in progress."
5. Known trouble-makers near large gatherings.
6. Persons who attempt to avoid or evade the officer.
7. Exaggerated unconcern over contact with the officer.
8. Visibly "rattled" when near the policeman.
9. Unescorted women or young girls in public places, particularly at night in such places as cafes, bars, bus and train depots or street corners.
10. "Lovers" in an industrial area (make good lookouts).
11. Persons who loiter about places where children play.
12. Solicitors or peddlers in a residential neighborhood.
13. Loiterers around public rest rooms.
14. Lone male sitting in car adjacent to schoolground with newspaper or book in his lap.
15. Lone male sitting in car near shopping center who pays unusual amount of attention to women, sometimes continuously manipulating rearview mirror to avoid direct eye contact.
16. Hitchhikers.
17. Person wearing coat on hot days.
18. Car with mismatched hub caps, or dirty car with clean license plate (or vice versa).
19. Uniformed "deliverymen" with no merchandise or truck.
20. Many others. How about your own personal experiences?
From Thomas F. Adams, "Field Interrogation," Police (March–April 1963): 28.
2 Colin MacInnes, Mr. Love and Justice (London: New English Library, 1962), p. 74.
3 James Baldwin, Nobody Knows My Name (New York: Dell, 1962), pp. 65–67.
4 MacInnes, Mr. Love, p. 20.
5 Thomas R. Brooks, "New York's Finest," Commentary 40 (August 1965): 29–30.

The Coop

GENE RADANO

A coop is a shelter where cops go to sit down, grab a smoke, escape the weather, or to lie down. Some coops are good coops, in terms of comfort, but most leave much to be desired. Maybe it's because no one pays any rent. Cops move in like the proverbial camel nosing his way into the tent, and soon squatters' rights prevail.

"Where's the coop?"

"You got keys to the coop?"

"There's no heat in this coop."

As you can see, coop is a word that lends itself easily to any cop conversation.

"Stay out of the coop. I'm having company."

"A broad?"

"I don't have to answer any questions by you. You're not paying me home relief."

Cops are always coming and going, and because of that a cop may often find himself alone in a coop; sometimes there'll be one other cop; other times there may be as many as three, four, or five. Usually there isn't much to do in a coop so cops just sit there. Instead of being on the sidewalk doing nothing they sneak into the coop and do nothing. Sometimes they swap stories; humorous ones, dirty ones, some tragic ones, but most often cynical ones.

This particular day Paul was one of five cops in a coop. Paul was a rookie, fresh out of the Police Academy. The job was still springtime to him so he would have preferred to remain on the street. However the cop working the beat alongside of him interpreted his reluctance to "hit the coop" to a more sensible reason.

"Don't worry about the Sergeant, kid," he advised. "He won't be around. He's covering a D.O.A."

(Covering a D.O.A. doesn't mean the Sergeant is placing a warm woolen blanket over someone or something. It means he is assigned to the case of a person just found dead on arrival of the police.)

This coop that Paul was led to was located in the cellar boiler room of a neighborhood movie house. It wasn't a good coop. A thick layer of dust created many problems there. One had to be careful where one sat or where one leaned. One of the policemen had solved the dilemma by spreading newspapers along a narrow wooden bench. Then he lay down on them and tried to relax.

Paul's side partner, on seeing the cop stretched out, philosophically remarked, "If you can do your tour of duty sitting down, fine. If you can do it lying down, great!"

Talk in coops is the usual man talk: sex, politics, hemorrhoids, the Sergeant. Not always in that order.

One cop was talking. He pretended he was addressing another cop; actually he was speaking for everyone's benefit.

"Jack, what were the first words you said to her?"

The cop to whom the question was addressed was the one stretched out on the newspapers. He may have been sleeping because he didn't answer.

"For the past year I've been asking him this but he won't tell me. He's made a mystery out of it! Jack, what were the first words you said to her?"

Silence. He couldn't be dead: his big stomach was going up and down. Up and down.

The first cop, the one who was standing, continued: "I was riding a radio car with this guy"—indicating the prone Jack—"and we get a radio run. Family trouble. When we arrive there's this blister and her husband. She's waving a kitchen knife like it was the American flag and he's trying to use a pot for a hammer. Several neighbors are acting as referees. Everybody is screaming. The place is jumping, a real tumult! We chase the neighbors out. . . ."

Jack opened his eyes at this point. "Why don't you shut up?" he grumbled.

The cop who was standing ignored the interruption. "We chase the neighbors out. . . ."

Jack closed his eyes.

"We chase the neighbors out and I push the husband into a bedroom. Jack corners the wife in the living room." To the man lying down: "You cornered her all right, didn't you, Jack?"

At this point Jack rolled over on his side. His eyes were still closed.

"Well," continued the cop who was standing, "the husband turns out to be one of those would-be tough guys. He's going to do this: he's going to do that. He tries to get by me to get at her. I got to block the doorway. One time he got me so mad I'm ready to belt the bum. Finally he tells me what it's all about. His wife is jealous. Smells his clothes when he comes home to see if he's been with another blister. Things like that. I take a good look at this guy. A monkey! He has a bean belly, a head shaped like a football, and he's so small if you spit on him you drown him!

"I ask him, 'You a ladies' man?' He winks. Then he says, 'A woman gives me the signal what can I do? I wouldn't be a man unless I accepted the challenge!' And he meant it! He meant it! . . .

"Now that I got the facts I can make the pitch. I tell him, 'Your wife is home slaving and you go out, get a bag on, and come home and make her think God knows what. Then 'cause she gets suspicious you take it out on her. I don't know why she stays with you. If she was my sister I'd tell her to get out!'

"Little by little Football-head quiets down. He even tells me he's sorry. I listen for Jack and the blister; everything seems to be quiet in the living room. But I can't really tell 'cause Jack has the door closed. I finally tap on the living room door. 'Jack,' I ask, 'how's it going?'

" 'Good. Good,' he answers. 'Give me a minute.'

"It took more than a minute. I go back to talk to Football-head. We grab a smoke together. Turns out his father and my father were in the same line: cement masons. Small world! After a while the living room door opens. Jack walks out with the wife. She's quiet. Subdued. Domesticated. She's really tame. Jack did a good job on her! Didn't you, Jack?

"I make a speech. It's a speech I've worked out myself and I use it on family problems. 'You're two grown people,' I tell them. 'You've married for better or for worse. You have to learn to trust each other. You have a family. It's not nice to argue in front of the kids. Think how they must feel.

You've made a bargain; now make the best of it!'

"They thank us. Football-head and the blister both thank us. With that we leave. Case closed! Right? We get in the radio car and we start to cruise around. Suddenly I notice that this guy, Jack, his fly is open. I don't know what made me look—normally I don't—but there it is *unzippered!*

" 'Hey!' I point. 'What gives, Jack? Has the fly flown?'

" 'Excuse me,' he says and zippers his fly. Then he winks at me and leans his head against the side of the car. He starts to doze."

The cop who had been doing all the talking now turned his attention to the cop who was lying down. "I know she was screaming when she went into that room with you. I don't want to know what happened in there. All I ask is, what, in your opinion, were the first words you spoke that changed her from a raving, jealous bitch into a docile housewife? What were the opening words? Not that I want to pry; I only ask so that I too can learn proper, proven police action during family fights. Then if it works for me I'll recommend it be included in the official Manual of Procedure. That's how progress is made."

The cops all laughed. Jack ignored the man who was standing over him.

The rookie found a fairly clean spot on another bench and sat down cautiously. He wondered what would happen if the Sergeant found out about the coop and walked in on them. Surely someone would get a complaint. His mind drifted back to his first day in the Police Department. The rookies had all been herded into a big armory and one of the Department chaplains had addressed them.

"Welcome, men!" said the Chaplain. "We're glad to have you with us. You're not starting on a job; you're starting on a career! It is difficult, dangerous, and filled with problems that would challenge a saint. One of the worst problems is drinking. For some it's a curse! I ask you to make a vow, here and now, never to touch one drop for the first five years in the Department! If you do that I can assure you drinking will never become your problem.

"Then there's temptation! No man outside the Department will ever have to face what you'll face each and every day. Temptation is probably the most severe test you will ever encounter. And it takes many different shapes. Turn away from it, I say. Turn away. Avoid beginnings and you won't be swept under! But if you must look then don't look at the face it shows you. Temptation has one face it tries to hide. Find *that one* and look into it. You'll run away in terror!

"And now we come to sex! I use the word to wake up anyone who might be dozing. I suggest, I recommend, that you men who are now single, I strongly recommend you get married. As soon as possible. You men who *are* married: my advice is this—after work don't stop for a quick one with the boys. Go home. She's waiting for you—your wife. And help around the house! All day long you've been helping other people solve their problems; now do the same at home. Help out! And take the baby for a walk. Nobody's going to question your manhood! You prove your manhood every day!"

Authoritarian Police Personality

ARTHUR NIEDERHOFFER

There is a social process at work within the police system that precipitates the most authoritarian type into the authoritarian role at the lowest level of the hierarchy, pounding the beat. Only after many years, when he is too old to stand the pace, is the policeman rewarded with a quiet job in the station house as messenger or attendant. There, as an elder statesman, he transmits his reverence for toughness to each new generation of recruits.

The doctrine of the professional movement advocates education, a nonpunitive orientation, strict legality in every phase of police work, and, most important of all, good public relations. These principles create an atmosphere in which only the professionally directed police officer can operate successfully. On a lower plane within the hierarchy exists the tough-minded, authoritarian working class of the police society. Conditions at this level foster an outlook that exalts power and force, and is contemptuous of the so-called unrealistic, soft-minded, and even subversive ideas of the professionals. Different value systems, ranks, and assignments create the two poles: the most authoritarian policemen work at the bottom of the police occupation in the streets; the most professional generally rise to the higher ranks and the preferred administrative assignments.

Although the two classes are constantly

From *Behind the Shield* by Arthur Niederhoffer, pp. 131–136 and 139–142. Copyright © 1967 by Arthur Niederhoffer. Reprinted by permission of Doubleday & Company, Inc.

at odds, this internecine struggle must be kept under cover; at all costs a united front must be presented for public inspection. The salary raises and legal concessions both groups desire depend on how well this united image is accepted by the public. The dilemma of the contemporary urban police system is that it must produce both classes and inevitably polarize them. Law enforcement oscillates from one philosophy to the other.

The source of police authoritarianism is a recurrent question. I have taken the position that authoritarianism develops after appointment as a result of socialization and experience in the police social system. The opposing view is that long before appointment, a self-selection process predisposes those who are authoritarians to police work. This latter thesis ascribes police authoritarianism to the personality variable rather than to factors of the social system.

Because there are few definitive related studies and because social scientists have had limited intimate experience in this area, the fundamental source of evidence necessarily depends upon the general sociological and psychological characteristics of the group in question.[1]

Police candidates are male. They are young, ranging from the late teens to the late twenties. They are physically above average, strong, and athletic. The great majority have high school diplomas or the equivalent. Most come from working-class backgrounds. In general, they are white, predominantly Catholic, and to a lesser degree Irish. All know that they have chosen to enter a quasi-military occupation that requires the use of force and lethal weapons. Preliminary investigation of their backgrounds eliminates radicals and applicants with criminal records. Of all the hopeful aspirants only 10 to 15 percent are eventually appointed. The most popular motivations for choosing the police occupation include security, public service, adventure, family tradition, and the appeal of the uniform and the authority it connotes.

Fortunately, most of these descriptive categories—sex, age, religion, physique, intelligence and education, motivation and class—have been studied in connection with authoritarianism. From the published reports we can make some legitimate deductions about police candidates.

Among the few who might advance the hypothesis that authoritarianism can be completely equated with masculinity is Simone de Beauvoir. She asserts that men are aggressors because they subjugate women by the position assumed in the sexual embrace.[2] If this is so, then every male occupation is by definition authoritarian. It is of some interest that men do score slightly higher than women on the F scale, thereby creating circumstantial evidence that men are more authoritarian; however, researchers advise that the results "may not reflect a true sex difference since they are not based on comparable groups of men and women."[3] Even if men are more authoritarian than women, this fact does not justify any assumption about the range of authoritarianism among men.

Age is another factor that correlates positively with authoritarianism. In a careful replication study of authoritarianism, Morris Janowitz and Dwaine Marvick found that, "First there was a statistically significant tendency for younger people to register as 'low

authoritarians' more frequently than did older people."[4] Therefore, the youth of the neophyte policemen would reduce the probability of high authoritarianism.

Religion may have some bearing on the case, especially because Catholics are heavily represented on the major urban police forces, but there is conflicting evidence on this point. Adorno and his colleagues found that "The factor of religious denomination does not prove to be very significant. Among the largest denominations no differences of any significance appear."[5] In a study by Daniel J. Levinson and Phyllis E. Huffman, Catholics were found to be more authoritarian than other religious groups but showed great variation among themselves.[6]

The stereotype of the policeman with the Irish brogue happens to be based on fact. Irishmen are strongly attracted to the police force. Cultural tradition almost requires one son of an Irish American working-class family to be a policeman, another a priest, jobs that have striking parallels. The police force has been called "the classic stronghold" of the Irish.[7] Former New York City Police Commissioner Francis Adams remarked, half seriously, that "If it weren't for the Irish, there would be no police. And if it weren't for the Irish, there would be no need for them."[8]

It is very difficult to obtain exact figures on the racial, ethnic, or religious composition of a large police force. However, it is possible to make an educated guess in the case of the New York City Police Department. *Spring 3100* publishes membership figures of officially recognized police organizations. The major religious and ethnic groups have their own social and fraternal associations whose members have joined them for various reasons. Each organization usually includes a small percentage of retired policemen. For this reason the figures give only an approximation but withal a fairly reliable basis for comparison, as shown in Table 1.

Table 1

COMPARISON OF MEMBERSHIP
OF SELECTED POLICE SOCIETIES

Name of Association	*Background of Membership*	*Number of Members*	*Percentage*
Emerald Society	Irish	8,500	42
Columbia Association	Italian	5,000	25
Shomrim Society	Jewish	2,270	11.2
Steuben Association	German	1,500	7.4
Guardians Association	Negro	1,320	6.5
Pulaski Association	Polish	1,100	5.4
St. Paul Society	Greek and Russian	300	1.5
Hispanic Society	Puerto Rican and Spanish	250	1
Totals		20,240	100

Source: *Spring 3100* **36** (March 1965): 21–26.

It was estimated that approximately eleven thousand members of the police force (40 percent) are Irish.[9] In comparison, the Irish ethnic group numbers only 10 percent of the total New York City population.[10]

Since it has not yet been proved conclusively that the Irish are more authoritarian than other ethnic groups, the predominance of Irish in the police force does not resolve the problem of police authoritarianism. There is no reason to suppose that Irishmen join the force for any motive other than se-curity, as do the other applicants. The author of a popular book describing American-Irish life and customs agrees that the reason "why so many Irish have joined the police force, down through the years, is that lacking capital, often the victims of prejudice, they sought security." [11]

There may be some question about a police candidate modal personality; there can be none about the basic physique of the candidate group. It falls perfectly into the mesomorph, or average body build, classification assigned to this somatotype by William H. Sheldon, the controversial constitutional psychologist. According to Sheldon, mesomorphy is highly correlated with the temperament he has designated as Somatotonia.[12] This temperament is characterized by assertiveness, dominance, lust for power, competitive aggressiveness, ruthlessness, and several other qualities associated with authoritarianism.[13] However, it must be noted that Sheldon's work has been widely criticized, and it is still too early to conclude that the modal mesomorph physique of police candidates indicates their authoritarian orientation.

*   *   *

The next variables to be examined are intelligence and education. The educational background of police candidates offers no real clue, either. Graduation from high school is not remarkable one way or the other, nor is the fact that most members of the group invariably have an I.Q. of 100 to 105. From all that is known about the selection process, we may assume that the most educated and most intelligent police candidates will survive the various hurdles with greater frequency than those with less education and intelligence, that is, that those who have the qualities associated with a lower degree of authoritarianism are more likely to be chosen.[14]

In the preliminary character and background investigation, applicants who reveal extreme deviance are eliminated. Among authoritarian individuals certain syndromes often occur that preclude the appointment of such types as the rebel, the tough guy, the hoodlum, the asocial, the fascist, the crank, and the psychopath.[15] A report covering the period 1953–1956 indicated that 11 percent of the applicants for the Los Angeles Police Department were rejected because they did not meet acceptable psychiatric standards. Some of those rejects failed because they were aggressive personalities.[16] However, it should not be assumed that those remaining are highly submissive to authority—a trait that is connected with authoritarian personality.

If it could be shown that men are drawn into the police force through a desire to arrest criminals, demonstrate power, fight crime, regulate or prevent public action, or that they are lured by the potential adventure and glamour of police work we might conclude that police work mainly attracted authoritarians. But the fact that security is the most frequent reason for the choice invalidates this assumption. Eli Ginzberg and his colleagues maintain that there is a definite relation between occupational choice and personality needs. It is instructive to note that they report an interview with a working-class teenager who intended to become a policeman. As his responses indicate, security first, then service, determined his choice.

Q. What are the advantages of being on the police force?
A. You serve twenty years and then get a pension; you carry hospitalization for the family.
Q. If you had no need to make money, what would you consider an ideal job?
A. Still the police force.
Q. What do you like about it?

A. Just the idea to help somebody in some way or another. You're always bound to help somebody. I've talked to cops.[17]

In a series of studies conducted at the New York Police Academy from 1957 to 1961, security was the principal motivation that merged in at least 60 percent of the cases. Robert Bird in 1960 wrote an interesting series of articles on the New York City Police Department, which appeared in the New York *Herald Tribune* under the title, "Cops or Social Scientists?" He questioned such experts as Stephen P. Kennedy, then Police Commissioner, Deputy Police Commissioner Alexander Aldrich, and other leading officials about this very subject and received similar replies: "Police officials say that when these men are asked why they want to join the police force, the overwhelming majority answer because of security. When asked what they mean by security, they explain, freedom from lay-offs." [18]

Dr. James Rankin, who has interviewed and tested thousands of candidates for the Los Angeles Police Department, concludes that "A high percentage of applicants for police jobs are attracted by 'security' advantages." [19] And from studies in the Midwest there is another echo: "The preceding material suggests that men who decide to join the police department are drawn from large, working-class families . . . and emphasize security as a major reason for joining the department." [20] Security, particularly economic security, may well be the motivation for joining. But what about the cognitive component? Police candidates know that their duties require the use of lethal weapons, and that force and violence are the stock in trade of the successful patrolman. Does not this indicate that they are incipient authoritarians? Contact with thousands of recruits shows that most new recruits accept the revolver and the nightstick with a neutral attitude which they display from the first day of service and which, we may suppose, reflects and continues their feelings before appointment. Moreover, when the candidates learn the terrible responsibility of safeguarding the gun, this symbol of authority loses whatever glamour it may have possessed. It would thus seem unwarranted to conclude that accepting the responsibility and necessity for authority and force demonstrates an eagerness to use them. It is more tenable to maintain that force is a necessary evil which is one of the more unattractive aspects of the police job.

NOTES

1 Most of the reported research concerns subjects who were already policemen at the time of the study. There have been reports by psychiatrists hired by police departments to screen applicants. But they usually end up by rejecting candidates with unfavorable personality syndromes, and this would include extreme authoritarianism.

2 Simone de Beauvoir, *The Second Sex* (Alfred A. Knopf, 1953).

3 T. W. Adorno et al., *The Authoritarian Personality* (New York: Harper, 1950), p. 138.

4 Morris Janowitz and Dwaine Marvick, "Authoritarianism and Political Behavior," *Public Opinion Quarterly* 17 (Summer 1953): 191.

5 Adorno et al., *Authoritarian Personality,* p. 220.

6 Daniel J. Levinson and Phyllis E. Huffman, "Traditional Family Ideology and Its Relation to Personality," *Journal of Personality* 23 (1955): 265. Rokeach cites studies of a similar import. See Milton Rokeach, *The Open and Closed Mind* (New York: Basic Books, Inc., 1960), pp. 110–119.

7 Nathan Glazer and Daniel P. Moynihan, *Beyond the Melting Pot* (Cambridge: The M.I.T. Press and Harvard University Press, 1964), p. 261.

8 Statement made by former Commissioner Francis Adams on TV program entitled "Crime and the Cities," May 17, 1964.

9 Personal conversation with high officials and delegates of the Emerald Society.

10 Glazer and Moynihan, *Melting Pot,* p. 19.

11 Bob Considine, *It's the Irish* (Garden City, N.Y.: Doubleday & Co., 1961), pp. 110–111. On the other hand, James Wilson suggests that some Irish candidates join the force because they have better chances of being promoted. However, this would not apply to the New York police force because promotion at least through captain depends on civil service examinations. See James Q. Wilson, "Generational and Ethnic Differences among Career Police Officers," *American Journal of Sociology* 69 (March 1964): 522–528.

12 William H. Sheldon, *The Varieties of Temperament: A Psychology of Constitutional Differences* (New York: Harper, 1942), p. 400.

13 Ibid., p. 26.

14 Richard Christie and Marie Jahoda, eds., *Studies in the Scope and Method of the Authoritarian Personality* (Glencoe, Ill.: The Free Press, 1954), pp. 167–172.

15 T. W. Adorno et al., *Authoritarian Personality,* pp. 762–767.

16 James H. Rankin, "Preventive Psychiatry in the Los Angeles Police Department," *Police* 1 (July–August 1957), p. 4.

17 Eli Ginzberg et al., *Occupational Choice: An Approach to a General Theory* (New York: Columbia University Press, 1951), pp. 156–157.

18 Robert S. Bird, "Cops or Social Scientists?" New York *Herald Tribune,* July 17, 1960, p. 16.

19 Rankin, "Preventive Psychiatry," p. 6.

20 Westley, "The Police: A Sociological Study of Law, Custom, and Morality" (doctoral diss., University of Chicago, 1951), p. 83.

Selecting for a Police Subculture

THOMAS C. GRAY

The idea of socialization connotes the development of an individual from a prior state to a future one. The individual is taught, develops, and is transformed from, say, a child to an adult. Obviously, however, such a notion is oversimplified. All children are not taught the same things, nor do they develop in the same way. Children are socialized into different cultures, and children resist socialization as well. An understanding of the process demands close and careful observation and analysis. This sort of analysis is undertaken here to understand the first stage of the transformation of civilians into policemen, the stage of selection.

The selection process does not recruit full-fledged members of the police department or the police subculture. Those selected become recruits, that is, individuals who possess an *affinity* for membership for both the formal organization and informal culture. The concept of affinity requires clarification if we are to understand it as the necessary first step in the socialization process of police recruits. Affinity represents a predisposition to adhere partially to a set of distinctive sentiments that can be expanded and reinforced by training and socialization. Affinity suggests the identifiable raw material from which policemen are made. However, the idea of affinity is too remote to employ as an explicit concept on which to base formal selection criteria. Nevertheless, close observation of selection practices strongly suggests that affinity is the *operative* concept. It is this concept that permits senior police officials to separate those who are *technically* qualified to become police officers from those who will probably be able to absorb the requirements of the legal system, the formal police organization, and the police subculture.

JOB DESCRIPTIONS AND SELECTION

An analysis of the police selection process illuminates several major problems confronting the police and those who would understand the police. The first of these is the lack of a job description for police, and the second is police subcultural influence and, in some cases, control of official policy.

Ideally, selection of employees for most occupations is based on the minimum technical skills necessary to do the work. Beyond this, the applicants may be selected on personality traits that will allow them to fit into the existing social structure of the organization. A hod carrier is selected because he knows how to mix cement and has the physical strength to carry hod. A lawyer is selected because he has demonstrated minimal competence by completing his course of studies and passed a bar examination. College students are selected because they have demonstrated a minimal ability to learn. The criteria for selecting police, however, are based on an assumption that applicants will not possess even minimal technical skills required of the work to be done. The criteria, consequently, are based almost entirely on certain suggestions of character indicating the kind of person the recruit can become.

One reason for selecting individuals on the basis of character resides in the diffuse nature of police work and the fact that all police first become patrolmen, a job that defies an adequate concrete description and is very different from the job of investigator. Michael Banton has written:

> A division is becoming apparent between specialist departments within the police forces (detectives, traffic officers, vice and fraud squads, etc. ...) and the ordinary patrolman. The former are "law officers" whose contacts with the public tend to be of a punitive or inquisitory character, whereas the patrolmen ... are principally "peace officers" operating within the moral consensus of the community. Whereas the former have occasion to speak chiefly to offenders or to persons who can supply information about an offense, the patrolmen interact with all sorts of people and more of their contacts center upon assisting citizens than upon offenses.[1]

If selection were aimed at filling various positions within the police organization, definitive job descriptions for these positions would be possible. An example of this is the job of a burglary detective. A job description for this position might read:

> Needed: a person to investigate the illegal entry into closed structures or locked vehicles from which some object of real or intrinsic value has been taken. The duties of this individual include the following: developing legal evidence that places responsibility on a person or persons for the theft, testifying in court as to the nature of that evidence and the means by which that evidence was obtained, working with district attorneys and judges, developing a system of informants within the community who can aid in the gathering of evidence or apprehension of the responsible party. Individuals hired for this position will be given extensive training in criminal law, criminal evidence, search and seizure, psychology, and sociology.

Specialized tasks, as can be seen, are better fitted for definitive descriptions than generalized tasks. As a result of its diffuseness, the patrolman's job is often described through slogans such as, "to protect and serve," "enforce the law," or "keep the peace," all of which beg the obvious questions of protect who and serve what, enforce which laws under what circumstances and against whom, keep whose peace at whose expense?

Examining the job requirements for police personnel gives no indication of the kind of work an individual will be engaged in. In 1960, California created a Commission on Peace Officers Standards and Training (POST). This commission recommended the following minimal criteria for selecting police personnel:

1. Citizen of the United States.
2. Minimum age of 21 years.
3. Fingerprinting of applicants, with a search of local, state, and national fingerprint files to disclose any record.
4. No felony convictions.
5. Good moral character.
6. High school graduate or equivalent.
7. Free of physical defects with minimum height of 5'7" and weight of 150 lbs. and free of emotional problems.
8. A written test and an oral examination conducted by the hiring agency.[2]

The criteria for hiring individuals provide minimal information about the job being offered. That the hiring agency is particularly concerned with the past of its prospective employees is extremely clear. It is also evident that the criteria are subjective. Despite the fact that these standards have been widely criticized in the literature dealing with police selection, the criteria for employment have not been significantly altered. One reason is the fear of police administrators that their officers, if they have shown any character flaws in the past, will succumb to the temptations of corruption. In fact, the best this procedure can do is to determine if a person has been *caught* in the past for some immoral or illegal act.

An inadequate job description may also be attributable to the unpleasant or distasteful aspects of the patrolman's work. Fatal traffic accidents, suicides, insane people, severely injured people, and the use of violence are unattractive elements of any job description. Perhaps a description advertising these features of patrol work would offend the public and attract violent or sadistic applicants. Consequently, a specific job description may be abandoned in favor of a description of the desired character of the applicant.

On the surface, police selection seems to be irrational or at best nonrational. Certainly Blum et al. point out the irrational components of the selection criteria.[3] However, their analysis is from the perspective of the formal organization and fails to take into account the requirements of the legal system and the police subculture. In the following paragraphs the selection criteria of police recruits will be examined as a process for selecting individuals into a police subculture. Analysis from this perspective graphically illustrates the extent of the police subculture and its influence on the formal police organization. In addition, it illustrates the police subculture's potential for later socialization of police recruits.

The legal authority under which the police conduct themselves sometimes requires the use of violence, violation of privacy, deception, and the denigration of an individual's character. For example, the process of arrest permits, and sometimes requires, force from simply touching to maiming or killing; similarly, search warrants require violation of privacy, and investigations sometimes require deception and the denigration of an individual's character. Normally such conduct is legally restricted to the enforcement of laws, and when no laws are being enforced this very conduct is illegal. This has resulted in a subculture whose members share an acute sense of masculine identity, especially in a lack of squeamishness, that is, the ability to withstand the shock of seeing gory, violent, or ugly scenes, a willingness to accept personal risk, plus a high value on the exercise of authority, secrecy, and group solidarity. This subculture, with its associated psychic identifications, internal morality, and political direction encourages its participants to view the world as a hostile and potentially violent place.

Given these considerations and the attendant view of the world, the selection criteria for the police become meaningful. The criteria allow for selection of individuals who are potentially trustworthy and physically able to subdue violent individuals. The twist in this criteria is the word "trustworthy" instead of "competent." The criteria for selection are designed to identify individuals with an investment in the status quo and who, as a result, are likely to be politically conservative because change invariably upsets the established social and political order.

Not all individuals who support the status quo are selected for police work. Other considerations are of equal importance, particularly in light of the legal system's requirements and the strong sense of masculine identity within the police subculture. This conception of masculinity becomes the cutting edge of selection when an applicant reaches the point of an oral interview. This can be best illustrated by observations made of oral interviews of police candidates.

METHODOLOGY

As a law enforcement practitioner and a student of the police, I have had the opportunity to observe some 83 interviews of police candidates. These observations were made, in part, while I was a deputy sheriff for Los Angeles County (38 observations). I made others as a consultant to the Pittsburg, California, Police Department (25 observations), as a consultant to Berkeley, Police Department (12 observations), and while doing research at the Oakland Police Department (8 observations). In addition to these observations, I have interviewed those officers responsible for selection at Los Angeles, New York, Las Vegas, San Diego, and the Odessa, Texas, Police Departments.

For my doctoral dissertation, which is a study of socialization in the Oakland Police Department, I have selected the eight interviews conducted there during the month of September 1972. Selecting only eight interviews from one police department would present some methodological problems if the study were quantitative in nature. The eight interviews selected, however, were typical of my other observations. I restricted my examples to the Oakland Police Department because the objective was to describe rather than quantify the process of police selection.

Each interview took on the average from one to one and one-half hours to complete, including all paper work. I have reviewed these in light of my other observations of recruitment interviews and consider them to be typical. The subculture of police is remarkably constant despite variations in size and organization of police departments. As an indicator of this constancy, one need only peruse magazines of the trade, such as *Police Chief* and *Law and Order*.

I sat at the table where the interviews took place. I did not, however, ask any questions of the applicants, nor did I offer any advice to the members of the oral board. Prior to the actual interviews I read the applicant's employment, educational, and psychiatric reports. All eight applicants had passed the written, medical, background, and psychiatric phases of the pre-employment process. In short, they were qualified applicants with only the police selection board separating them from employment.

Of the eight applicants, three interviews resulted in acceptance and five in rejection. In either case the decision was made in my presence. Thus, I was allowed to know why and how a decision had been reached. If the reasons for a particular decision were unclear, I asked the board members for clarification, and they would restate the reasons for the decision. After each interview I was allowed to read each board member's notes which were written during the applicant's interview. In that way I was able to compare the stated reasons and unstated reasons for a particular decision.

THE ORAL INTERVIEW

The Oral Board consisted of two police officers and an employee of the Civil Service Commission. One officer was a black patrolman and the other a lieutenant or sergeant. All three members of the board had equal status during the examination. This in effect meant that two members of the board could generally pass a candidate. Before each interview the candidate's job application was reviewed by the Board members. This was done so that specific questions could be asked, particularly about past arrest records, frequent job and residence changes, and any civil law suits that he had been party to. Once this information had been read, the candidate was called into the interview room.

As is typical of most interviews where the applicant will meet the public, the first item noticed was the appearance of the applicant. How did he "carry himself," how was he dressed, was he clean shaven, what expression was on his face—in short, what kind of image did he project to the board? Few applicants were able to overcome a poor initial self-presentation.

A poor presentation of self was indicated by certain types of bearing, for example, entering the room with eyes averted from the board members, walking stoop-shouldered, not picking up feet when walking, and showing undue apprehension in facial expression and hand gestures. As a criterion, bearing was followed closely by dress. Dirty, wrinkled, loud, or otherwise unusual clothing were all considered a poor indication of potential for police work.

Any member of the board could and would start the actual interview. Normally, the first few questions related to the facts of the applicant's prior work experience. At this point, the attitude of the board members was nonaggressive, almost informal. As the interview progressed, however, questions became more probing of possible actions and attitudes on the job. Board members asked about when the applicant would or would not invoke police powers, when and under what circumstances he would use deadly force, what specifically did he know of the racial composition of the city, what his attitudes were toward members of other racial groups, and why he wanted to be a police officer. If the candidate had an arrest record, questions centered on the circumstances surrounding the arrest and the disposition of the case after the arrest.

Of eight candidates interviewed in my presence, three passed the examination. The other five were rejected for the following rea-sons, as stated by the members of the Selection Board. The first appeared for the interview dressed in a high school athletic jacket, dirty dungarees, and a T-shirt. On entering the room, he made no eye-to-eye contact with the board members but instead fixed his eyes on the chair he was to be seated in. Furthermore, the interview revealed that he had applied for the position on a whim. Finally, the applicant was facetious, stating to the board members that he should be hired because he would either be a thief or a police officer. The interview was terminated at this point.

The second applicant was visibly shaken by the interview and began to perspire and fidget with his hands as soon as seated. When asked why he wanted to become a police officer, he stated that he had a strong sense of morality and he wanted to be in a position where he could make sure people did what was "right."

The third candidate proved the most interesting. He made an excellent presentation of self both in his appearance and bearing on entering the room. His reactions to the questions posed by the board were calm and deliberate, and his answers reflected some prior thinking on the role of the police. His answers were slow, however, and there seemed an interminable silence between question and answer. His voice was soft and laconic. The turning point in the interview came when the following question was posed:

"Suppose you are in uniform and you've been asked to check a bar and a man 6'4" and 230 pounds is blocking your way and refuses you entrance to the bar, what would you do?"

The candidate said he would ask the man to move.

The members of the board asked: "What would you do if the man refused?"

"I would go," he said, "to the back door of the bar."

"But suppose," the candidate was asked, "the man stopped you from entering?"

The candidate replied: "I would physically remove the man if he wasn't too big."

The board rejected this applicant on grounds that he lacked the verbal skills and aggressiveness to become what they considered a "good cop."

The fourth candidate lied to the board members concerning a past arrest record. He had failed to report an arrest for assault which took place some five years prior to the interview. When asked about the arrest the candidate said he hadn't thought it important and therefore didn't report it. The board rejected him for failing to report his past arrest record.

The fifth candidate was rejected because he told the board that he did not want a permanent position. His real interest was in law, and he said that he would leave the force as soon as he was admitted to law school. The board rejected him because they felt that a permanent employee would be preferable.

REJECTION VERSUS ACCEPTANCE

If the criteria for rejection are held up against the value system of the police subculture, they fit neatly. To one degree or another, all of the rejected candidates displayed a potential for violating the value system of the police subculture. The first displayed a lack of potential loyalty to the group, the second displayed a moral squeamishness, the third a strong internalization of prohibitions against the use of violence, the fourth a lack of trustworthiness, and the fifth a potential lack of commitment. Any one of these factors would offer a threat to the police subculture and hence (if the explanation is valid) would render an applicant unfit for employment.

The selection process can now be seen as the interface between the formal and informal organization and, further, the requirements of the legal system. Acceptability on any one factor does not automatically imply acceptability for the others. The candidate must in fact prove acceptable to all three systems. This conclusion is illustrated by the examination of the candidates who were selected. Acceptable candidates were all conservatively dressed in suits and ties, made eye contact with the members of the board, walked directly to the board and shook the hands of the board members. These candidates answered the questions in a calm, straightforward manner looking the board members in the eye. None displayed reservations concerning the use of violence, violation of privacy, deception, or the denigration of an individual's character, and all conveyed a high sense of loyalty to their present group of acquaintances.

Also noticeable as a subtle undercurrent in the interview was the willingness of individuals to accept direction and physical violence as well as maintaining a generalized suspicion of others. The applicant would be asked, for example, if he were in combat and a superior officer ordered him to shoot a fleeing enemy soldier who had just "knocked out" a machine gun nest, would he do so? Or an applicant might be asked if an individual (who to the applicant's knowledge had not committed a crime) ran on seeing him in uniform, would he pursue that individual? The successful applicants answered yes to both questions. Given their willingness to follow directions, the candidates may also be inclined to follow the orders of their superiors even when those orders are illegal, unconstitutional, or immoral. There appeared, however, to be limits on the acceptable potential to use violence. One successful candidate had been an officer in special forces and had spent approximately two years in combat. The board members expressed concern that the applicant might, because of his past training and experience, use fatal force when it wasn't necessary. This objection, however, was of little consequence in the overall rating of the applicant.

THE MARK OF AFFINITY

On the basis of these interviews, what concrete factors seem to suggest an affinity for police work? One such factor is an individual's personal history from which is inferred a predisposition to engage in certain types of conduct. For example, a past largely made up of conviction and incarceration for serious crimes is unlikely to suggest an affinity for police work; nor is such a past likely to produce an affinity for the values of a police subculture. Conversely, absence of such a past does not necessarily indicate an affinity for the values of the police subculture. It is experience with some elements of police subculture, such as engaging in contact sports, that suggests an affinity for police work. For example, playing football provides an individual with an experience that contains some elements of the police subculture: (1) controlled use of violence, (2) teamwork and group loyalty, (3) memorization of codes, (4) uniform behavior, (5) experience with personal pain, (6) a willingness to inflict pain on others, (7) dirty tricks, and (8) authoritarianism (leading or being led).

A further clarification of affinity is made by separating it from the technical requirements of police work. Affinity is the predisposition toward certain values, not the technical competence of the candidate to read or write or the abilities to meet the minimum physical requirements of the job.

Possessing a predisposition for police work appears to be a necessary but not a sufficient requirement for employment as a police officer. This is illustrated by the fact that certain individuals possess all of the necessary technical skills and the necessary predispositions but still are not seen as potential members of either the formal police organization or the police subculture. Women fall into this latter category. This observation reinforces the earlier contention of masculine identification as part of the basis upon which the police subculture is built. Women in their presentation of self are hard-pressed to overcome the impact of their physical makeup regardless of their capacity to do the job. In short, women would, if hired for patrol, potentially undercut the basis of male solidarity.

The salient observations, then, revolve around not what the formal requirements say but rather what they don't say. In recruiting police officers an adequate job description is lacking primarily because individuals are recruited to do a number of diffuse tasks, and consequently the division of labor within the police is largely ignored when selecting police candidates. The result of such a selection process is to place an emphasis on the individual's past and his potential to become something different from what he presently is.

Selection of police personnel on the basis of their potential to internalize the requirements of the police subculture may help to explain some of the apparent contradictions between impressions of police as "authoritarian" and findings suggesting that police are "normal." For example, Skolnick writes:

> It is hard to say why men join the police force, but the evidence we have indicates that police recruits are not especially sadistic or even authoritarian, as some have alleged. On the contrary, the best evidence that we have been able to accumulate from

works of such police authorities as Niederhoffer and McNamara suggests that the
policeman is usually an able and gregarious
young man with social ideals, better than
average physical prowess, and a rather conventional outlook on life, including normal
aspirations and self-interest.[4]

An understanding of the paradoxical demands of police work should help us to understand some of the apparent contradictions
in police personality, and also to be skeptical
regarding certain solutions proposed to correct police conduct. Thus, the solutions usually advanced when the police are found
to be corrupt, brutal, or unresponsive to the
needs of the community are to change hiring
policies, retrain the police, and get rid of the
offending officers. In light of the legal system's requirement that the police use violence, violate privacy, practice deception, and
denigrate an individual's character, such
measures seem to be at best of only temporary value.

The difference between behavior required of the police by the legal system and
behavior required to engage in corrupt, brutal, or indifferent conduct is more one of
degree than of kind. As Matza has suggested
regarding juvenile delinquency:

> The major bases of negation and irrespon-
> sibility in law rest on self-defense, insanity,
> and accident. . . . The restraint of law is
> episodically neutralized through an expan-
> sion of each extenuating circumstance be-
> yond a point countenanced in law. Each
> point of law is extended and in that sense
> distorted.[5]

CONCLUSION

Literature on police selection focuses on the
requirements of the formal police organization for intelligent, mature, and emotionally
stable individuals. Such a focus, although

necessary, is incomplete. Police are selected
on three levels, each involving distinct norms
and values—the levels of legal norms, formal
police organization, and the police subculture. As the following excerpts from the literature on police selection suggest, there is an
implicit recognition of the involvement of
legal requirements and police subculture.

Typical of the literature is the American
Bar Association's *Recommended Selection
Standards for the Police.* It reads, in part:

> In view of the broad diversity of the po-
> lice rule, experiments should be conducted
> which make use of different levels of entry
> for personnel and standards particularly
> relevant for the various levels. Such re-
> cruitment should be related directly to the
> requirements of various police tasks and
> should reflect a great degree of concern for
> such factors as judgmental ability, emo-
> tional stability, and sensitivity to the deli-
> cate and complicated nature of the police
> role in a democratic society.[6]

As the following quote indicates, when confronted with the problems imposed by the
legal system and the requirements of a police
subculture, the Bar Association abandons
specific recommendations in favor of admitting ignorance. "It is not feasible here to attempt to be any more specific regarding the
mechanisms to be employed in the screening
of police applicants." [7]

The irony of the Bar Association's recommendations is a footnote following this
quote directing the reader to the Task Force
Report on the police of the President's Commission on Law Enforcement and the Administration of Justice. The Task Force Report also concentrates on the formal police
organization's needs and recommends hiring
intelligent, mature, and emotionally stable
individuals for police work. However, the
Task Force Report recognizes that a set of
rigid standards for police personnel selection

eliminates many qualified applicants. The report reads, "Seventy percent of all police departments require a police candidate to have a high school diploma. From the point of view of recruiting college graduates and minority group personnel of the requisite quality, this standard is both too low and too high." The report goes on to recommend hiring on three levels of police duties, for example, community service officer, police officer, and police agent. Each of these groups would have different standards of selection applied to them, the police community service officer having the lowest educational standard and the police agent the highest.[8]

W. A. Leonard in *Police Organization and Management* also recommends hiring intelligent, mature, and emotionally stable individuals. Leonard, however, recognizes that, "There are many men of intelligence, character and ability who never under any circumstances can become good police officers; they may work hard, long, loyally and faithfully and yet prove incompetent." [9]

What these writers have done is to ignore the very nature of the work for which they are recommending personnel selection standards. Leonard, however, seems to recognize at least implicitly that more than just the requirements of the formal police organization operate in the selection of police personnel.

This paper has advanced the theory that police selection practices are based upon the convergence of three needs: (1) the legal system's need for individuals who can engage in violence, violate privacy, use deception, and denigrate the character of another; (2) the formal police organization's need for competent personnel; and (3) the police subculture's need to protect its value system. In short, police personnel selection is the selection of individuals who demonstrate, by a number of subtle cues, an affinity for pursuing the sometimes inconsistent—that is, deviant yet legal—dictates of a policeman's life-style.

NOTES

1 Michael Banton, *The Policeman in the Community* (London: Tavistock Publications, 1964), p. 20.
2 *California Commission on Peace Officers Standards and Training,* Academy Reimbursement Manual (1970), p. 8.
3 Richard H. Blum et al., *Police Selection* (Springfield, Ill.: Charles C Thomas, 1964), pp. 44–70.
4 Jerome H. Skolnick, *The Politics of Protest* (New York: Clarion Books, 1969), p. 252.
5 David Matza, *Delinquency and Drift* (New York: Wiley, 1964), p. 74.
6 Frank J. Remington et al., *Recommended Selection Standards for the Police* (American Bar Association, 1972), pp. 197–198.
7 Ibid., p. 200.
8 President's Commission on Law Enforcement and the Administration of Justice, *The Challenge of Crime in a Free Society* (Washington, D.C.: U.S. Government Printing Office, 1967), pp. 106–109.
9 W. A. Leonard, *Police Organization and Management,* 2nd ed. (New York: The Foundation Press, Inc., 1964), pp. 106–107.

District of Columbia officer introducing his police dog to neighborhood
children during a visit to an area school

II

The Role and Function of Police

THE CENTRALITY OF FORCE

Recruits in a Washington, D.C. self-defense class learning to use physical fitness as an alternative to weapons.

The capacity to use force is unquestionably a central feature of police work. Stressing this feature, Egon Bittner argues that the best way to understand the role of the police in society is as a mechanism for distributing force in accord with an intuitive grasp of situational needs. In other words, Bittner is arguing that police learn on the job when force is properly to be used; and that the core of the police work is in learning when and how to use force. Bittner contrasts this aspect of the policeman's job with police activities dedicated to law enforcement, pointing out quite correctly that only a small part of police activity is dedicated to that end. But Bittner's thoughtful and provocative article may raise more questions than it answers. If the police are best understood as a mechanism for distributing force, to what extent is their use of force governed by legal authority? That is, if police were not officers of the law, would they then be empowered to employ force? And if police are so empowered, should the dictates of the police subculture govern the policeman's understanding of when to use force? Or should this understanding be governed by a body of laws set out through the legislative and interpreted by the judicial branch of government?

Anyone who has been a policeman or who has studied police learns that lawful strictures on police activities are mediated through the police subculture, plus the perceived requirements of police organization. Nevertheless, a continuing and relevant question for police and police organizations is how to interpret and communicate authoritative ideas about the nature and limits of the use of force. For example, it is possible to have several different legal standards pertaining to police. One might be that police can use force to apprehend any person who has committed a crime of any kind, whether the most serious felony or the most innocuous misdemeanor. Another position might be police can apprehend any fleeing person whom they honestly feel has committed a felony. A third position, which was the law in New York state for a couple of years in the 1960s and was fought by organized police organizations, is that police may use force to apprehend felons only when fleeing felons present a danger to life, either to themselves or to others. One question for discussion is: Which of these standards is most appropriate? Another issue is: Whatever the standard, how should the police organization go about communicating it and enforcing it?

This issue is discussed in the other two articles in this chapter. Jonathan Rubinstein points out that the policeman's body is his principal tool. A policeman uses his body and its extensions, such as a gun or a nightstick, to control other people. In this the policeman exercises considerable discretion. But the questions for the policeman and the public are: What should be the limits of that discretion? And what sanctions should be employed to ensure that these limits are followed? For example, many policemen regard an insult by a citizen as sufficient to justify the use of physical force, even though no jurisdiction gives the policeman that lawful authority. Should police be permitted to strike people who insult them? Should insulting a policeman be a crime? If police do hit people who insult them, what should be done about it?

In his article on false arrest and cover charges, Paul Chevigny argues that police, at least some police, do routinely use force as a means of protecting their own perceived conceptions of authority, and that moreover they use the authority vested in them by the criminal law as a way of covering up their own illegal activities. Is such police conduct necessary? Is it desirable? If not, what can be done about it at the level of (1) police training in the academy, (2) police training in the street, (3) controls from within the police department, and (4) the voting public?

The Capacity to Use Force as the Core of the Police Role

EGON BITTNER

The quest for peace by peaceful means is one of the culture traits of modern civilization. This aspiration is historically unique. For example, the Roman Empire was also committed to the objectives of reducing or eliminating warfare during one period of its existence, but the method chosen to achieve the *Pax Romana* was, in the language of the poet, *debellare superbos,* that is, to subdue the haughty by force. Contrary to this, our commitment to abolish the traffic of violence requires us to pursue the ideal by pacific means. To support this contention, we need only consider our elaborate system of international diplomacy, whose main objective it is to avoid war, and those changes in internal government that have resulted in the virtual elimination of all forms of violence, especially in the administration of justice. That is, the overall tendency is to withdraw the basis of legitimacy not merely from all forms of provocative violence but even from the exercise of provoked force required to meet illegitimate attacks. Naturally this is not possible to a full extent. At least, it has not been possible thus far. Since it is impossible to deprive responsive force entirely of legitimacy, its vestiges require special forms of authorization. Our society recognizes as legitimate three very different forms of responsive force.

From *The Functions of the Police in Modern Society* by Egon Bittner, pp. 36–44, 46–47. Printed in 1970. Reprinted by permission of the National Institute of Mental Health.

First, we are authorized to use force for the purpose of self-defense. Though the laws governing self-defense are far from clear, it appears that an attacked person can counterattack only after he has exhausted all other means of avoiding harm, including retreat, and that the counterattack may not exceed what is necessary to disable the assailant from carrying out his intent. These restrictions are actually enforceable because harm done in the course of self-defense does furnish grounds for criminal and tort proceedings. It becomes necessary, therefore, to show compliance with these restrictions to rebut the charges of excessive and unjustified force even in self-defense.[1]

The second form of authorization entrusts the power to proceed coercively to some specifically deputized persons against some specifically named persons. Among the agents who have such highly specific powers are mental hospital attendants and prison guards. Characteristically, such persons use force in carrying out court orders; but they may use force only against named persons who are remanded to their custody and only to the extent required to implement a judicial order of confinement. Of course, like everybody else, they may also act within the provisions governing self-defense. By insisting on the high degree of limited specificity of the powers of custodial staffs, I do not mean to deny that these restrictions are often violated with impunity. The likelihood of such transgressions is enhanced by the secluded character of prisons and mental institutions, but their existence does not impair the validity of this definition.

The third way to legitimize the use of responsive force is to institute a police force. Contrary to the cases of self-defense and the limited authorization of custodial functionaries, the police authorization is essentially unrestricted. Because the expression *essentially* is often used to hedge a point, I will make fully explicit what I mean by it. There exist three formal limitations of the freedom of policemen to use force, which must be admitted even though they have virtually no practical consequences. First, the police use of deadly force is limited in most jurisdictions. Though the powers of a policeman in this respect exceed those of citizens, they are limited nevertheless. For example, in some jurisdictions policemen are empowered to shoot to kill fleeing felony suspects, but not fleeing misdemeanor suspects. It is scarcely necessary to argue that, given the uncertainties involved in defining an offense under conditions of hot pursuit, this could hardly be expected to be an effective limitation.[2] Second, policemen may use force only in the performance of their duties and not to advance their own personal interest or the private interests of other persons. Though this is rather obvious, I mention it for the sake of completeness. Third, and this point too is brought up to meet possible objections, policemen may not use force maliciously or frivolously. These three restrictions, and nothing else, were meant by the use of the qualifier *essentially*. Aside from these restrictions there exist no guidelines, no specifiable range of objectives, no limitations of any kind that instruct the policeman what he may or must do. Nor do there exist any criteria that would allow judgment of whether some forceful intervention was necessary, desirable, or proper. And finally, it is ex-

ceedingly rare that police actions involving the use of force are actually reviewed and judged by anyone at all.

In sum, the frequently heard talk about the lawful use of force by the police is practically meaningless, and, because no one knows what is meant by it, so is the talk about the use of minimum force. Whatever vestigial significance attaches to the term *lawful* use of force is confined to the obvious and unnecessary rule that police officers may not commit crimes of violence. Otherwise, however, the expectation that they may and will use force is left entirely undefined. In fact, the only instructions any policeman ever receives in this respect consist of sermonizing that he should be humane and circumspect, and that he must not desist from what he has undertaken merely because its accomplishment may call for coercive means. I might add, at this point, that the entire debate about the troublesome problem of police brutality will not move beyond its present impasse, and the desire to eliminate it will remain an impotent conceit, until this point is fully grasped and unequivocally admitted. In fact, our expectation that policemen will use force, coupled by our refusals to state clearly what we mean by it (aside from sanctimonious homilies), smacks of more than a bit of perversity.

Of course, neither the police nor the public is entirely in the dark about the justifiable use of force by the officers. I have alluded to the assumption that policemen may use force in making arrests. But the benefit deriving from this apparent core of relative clarity is outweighed by its potentially misleading implications. For the authorization of the police to use force is in no important sense related to their duty to apprehend criminals. Were this the case then it could be adequately considered as merely a special case of the same authorization that is entrusted to custodial personnel. It might perhaps be considered a bit more complicated but essentially of the same nature. But the police authority to use force is radically different from that of a prison guard. Whereas the powers of the latter are incidental to his obligation to implement a legal command, the police role is far better understood by saying that their ability to arrest offenders is incidental to their authority to use force.

Many puzzling aspects of police work fall into place when one ceases to look at it as principally concerned with law enforcement and crime control, and only incidentally and often incongruously concerned with an infinite variety of other matters. It makes much more sense to say that the police are nothing else than a mechanism for the distribution of situationally justified force in society. The latter conception is preferable to the former on three grounds. First, it accords better with the actual expectations and demands made of the police (even though it probably conflicts with what most people would say, or expect to hear, in answer to the question about the proper police function); second, it gives a better accounting of the actual allocation of police manpower and other resources; and, third, it lends unity to all kinds of police activity. These three justifications will be discussed in some detail in the following pages.

The American city dweller's repertoire of methods for handling problems includes one known as "calling the cops." The practice to which the idiom refers is enormously widespread. Though it is more frequent in some segments of society than in others, there are very few people who do not or would not resort to it under suitable circumstances. A few illustrations will furnish the background for an explanation of what "calling the cops" means.[3]

Two patrolmen were directed to report to an address located in a fashionable district of a large city. On the scene they were greeted by the lady of the house who complained that the maid had been stealing and receiving male visitors in her quarters. She wanted the maid's belongings searched and the man removed. The patrolmen refused the first request, promising to forward the complaint to the bureau of detectives, but agreed to see what they could do about the man. After gaining entrance to the maid's room they compelled a male visitor to leave, drove him several blocks away from the house, and released him with the warning never to return.

In a tenement, patrolmen were met by a public health nurse who took them through an abysmally deteriorated apartment inhabited by four young children in the care of an elderly woman. The babysitter resisted the nurse's earlier attempts to remove the children. The patrolmen packed the children in the squad car and took them to Juvenile Hall, over the continuing protests of the elderly woman.

While cruising through the streets a team of detectives recognized a man named in a teletype received from the sheriff of an adjoining county. The suspect maintained that he was in the hospital at the time the offense alleged in the communication took place and asked the officer to verify his story over their car radio. When he continued to plead innocence he was handcuffed and taken to headquarters. Here the detectives learned that the teletype had been canceled. Prior to his release the man was told that he could have saved himself grief had he gone along voluntarily.

In a downtown residential hotel, patrolmen found two ambulance attendants trying to persuade a man, who according to all accounts was desperately ill, to go to the hospital. After some talk, they helped the attendants in carrying the protesting patient to the ambulance and sent them off.

In a middle-class neighborhood, patrolmen found a partly disassembled car, tools, a loudly blaring radio, and five beer-drinking youths at the curb in front of a single-family home. The homeowner complained that this had been going on for several days and the men had refused to take their activities elsewhere. The patrolmen ordered the youths to pack up and leave. When one sassed them they threw him into the squad car, drove him to the precinct station, from where he was released after receiving a severe tongue lashing from the desk sergeant.

In the apartment of a quarreling couple, patrolmen were told by the wife, whose nose was bleeding, that the husband stole her purse containing money she earned. The patrolmen told the man they would "take him in," whereupon he returned the purse and they left.

What all these vignettes are meant to illustrate is that whatever the substance of the task at hand, whether it involves protection against an undesired imposition, caring for those who cannot care for themselves, attempting to solve a crime, helping to save a life, abating a nuisance, or settling an explosive dispute, police intervention means above all making use of the capacity and authority to overpower resistance to an attempted solution in the native habitat of the problem. There can be no doubt that this feature of police work is uppermost in the minds of people who solicit police aid or direct the attention of the police to problems, that persons against whom the police proceed have this feature in mind and conduct themselves accordingly, and that every conceivable police intervention projects the message that force may be, and may have to be, used to achieve a desired objective. It does not matter whether the persons who seek police help are private citizens or other government officials, nor does it matter whether the problem at hand involves some aspect of law enforcement or is totally unconnected with it.

It must be emphasized, however, that the conception of the centrality of the capacity to use force in the police role does not entail the conclusion that the ordinary occupational routines consist of the actual exercise of this capacity. It is very likely, though we lack information on this point, that the actual use of physical coercion and restraint is rare for all policemen, and that many policemen are virtually never in the position of having to resort to it. What matters is that police procedure is defined by the feature that it may not be opposed in its course, and that force can be used if it is opposed. This is what the existence of the police makes available to society. Accordingly, the question, "What are policemen supposed to do?" is almost completely identical with the question, "What kinds of situations require remedies that are non-negotiably coercible?" [4]

The second justification for preferring the definition of the police role I proposed to the traditional law enforcement focus of the role requires us to review the actual police practices to see to what extent they can be subsumed under the conception offered. To begin, we can take note that law enforcement and crime control are obviously regarded as calling for remedies that are non-negotiably coercible. According to available estimates, approximately one-third of the manpower resources of the police are at any time committed to dealing with crimes and criminals. Though this may seem to be a relatively small share of the total resources of an agency ostensibly devoted to crime control, it is exceedingly unlikely that any other specific routine police activity, such as traffic regulation, crowd control, supervision of licensed establishments, settling of citizens' disputes, emergency health aids, ceremonial functions, or any other, absorb anywhere near as large a share of the remaining two-thirds. But this is precisely what one would expect on the basis of our definition. Given the likelihood that offenders will seek to oppose apprehension and evade punishment, it is only natural that the initial dealings with them be assigned to an agency that is capable of overcoming these obstacles. That is, the proposed definition of the role of the police as a mechanism for the distribution of non-negotiably coercive remedies entails the priority of crime control by direct inference. Beyond that, however, the definition also encompasses other types of activities, albeit at lower levels of priority.

Because the idea that the police are basically a crime-fighting agency has never been challenged in the past, no one has troubled to sort out the remaining priorities. Instead, the police have always been forced to justify activities that did not involve law enforcement in the direct sense either by linking them constructively to law enforcement or by defining them as nuisance demands for service. The dominance of this view, especially in the minds of policemen, has two harmful consequences. First, it leads to a tendency to view all sorts of problems as if they involved culpable offenses and to an excessive reliance on quasi-legal methods for handling them. The widespread use of arrests without intent to prosecute exemplifies this state of affairs. These cases do not involve errors in judgment about the applicability of a penal norm but deliberate pretense resorted to because

more appropriate methods of handling problems have not been developed. Second, the view that crime control is the only serious, important, and necessary part of police work has deleterious effects on the morale of those police officers in the uniformed patrol who spend most of their time with other matters. No one, especially he who takes a positive interest in his work, likes being obliged to do things day in and day out that are disparaged by his colleagues. Moreover, the low evaluation of these duties leads to neglecting the development of skill and knowledge that are required to discharge them properly and efficiently.

It remains to be shown that the capacity to use coercive force lends thematic unity to all police activity in the same sense in which, let us say, the capacity to cure illness lends unity to everything that is ordinarily done in the field of medical practice. While everybody agrees that the police actually engage in an enormous variety of activities, only a part of which involves law enforcement, many argue that this state of affairs does not require explanation but change. Smith, for example, argued that the imposition of duties and demands that are not related to crime control dilutes the effectiveness of the police and that the growing trend in this direction should be curtailed and even reversed.[5] On the face of it this argument is not without merit, especially if one considers that very many of those activities that are unrelated to law enforcement involve dealing with problems that lie in the field of psychiatry, social welfare, human relations, education, and so on. Each of these fields has its own trained specialists who are respectively more competent than the police. It would seem preferable, therefore, to take all those matters that belong properly to other specialists out of the hands of the police and turn them over to those to whom they belong. Not only would this relieve some of the pressures that presently impinge on the police, but it would also result in better services.[6]

Unfortunately, this view overlooks a centrally important factor. While it is true that policemen often aid sick and troubled people because physicians and social workers are unable or unwilling to take their services where they are needed, this is not the only or even the main reason for police involvement. In fact, physicians and social workers themselves quite often "call the cops." For, as in the case of the administration of justice, on the periphery of the rationally ordered procedures of medical and social work lurk exigencies that call for the exercise of coercion. Since neither physicians nor social workers are authorized or equipped to use force to attain desirable objectives, the total disengagement of the police would mean allowing many a problem to move unhampered in the direction of disaster. But the non-law-enforcement activities of the police are by no means confined to matters that are wholly or even mainly within the purview of some other institutionalized remedial specialty. Many, perhaps most, consist of addressing situations in which people simply do not seem to be able to manage their own lives adequately. Nor is it to be taken for granted that these situations invariably call for the use, or the threat of the use, of force. It is enough if there is need for immediate and unquestioned intervention that must not be allowed to be defeated by possible resistance. And where there is a possibility of great harm, the intervention would appear to be justified even if the risk is, in statistical terms, quite remote. Take, for instance the presence of mentally ill persons in the community. Though it is well known that most live quiet and unobtrusive lives, they are perceived as occasionally constituting a serious hazard to themselves and others. Thus, it is not surprising that the police are always prepared to deal with these persons at the slightest indication of a possible emergency. Similarly, though very few family quarrels lead to serious consequences, the fact that most homicides occur among quarreling kin leads to the preparedness to intervene in situations that might represent incipient problems.

In sum, the role of the police is to address all sorts of human problems when and insofar as their solutions do or may possibly require the use of force at the point of their occurrence. This lends homogeneity to such diverse procedures as catching a criminal, driving the major to the airport, evicting a drunken person from a bar, directing traffic, crowd control, taking care of lost children, administering medical first aid, and separating fighting relatives.

There is no exaggeration in saying that there is topical unity in this very incomplete list of lines of police work. Perhaps it is true that the common practice of assigning policemen to chauffeur mayors is based on the desire to give the appearance of thrift in the urban budget. But note, if one wanted to make as far as possible certain that nothing would ever impede His Honor's freedom of movement, he would certainly put someone into the driver's seat of the auto who has the authority and the capacity to overcome all unforeseeable human obstacles. Similarly, it is perhaps not too farfetched to assume that desk sergeants feed ice cream to lost children because they like children. But if the treat does not achieve the purpose of keeping the youngster in the station house until his parents arrive to redeem him, the sergeant would have to resort to other means of keeping him there.

*   *   *

To summarize: Because only a small part of the activity of the police is dedicated to law enforcement and because they deal with the majority of their problems without invoking the law, the concept of the police as "law enforcers" does not seem to reflect accurately the role they play in society. In light of what the public appears to expect of the police, the range of activities police actually engage in, and the theme that unifies all these activities, I have suggested that *the role of the police is best understood as a mechanism for the distribution of non-negotiably coercive force employed in accordance with the dictates of an intuitive grasp of situational exigencies.*

It is, of course, not surprising that a society committed to the establishment of peace by pacific means and to the abolishment of all forms of violence from the fabric of its social relations, at least as a matter of official morality and policy, would establish a corps of specially deputized officials endowed with the exclusive monopoly of using force contingently where limitations of foresight fail to provide alternatives. That is, given the melancholy appreciation of the fact that the total abolition of force is not attainable, the closest approximation to the ideal is to limit it as a special and exclusive trust. If it is the case, however, that the mandate of the police is organized around their capacity and authority to use force, that is, if this is what the institution's existence makes available to society, then the evaluation of that institution's performance must focus on it. While it is quite true that policemen will have to be judged on other dimensions of competence, too—for example, the exercise of force against criminal suspects requires some knowledge about crime and criminal law—their methods as society's agents of coercion will have to be considered central to the overall judgment.

The proposed definition of the police role entails a difficult moral problem. How can we arrive at a favorable or even accepting judgment about an activity which is, in its very conception, opposed to the ethos of the polity that authorizes it? Is it not well-nigh inevitable that this mandate be concealed in circumlocution? While solving puzzles of moral philosophy is beyond the scope of this analysis, we will have to address this question in a somewhat more mundane formulation: namely, on what terms can a society dedicated to peace institutionalize the exercise of force?

It appears that in our society two answers to this question are acceptable. One defines the targets of legitimate force as enemies and the coercive advance against them as warfare. Those who wage this war are expected to be possessed by the military virtues of valor, obedience, and *esprit de corps.* The enterprise as a whole is justified as a sacrificial and glorious mission in which the warrior's duty is "not to reason why." The other answer involves an altogether different imagery. The targets of force are conceived as practical objectives and their attainment a matter of practical expediency. The process involves prudence, economy, and considered judgment, from case to case. The enterprise as a whole is conceived as a public trust, the exercise of which is vested in individual practitioners who are personally responsible for their decisions and actions.

Reflection suggests that the two patterns are profoundly incompatible. Remarkably, however, our police departments have not been deterred from attempting the reconciliation of the irreconcilable. Thus, our policemen are exposed to the demand of a conflicting nature in that their actions are supposed to reflect both military prowess and professional acumen.

NOTES

1 "Justification for the Use of Force in the Criminal Law," *Stanford Law Review* **13** (1961): 566–609.

2 "At common law, the rule appears to have been that an officer was entitled to make a reasonable mistake as to whether the victim had committed a felony, but a private person was not so entitled. Thus strict liability was created for the private arrester, and he could not justifiably kill, if the victim had not actually committed a felony. Several modern cases have imposed this standard of strict liability even upon the officer by conditioning justification of deadly force on the victim's actually having committed a felony, and a number of states have enacted statutes which appear to adopt this strict liability. However, many jurisdictions, such as California, have homicide statutes which permit the police officer to use deadly force for the arrest of a person 'charged' with felony. It has been suggested that this requirement only indicates the necessity for reasonable belief by the officer that the victim has committed a felony." Ibid., pp. 599–600.

3 The illustrations are taken from field notes I have collected over the course of fourteen months of intensive field observations of police activity in two large cities. One is located in a Rocky Mountain State, the other on the West Coast. All other case vignettes used in the subsequent text of this report also come from this source.

4 By "non-negotiably coercible" I mean that when a deputized police officer decides that force is necessary, then, within the boundaries of this situation, he is not accountable to anyone, nor is he required to brook the arguments or opposition of anyone who might object to it. I set this forth not as a legal but as a practical rule. The legal question whether citizens may oppose policemen is complicated. Apparently resisting police coercion in situations of emergency is not legitimate; see Hans Kelsen, *General Theory of Law and State* (New York: Russel & Russel, 1961), pp. 278–279; and H. A. L. Hart, *The Concept of Law* (Oxford: Clarendon Press, 1961), pp. 20–21. Common law doctrine allows that citizens may oppose "unlawful arrest," 6 *Corpus Juris Secundum,* Arrest #13, p. 613; against this, the Uniform Arrest Act, drafted by a committee of the Interstate Commission on Crime in 1939, provides in Section 5, "If a person has reasonable grounds to believe that he is being arrested by a peace officer, it is his duty to refrain from using force or any weapons in resisting arrest regardless of whether or not there is a legal basis for the arrest." S. B. Warner, "Uniform Arrest Act," *Vanderbilt Law Review* **28** (1942): 315–347. At present, at least twelve states are governed by case law recognizing the validity of the Common Law doctrine, at least five have adopted the rule contained in the Uniform Arrest Act, and at least six have case law or statutes that give effect to the Uniform Arrest Act rule. That the trend is away from the Common Law doctrine and in the direction of the Uniform Arrest Act rule is argued in Max Hochanadel and H. W. Stege, "The Right to Resist an Unlawful Arrest: An Outdated Concept?" *Tulsa Law Journal* **3** (1966): 40–46. I am grateful for the help I received from 35 of the 50 State Attorney General Offices from whom I sought information concerning this matter.

5 Bruce Smith, *Police Systems in the United States* (New York: Harper, 1960), 2nd ed. rev., p. 3.

6 The authors of the *Task Force Report: The Police* note that little has been done to make these alternative resources available as substitutes for police intervention; see the President's Commission on Law Enforcement and Administration of Justice, *Task Force Report: The Police* (Washington, D.C.: U.S. Government Printing Office, 1967), p. 31.

Cops' Rules

JONATHAN RUBINSTEIN

*Son: You know, Dad, I think I'll be able
to take you in a couple of years.*

*Father: You think so, boy? Listen, when
we fight, it ain't gonna be any of that
stuff they teach you in the Boy
Scouts. We fight cops' rules.*

Son: Hey, that ain't fair.

Father: Why not?

*Son: Because policemen fight dirty, you
told me that.*

*Father: That's right, boy, and don't you
forget it. Just remember, cops always
win.*

A policeman and his son

The policeman's principal tool is his body. He shares with many persons the use of their bodies as a piece of equipment essential to the performance of their trades. He is similar to a mountain climber; to athletes whose success is rooted in physical prowess rather than the skillful use of equipment; to runners, circus acrobats, sexual performers, laborers, and peasants. He also has, in common with people in many trades, a set of skills that are needed for the effective use of tools expressly provided to expand the effectiveness of his body. For him a gun and a nightstick are not simply weapons that terrify some and intrigue others but extensions of himself whose use (and non-use) is linked to his notions about how he uses his body

to do his work. But unlike anyone else whose body is the tool of his trade, the policeman uses his to control other people.[1]

Despite careful restrictions designed to establish firmly the boundaries of his authority, the policeman is endowed with quite extraordinary power. Even in communities where there is intense conflict between policemen and citizens, there is little resistance to the notion that there ought to be people patrolling the streets, licensed to regulate public traffic and even forcibly to restrict and restrain people. The policeman's power and skills are not authorized and encouraged for the purpose of entertainment or production but for the maintenance of order and the preservation of authority. But whatever the functions assigned to him, whatever uses are made of him by the government, the policeman views his work in personal terms. Whether he works alone or in the company of a partner, everything he does is measured in terms of his individual capacity. The manner in which he works and the tactics and techniques he employs are greatly affected by the policies of his department and the attitudes of his city's government toward its citizens, but whatever style he uses, he is motivated by his need to keep whole his notion of himself as an effective and capable worker.

The policeman is a unique kind of user of the city streets. He develops an intimate knowledge of the places he works, a knowledge of his territory not matched by many of the people who live there. He knows it better than his own neighborhood, but he is not "at home" there. He does not know most of the people he sees or is called to assist, but everyone knows that he is a policeman. Every aspect of his appearance has been calculated to assure that there can be no mistake about his social identity. His uniform not only makes him visible to people who wish to find him but limits his snooping directly in the private lives of citizens; it also gives an unequivocal statement to everyone that the person intervening in their lives is not a private person but a cop.[2]

Out of uniform he betrays a self-consciousness on the streets he polices which expresses his own understanding of the special character of his place in public. When he's on patrol, people feel free to approach him for advice or help, but if he approaches them, there are inevitably tensions and unease that cannot be masked, even if the encounter is not marked by displays of incivility. The person approached cannot know what the policeman wants of him, and the policeman, if he is suspicious of someone, does not know whether his feelings are accurate. Every encounter the policeman has in public, except when he is called to aid someone, must begin with an abridgment of personal freedom. Regardless of how much experience he has accumulated in dealing with people, reading their demeanor and attitudes, he cannot know how they will respond to him. He is a public stranger whose authority allows him to do things that private persons normally avoid doing at all costs, but whose powers do not diminish the tensions created when strangers meet.

When a policeman stops someone on suspicion, their relationship closely parallels the contact between a common street criminal and his victim. While the person stopped may not be surprised by the intervention of the policeman—people in some neighborhoods are stopped frequently—he does not

anticipate its occurrence. Once the policeman has committed himself to an investigation, he is also revealing the purpose and intent of his actions, although this is incidental to his main concern. A criminal tries to initiate his contact with a victim covertly, taking him by surprise, but at some point he must reveal his intentions to the intended victim (unless he is a pickpocket, who relies on skill and deception). While the policeman is legally empowered to make a stop (and in some places citizens are lawfully deprived of the right to resist even the unlawful actions of policemen) and the criminal's actions are sanctioned only by his willingness to risk his liberty and to use force to accomplish his purposes, both are strangers who suddenly intervene in another person's life, absolutely depriving him of his freedom, at least momentarily. The criminal naturally seeks to minimize the time between the initiation of contact and his departure from the scene, while the patrolman's purpose is to detain the person for as long as he feels necessary to conduct his investigation. Both must be prepared to honor any actions necessary to carry out their purposes, unless they are willing to fail. A policeman has no guarantee that after he has established contact with someone and even explained the purpose of his stop that the unease and tension created will decline. They may well increase. The person stopped may have something to conceal from the police, or he may object in principle to the restriction of his liberty. The policeman's knowledge of his legal powers encourages him to proceed with actions that he knows arouse considerable hostility, but he also recognizes that the law does not prevent people from objecting and even resisting him.

A suspicion stop is only the most extreme form of engagement which comprises most of the work a policeman does. When he is hailed on the street or summoned by the dispatcher, there exists between the policeman and the person requesting his aid a consensus regarding his function, but even in these instances, the bonds of agreement do not often run deep and are easily overturned. He assumes that what the dispatcher tells him is the truth as it is known to him, but the patrolman recognizes that he may have been misinformed or misled, or the situation may have changed between the time the call was made and the time he arrives at the scene. When he is stopped on the street, he is attentive to what people tell him, but he does not necessarily believe what they say. He has been lied to too often and has come to recognize that people are willing to use him in ways they would not use someone they knew personally. When he responds to a call, the action he takes may not be the one that those who summoned him want, and they are not unwilling to express their dissatisfaction to him. Even when he stops people for a traffic violation or some other minor matter, he cannot know whether the person he is approaching will treat the moment casually; he does not know whether he might be stumbling into a situation that is explosive for reasons he cannot anticipate. The policeman may think his actions are not to be regarded with great seriousness, but the other party to the encounter may feel wronged, may misjudge entirely what the officer's purposes are, or, occasionally, when the patrolman's intentions are to advance his private interests under the cover of public law, may understand him too well.

The policeman brings to almost all of his encounters some degree of suspicion and uncertainty. The law formally recognizes that he must assume risks that citizens normally do not undertake and provides him with the means to protect himself. The potential danger that arises each time he places himself in contact with someone suspected of criminal acts or intentions can be reduced by exercising his defensive right to assure himself that the person is not armed. He may not only circumscribe a person's liberty by stopping him on the street, he may also completely violate the suspect's privacy and autonomy by running his hands over the man's entire body. The policeman knows that a frisk is a humiliation people usually accept from him because he can sustain his authority by almost any action he feels necessary. While he does not frisk people often just to humble them, he can do so; when he feels obliged to check someone for concealed weapons, he is not usually in a position to request their permission, even if this were desirable.

The policeman also carries powerful weapons that he may use only to defend himself, to defend others who are threatened physically, or to prevent the flight of persons known to be felons and impossible to halt in any other manner. These limitations on his right to use force are relaxed only in the most unusual circumstances. Only when martial law is decreed is the policeman authorized to exercise force without limitation, and these measures are generally accompanied by the introduction of soldiers, whose training and equipment prepare them to control people by brute force. But when a policeman shoots someone in a dirty, dark alley, no declarations are required. In some cities the entire matter is covered over, while in others there are careful investigations designed to probe the patrolman's motives and to remind his colleagues that the limitations are real and the boundaries of their authority are being patrolled. In either case, the policeman does not have to request permission to use his weapons. He is authorized by the community, theoretically, to carry them and to exercise judgment about their use. They are not only a protection and a comfort to him (as well as a heavy weight that strains his stomach muscles over the years) but also serve to remind him, if any reminder is required, that each time he knocks on a door, approaches a person, or answers a call, there is potential trouble. He does not go about his work in a constant state of anxiety, but he must be alert for signs of danger and threat.

A policeman has many responsibilities and opportunities to perform, but he measures his capacity to "do the job" (and is judged by his colleagues) by his success in policing people. He gets little comfort and pleasure from being a watchman patrolling empty streets, looking at rows of darkened buildings. That is why many patrolmen hate last out and go to sleep unless constantly prodded by their supervisors. Those who do not sleep may continue patrolling, but unless they are given a job and kept involved, they too become bleary-eyed and indifferent. However, a single call from the dispatcher awakens all but the soundest sleeper, mobilizing them for action. People interest him, or signs of mistreated or misappropriated property. An empty street offers him no challenge, nor is he comforted by the possibility that its being empty means there is nothing for him to be concerned about.

Although a policeman seldom becomes involved in fights, he carefully assesses the physical assets of all the people he approaches. He is always making appraisals of a man as he comes near, deciding whether he can "take him" if he must. This is not an expression of his lust for combat but a recognition of his place in the scheme of things. When he approaches an individual or a group, the patrolman is not only risking injury and pain, he is also placing on the line his capacity to do his job. Since his body is his principal tool, he cannot separate its protection and defense, which are instinctive, from his need to use it in the performance of his work. Each time he does a job of police work, he enters a situation where violent conflict is a possibility.

The moment he accepts the responsibility of being a policeman, he assumes the risks of physical combat. Regardless of his personal inclinations toward fighting, he takes it as a matter of course that he will be hit and in turn will hit back. If he has any doubts, they are quickly put to rest in his initial contacts with veterans. "None of you has been hired to go out and get yourselves killed, but you will take your lumps. If you aren't ready for that, stroll out now and get a job in a shoe store," a lieutenant suggested to a class of recruits on their first day at the academy. Several weeks later the same class was being lectured on testifying in court when one student asked whether a man who had been assaulted had to appear in court. The instructor sensed something inappropriate about the sentiment that prompted the question and, ignoring it, replied, "Listen, if you guys aren't ready to take your shots, you better quit right now. Because I'm tellin' you, somewhere along the line someone is gonna lay it to you. I don't care how tough you think you are. It happened to me, it's happened to everyone. With me it was my own fault, I was takin' a broad down a flight of stairs and I got a little careless. She jumped me and worked me over with a shoe before I punched her in the mouth. And dealing with a woman is the worst." Few policemen seek to hide the fact that they have been beaten. While many men conceal embarrassments, failures that resulted from their being outsmarted or from a personal lapse, they do not try to hide admissions of defeat from others or themselves.

Perhaps it is a way of reminding themselves of errors made, of things learned and not to be forgotten, a reaffirmation of their mortality. "See that bar? My first night on the street they put me in the hospital. I was out for two weeks. The sergeant took me from roll call and drove me to that garage down the street and told me to stay put until he came for me. Shit, I wasn't gonna sit inside all night. So I started walkin', and right in front of this bar I got jumped by four guys. They really beat the shit out of me. I never been beat like that since. But I sticked a couple of them pretty good before I went out. I guess that old sergeant knew what he was talkin' about," the sergeant said, with a wry smile.

A patrolman approaches people in a variety of situations. He comes upon them driving and walking; he sees them in places where he has responded to calls for help; he is approached by strangers for advice and aid, goes with them into houses to break up fights and settle accounts. He enters crowded public places and deserted private ones, looking for the source of trouble that has brought him there. Since he must constantly confront people under widely differing circumstances, he cannot develop a single approach to all situations. He behaves differently when he is working alone than when he is with a partner who understands his manner. If he is a frightened man unwilling to take the easy way out of his dilemma by resigning or feigning work, he can allow the fears that assail even the bravest to control him. He may approach every situation with his holster unsnapped and his stick poised, but his colleagues will shun him and he cannot long remain on the job, although he may stay for enough time to cause pain and grief to himself, his colleagues, and whoever has the misfortune to cross his path.

He must learn to control his fears and anxiety by looking for signs of danger in the places and people he approaches; he must learn to examine people for signs of resistance, flight, and threat, to limit their chances of hurting him or creating situations he cannot control or can control only with the use of force which is inappropriate to the circumstances. He must learn to use his body as a tool, positioning himself in an unobtrusive manner so that he is always able to retaliate with force if attacked, while not giving a threatening and provoking appearance. He must learn to use the powerful weapons he carries, so they will do what they are supposed to do and no more. He must learn when to hit people and when not to hit them. He must also learn how to establish and express his authority by cajoling, requesting, threatening, "bullshitting them," as patrolmen say, to avoid using force. He must learn to use his body to express with his whole self the authority represented by the appearance he presents; he must learn to use it as a weapon when the occasion demands. He must learn when to mobilize his physical resources and when to let them slumber, allowing his legal power to act for him. In all of his actions he must learn to acquire a quickness, resolution, and decisiveness that urge him forward when others withdraw. He must accept and welcome the fact that, as a policeman, he must be in control of the situation lest it be in control of him.[3]

Although the police assume that force and violence are an inevitable part of their work, there is a noteworthy absence in their training of emphasis on the techniques and uses of force. There is no way of instilling in a man a set of sophisticated tricks without also encouraging him to use them. While many policemen consider the threat of force to be the most useful technique available to assure their success, the administrators of the police recognize that unless there is careful regulation of attitudes toward force, the men can easily get out of hand. Little time is devoted to physical training or contact exercises. The men are taught a few basic "come-alongs," handholds,[4] which are designed to move drunks, to walk an unsecured prisoner, and to disarm an assailant. There is no special judo training or suggestion that a policeman should develop sophisticated combat skills. The instructors warn the men that they are given only basic moves to be used in emergencies. "We don't teach anything fancy because if you don't practice you forget them, and when you get to the district there's no time for that. Just remember, if you're rolling around the street with someone and everything else fails, go for the guy's jewels, that's the basic rule," the instructor laconically explained. The essence of physical training is street fighting, and this basic form of urban combat depends almost entirely on a person's willingness to hit and to be hit.

"The last thing you want to do is to pull your gun, but you'll learn when to pull and when to leave it alone," the instructor said, emphasizing the special character of the gun, a theme constantly stressed in police training. "If a guy comes at you with a knife, you must decide whether he is a drunk who can be knocked on his ass with your stick or someone who knows how to handle it. If he keeps shifting it, weaving the knife in front of you, putting it behind his back, you don't want to fuck with him. You pull your gun and aim for his chest. If he keeps coming, bury him. But you'll learn when to pull it and when to leave it alone."

The lack of emphasis on combativeness and physical prowess suggests that the police presume that any man who wants to be a policeman has the physical assets necessary to do the job. The men are told bluntly and often, formally and informally, that they will find themselves in situations where the use of force is necessary, unavoidable, and occasionally desirable. But every time they are taught a technique or introduced to a new weapon, their instructors stress the limitations that the law imposes and remind everyone how easy it is to go over the fine edge between defense and terror. There is never a hint that violence is to be treated casually.

"We are trying to make this job into a profession, not some Irish goon with a stick like it used to be," the instructor said, with a grin. "You can hit a man who resists arrest and you can keep hitting him until he submits. But once he is subdued, you cannot hit him—then it's brutality. If you hit a man who is cuffed, if you beat someone in the station, even if you give a guy a shot after he gives up because he hurt you, it's illegal. You're not much of a man if you do. You'll see guys out there who do these things, fewer every year, but there are still some, and in this business I guess there will always be some. But don't you be one of them."

The department also wants everyone to go on the street confident of his ability to meet any challenges, able to stand up and learn the job. Nobody is discouraged from thinking that physical prowess and courage are not necessary elements in the patrolman's make-up. On the contrary, the men are warned that some of them will not be able to handle the strain of the job and will quit soon after they leave the academy. But they are discouraged from looking for a routine way of handling problems. They are urged to understand the difference between a man who is willing to use force and one who is eager to do so. It is this willingness that experienced policemen look for in new men, and every recruit is made to understand this.

One afternoon, a visiting psychologist gave a lengthy lecture on human relations.

The supervising sergeant openly slumbered at the back of the room, displaying his contempt for the discussion. At one point the lecturer asked the recruits how they would react to being called certain kinds of names. When several responded correctly, saying they would ignore personal epithets designed to undermine their professional calm, the sergeant rose and began pacing about the room. He started to say something but caught himself and returned to his seat. A burly Puerto Rican recruit rose and in halting English expressed his feelings. He was well liked by all for his willingness to take part in any classroom demonstrations and for his bluff attitudes toward the academy, which most men despise by the end of the first month of training. "I don't care what anyone call me, spick or anything," he said, "just as long as they don't touch my body. They touch my body, I care, I care a lot." The sergeant bounded up from his seat, beaming. "That's a policeman talking. I want you in my platoon, boy. Keep your hands off my body, I like that. Oh boy, I just can't wait to see you guys on the street," he said, beaming.

NOTES

1 I have benefited greatly by a reading of Erving Goffman's essay, "Where the Action Is," in *Interaction Ritual: Essays on Face-to-Face Behavior* (Garden City, N.Y.: Anchor Books, 1967), pp. 149–270.
2 It is reported that New York City patrolmen complain that they are sometimes mistaken for private guards because a number of private agencies have designed uniforms quite similar to the official police uniform.
3 "If one examines moments when an individual undergoes . . . chances, whether as part of serious work or dangerous play, certain capacities, certain properties of his make-up, appear to be of intrinsic or 'primary' relevance: in high construction work, care and balance; in mountain climbing, timing and perceptual judgment; in game hunting, aim; in gambling, a knowledge of the odds; and in all cases, memory and experience." Goffman, "Where the Action Is," p. 216.
4 David H. Gilston and Lawrence Podell, *The Practical Patrolman* (Springfield, Ill.: Charles C Thomas, 1959), pp. 13–15.

Force, Arrest, and Cover Charges

PAUL CHEVIGNY

Any person who defies the police risks the imposition of legal sanctions, commencing with a summons and continuing on up to the use of firearms. The sanction that is imposed depends on at least three factors: the character of the officer, the place where the encounter occurs, and the character of the person with whom the encounter is had. The police may arrest *anyone* who challenges them (as they define the challenge), but they are more likely to further abuse anyone who is poor or who belongs to an outcast group.

Members of outcast groups, by their mere presence, seem to offer an affront to order such that the police will themselves initiate action against them by ordering them to move along, breaking into a party, or some similar action. To the police, the ordinary citizen begins to assume the status of an outcast only when he actively defies the police, whereas a member of an outcast group need take no such action.

John McNamara, reviewing "critical incidents" involving police and citizens in his work with New York City police recruits, was "struck by the extent to which the handling of relatively minor incidents such as traffic violations or disorderly disputes between husbands and wives seemed to create a more serious situation than existed prior to the police attempt to control the situa-

tion." [1] In many of our cases, the police have gone further and caused a situation to degenerate into an argument when it was scarcely a dispute at all to begin with. McNamara attributes the phenomenon to mistaken assumptions on the part of the police about how they ought to behave toward the public. For example, he found that 39 to 40 percent of policemen agree with the proposition that "a patrolman can be pretty sure he will gain compliance from a person who appears to be somewhat frightened of the patrolman," as well as with the proposition that "when patrolmen indicate they will use the force necessary to gain compliance from a citizen, they are helped considerably if the citizen thinks they are getting angry." [2] These police opinions are so potentially dangerous, and in many cases so catastrophically applied, that it is not enough to think of them only as mistaken assumptions. The reason that policemen act so aggressively as to exacerbate street situations is, of course, that they seek to establish their authority by such transactions. The answers to McNamara's questions indicate that a large percentage of policemen will usually try to obtain compliance by an unconditional demand or the use of force. Many people wonder whether police work attracts young men who already have such attitudes, or whether the police role develops those attitudes in them. Most authorities who have studied the problem intensively seem to agree that the second alternative is the correct one. Police recruits are much like other young men of a similar background; it is police customs and the police role that make them adopt police attitudes.[3]

In the typical street encounter there are three steps:

1. *Police perception of a challenge to authority.* In the case of a member of an outcast group this step is eliminated or at least minimized.
2. *Police demand for submission.* This is most commonly enshrined in the question, "So you're a wise guy, eh?" . . .
3. *Response to the demand.* The citizen in effect either admits that he is a wise guy, or denies it by complying with the police demand, if it involves an action like moving along, or by apologizing to the policeman if no action is demanded.

People in minority and outcast groups, who are the most likely to be subjected to a police demand for submission, at the same time find it hardest to comply with it. The middle-class man thinks nothing of saying, "Sorry, officer," but to the oppressed and downtrodden those words are galling. It is especially hard for a black, for whom such an act seems just one more token of submission. The combination of being an outcast (step one) and refusing to comply in step three is explosive; thereby hangs the tale of many police brutality cases.

The police rationale for this three-step process is that people who present a challenge to them are troublemakers, as the police might put it, or "symbolic assailants," as Skolnick calls them. They are, quite literally, potential offenders, and so to arrest one of them is at least the ethical (if not the legal) equivalent of arresting a criminal. The policeman will go on to say that he must maintain his authority against those who challenge it in order to enforce the laws effectively. In short, his authority over others will be lost if he backs down with one person. It inevitably follows that his authority as a policeman is asserted in situations which are personal disputes or at least have a personal dimension. In some of these cases, the provocation comes principally from the citizen, and in others, principally from the police. The point is that they are street arguments, not so very different from those which arise every day between private citizens when one insults another or tries to get him to do something he does not want to do. Although it is true that policemen take umbrage very easily, and that they sometimes see a threat where there is none, it is equally clear that in many instances some sort of retaliation is almost inevitable. The chief difference is that one of the parties is a policeman, and for him no dispute is purely personal. It is no accident that in old-fashioned journalistic parlance the officer was personified as "John Law" or the "long arm of the law." Policemen apparently do see themselves as personifying authority, and a challenge to one of them (or to all of them, as in the case of civilian review) is a challenge to the Law. Everybody knows that when you defy the Law, you go to jail.

The apparently irrational and sometimes provocative behavior of the police in street conflicts has often raised the question whether the police deliberately encourage violence or at least disorderly behavior from a troublemaker, in order to show that he really is an offender and to provide grounds for removing him from the street by arrest. This is one of the unresolved questions about police behavior, and one that is central to an understanding of police abuses. If the police react in a rough manner to provocation from citizens, if they in fact themselves behave in a rude fashion, that is one problem, but it is quite another if the police deliberately provoke violence in people they believe to be troublemakers. Westley, in his research on a Midwestern police department, felt that there was a tendency for the police to provoke anyone who was disrespectful until there was an assault and then to retaliate with violence.[4] Werthman and Piliavin detected the same thing in their work on police treatment of juveniles,[5] and at least one writer in the professional journal, *Police,* has criticized the practice, while carefully labeling it "unusual." [6]

*   *   *

The consensus among the authorities who have studied the problem is that the police do sometimes try to provoke violence in order to make an arrest. It is logical to think that policemen will try such things with outcasts, whom they fear and dislike and would prefer to see in jail. One young black in a ghetto neighborhood in Brooklyn, who had the reputation of being a "cop fighter," complained that the police would not let him alone. Whenever they saw him on the street they slowed down their cars and asked him if he wanted to fight. In New York City today, however, I think that the challenge by a policeman to physical combat, or even to a public disturbance, is the exception. . . . In most cases, even if a policeman wanted to use such crude tactics, they would not be necessary. The New York police are sophisticated enough in drawing charges and making them stick not to need an actual act of physical violence to arrest anyone. If they feel that a man is a troublemaker, they can, unfortunately, charge him with resisting arrest, without the necessity of risking injury to an officer.

The worst problem in street-corner incidents is not that of police quarrelling with citizens. Most such quarrels, while never admirable, are at least understandable; they are much like quarrels between private citizens. The worst abuse is not even the police hitting people in such quarrels; pugnacious citizens hit others in private disputes every day. The root problem is the abuse of power, the fact that the police not only hit a man but arrest him. Once they have arrested him, of course, lying becomes an inevitable part of the procedure of making the quarrel look like a crime, and thus the lie is the chief abuse with which we must come to grips. If the police simply hit a man and let him go, there would be an abuse of the authority conferred by the uniform and the sick but not the compound abuse of hitting a man and then dragging him to court on criminal charges, really a more serious injury than a blow. One's head heals up, after all, but a criminal record never goes away. There is no more embittering experience in the legal system than to be abused by the police and then to be tried and convicted on false evidence.

Police abuse and consequent conviction on false evidence are a combination which feeds the impulse to riot; once respect for the legal process is gone, grievances can be expressed only by force. Despite these obvious repercussions upon community relations, it is rare that anyone is abused without being criminally charged, not only because of the rationale for such abuse ("he was guilty anyhow") but because the policeman is likely to get into trouble if he lets an abused person go free. There is nothing to cover a later accusation of abuse if an arrest has not been made.

There can be no doubt that police lying is the most pervasive of all abuses. . . . In the police canon of ethics, the lie is justified in the same way as the arrest: as a vindication of police authority, by proving that defiance of the police is a crime in fact if not in law. A member of an outcast group, or anyone who defies the police, being guilty at heart and sometimes potentially guilty in fact, deserves to be punished out of hand. Besides, the police dislike such people so much that they consider them unworthy of the protection of the law. By lying, the police enforce these folkways of their own, while preserving the shell of due process of law.

Not surprisingly, police lying is a problem about which little reliable research has been done. William Westley, after breaking ground upon the police use of violence in his first article, went on to open the problem of lying in "Secrecy and the Police." [7] He found that 11 out of 15 men said they would not report a brother officer for taking money from a prisoner, and 10 out of 13 said they would not testify against the officer if he were accused by the prisoner. Comments on police honesty since the publication of Westley's article have often taken the form of warnings in the professional journals. Richard H. Blum wrote in *Police:* "The conflict of loyalty versus lawfulness is always with the officer, as he is faced with wanting trust, friendship and reliability on the one hand, while wanting to be lawful on the other." [8] Both Blum and Westley deal with honesty about the conduct of a fellow officer; obviously the temptation is even stronger for an officer to cover up when he himself is in trouble, as he usually is when he has abused a citizen.

Once an arrest is made, the police begin to consider what testimony is necessary for a conviction and what charges are necessary to create pressure on the defendant for a plea of guilty. The Criminal Court is viewed not as a tribunal for the determination of fact but as a sort of administrative adjunct to the police station for the purpose of obtaining desirable results. Lying is a litigation tool much like, say, investigation. Once the police have arrested a man, particularly under circumstances when charges have been made against an officer, the only real objective is conviction, and the police feel that they have made a mistake if they fail to obtain the conviction, not if they lied to obtain it. The arresting officer who has abused a citizen makes it his business to get out of trouble, as does any other accused party, and his original aim of "preserving police authority" becomes little more than a rationalization. The lie serves the double purpose of preserving his authority and his job.

It seems that there is some sort of folklore or underground standard circulating in the police department, according to which charges are drawn to cover abuses. Lying to cover a mistake and the use of a criminal charge to buttress the lie are such a natural development that it would hardly seem necessary to do more than give a patrolman a hint. Charges are so invariably preferred, however, and the charges are so much alike from one case to the next, that I am constrained to believe that something a little more definite than a hint is at work. At some level in the department, something close to this standard has been accepted: "When a citizen is injured by a policeman, he must be charged with resisting arrest, together with the underlying crime for which he was arrested. If there was no crime, but rather a personal dispute with the policeman, then the defendant must be charged with disorderly conduct and resisting arrest." Other, more serious charges become something of a matter of taste. Experienced men tend to add other charges, in order to increase the pressure for a plea of guilty to one of the charges. I once heard two transit policemen arguing in the hallway outside the courtroom after a man had refused to plead guilty to disorderly conduct in exchange for a dismissal of the charge of resisting arrest. The more experienced of the two was saying, "You see? He wouldn't take it. I *told* you you should have charged him with felonious assault." These charges—disorderly conduct, resisting arrest and felonious assault, or all three—together with a story to establish them, constitute the system for covering street abuses. According to a task force of the President's Commission on Law Enforcement, the system exists in many other cities with conditions similar to those of New York, notably in Philadelphia.[9]

It is my guess that the system is perpetuated at the middle level, among the sergeants and possibly the lieutenants. . . . Investigators for a field survey of the President's Commission, covering police departments in major cities outside New York, have reported observations that support the theory that it is the officers at the middle level who tend to cover for the abuses of the men working under them.[10] This cover may take the form of advice about criminal charges or simply of keeping quiet about abuses; in any case, it is characteristic of the extreme solidarity and secrecy of policemen in every city. No doubt the solidarity is as tight as it is because every ranking officer in the typical urban police department has come up through the ranks and shares the mores of the men below him. By the same token, it follows that the introduction of new men at the middle level, specially trained for their jobs rather than drawn from the ranks, would be the most effective way of breaking through the police secrecy. Under present civil service laws, in New York as well as most other communities, it is difficult to alter the system of seniority, but any limitation on

the protection of underlings by superiors may be impossible without it.

The Review Board and other institutions in the New York City Police Department do little to discourage the system of cover charges. The Review Board does not hold a hearing until after criminal charges against the complainant have been disposed of, and the charges at a departmental trial are always artfully drawn to avoid any conflict with criminal charges made by the officer involved, even when they have been disposed of. These practices encourage officers to believe that if they can cover themselves by a criminal charge, they will escape censure. If the department were vitally concerned about seeing justice done, it would make sure that criminal charges were dropped against citizens when a departmental investigation showed that they were unwarranted. Instead, the department sits back to see whether the officer can make his criminal case stick before proceeding against him.

It is worth mentioning here that the ironclad system of cover charges exists in New York City partly because certain other abuses do not. For example, the New York City Police Department does not permit arrests on "suspicion," a practice allowed by departments in other cities such as Detroit, where 13 percent of the arrests in 1964 were for "detention."[11] Dragnet arrests for suspicious persons do occasionally occur after serious crimes in New York, but in general, if a city policeman has a defendant in custody, he must try to show probable cause for arresting him, and if he is to account for a defendant's injuries by resistance to arrest, he must commence his explanation with a lawful arrest. Hence the elaborate lies about disorderly conduct. It is because the men at the top of the department are trying to maintain a façade of probable cause for arrest that the men in the middle and at the bottom go to such lengths to cover their mistakes. To be an oppressor is a tricky business in New York, this most liberal of all possible worlds. In jurisdictions where no attempt is made to maintain the requirements of probable cause, the system of cover charges is correspondingly less deeply entrenched.

Furthermore, in other jurisdictions a policeman can afford to be a little lax in covering himself because he can rely on the district attorney to help him out if he makes a mistake. In the District of Columbia, for example, the authorities have in the past preferred charges of filing a false report against people who made complaints about policemen.[12] In one case from that jurisdiction the District Attorney started a prosecution upon minor traffic charges three months after the events were supposed to have occurred, and solely because the defendant had complained against the police officer involved in the incident.[13] If there is an instance of equal skulduggery perpetrated by any of the five New York City district attorneys, I have not heard of it. The only incident in my experience which approaches these in depravity was a threat by a prosecutor, after he had consented to a dismissal of the charges against two out of three codefendants, to reinstate the charges against them if they testified in defense of the third. That is an exceptional incident, however, and it is generally up to the New York City policeman to provide his his own cover for his mistakes. If he does not make his accusation at the time of the occurrence, the prosecutor is not likely to look upon the case with favor. The system is the policeman's only solution.

If officials outside the police department in New York do not participate directly in protecting police officers, they do so by their silence. The judges, the prosecutors, even the commissioner himself, cannot appear to condone slipshod police work or police abuses. On the other hand, they know that there is such poor police work, and although they would not participate in it, they do not expect to do very much to improve it. The district attorneys go right on taking waivers of damage claims in return for the dismissal of criminal charges, the remedies for abuses continue to be inadequate, and all in all, with some exceptions, the system works nearly as effectively as if all the other officials participated in it. They become parties to the system in the sense that they know, or should know, that the policeman is covering his mistakes by lying, and they are content to let him go on doing it. They maintain the rigid standards of due process required in a modern liberal society by letting the patrolman vary the facts to fit the case. They have helped to make the policeman the target for much of the hostility in the city by making him do all the dirty work.

Ironically, the vigilance and sophistication of citizens in pursuing what few poor remedies are open to them have probably helped to make the system as rigid as it is. In rural communities and small towns, where abused citizens are satisfied to forget the whole thing if the police will forget it, criminal charges may not be used by the police as a cover; but in New York, where many abused citizens are very likely to complain to the department and perhaps even bring a lawsuit, criminal charges are almost invariably preferred. One thoroughly puzzled woman who complained of being manhandled in a welfare center by a policeman told me that the officer had later bought her lunch and said that he would like to drop the charges, but he dared not because she might sue the city. She tried to convince him that she would not sue, but he felt that he could not trust her; regardless of the promises she made while she was under arrest, she might

change her mind later. The system was too ironclad for him to let her go.

NOTES

1 John H. McNamara, "Uncertainties in Police Work: The Relevance of Police Recruits' Background and Training," in David Joseph Bordua, ed., *The Police: Six Sociological Essays* (New York: Wiley, 1967), p. 168.
2 Ibid., pp. 226, 228.
3 Ibid., p. 194; Arthur Niederhoffer, *Behind the Shield: The Police in Urban Society* (New York: Doubleday, 1967), Ch. 5.
4 William A. Westley, "Violence and the Police," *American Journal of Sociology,* LIX (August 1953): 39.
5 Carl Wertham and Irving M. Piliavin, "Gang Members and the Police," in David Joseph Bordua, ed., *The Police: Six Sociological Essays* (New York: Wiley, 1967), p. 93.
6 Richard H. Blum, "The Problems of Being a Police Officer," *Police* (January 1961): 12.
7 William A. Westley, "Secrecy and the Police," *Social Forces* **34** (March 1956): 254.
8 Blum, "Problems of Being a Police Officer," p. 10.
9 President's Commission on Law Enforcement and the Administration of Justice, *The Task Force Report on the Police* (Washington, D.C.: U.S. Government Printing Office, 1967), p. 195.
10 President's Commission on Law Enforcement and the Administration of Justice, *Field Survey V*, pp. 189ff.
11 *Task Force Report,* p. 186.
12 Ibid., p. 195.
13 *Miller Dixon* versus *District of Columbia,* D.C. Cir. Dkt. No. 21084/67.

POLICEMAN'S CHOICE

Woman officer-in-training issuing parking violation tickets as part of her routine beat.

Every police department of some size is a complex social organization, with different lines of authority and control, including the chief, the heads of divisions, special units, and patrolmen. Presumably, police departments are hierarchically organized, with the chief at the top setting the priorities for the patrolman at the bottom and all those in between. Yet this model of hierarchical control from top to bottom is rarely realized in practice. Some observers of police have argued that it is virtually impossible to attain, and that any notion of control from top to bottom is quite unrealistic. As Bruce Smith wrote years ago:

> The policeman's art . . . consists in applying and enforcing a multitude of laws and ordinances in such degree or proportion and in such manner that the greatest degree of protection will be secured. The degree of enforcement and the method of application will vary with each neighborhood and community. There are no set rules, nor even general principles, to the policy to be applied. Each policeman must, in a sense, determine the standard to be set in the area for which he is responsible. Immediate superiors may be able to impress upon him some of the lessons of experience, but for the most part such experience must be his own. . . . Thus he is a policy-forming police administrator in miniature, who operates beyond the scope of the usual devices for control. . . .[1]

Smith may be making his point too strongly. Nevertheless, as all writers in this section indicate, both police chiefs and patrolmen must exercise discretion. It is useful, though, to distinguish between delegated discretion, that is, discretion clearly given to the policeman, and unauthorized discretion, that is, discretion which is exercised by a patrolman but for which he may not have authority. If the patrolman is given discretion by police officials, then the question becomes whether the officials themselves have the authority under law to offer patrolmen the discretion. But if the patrolman acts on his own outside of a discretionary authority, as he sometimes may do, should he be subject to sanctions, and if so, what kind? If policing is an art, as Bruce Smith suggests, does it require the policeman to be a policy-making administrator in miniature? Is police discretion different in quality from the discretion exercised by doctors, lawyers, and other professionals? In light of the readings by Banton, Goldstein, and Wilson, what limits should be imposed on police discretion and by whom? In considering this question, it will also be useful to ask whether authority can be vested in an organization or an individual without allocating some degree of discretion. Is the discretion exercised by the chief of police qualitatively different from that exercised

by the patrolman, and should it be? Does a chief in fact have more discretion than a patrolman, given the low-visibility operations of patrolmen?

Certain pressures both within and outside police organizations serve
to limit discretion. It is useful to consider what these might be and how
they might be influenced and changed, if at all. It is also useful to ask
whether there is a relationship between police discretion and police malpractice and, if so, what kind of relationship it is. In the preceding chapter, the articles discussed the centrality of force as an inherent feature of
the policeman's role. At what point do police discretion and the use of
force become police abuse, and what agency should determine that point?

Ultimately, the issue of police discretion is the other side of the coin
of police control. We must continually ask ourselves how far and how
well we can control through the instruments of organization, legal sanction, education and socialization, and community pressure. In other
words, can we devise some system for enforcing a multitude of laws that
does not ultimately depend on the competence of the individuals who are
doing the enforcing?

NOTE

1 Bruce Smith, *Police Systems in the United States* (New York: Harper and
Brothers, 1960), p. 19.

Police Duty

MICHAEL BANTON

Quite separate from the question of whether the police should have any discretion in law enforcement is the question of how they in fact exercise the discretion they are acknowledged to possess.

At some times and in some districts, the police enforce legislation more strictly than the letter of the law allows. In the rougher neighborhoods they will disperse groups from the street corners to prevent the conditions arising in which fights and disturbances most easily start. A larger group on the pavements at the end of a church service or in a middle-class neighborhood will be left undisturbed. Offenses such as obstructing the highway, loitering, and vagrancy are difficult to define objectively, and the laws governing them are used by the police to frustrate activities that seem likely to cause trouble. The police will also utilize the law more rigorously in dealing with known criminals, for it may be dangerous to allow them the same latitude as the law-abiding citizens.

*   *   *

LaFave describes seven cases in which the police arrested or charged a particular offender though they would not normally have invoked the law for the offense in question. These cases were ones that came to attention in the American Bar Foundation survey of the administration of criminal justice, and

they illustrate not overenforcement in particular cases so much as underenforcement in the majority of instances. They fall into five categories: arrest to avoid a strain on police resources (arrests made at a domestic dispute because brawls in the household had necessitated police calls in the past); charges to maintain respect for the police (abusive motoring offender); arrest to maintain public image (social gamblers who made no attempt to conceal their activity); arrest because of an opportunity to punish a criminal who had been able to avoid convictions on more serious charges; arrest to aid in investigation of another offense (murder suspect arrested on vagrancy charge). In the same survey, cases were also recorded of nonenforcement: because of ambiguity in legislation or doubt as to the legislature's intentions; because a warning was considered sufficient; because the conduct in question was common among the offender's section of the population; because the victim did not desire prosecution or the offender's own conduct invalidated his claims; because the prosecution would achieve nothing, would lose the police public respect and support, or would entail disproportionate punishment for someone guilty of only a minor offense.[1]

It seems clear from LaFave's discussion and from my own experience that in both Britain and the United States, where minor offenses are concerned, underenforcement is a general rule. It is advisable, however, to distinguish between cases in which the policeman does not invoke the law because of the nature of the offense and those in which he fails to do so because of the character of the offender. Regarding the first category, policemen feel that it is fruitless to proceed against offenders if the courts are unwilling or reluctant to convict people for the offense in question. Thus in both countries, officers complain that it is difficult to get a conviction for dangerous driving unless such driving contributed to an accident. Carolina City officers had many tales to tell of how persons convicted of a motoring offense would fight to retain their driving license, and of how juries were sympathetic toward them; the prospect of a long tussle in the courts may make the police reduce the charge in the belief that this improves their chance of getting a conviction that will not be reversed on appeal. They also said that it was no longer much use bringing charges for loitering or vagrancy. A different illustration of the same principle is found when a man charges larceny against a woman to whom he has given money, expecting her services as a prostitute in return, and he has been tricked. In such cases it is considered that the complainant does not come to court with "clean hands," and either the court may be unwilling to treat it as a case of larceny or the police may be unwilling to prosecute.

Social control cannot be maintained by enforcement of the criminal law alone. There are many instances of wrongful behavior which can only be punished by civil actions. Frequently members of the public are unwilling to take such action either because the matter at issue is too trivial or because they do not have the public good at heart. Certain it is, though, that they often expect the police to act for them. LaFave writes:

> When a woman called precinct headquarters and reported that in the course of paying for her meal in a restaurant she had been bilked out of some money, the lieutenant answering the call suggested she re-

port to the station so that a complaint could be made out against the person who had cheated her. When the woman indicated she only wanted her money back, the lieutenant said, "Then, madam, you have the wrong department. Please call the lonely hearts club." He then hung up the phone.[2]

Similarly, in Georgia City a man came up to a police lieutenant and reported that he was unable to collect his property from an apartment where he had been living because of threats from his former landlord. The officer suspected that the complainant had been living in a homosexual relationship with the other man and thought that it was not the job of the police to do private citizens' dirty work, so he declined to take any action. How far enforcement of the law in some of these borderline cases is a responsibility of the police rather than of private citizens is open to argument.

At times, strict enforcement of the law would be contrary to public policy or to the ideas that once were termed "natural justice." Thus policemen everywhere have discovered that if a woman complains on a Saturday night that her husband has come home drunk and has assaulted her, it is often futile to arrest the husband. Many policemen who have done this have found the man difficult to subdue and before they have got him out of the house they have received a hearty crack over the head from the now doubly aggrieved wife who has changed sides and come to the aid of her ill-used spouse. Whatever happens on the Saturday night she may well appear at the jail next morning with his breakfast and the announcement that she is unwilling to give evidence against him—for she, after all, has to live with the man, and it may be long enough before he forgives her for having called in the police. Should the case go to trial, however, and the man be convicted, it is certain that the wife and children will have to bear most of the financial burden of the sentence imposed. Policemen naturally doubt whether the ends of justice are served by prosecution in cases like these. An officer in Felsmere City said jocularly that the law of assault and battery was suspended on Christmas Eve—not because assaults were frequent, but because no court sat on Christmas Day and the police had no authority to allow bail on this charge. Being unwilling to keep a man away from his family over Christmas they preferred, if his behavior had not been particularly objectionable, to charge him with disorderly conduct or some minor offense that permitted bail. Not only the time and season but the place as well may be relevant to a decision whether or not to enforce the law. The police will turn a blind eye upon drunks and revelers in some neighborhoods, who, if they were to appear on the main streets of the town or amid the traffic, would be arrested immediately.

*   *   *

Sometimes police treatment of an offender is influenced by his personal characteristics. Some citizens try to obey the law because they believe that they should, and not because they fear the police (though they may do that too). If they make a genuine mistake (a traffic offense, perhaps) and are treated in the same fashion as a persistent offender who simply took a chance on it, they feel insulted and may in the future concentrate upon dodging the police instead of upon observing the law. If the police enforce traffic laws rigidly they may reduce motorists' commitment to the prescribed norms, and the level of observance will fall. Every society acknowledges the additional claims of the person with a good record, and the principle is acknowledged in court when a first offender with a notable war record is given a lighter sentence. People do not see the law

as concerned only with shortcomings; they expect previous good behavior to tell in their favor, but there is no good means whereby the police or the courts may calculate people's moral credit. The law-abiding citizen also gains psychological rewards from his good conduct, paid in the coin of self-esteem; if he is prosecuted, this is apt to destroy his image of himself as a good citizen. Whether or not the law has been fairly administered, if the offender feels unfairly treated he is no longer so strongly motivated to obey the law. An awareness of the feelings of their fellow citizens underlies the belief of many Scottish policemen that traffic offenses are often best dealt with by a verbal warning. Sometimes they only draw the driver's attention to his mistake and say no more.

This view of the relation of law to morality is particularly relevant to traffic offenses. It seems reasonable to suppose that there is a point in traffic regulation beyond which increased enforcement provides only diminishing returns. The uniform treatment of all offenders leads motorists to regard a traffic citation as a natural hazard, and to have a citation issued against oneself is merely bad luck and not a criticism of one's performance as a citizen.

*   *   *

The action policemen take after stopping a motoring offender is often influenced by the demeanor of the driver. If he adopts an abusive attitude he is more likely to be charged. In the United States policemen may justify their taking a stricter line in such cases by arguing that it is necessary to maintain respect for the police.[3] In Britain police officers do not have to be so concerned with this aspect of the matter, and a different interpretation seems necessary. If a constable approaches an offender knowing that he can either administer a caution or put him on a charge, he needs, in order to make his decision, some additional information about the driver and the circumstances that caused the offense. If, say, he finds that the driver passed the "Halt" sign because his daughter in the back seat had just been stung by a bee, he may well take no further action. But if there are no special circumstances he is inclined to ask whether, if he lets the man off, he will be more careful or less careful next time. If the driver is quiet and apologetic the odds are that a warning will be more effective, but if he is one of the loud-mouthed type this is less likely: such a driver may conclude that if only he is belligerent enough, he can shout himself off, and that therefore he need not be careful. The offender's demeanor supplies the policeman with information relevant to the decision he has to make, and the decision, though on a subordinate level, is of a judicial character.

Other factors also make for underenforcement. The volume of legislation today is such that no one individual can possibly remember all the actions that have been declared criminal. In Britain the road traffic law is now so complex that an ordinary patrol officer will be able to recollect only its more important provisions, and it may well be that some officers take action on matters that others believe unexceptionable. As he is personally liable for his decisions and can be made to pay damages if a civil action charging false arrest is upheld against him, the policeman who is unsure of the law may prefer not to take action.[4] Some citizens also receive preferential treatment because of their special relation to the police: local politicians, the police chief's wife, brother officers, and so on. In a good police department any one of these would be prosecuted if he or she committed a serious offense, and they can never be certain of preferential treatment even in minor matters. The Scottish press recently reported that in a routine check two constables stopped a car and found that the driver had not signed her driving license. As the driver was the wife of their inspector they did not report her but told her to show her license to her husband. The inspector summoned the constables and reprimanded them for failing to report an offense. . . . Normally, however, there is a risk that if the police prosecute someone close to them for a minor misdemeanor like a parking offense or a smoking chimney, it may put too much strain on the human machinery by which more important laws are enforced. Around almost every occupation there seems to be a little cluster of privileged persons who get some benefits—like cheaper services—from the people who practice the occupation. With the police, as with other occupations, to try and cut this away completely would not only be extremely difficult but would also reduce the effectiveness of the people on the job. . . .

Another aspect of the problem which is more relevant to circumstances in some American towns arises from social differences within the community. In some lower-class neighborhoods different standards are customary, and if the police try to enforce the norms of the wider society this only induces the local people to cover up for one another because they do not wish the police to intervene in such matters. . . . The sociologist William Foote Whyte in his account of the social structure of racketeering in a Massachusetts Italian neighborhood observes that there is a contradiction between the policeman's formal obligations and the relationships he needs to build up in such a community if he is to keep the peace. The policeman who takes a strictly legalistic view of his duties cuts himself off from the personal relations necessary to enable him to serve as a mediator of disputes in his area. Yet the policeman who develops close ties with the local people is unable to act against them with the vigor prescribed by the law.[5]

In order to determine the best course of action in any particular case, a policeman must be able to separate the sheep from the goats. For the village policeman this is relatively easy; he knows the people he sees on his rounds, and he has a good idea of their character. The city officer, however, meets many people he has never seen before, and it is harder for him to tell from their appearance and behavior what manner of men they are. He has insufficient information about many of the people he has to deal with, so it is very important that he should have good judgment in handling them. The most common complaint of supervising officers in urban police departments seems to be about what they consider the stupidity of some of their younger officers, whose lack of judgment creates problems for their colleagues and supervisors. This question came up in a recorded group discussion with some Scottish probationary police officers, and I reproduce some extracts (slightly edited) from it which are relevant to the present chapter ("I" signifies the author):

I What sort of case had you in mind when you spoke of special constables (that is, reservists) who wanted to go booking everyone?

E Well, there was a drunk. In my opinion he was fit enough to get himself home but the special wanted to lift him. I just told him that you don't lift any person that you see staggering.

I This question of lifting somebody who is drunk but not too drunk is an interesting case because it bears upon the exercise of your discretion, doesn't it?

E Yes. It's just something you pick up.

I Now this is something you've learned on the beat, is it not? How much were you told about the use of discretion in your training? (*Looks round the table.*)

C It's just common knowledge.

A It comes to you every time you're on, more or less.

B It's something you pick up that you're no' told, it's just . . .

E What I mean, you just seem to be able to judge straight, you just look at the person, it just sort of comes to you, "Oh, he'll make it O.K."

D Most of police work anyway is common sense.

C Common sense, aye.

D I was out with a special one day, it was on one of the outlying beats, and there was this chap and he was drunk, lying on the ground. Well, I knew that the chap lived in that area. The special was all for taking him down to the box to get a van out to take him in. I spoke to the chap and after a while I managed to get his address and took him home. The special was gey quiet after that. He would rather have seen the police take him in.

E What did you do after you'd taken him home, like?

D That was it finished.

C We do that quite often in our force, too.

D You would take him home?

B (*Interrupting*) We never do that. We get a bloke drunk and incapable, and suppose he was lying outside his own doorstep, in the roadway, we take him home and go back the next day and book him for being drunk and incapable.

E I wouldn't agree to that.

D   If you know a person is near his home I think it's unfair.

B   What do you lift a drunk for? Because he is a danger to himself is one of the reasons. I mean he could be run over lying outside his own gate as lying five or six hundred yards away . . . and you find next Saturday night he's lying outside his door again.

D   I don't mean to say that if it were a regular habit I'd let him off with it. . . .

I   This may be a difference of opinion or it may be a difference in practice between two different forces. Where would you say (*to* D) that you picked up this idea that you should take this sort of customer home? Wouldn't you have picked it up from older men?

D   I picked it up from a constable that got on very well with the public.

I   (*to* B) But you, in your force, must have seen other police officers going round and charging the man the day after?

B   Well, that was the habit. As far as I'm concerned, I mean.

D   That's your procedure.

B   This is my own opinion. I mean, I'm no' wanting to be number one popularity boy in the town. I've got to do the job. When I came into the force I swore I would discharge the duties of constable. The thing as far as I can see it is, it's all right to be lenient. I mean, if you catch a boy stealing apples, you're no' going to drag him to the office and charge him with theft. I don't know about the rest of you but back to when I was a boy, I ken I've stolen apples: it was part of the process of growing up. But a bloke lying in the middle of the road is a danger to himself plus a danger to other road users. (*To author*) You're a civilian, let's bring you into this. You drive along the road and you don't see the bloke on the dark side and you run over him. You'll remember that for the rest of your life. You've always got it on your conscience that you've killed this bloke. I think that you are duty bound to charge him.

D   I don't say I'd blame you for that, but I've found that any person I've helped is a good source of information regarding any other inquiries I've got.

B   Can you honestly sit there and tell me that some drunk that you've helped into a house has ever benefited you later on?

D   Yes, that beat I was referring to is one of our roughest beats and there's a lot of. . . .

B   (*Interrupting*) And how does this bloke come to give you information?

D   Well, you see, if I meet the chap and I have an inquiry, I'll maybe ask him, "Have you heard anything?"

B   How did he ken it was you helped him that night?

D   Because his wife pointed me out to him one day.

I   (*A few minutes later*) If, let us say, you picked up a man drunk who occupied a fairly responsible position in the community and you thought, "Now, if I put this man on a charge this is going to be a far more serious matter for him than it would be for someone who was a farm laborer. Everybody is going to hear about this; the man's reputation will sink and it will be a very severe blow to him." Would you be inclined to exercise your discretion differently? (*Turns to* C, *from a country station.*)

C   No. We find that it's entirely the same, no matter who they are. If you do that once you may as well pack up and go.

D   Quite. Why do you think he should be favored anyway?

I   I'm not sugesting that he should be.

B   Why should they be? Because one bloke's got £50 in his pocket and another one's got five shillings and the two of them's committing the same offense, you're no' going to say that the one's a decent bloke because he's got £50.

I   No. The argument would be that it was a more severe punishment for the one man than for the other.

B   Oh yes. I mean I'm agreeing with you there. I mean his status in life is probably far better, but that is out with the police; we have nothing to do with that.

E   We had a case when we were instructed to go round and book those who had no parking lights and the Provost was one of them. He was booked for it and the constable who booked him was up in front of the chief constable the following morning. I disagree with that. The Provost was committing an offense the same as any other person. . . .

This extract points up some of the possible differences in the way young constables define the social situations they encounter. It mentions something that many officers can corroborate: a minor kindness to an offender may dispose him to supply useful information on other occasions. The range of situations with which the new constable may be confronted is so varied that instructors cannot cover every contingency, and they have to depend on the constable's common sense. How, the supervisor will ask, can you teach a man common sense? Either he has got it or he hasn't. The usual policy is to rely upon his picking up the general principles by accompanying more senior men. From the recruit's point of view, also, this delicate balance between contrary obligations may be a source of embarrassment. "Everything about this job's so vague," one complained, "no matter what you're doing you can always be told you should be doing something else." The regulations all too often tell a policeman what he must not do, and fail to indicate what positive steps should be taken. Yet this quality of judgment which is so difficult to teach or to measure is nevertheless one of the things that are looked for when promotions are to be made. A Carolina City supervisor commented on a patrolman who had recently asked him whether, if he saw a man driving a vehicle late one evening, with a dealer's registration plates and two women inside (in other words, presumably using a motor dealer's registration for pleasure and not for purposes of trade), he would give him a ticket. The supervisor said that his action would depend upon what the man said. Whereupon the patrolman remarked that he would certainly give him a ticket; the law was clear and his job was to enforce it. The supervisor replied that this attitude of his explained why he was still a patrolman after fifteen years' service.

It is important, therefore, to consider the sources from which policemen draw their ideas as to the way in which they should exercise their discretionary powers. Apart from their training, the example of their colleagues, and the advice or instruction of their supervisors, two sources are especially influential. In the first place there are the courts. In the long run a police officer can go only as far as the courts will let him; the man who lacks a sense of judgment will probably come to grief in court some day. The courts provide a good expression of the consensus of responsible opinion, and to a certain extent (more marked when the police view and public opinion differ) they tend to sit in judgment on the arresting officer. The policeman learns in court what cases the court will accept. For example, an American officer said that a judge had once thrown out a prosecution of a motorist who had turned out of the center lane of traffic; there had been a violation, but since there had been no accident or hindrance to other drivers, the accused was discharged. The policeman soon discovers—if he did not know it already—that offenders who have the money to engage an attorney are treated with more consideration and have a better chance of acquittal. In this way he learns the values by which his society is really ruled (as opposed to the ones praised in ceremonial speeches) and how to operate within this context. Policemen generally agree that there is one law for the rich and another for the poor; many of them accept this as one of the facts of life without in any way approving it. The police officer is frequently a critic of society; through what he sees in the courts, as well as on the beat, he is in an unparalleled position to observe the machinery of society in operation. It also seems as if the procedure of the courts has an indirect effect upon the culture of the police occupation. Several times when I have been with a group of policemen I have been struck by the readiness of members of the group to argue against almost any proposition stated by one of their number or to point out other interpretations of his facts. The policeman knows that any of his decisions may later be judged in court, and he gets used to anticipating arguments that could be advanced against them. In the same way he will readily play devil's advocate to one of his colleagues.

In the second place, a policeman derives much of his sense of judgment from his participation in the society he polices. Out of uniform he is subject to exactly the same controls as any other citizen. He mixes with other citizens on an equal footing and soon hears what they think about the police. British and American officers will readily comment upon the way the press and the public fail to appreciate their problems and rush in with criticisms; they are very conscious of this criticism, and much of it impinges on their private lives. The resulting awareness of the public's point of view influences many of a policeman's decisions in the course of his daily work. Many times, when discussing his treatment of an offender, has an officer observed: "I know that if I were in his place I should feel so-and-so." In a colonial or military-style police, where the officers live in barracks and do not mingle with the public, this kind of understanding must be greatly reduced. The influence of a policeman's private roles upon how he performs his public role is of the utmost importance, and it is not limited to his off-duty experiences. While on patrol the policeman learns a great deal about human nature which may later stand him in good stead.

Like so many aspects of police work, the question of discretion in law enforcement is not something that can be considered apart from the topic of supervision or from the policeman's role in society. . . . Indeed Roscoe Pound, the great lawyer, once wrote: "A balance between rules of law . . . and discretion, which will give effect both to the general security, and the individual life, with the least impairment of either, is perhaps the most difficult problem in the science of law." [6] And LaFave concludes his survey of American practice:

> The first step is to elevate police discretion from the *sub rosa* position it now occupies; the role of the police as decision-makers must be expressly recognized. Then, as has been found possible with respect to other administrative agencies, the areas in which discretion properly may be exercised must be delimited, principles to govern its exercise must be discovered. Only then can it be said with certainty that police non-enforcement does not contravene some of our most cherished democratic values. [7]

The British sociologist is bound to feel that even this is insufficient. Consider a recent English case in which Miss Pat Arrowsmith, the advocate of nuclear disarmament, was prosecuted under the Highways Act for obstructing the highway. She addressed a crowd in a place often used for open-air meetings. The police asked her to call the crowd in closer so as to minimize the obstruction; she and the crowd complied, leaving some of the road clear. The partial obstruction continued for twenty minutes, after which she was charged. On appeal it was argued among other things that many meetings were held in that place, and that the police often helped by keeping a free passage for traffic. The Lord Chief Justice said he could not concern himself with "what happened on other occasions." The police, he added, "cannot prosecute every obstructor of the highway but must exercise a wise discretion when to prosecute." [8] Was Miss Arrowsmith given the same latitude as other offenders? No administrative principles can ensure equity in circumstances so dependent on the vagaries of human judgment. The only long-term solution to the problem of police discretion is for the police and the public to share the same norms of propriety. Some modern tendencies, however, are making this ideal more and more difficult to realize.

NOTES

1 Wayne R. LaFave, "The Police and Nonenforcement of the Law," *Wisconsin Law Review,* 1962, pp. 104–37, 179–239.
2 Ibid., p. 212n.
3 Ibid., p. 231.
4 Ibid., p. 190.
5 William Foote Whyte, *Street Corner Society* (Chicago: University of Chicago Press, 1943), p. 136.
6 Roscoe Pound, *Criminal Justice in America* (1930), p. 116 as quoted by LaFave, 1962, pp. 40–41.
7 LaFave, "Police and Nonenforcement," p. 239.
8 *Arrowsmith* v. *Jenkins,* Queen's Bench Division, 6 March 1963, as reported in the *Police Review,* 23 August 1963.

Police Discretion: The Ideal versus the Real

HERMAN GOLDSTEIN

Parking meters are a common source of irritation to both the public and the police. They were a particular source of annoyance to a city manager-friend of mine whose council membership included one man whose sole concern in life appeared to be those vehicles parked alongside meters on which the time had expired. After repeated criticism of the police department for its failure to achieve a greater degree of compliance and enforcement, the city manager was moved to speak on the issue. He offered the councilman a choice from among what he referred to as levels of enforcement. He suggested that the city could assign one police officer to enforcing all of the meters throughout the city. If this was done, he anticipated that the frequency of checks would be low and the number of overtime violations and red flags would increase. On the other hand, he could assign one police officer to each parking meter in the city. With such extensive coverage, there would be reasonable assurance that a summons would be issued at the moment the meter expired. The city manager then suggested that the council determine through its appropriation, just how many police officers were to be provided and what level of enforcement was desired as between the two extremes. The point was well made.

Without full recognition on his part, the

From *Public Administration Review,* Journal of the American Society for Public Administration, **23** (September 1963): 148–156. Reprinted by permission.

city manager was addressing himself to one of the very basic problems in law enforcement today. We need only substitute people for parking meters and the broader categories of crime for red overtime flags. Given the total amount of criminality in a community and the resources with which to cope with it, what is the position or policy of the local law enforcement agency? Is the agency committed to a concept of "full enforcement" of all laws, or is it committed to something less than full enforcement?

A policy of "full enforcement" implies that the police are required and expected to enforce all criminal statutes and city ordinances at all times against all offenders. It suggests that the police are without authority to ignore violations, to warn offenders when a violation has in fact occurred, or to do anything short of arresting the offender and placing a charge against him for the specific crime committed. It views the police function to be that of relating the provisions of the law to a fine measurement of the quantum of evidence. Out of this cold and somewhat mechanical calculation evolves an answer which provides the basis for police action.

The exercise of discretion, on the other hand, suggests that the police are required, because of a variety of factors, to decide overtly how much of an effort is to be made to enforce specific laws. It recognizes that actions short of arrest may achieve the desired goal. It implies that a police officer may decide not to make an arrest even in those situations in which an offense has been committed and both the offender and the evidence are at hand. It tends to portray police officers as something other than automatons —as reasonable men whose judgment is essential in determining whether or not to invoke the criminal process.

To date, this dilemma has been of principal concern to those interested in the total system for the administration of criminal justice—those interested in the working of the prosecution, the courts, and the correctional agencies as well as the police. To understand how the system functions in its entirety, these students of criminal law have necessarily focused their attention at that point where it is most commonly determined whether or not a person is to be subject to the system—on the initial screening function performed by the police. If a person is arrested, he enters the system, and the path which he takes, in large measure, is established. If he is not arrested, the action of the police terminates the case before the person enters the system, and the action is not subject to further review.

The bibliography of thinking on this subject is rapidly increasing. This body of thought and analysis is of more than academic interest to the police. It has some very practical implications.

What is the position of the average police administrator in these deliberations? He is most likely to support the view—somewhat hesitantly—that he is committed to a policy of full enforcement. It is, after all, the policy most commonly enunciated by police agencies. In contrast, the mere suggestion that a police administrator exercises discretion in fulfilling his job may be taken as an affront —an attack upon the objective and sacrosanct nature of his job—that of enforcing the law without fear or favor. Here too, there is a little hesitation—an awareness that

discretion must be and is exercised. But like planned parenthood, it may be something you practice; it is not something you admit or even discuss.

This awkward position, in my opinion, places the average police official in a most embarrassing situation. What are the facts?

Do we have full enforcement, as the term is defined here? Obviously, we do not. How often have law enforcement personnel released a drunk and disorderly person without charging him? released a juvenile offender to his parents? warned a driver who had clearly committed a violation? ignored the enforcement of some city ordinances? chosen not to arrest an individual known to have committed fornication or adultery? arranged for the release of a narcotic addict in exchange for information? dropped charges against an assailant when the victim failed to cooperate in the prosecution? ignored Sunday blue laws or simply been instructed not to enforce a specific law?

And yet, in acknowledging that some or all of these practices exist, police officials feel a sense of guilt; that these actions were not quite proper; and that they had no basis in law. Why, then, do police officials do these things? Because they are, consciously or unconsciously, acknowledging what they do not wish to proclaim—that the police must exercise discretion.

THE EXERCISE OF DISCRETION

Why must discretion be exercised? Let us take a look at some of the laws under which the police operate, some of the procedures which must be followed, and some of the pressures which exist in the typical community which the police serve.

Examine, for example, the criminal code of any one of our states. By its action, the legislature has attempted to establish those forms of conduct which its members desire to be declared criminal. But this action, as reflected in the statement of the criminal law, is often expressed in such broad terms as to render a clear interpretation of the legislature's intentions most difficult. Ambiguity may be intentional so as to provide greater flexibility in enforcement; it may result from a failure to envisage the day-to-day problems encountered by the police; or it may simply be a result of language limitations. Whatever the basis for the broad statement of the law, the need for resolving these ambiguities frequently places the police in the position of having to determine the forms of conduct which are to be subject to the criminal process.

The State of Illinois has a typically broad statute defining gambling. Under its provisions, the flip of a coin to determine who shall purchase coffee or the playing of penny-ante poker must be considered a violation. As a general policy, the Chicago Police Department devotes its efforts to seeking out gambling activities which are part of an organized operation. We do not devote manpower to ferreting out social card games conducted in the privacy of a home. But, upon complaint, we have an obligation to conduct an investigation of any alleged gambling activity.

In March of this year, the department received a complaint of gambling in the basement of an American Legion Post. Three police officers were sent to investigate. They quickly established that the affair was being run by the post auxiliary as a benefit and that a variation of bingo was to be played with the proceeds going to the men at a veterans' hospital. The officers politely warned against any activity which would be considered gambling and left. The patrons of the social, however, got panicky, grabbed

their hats and coats and fled. The expected flurry of letters and newspaper articles followed. One such article concluded with this statement addressed to the Superintendent: "Most of the people of Chicago don't want you or your men to raid a women's social. They want you to go chase some crooks and leave the good people alone."

Both state statutes and city ordinances may be explicit in defining conduct to be considered criminal, but there may be little expectation on the part of those who enacted the laws that they be enforced to the letter. The statute or ordinance may be stating the ideals of the community; that adulterous activity, for example, will not be tolerated. Through this action, the community is placed on record as opposing a form of conduct considered morally wrong. Lawmakers and citizens alike derive a certain degree of comfort from having legislated against such activity. Should this false sense of comfort be a source of concern to the conscience of a legislator he is faced with a dilemma: he might more easily choose to seek full enforcement than to be caught supporting the repeal of such a prohibition. Since few legislative consciences are upset, it falls to the police agency to live with the law without enforcing it.

The problem does not always stem from a double standard in matters of morality. Often it stems from mere obsolescence. Earlier this year, the Chicago Police Department was subject to the wrath of the community for having arrested a driver of a jeep, equipped with a snow plow, which was used in the plowing of neighborhood sidewalks as a friendly gesture and without charge. The young officer who made the arrest had been confronted with a complaint. The benevolent driver had piled snow in a driveway to the displeasure of its owner. The officer was unable to find an ordinance that prohibited piling snow in driveways, but he did find an ordinance which prohibited four-wheeled vehicles from being driven on sidewalks. The public became enraged as news of this action spread, and we were once again asked if we had run out of honest-to-goodness crooks in need of apprehension. Members of the department no longer arrest the drivers of four-wheel sidewalk plows; the ordinance, however, remains on the books. We have just decided not to enforce it.

Another major factor which forces the exercise of discretion is the limitation on manpower and other resources. Few police agencies have the number of personnel that would be required to detect the total amount of criminality which exists in a community and to prosecute all offenders. Rarely is consideration given to the relationship between the volume of what can be termed criminal acts and the resources available to deal with them. New legislation declaring a form of conduct to be criminal is rarely accompanied by an appropriation to support the resources for its enforcement. The average municipal administrator who has budget responsibilities brings a different orientation to the problem than does the police chief: his determination as to the size of the police force is based more directly upon a value judgment as to what the tax structure can afford rather than upon a determination of the degree to which the community wishes to enforce the criminal laws; he is more concerned with efficiency, production, and quality of service in handling the routine tasks which accrue to the police and which are so important to the citizenry; he has only a slight interest in or knowledge of the provisions of the criminal law.

Since there are no established priorities for the enforcement of laws prohibiting one type of conduct as against another, the police official must determine the manner in which available manpower and equipment will be used. The daily assignment of manpower is, therefore, perhaps the most easily identifiable exercise of discretion on the part of the police.

This need for discretion was acknowledged in at least one case adjudicated in 1909 in the State of Michigan. The Michigan Supreme Court held:

> The [police] commissioner is bound to use the discretion with which he is clothed. He is charged not alone with the execution of the liquor laws of the State within the city of Detroit, but he is likewise charged with the suppression of all crime and the conservation of the peace. To enable him to perform the duties imposed upon him by law, he is supplied with certain limited means. It is entirely obvious that he must exercise a sound discretion as to how those means shall be applied for the good of the community.[1]

In establishing priorities of enforcement, greater attention is ordinarily given to more serious crimes. A determination not to arrest is most common at the level of the petty offender—and especially if the offender is an otherwise law-abiding citizen. Policies—albeit unwritten—begin to evolve. Just as social gamblers may be arrested only if their activities become organized and move into public places, so drunkards may be arrested only if they are belligerent and homeless as distinct from those who are cooperative and long-established residents.

Discretion may be exercised on the basis of a police officer's particular assignment. Many police agencies have officers assigned to specific types of investigations, such as those relating to homicide, burglaries, or narcotics. Officers so assigned understandably consider their respective specialized function as being of greatest importance to the department. The generalization can be made that police officers frequently refrain from invoking the criminal process for conduct which is considered of less seriousness than that which they are primarily responsible for investigating. A group of officers, intent on solving a homicide, for example, will complain bitterly of the lack of prostitutes on the streets from whom they may obtain information. Narcotics detectives will likewise make frequent use of gamblers and may even tolerate petty larcenies and minor drug violations on the part of their informants. Whatever the merits of the practice, the goal is an acceptable one: that of solving the more serious crime.

Where the volume of criminal activity is high, it is common to observe police policies which result in the dropping of charges against minor assailants when the victim is unwilling to testify. Without a complainant, the case cannot usually be prosecuted successfully. While an effort can be made to prosecute in the name of the state, the mere volume of work demanding attention ordinarily rules out a decision to do so. The determination not to proceed is clearly an exercise of discretion and terminates at this early stage in the process a case in which an offense has clearly occurred and an offender was identified and apprehended.

Discretion is often exercised by the police in a sincere effort to accomplish a social good. This is a sort of humanitarian gesture in which the police achieve the desired objective without full imposition of the coldness and harshness of the criminal process. The drunk may be ushered home; the juveniles turned over to their parents; the new driver warned of being found headed in the wrong direction on a one-way street. It is the exercise of discretion such as this to accomplish a desired goal to which others refer when they exhort the police to enforce the "spirit" rather than the "letter" of the law.

These are some of the reasons why the police do, in fact, exercise discretion not to invoke the criminal process in many cases. These same considerations provide ample indication that the police do not, in fact, engage in full enforcement. Why then are the police so reluctant to acknowledge that discretion is exercised?

REASONS FOR NOT ACKNOWLEDGING THE EXERCISE OF DISCRETION

To acknowledge that law enforcement officials do exercise discretion requires an overt act—the articulation of a position—an action which is rare among those in the police field. Most law enforcement officials long ago resigned themselves to the role of the underdog upon whom the unsolved problems of society were piled high. Having developed what might best be termed a defensive posture, the police have, for example, widely accepted responsibility for all that is criminal, despite the fact that crimes are not committed by the police, but rather by the citizens of the community they serve. How often do we hear a police official admonish a community for a rise in crime? How often does a police official point an accusing finger at conditions which produce crime and criminals? Instead, whenever the publication of crime statistics indicates a rise in crime, he feels that he has in some way failed and that his department has failed. In carrying such a burden, the average police official sees nothing especially strange about having to carry responsibility for a type of enforcement he is unable to fulfill. He has learned two characteristics of his job: he must bear this burden well and he must refrain from discussing it lest it be a source of embarrassment to him and the community.

If he should have the urge to discuss his problem of achieving full enforcement, the average police official would not wish to do so in public. To acknowledge the exercise of discretion belies the very image in which he takes such pride and which he strives so hard to achieve. This is the image of total objectivity—of impartiality—and of enforcement without fear or favor. A cursory examination of the typical oath of office administered to police officers, the rules and regulations of police departments, and the several codes governing police conduct give the general impression that strict adherence to the "letter of the law" has come to be the ideal toward which all well-intentioned police officers should strive. There is great difficulty in recognizing that discretion can be exercised without being partial. It is, of course, extremely important that police officers be impartial in their enforcement policies, but it is possible for them to be so and still exercise discretion.

Impartiality requires the establishment of criteria for uniform action—a difficult task and one which perhaps constitutes the most valid objection to acknowledging discretionary powers. It is easy, from an administrative standpoint, to support a program of full enforcement. Instructions and training are simple. One need only teach the difference between black and white. If discretion is to be exercised, criteria become essential. And here the problems begin: (1) there is a general reluctance to spell out criteria as to those conditions under which an arrest is to take place lest this written modification of existing laws be attacked as presumptuous on the part of an administrative agency and contemptuous of the legislative body; (2) in the absence of written instructions, it is extremely difficult to communicate to large numbers of policemen the bounds of the discretion to be exercised; (3) an officer cannot be forced to exercise discretion, since the broad oath which he takes places him under obligation to enforce all laws, and he can maintain that he is adhering to this higher authority; and (4) if a written document is desired, the preparation of criteria for the exercise of discretion requires an expert draftsman—one more skilled than the legislative draftsman who may have tried and failed. Is it any wonder that the typical reaction of the police administrator to the mere suggestion that discretion be acknowledged is likely to be, "It isn't worth the trouble!"?

Broadly stated laws are, after all, one of the lesser concerns of the police. Most attention of law enforcement officers in recent years has focused upon legal provisions which are too narrow. The average police official is not very concerned about having the authority to enforce adultery statutes and not having the manpower or the community support necessary to do so. He is much more concerned because of his inability to attack organized crime effectively. And there may be an occasion upon which he can use an obscure or otherwise unenforced law to launch an oblique attack against a situation or activity which he feels warrants action on his part. His attitude is often that the law should be left on the books; it may come in handy sometime. Why impose self-limitations on police authority beyond those established by the legislature?

Another contention is that discretion breeds corruption and for this reason should be denied. This constitutes another strong administrative argument against acknowledging its existence. The average police administrator spends a considerable portion of his time worrying about the integrity of his force. Corruption, when it does exist, usually stems from the misuse of authority in order to attain selfish ends or from restraint from exerting authority in exchange for personal gain. It is always difficult to investigate. But it is easier to do so if policemen are expected to function on a black or white basis. If regulations require that an officer make an arrest when a violation occurs, the officer who does not do so is suspect. If, on the other hand, an officer is told that his decision to arrest should weigh a number of factors, it is difficult to determine if his failure to act was an exercise of good judgment or an exchange for a favor or a bribe. If the exercise of discretion is sanctioned by a department's administration, it becomes known both to the violator and the officer and creates the atmosphere and bargaining power for a corrupt act. It is the fear of this possible consequence that constitutes another strong reason that open acknowledgment of discretionary authority is frowned upon by most police administrators.

To the several arguments already stated, the police will usually add the contention that whatever their practice, they are required by law to subscribe to full enforcement. Indeed, in response to a suggestion that discretion in the area of traffic enforcement be acknowledged, the objection was raised that such an assumption on the part of a police department would be "unconstitutional." Some jurisdictions do go so far as to impose a penalty upon police officers who fail to take action upon learning of a crime, but there is no indication that such jurisdictions provide a higher level of enforcement than do those without such provisions.

There is, among police officers, a healthy respect for "the law" in its generic form, whatever the attitude may be toward specific provisions of either the substantive or procedural codes. It is one thing to ignore a law; it is much more serious to acknowledge publicly that it is being ignored.

One factor that results in a healthy respect for the law is the knowledge on the part of every police officer that he may personally be held accountable in a legal suit for actions which he takes as a police officer. Should he be subject to legal action, he knows that a literal interpretation of his authority and his actions will determine the outcome; and that any exercise of discretion on his part is, in the eyes of the court clearly outside the law. Concern for legal actions fosters support for a concept of full enforcement.

There is some basis to the concern expressed for the legal obligation to enforce all laws without the exercise of discretion. In 1960, the Police Commissioner of Philadelphia asserted that for lack of funds and personnel, he would limit initial enforcement of the Sunday closing law to large retail establishments. When a Pennsylvania court reviewed this action, they ruled in favor of one of the large retail merchants and stated:

> The admitted discrimination in enforcement is a calculated result of a definite policy on the part of a public official and thus results in a denial to the plaintiff of the equal protection of the law to which it is entitled by virtue of the fourteenth amendment of the United States Constitution.[2]

Strong as is the fear of legal entanglements, the fear of public reaction to an announced policy of selective enforcement is even greater. Since the police know how difficult it is to meet accusations of nonenforcement when they profess full enforcement, they fear that acknowledging a policy of nonenforcement is even less defensible. The average police official recognizes that no amount of explanation will placate the citizen who, for example, is obsessed with the need for strict enforcement of an ordinance requiring that bicycles not be ridden on sidewalks. He must simply be politely "brushed off." But, what does one tell the citizen who feels that too much effort is going into traffic enforcement and not enough into apprehending burglars? What is said to the citizen who demands additional manpower to apprehend disorderly youths congregating in park areas? And what does one tell the citizen who argues in favor of tripling the effort presently directed toward apprehending narcotics peddlers?

To answer such questions intelligently, the police official must have a defensible formula for the distribution of his manpower. Such a formula rarely exists because of the reluctance of the average police official to make value judgments. He, understandably, is unwilling to decide what should be of greatest concern to the community. The whole thought of trying to defend a policy of selective enforcement is a bit frightening. It is asking for trouble. So, he often concludes that it is, in his opinion, much safer to maintain he has no discretion in these matters.

THE ADVANTAGES OF A POLICY
OF RECOGNIZING THE EXERCISE
OF DISCRETION

Some of the arguments in behalf of a denial of discretion are convincing arguments. They lend strong support to those who advocate a policy of full enforcement. If there was any indication that the breach between actual practice and the concept of full enforcement was narrowing, one might be encouraged to lean even more strongly in the direction of supporting a policy of full enforcement. The opposite, however, is true. The gulf between the ideal and reality in criminal law enforcement is growing wider. Every police official is keenly aware that the demands for his services are constantly increasing and that he is not given a proportionate increase in the resources with which to meet these demands.

Crime is on the increase and gives no sign of leveling off. But, beyond this, there is evidence of a growing concern on the part of the public for a problem toward which there has more commonly been an attitude of complete apathy. The public no longer tolerates mental illness, unemployment, poor housing, or dropouts from high school. They do something about these social problems, and there is an increasing indication that they intend to do more about crime. As this concern increases, the demands on law enforcement agencies will similarly increase.

How, then, does the dilemma posed here relate to improved law enforcement? How would its resolution better enable us to cope with present problems and those which develop in the future?

Law enforcement agencies cannot make progress so long as they remain on the defensive. They cannot win public support if they fail to level with the public. They cannot solve their problems if they fail to identify these problems.

There are a number of advantages to be gained by the police by being forthright in acknowledging the role which the police play in determining whether or not to invoke the criminal process. Let us examine the major ones.

Once and for all, acknowledging discretion would enable the police to climb out from underneath the impossible burden which has been placed upon them and which has placed them on the defensive in dealing with the public. And they would be doing so, not by abdicating their legal responsibilities, but by simply acknowledging the true magnitude of their responsibilities. It is the function of the police to demonstrate the impossibility of full enforcement to the community—making citizens aware that the enactment of laws does not cure a problem unless consideration is given to the means for enforcement. An appeal must be made to the public to accept the best judgment and efforts of the police in their approach to the total problem of criminal law enforcement. The community can be given the alternatives of providing additional funds for a level of enforcement closer to full enforcement, of relieving the police of nonpolice functions which deplete the effort devoted to criminal law enforcement, or of providing the police with more realistic legal guidance in how to fulfill their broad responsibilities. Citizens will choose a level of enforcement, if it is put to them in terms of cost. Somewhere between the extremes of having a police officer for each citizen and having none, a determination must be made as to the number of officers to be employed. Placed in these terms, the degree to which full enforcement can be achieved is a matter known not only to the police agency but to the community as a whole.

In the administration of governmental affairs, respect for the law takes a second place only to the need for honesty in dealing with the public. Because police officials have been placed in so awkward a position for so long and have felt compelled to deny the obvious, the public typically reacts with initial shock and subsequent pleasure when a police official is refreshingly forthright in his public pronouncements. Keeping the public well informed on police problems, including police shortcomings, clearly develops support for good law enforcement—and public support is the key to the solution of most police problems.

What are some of the specific implications of a policy which recognizes the discretion exercised by the police? At the present time, new legislation is enacted without regard to its enforceability. The assumption is that the police will, as always, assume responsibility for the new task much as a sponge absorbs water. Rarely is consideration given to possible problems of enforcement —or to the manpower which may be required. If the police speak out on such occasions, legislative groups may be less likely to act without regard to considering enforcement.

It is not, in the long run, to the advantage of law enforcement agencies to have laws on the books which are widely ignored. The police have an obligation to help build respect among all citizens for law and order. A law which is known to exist and which is honored more in the breach than by compliance, tends to breed contempt for law enforcement—and usually among the very element in whom there is the greatest need for building respect. Knowledgeable in the techniques of enforcement, the police are probably in a better position to seek repeal of an obsolete or unenforceable law than any other element in the community. Their position need not be based on whether the conduct ought to be criminal, but rather on what are the practical aspects of enforcement.

The unworkability or inappropriateness of a legislative provision becomes apparent to a law enforcement agency more rapidly than it does to a legislative body. To persist in adhering to these legal requirements is nonsensical; such a policy tends only to harass citizens and lessen respect for the police. Applause will greet the police administrator who takes what the community terms an enlightened approach to such problems— publicly acknowledging the inappropriateness of the legislative provision.

Until this past year, members of the Chicago Police Department issued a summons to any motorist having a faulty headlight. This policy had been followed for years. It was, after all, the law. Had an effort been made, it is doubtful if one could have devised a more effective way of antagonizing the public. The violator rarely was aware of his violation.

A department memorandum was issued. It said, in clear language, that a police officer need not arrest a motorist with a defective light when the police officer was of the belief that the light would be repaired immediately. And further criteria were set forth:

> Where more than one lighting fixture is inoperative, or where one is in such a state of disrepair as to indicate that it was not a recent, temporary malfunction, or where the lighting violation was the cause of an accident, or is only one of several violations, the operator will be cited.[3]

The reaction on the part of the press was that the public had cause to rejoice, that the department was "thinking big," that the policy was fair, and that the motorist who purposely breaks the law deserves to be punished. The police, they declared, were finally sensible about faulty car lights.

Taking the initiative in these matters has another advantage. A person who is unnecessarily aggrieved is not only critical of the procedure which was particularly offensive to him. He tends to broaden his interest and attack the whole range of police procedures which suddenly appear to him to be unusually oppressive; he may consider the police devoid of concern for civil rights; and perhaps, in moments of extreme delirium, he may even accuse them of fascist or communist tendencies. Regrettably, such a person usually resorts to the therapy of letterwriting to vent his emotions, with carbon copies clearly labeled and sent in all directions. The pattern is a familiar one.

Police officials too often fail to recognize that there are many in the communities which they serve who have an inherent distaste for authority—and especially police authority. Joining with others of the same

view and those whose beliefs are more firmly grounded in a support for our democratic processes, these people closely guard against the improper use of authority by the police. It behooves law enforcement officials to refrain from unnecessarily creating a situation which annoys such individuals. Such situations can often be avoided through the exercise of proper discretion.

One of the greatest needs in law enforcement is effective leadership. Presently, because of its defensive posture, law enforcement agencies have too often cultivated a form of defensive leadership. Many law enforcement officials today fulfill the need for defensive leadership in their respective organizations but are not equal to the challenge of the times. Unfortunately, this type of need places a premium on the police administrator who can successfully dodge the issue of why he fails to provide full enforcement, who can create the impression that he is endeavoring to enforce all of the laws all of the time, who can take repeated attacks and onslaughts of public criticism, and who can be devious and less than forthright in his dealings with the public. While such leadership may have served some purpose in the past, it has not given law enforcement the type of guidance and impetus which is required to meet the problems of the 1960s.

Open recognition of basic police problems gives the police leader a clean atmosphere in which to operate. He becomes a leader rather than a defender. Police service today demands a bolder, more aggressive individual who is adept at articulating police problems in a forthright manner and developing community support for their solution.

The police have sought professional status. But, professional status does not normally accrue to individuals performing ministerial functions. One of the marks of a true profession is the inherent need for making value judgments and for exercising discretion based upon professional competence. To deny that discretion is exercised gives support to those citizens who maintain that the job of a police officer is a simple one, that it requires little judgment, and that it is not worthy of professional status. Acknowledging the discretionary role the police do play will give impetus to the drive toward a higher degree of respect and recognition for law enforcement personnel.

THE CHOICE OF THE TASK

The real choice for a police administrator is not between "full enforcement" and "discretion" but rather more precisely between the ideal and the real. As the public becomes increasingly intolerant of crime, pressures will develop to improve and streamline not only our police organizations but the laws and procedures under which they operate. An essential first step will then be to inform the public, to challenge some of our basic concepts, to take stock of the total responsibilities of the police, to recognize the limitations under which the police operate, and to acknowledge the need for the exercise of discretion. It is then likely that a new atmosphere will be created which will foster some new thinking and some new developments to aid in the improvement of the total system for the administration of criminal justice.

This is a big task. It is not a function for the police alone. Law—and the enforcement of law—is a vital element in our form of government. In law enforcement, one comes to grips with some of the basic legal, political, and social concerns and issues of our time. Clearly, it warrants more than it has received in attention from not only the public but from our universities and colleges as well. There is a need for a much greater body of knowledge and understanding of our present operations. Such knowledge and understanding are essential if we are to develop intelligent solutions to our present and future problems.

NOTES

1 *Gowan* v. *Smith* [157 Mich. 443, 473, 122 NW 286, 297 (1909)].
2 *Bargain City U.S.A. Inc.* v. *Dilworth* [29 U.S. Law Week 2002 (Pa.C.P. June 10, 1960)].
3 Chicago Police Department, Department Memorandum No. 63–35.

The Police Administrator

JAMES Q. WILSON

The police administrator—variously called chief, superintendent, commissioner, or captain—has in common with all other executives, especially those of governmental organizations, responsibility for the policies of his agency. In principle, he is supposed to "set policy" and, having set it, to obtain resources (money, manpower, public support) from the community in order to carry it out. Ideally, performing this function requires that the administrator have sufficient knowledge about and control over the rank-and-file members of his organization—especially the patrolmen—so that he can show what the police are doing and how well they are doing it, alter more or less precisely their behavior to accord with such policies as the community may agree to, and evaluate a particular officer's actions in the light of a specific citizen complaint. With respect to some members of his organization, and with respect to some aspects of the work of all members, the administrator does have knowledge and control. He knows, or can find out, whether his officers are tolerating the operation of a brothel and how many traffic tickets they are issuing. But with respect to how well they are preventing crime, catching criminals, and maintaining order, he has very little information.

The police share with most other public

From *Varieties of Police Behavior* by James Q. Wilson, pp. 57–64. Copyright © 1968 by the President and Fellows of Harvard College. Reprinted by permission of Harvard University Press, Cambridge, Mass.

agencies—the schools, foreign ministries, antipoverty organizations—an inability to assess accurately the effectiveness of their operations. Indeed, some writers, like Anthony Downs, have made the absence of an output that can be priced on a market, or otherwise given an objective, continuous evaluation, a defining characteristic of bureaucracy.[1] However they choose to interpret such measures, automobile dealers know how many cars their salesmen have sold, television producers know what audience ratings their programs have earned, and baseball managers know their clubs' standing and the batting averages of their players. But just as the school superintendent has only the most approximate measures of how well his schools are educating children, partly because "education" is so hard to define and measure and partly because the school's contribution to education however measured is so hard to estimate,[2] so also the police chief has only the most rudimentary knowledge of how well his patrolmen are preventing crime, apprehending criminals, and maintaining order. No police department, however competently led or organized, can know how much crime and disorder a community produces or how much would be produced if the police functioned differently (or not at all).

Most crime becomes known to the police through citizen reports, but the citizens are likely to underreport many kinds of crime for reasons of self-interest that the police and the community cannot easily change. The true rates for rape, robbery, assault, burglary, and larceny are many times higher than the reported rates; though some of the difference is due to police error or malpractice, most of it is due to the failure of citizens to notify the police. A third to a half of the assaults in one survey went unreported; because most assaults occur among people known, or even related, to each other, it is not surprising that half the victims who did not report these offenses gave as their reason that they felt "it was a private matter" or that they did not want to get the offender into trouble.[3] Between 40 and 60 per cent of all thefts and cases of malicious mischief were unreported; because these are largely crimes of stealth, they are rarely solved by the police. Thus, it is not surprising that well over half the victims who did not report them gave as their reason that the police could not do anything. The two crimes most accurately reported are murder, presumably because it is so serious and because most murderers *are* caught, and auto theft, presumably because insurance companies require such a report and because most stolen cars are recovered by the police.

If the self-interest of the citizen causes him to underreport certain crimes, it may cause him to overreport others. A false report of a theft may be filed in order to make an insurance claim; disorderly conduct may be charged against a neighbor with whom one has a grudge to settle or against teenage boys whose rowdy (but noncriminal) behavior one wants curbed. And ignorance may cause other distortions—a stolen purse may be presumed lost, an unmarried couple caught in a motel may be thought of as having violated a moral but not a legal code.

Even when the police have accurate information, it is often difficult or impossible to devise a strategy that would make the occurrence of a crime less likely. Many serious crimes—murder, forcible rape—are of this character: though they are often reported with minimum distortion or delay, they oc-

cur, in many cases, in private places, among people who know each other, and in the heat of an emotional moment. A police department may assign an officer to each street corner, but inside the buildings on those corners, a drunken husband may still maul or murder his wife's lover as though the police were a hundred miles away.

Crimes that occur in public places are more easily suppressed by police patrol, but the police can never know whether a crime suppressed in one neighborhood reappears in another, less closely patrolled neighborhood, or in another community served by a different police department, or within the same neighborhood but in a different form. Stealing cars parked along the curb may be reduced by intensive patrol, but car thieves may then go elsewhere to steal or, abandoning the streets to the police, burglarize stores by entering them from the alley.

The rate of certain crimes is determined to a significant but unknown degree by factors over which the police have little control. Street crimes are affected by the weather, crimes against property by the prevailing economic conditions, crimes against the person by the racial and class composition of the community, delinquency by the nature and strength of family and peer group controls. The police know these things—or think they know them—but they cannot estimate the magnitude of such factors, or distinguish their effect from that of police tactics, or bring these factors under police control.[4]

Though he may talk publicly a good deal about crime rates, the police administrator knows or senses that he cannot get really reliable figures and that if he could get them he would not be able to show that police work makes a visibly dramatic difference in them. He will tell a visitor that "the police don't cause crime" and the "police alone can't stop it," and of course he is right. If the apparent crime rate goes down, he will not object if the newspapers give him credit; if it goes up, he will point, perhaps with ample justification, to conditions over which the police have no control.

As a result, few police administrators show much interest in "planning" the deployment of their manpower and equipment. There is no information—and in the nature of the case, there can never be sufficient information—on the effects of alternative police strategies on the several kinds of crime. Some problems could be dealt with by rational analysis, however. The Task Force on Science and Technology of the President's Commission on Law Enforcement and Administration of Justice showed that the probability of apprehending a suspect increased as the response time of the police decreased.[5] Operations research techniques are available to show how response time can be reduced most economically in a given department. Controlled experiments could be performed to assess the effect on citizen reports of crime by systematically altering the number of patrolmen and the frequency of patrol in an area.[6]

But few police administrators take even those steps that might lead to modest gains in optimal resource allocation. No department visited for this study, for example, tried systematically to measure response time and the consequences of its variations. Some departments have experimented with varying the forces assigned to particular beats, or even the dimensions of these beats, in accordance with reported crimes and calls for service, but they are the exception.[7] It is even rare for a department to keep careful and long-term records on the effect of "saturation patrol" (by a tactical squad or the like) in one or more neighborhoods.

Adequate information is, of course, not all that would be needed for a "rational" allocation of police protection. Even if the administrator had perfect knowledge of the outcome of various police deployment strategies, he would also have to have a decision rule that would tell him which outcome to prefer. There are at least two such rules, and they are in conflict. One is the "crime minimization" criterion: allocate patrolmen so that the last one assigned would deter an equal amount of crime no matter where in the city he was placed. This criterion would produce the smallest total amount of crime in the city, but because the deterrence value of a patrolman varies by type of neighborhood, some neighborhoods would have more crime than others. The other rule is the "crime equalization" one: allocate patrolmen so that the probability of being victimized is the same in all parts of the city. This might well leave the total amount of crime high in the city as a whole—equalizing victimization rates may be achieved by concentrating police in the most crime-prone areas to drive down those rates while allowing the rates in relatively crime-free areas to rise. In short, the police administrator—like all administrators—must make decisions about equity as well as about efficiency.[8]

Even if he had a decision rule, a police administrator would rarely have the funds, the information, the extra manpower, or the professionally competent assistants to make its systematic application possible. But most police administrators show little interest in such projects—partly perhaps because they have not been trained to think in these terms, but partly because they see these things as largely irrelevant. The administrator does not believe he and his organization are judged by the public in these terms, nor does he believe they should be: no statistics can be devised that would fairly measure what the police and the public take to be the true worth of police work. Repeatedly, interviewers for this study were told, "You can't go by the statistics," or "You have to use judgment and you've either got it or you don't." Even those departments with the most modern technologies—including computers—were administered by men who by and large used the numbers thus produced merely to compile annual reports, satisfy the FBI's need for data, and keep track of payrolls and operating expenses. Most departments gather data the way the telephone company gathers phone numbers—individual by individual, to be filed alphabetically and consulted only when somebody needs to "look something up."

The police administrator must nevertheless deal from time to time with a public hue and cry about "rising crime rates" or the "lack of police protection." If he knew how to prevent crime, of course he would, but he is in the unhappy position of being responsible for an organization that lacks a proven technology for achieveing its purpose. (In this, he is somewhat like the superintendent of a mental hospital: he too must deal with a problem of great importance for which there is no generally effective cure.) What he can do about rising crime rates, of course, is to hire more men (although the productivity of the marginal officer is impossible to measure, it is generally assumed that more men will not make matters worse and may make them better) and to use the ones he has "more aggressively." "Aggressive" police practice means gathering more information about people who may be about to commit, or recently have committed, a crime. Because he cannot, except by due process of law, put people in private places under surveillance (and the opportunities for eavesdropping or wiretapping are being restricted by court decision to the point where *any* surveillance in a private place may soon be impossible), he must gather the information in public places by stopping and questioning "suspicious" persons, checking cars, searching (where possible) people and vehicles for

contraband, and keeping an eye on those locales—street corners or taverns in rowdy neighborhoods, for example—where criminal acts often occur.

In short, "doing something" about rising crime rates means putting more patrolmen on the street and ordering them to be more alert. This, of course, increases the likelihood of the patrolmen coming into an adversary relationship with citizens—innocent people, to say nothing of guilty ones, usually do not like being stopped, questioned, or frisked. Furthermore, the patrolman cannot stop everyone, and in deciding who "ought" to be stopped he will rely on whatever clues he can. Persons who appear to be lower class are more likely than others to commit crimes; blacks are more likely than whites to commit the crimes of violence about which the public is most concerned; young men are more likely than older ones to steal automobiles. Intensifying surveillance will be experienced by people in these categories as "harassment"; failure to intensify surveillance will be regarded by people not in these categories as being "soft" on crime.[9]

Even assuming that there are substantial benefits from aggressive patrol (as there may be), these may be offset by increased citizen irritation. Today, more citizens are aware of their rights, more organizations are prepared to articulate and defend those rights, and the local political system is more vulnerable to (that is, finds it harder to ignore) complaints about the violation of rights. Those people who are most likely to believe, rightly or wrongly, that they are being "harassed"—blacks, young adults, lower-income persons—are increasing as a proportion of many cities' population, and thus it will be more difficult than ever for the police administrator to carry out a crime prevention program based on aggressive patrol.

NOTES

1   Anthony Downs, *Inside Bureaucracy* (Boston: Little, Brown, 1967), Chap. III.

2   Coleman, et al., *Equality of Educational Opportunity* (Washington, D.C.: U.S. Government Printing Office, 1966), Chap. III.

3   President's Commission on Law Enforcement and Administration of Justice, *The Challenge of Crime in a Free Society* (Washington, D.C.: U.S. Government Printing Office, 1967), pp. 21–22.

4   In addition, of course, police departments vary considerably in the accuracy with which they report such crimes as are known to them. See Ronald H. Beattie, "Problems of Criminal Statistics in the United States," *Journal of Criminal Law, Criminology, and Police Science* 66 (July–August 1955): 178–186; Marvin E. Wolfgang, "Uniform Crime Reports: A Critical Appraisal," *University of Pennsylvania Law Review* 109 (April 1963): 708–738; President's Commission, *The Challenge of Crime*, pp. 25–27; James E. Price, "A Test of the Accuracy of Crime Statistics," *Social Problems* 14 (Fall 1966): 214–221; James Q. Wilson, "Crime in the Streets," *The Public Interest* (Fall 1966): pp. 26–35. The President's Commission found that crime reports are significantly affected by local police reporting systems. For eleven large cities that recently changed their system, the increase in major (so-called "Index") offenses *in one year* ranged from 26.6 percent in Miami to 202.0 percent in Kansas City, Missouri. The cities that have made such significant changes in their reporting systems since 1959 account for *nearly 25 percent* of all reported index crimes against the person committed in the United States.

5   President's Commission on Law Enforcement and Administration of Justice, *Task Force Report: Science and Technology* (Washington, D.C.: U.S. Government Printing Office, 1967), pp. 92, 93.

6   Such experiments are likely to have two weaknesses, however. One is that it is often difficult to know the effect of altering patrol practices on crime reports in parts of the city outside the experimental area. The other is the "Hawthorne effect" — citizens may report more crimes in experimental areas because they see more policemen about or because they are aware they are part of an experiment, even though the actual rate of crimes has not changed; conversely, they may report fewer because they feel more secure.

7   The procedures used to allocate patrol forces in Los Angeles, Oakland, and Cincinnati are described in Frank E. Walton, "Selective Distribution of Police Patrol Force," *Journal of Criminal Law, Criminology, and Police Science* 49 (1958): 165–171. The few such efforts as are made to allocate patrol forces rationally are critically evaluated in "Program Budgeting for Police Departments," *Yale Law Journal* 76 (March 1967): 822–838. The Boston Police Department authorized a study that used operations research techniques to find ways of reducing response time. See Richard C. Larson, *Operational Study of the Police Response System*, Technical Report No. 26 of the Operations Research Center of the Massachusetts Institute of Technology (December 1967).

8   Carl S. Shoup, "Standards for Distributing a Free Governmental Service: Crime Prevention," *Public Finance* 19, No. 4 (1964): 383–392.

9   In 1967 the liberal mayor of Detroit, Jerome P. Cavanagh, faced a campaign led by certain white groups to recall him from office on the grounds that he had not done enough to halt the growing crime rate. He had first been elected mayor in part by black voters, who felt they were being harassed by a police crackdown on crime led by the previous administration; see the *New York Times,* May 7, 1967, p. 66. Nor are blacks the only group who complain of street stops. A Yale law professor wrote an article expressing his dislike at being stopped on his late evening or early morning walks or while driving and, what was worse, at being called "Charlie"; see Charles A. Reich, "Police Questioning of Law Abiding Citizens," *Yale Law Journal* 75 (1966): 1161–1172.

Los Angeles policeman and a Watts resident engage in friendly sidewalk conversation.

III

Police and Public Order

5

POLICE-MINORITY RELATIONS

St. Augustine policemen protecting black swimmers at a newly integrated beach.

By 1967, riots in heavily black American communities had become so widespread and so destructive that the President of the United States convened a National Advisory Commission on Civil Disorders. This commission concluded that what lay behind the riots was a long historical pattern of racism on the part of whites in America.

The police are deeply implicated in the racism of America both as contributors to it and as objects of it. Perhaps more than any other public agency, police departments continually face the social consequences of the problems in the ghetto created by the failure of other white institutions. A report by the Group for Research on Social Policy at Johns Hopkins University puts the issue of the rule of police in racial minority communities very well.

> The distant and gentlemanly white racism of employers, the discrimination of white parents who object to having their children go to school with Negroes, the disgruntlement of white taxpayers who deride the present welfare system as a sinkhole of public funds but are unwilling to see it replaced by anything more effective—the consequences of these and other forms of white racism have confronted the police with a massive control problem of the kind most evident in the riots.
>
> In our survey, we found that the police were inclined to see the riots as the long range result of faults in the Negro community—disrespect for law, crime, broken families, etc.—rather than as responses to the stance of the white community. Indeed, nearly one-third of the white police saw the riots as the result of what they considered the basic violence and disrespect of Negroes in general, while only one-fourth attributed the riots to the failure of white institutions. More than three-fourths also regarded the riots as the immediate result of agitators and criminals—a suggestion contradicted by all the evidence accumulated by the riot commission. The police, then, share with the other groups—excepting the black politicians—a tendency to emphasize perceived defects in the black community as an explanation for the difficulties that they encounter in the ghetto.[1]

There are no easy, or even difficult, solutions to the problems of police-minority relations. The introduction to this volume discusses some shortcomings of the approach taken by Police-Community Relations Units. Obviously, pervasively historical and deeply structural problems do not lend themselves to solution by bureaucratic initiative. Yet it may be possible, by recruitment, by education, by structuring means for communication between minority communities and the police, by reordering the controls over police policy, to improve relations between police and minority communities.

And what *is* the scope of "minority" relations? Women, for example, traditionally were not considered by police organizations as a "minority" group with definite concerns and needs. Yet during the 1960s and 1970s the women's movement—largely inactive since agitation for suffrage—began to emerge very much like other protesting social movements. All women shared certain experiences. As in other protest movements, there were differences of opinion about goals, strategy and tactics. Yet the basic principle of affirmative action for the development of women's capacities and dignity is subscribed to by all women—and men—who have become conscious of the sometimes gross and sometimes subtle ways women are discriminated against by social tradition and action.

Since most police are men, they have been insensitive to the special needs of women as victims of crime—particularly the crime of rape—and the possibilities of the value of women as functioning members of a police department. The article "Rape Squad" deals with both of these issues and, in addition, suggests how the structure and attitudes of a police department can be changed through organized social protest.

Certainly, a number of questions are worth raising as an initial step. For example, patrol procedures and policies suggest certain assumptions that police have regarding minorities. The readings in this chapter examine some of these assumptions. You may inquire what they are and whether they can be factually tested. We can also ask further questions about community relations units. For example, in the absence of competent and fairly administered police departments, can such units help police and community understanding? Who should accept ultimate responsibility for police-community relations? Should it be patrolmen, high-ranking officials, other officials? What roles should organized minorities play in community relations? When a police department has particularly poor relations with minority groups, to what extent does that undermine other aspects of the administration of the police department? Is competent, fair, and unbiased police work the equivalent of good police-minority relations? If not, why not? Since minority groups often claim that police-community relations units are fraudulent, and policemen often see such units as against the best interests of the police, what alternatives to police-community relations units can be suggested? If you had the resources and the power, how would you go about altering the character of police-minority relations?

NOTE

1   David Boesel, Richard Berk, W. Eugene Groves, Bettye Eidson, and Peter H. Rossi, "White Institutions and Black Rage," *Trans-action* (March 1969): 31.

Police Deployment Theories and the Mexican American

ARMANDO MORALES

The heart of the police law enforcement effort is patrol, the movement around an assigned area, on foot, vehicle, or by helicopter of police personnel. Orlando W. Wilson once referred to patrol as the "backbone of police service" and the largest of police divisions. Although police experts agree that patrol is an essential activity, the issue of how many policemen, under what orders, and using what techniques to patrol what activity is a highly complicated, complex question. In this article, there will be a review of the literature regarding theories on police patrol deployment with some emphasis on Mexican American communities. Thereafter, a community case situation will be analyzed in light of the theory presented. This will be followed by a discussion, recommendations, and the raising of questions for further research and documentation.

All police departments have the problem of patrol force deployment, how many men to assign to each shift and to each precinct. Most departments assign men equally to all shifts, which reduces scheduling problems but is an inefficient use of manpower. Some police departments use a formula such as the proportional need theory, which weights the previous year's reported crimes, radio calls, population, etc., for each patrol area or precinct, and then assign the patrol force proportionately to the precinct's weighted score. A question arises, however, regarding what specific weights to assign to what specific crimes. The literature regarding police patrol deployment theory is rather modest—one possible explanation being that a small fraction of one percent of the criminal justice system's total budget in the United States is spent on research.

A law enforcement professional in recent years who began discussing factors underlying police patrol deployment was the late William H. Parker, Chief of the Los Angeles Police Department from 1950 to 1966. In his 1957 book he said:

> Every department worth its salt deploys field forces on the basis of crime experience. Deployment is often heaviest in so-called minority sections of the city. The reason is statistical—it is a fact that certain racial groups, at the present time, commit a disproportionate share of the total crime. Let me make one point clear in that regard —a competent police administrator is fully aware of the multiple conditions which create this problem. There is no inherent physical or mental weakness in any racial stock which tends it toward crime. But, and this is a "but" which must be borne constantly in mind—police field deployment is not social agency activity. In deploying to suppress crime, we are not interested in why a certain group tends toward crime, we are interested in maintaining order.

According to Parker, therefore, police deployment is heaviest in minority sections of the city because, based on statistical reasons,

From *ANDO SANGRANDO (I Am Bleeding): A Study of Mexican American-Police Conflict* (La Puente, California: Perspectiva Publications, P.O. Box 3563, 1972), pp. 47–57, by Dr. Armando Morales. Reprinted by permission.

he *believes* it to be a *fact* that racial minority groups commit more crime. Parker made these statements in an address delivered at the National Conference of Christians and Jews, Institute on Police-Community Relations, Michigan State University, in May, 1955.

In comparing the 1955 crime statistics in the low-socioeconomic, predominantly Mexican American community LAPD Hollenbeck Division with the middle-class, predominantly Anglo-Saxon LAPD Hollywood Division, there does not appear to be a statistically significant difference in the crime rates per ratio of population in the two communities. In the Mexican American police division there was a crime rate of 3,682.9 per 100,000 population compared to a rate of 3,681.1 per 100,000 population in the Anglo-Saxon area. This means that there were 1.8 more crimes per 100,000 population in the Mexican American community. Would this minute statistical difference warrant heavier police deployment in the ethnic minority community? Parker further stated:

At the present time, race, color, and creed are useful statistical and tactical devices. So are age groupings, sex and employment. If persons of one occupation, for some reason commit more theft than the average, then increased police attention is given to persons of that occupation. Discrimination is not a factor there. If persons of Mexican, Negro, or Anglo-Saxon ancestry, for some reason, contribute heavily to other forms of crime, police deployment must take that into account. From an ethnological point of view, Negro, Mexican and Anglo-Saxon are unscientific breakdowns; they are fiction. From a police point of view, they are a useful fiction and should be used as long as they remain useful. The demand that the police cease to consider race, color, and creed is an unrealistic demand. Identification is a police tool, not a police attitude.

Parker does not elaborate as to how ethnicity and creed may be a "useful fiction" from a police point of view, or how the police administration determines when this ceases to be a useful criteria in police deployment. He feels that race, color, and creed for identification purposes are a police tool and not the result of a police attitude. Might not these criteria be based on *attitudinal perceptions* that may or may not be based on fact? How is *fact* determined? Would it not be possible to heavily deploy police in an ethnic minority community as a response to a perceived fact or assumption which in turn has the result of making it appear as if indeed it is a fact? As Gilbert Geis has said:

A belief, based on real or imagined information, that a particular minority group commits more crimes than other groups will often lead to a greater saturation of this group's neighborhoods by police patrol. Such saturation will likely turn up more crime and produce a larger number of arrests of persons belonging to the group, though it will often inhibit some kind of criminal activity as well because of the increased likelihood of apprehension. But it is the police activity and not the behavior of the group itself which is conditioning the crime rates for the group as these eventually appear in the printed statistics.

The phenomenon described by Geis leads to what Robert K. Merton called a "self-fulfilling prophecy." Within this conceptual framework, it would be possible for law enforcement unknowingly to generate its own need for more services, thereby utilizing critical manpower that could have been used for some other activity.

Orlando O. Wilson advocates the use of "police hazards" as a theoretical basis for the deployment of police patrols in communities. He states:

The need for patrol service derives from police hazards. The total hazard in a community resulting in need for police service is the sum of a multitude of varied and complex conditions and situations, many of them intangible and difficult to isolate for purposes of analysis and measurement. However, hazards result in crimes, offenses, accidents, complaints, and arrests whose frequency may be taken as a measure of the hazards. The measure is made, not in terms of the hours and minutes spent in handling cases or in neutralizing or minimizing the hazards, but in terms of the proportional distribution of the incidents that result from those hazards among the various patrol areas and time periods.

The purpose of patrol, according to Wilson, is to achieve police objectives through the action of officers moving about within prescribed areas. Their tasks are divided into three classes: services called for (incidents requiring police action reported by a victim or witness or discovered by a patrolman), inspectional services (routine examination of business premises, etc.), and routine preventive patrol (directed primarily at diminishing less tangible hazards that are not readily isolated and identified).

While a formula has not yet been developed to determine the needed strength of a police department, states Wilson, the minimum number of men needed for the special divisions can be estimated on the basis of essential duties that must be performed; and the number needed for patrol may be estimated by ascertaining the number required to provide an amount of patrol service in terms of called-for service and routine patrol. The relative need for routine preventive patrol and called-for services, according to Wilson, may be measured in terms of the relative frequency of occurrence of Part I offenses (seven major crimes), Part II of-

fenses (all other crimes), accidents, reports, and arrests, because these are the incidents that routine patrol is intended to prevent, and their frequency establishes the extent of called-for services. Wilson suggests that the procedure for working out the patrol deployment is simplified if those factors which determine the relative need for called-for services and routine patrol are consolidated into a single factor, or index. The factors are then assigned weights. In describing this procedure, he states:

> A weight of one should be assigned to all incidents in each of the categories of arrests, accidents, and miscellaneous reports, since it is assumed that they are of approximately equal importance and that approximately equal time is required to deal with them. A weight of two should be assigned to Part II offenses, and a weight of four to Part I crimes. In applying the weights, Part I crimes should be multiplied by four and Part II incidents by two, since it is assumed that they are, respectively, four and two times more serious than incidents in the other three categories and that a similar increase in time is required to deal with them.

Thereafter, the weighted numbers of incidents in each type are added, and the proportion of the total on each shift to the total for the 24 hours of the day is computed. This percentage is then used to apportion the man-hours to be devoted to called-for services and preventive patrol among the shifts. This approach would meet the requirements of the "proportional need theory."

Within recent years, the Los Angeles Police Department Patrol Bureau has instituted its own theoretical rationale for the distribution of personnel within a geographic patrol division. The policy states that "by evaluating past experiences, the police administrator can anticipate the distribution of the need for his patrol force on the basis of the past distribution of the problem." This policy is also consistent with the proportional need theory. There is, however, no way of measuring the *validity* of the *original* theoretical base upon which later personnel deployment policies may evolve.

The LAPD distributes its manpower on the basis of criminal activity and called-for services. The manpower distribution is made on the basis of four factors: selected crimes, called-for services, felony arrests, and misdemeanor arrests. The following crimes are selected, tallied, and combined for machine tabulation: "burglary," "robbery," "theft from person," "auto theft," "burglary and theft from auto," "bicycle theft," "murder, rape and felonious assault," and "other thefts." The policy states that:

> These crimes were chosen as they are more susceptible to prevention by the presence of uniformed patrol officers, or because they are indicators of the need for police services, or both. Bicycle thefts were included because of their correlation to those "less serious" juvenile crimes not covered by the other selected crimes. A question arises as to the inclusion of murder and rape with felonious assaults. Murder and rape are crimes of passion and are not responsive to the mere knowledge that the police are in the area. However, simply because a crime falls into a group of crimes which we think cannot be prevented does not preclude its value as an indicator of a police problem area. Aggravated or felonious assault are to a certain extent susceptible to prevention, especially when those assaults might occur in a public place. Additionally, the general geographic location of such assaults is usually predictable when considered in volume of number and time. Murders, rapes, and felonious assaults tend

to indicate the need for the presence of uniformed officers in those areas which, because of socioeconomic or ethnic conditions, seem to present a much higher proportion of crimes of violence.

Again, as was the case with the late Chief Parker, the deployment policy is based upon a *belief* that socioeconomic and ethnic conditions lead to a much higher proportion of crimes of violence. There is no further clarification or elaboration of these ethnic, socioeconomic variables to demonstrate how this is true (or not true). The local police administrator in effect has to accept this premise as a "given" and thereafter plan accordingly. A weight factor is assigned to called-for services, felony arrests, and misdemeanor arrests. These three factors are combined and form *work units* and are used as a *single factor*. The percentage of work units and the percentages of crimes are then averaged to determine the workload by reporting district. The workload then is determined separately for each watch.

The operationalization of the LAPD patrol deployment policy should reveal that more police are assigned to those areas that reflect the most need based on LAPD criteria. To accomplish this, two police divisions were selected for contrasting purposes because one area was a low-socioeconomic, predominantly ethnic minority community, and the other a middle-class, predominantly Anglo-Saxon community. The LAPD Hollenbeck Division is comprised of 73.4 percent white, Spanish-surname persons with a median family income of $4,820. The LAPD Wilshire Division is comprised of 68.6 percent white, non-Spanish-surname persons with a median family income of $6,517. The basic crime profiles and the number of police in the two communities are compared in Tables 1 and 2.

Contrary to common belief, Tables 1 and 2 reveal that even though there is a higher incidence of crime in the middle-class Anglo-Saxon community, there is a greater amount of police deployment in the poorer, Mexican American community. One possible explanation might be that police administrators, by placing a greater emphasis on a historical policy belief—that lower-socioeconomic ethnic minorities commit a much higher proportion of crime—accordingly assign more police to those areas even though statistical analysis does not warrant this deployment. Does this therefore suggest that there is an element of *subjectivity* in police patrol deployment? N. F. Iannone in his 1970 book expresses this viewpoint when he states:

> The determination of proportionate need for the distribution of the patrol force depends upon the selection and use of factors

which indicate the extent of the police problem in a given city. Herein lies the element of subjectivity since the selection of factors which reflect the nature of the police problem is, in large part, a matter of opinion. Each administrator should select those factors which he believes most accurately reflect the police problem in his community.

The police administrator is very much alone in making those subjective decisions, and perhaps even more important, when functioning under the proportional need theory, the greatest shortcoming of this theory is that there is no provision for feedback and control. In other words, not only is there no direct relationship between the deployment scheme and the activities of the officers in the field, but also there is no method by which the activities of the officers in the field can be related to the achievement of the ob-

Table 1

LAPD SELECTED CRIMES USED FOR DISTRIBUTION OF PERSONNEL
WITHIN A GEOGRAPHIC PATROL DIVISION

Division	Population	Burglary	Robbery	Larceny and Theft from Person	Auto Theft	Bicycle Theft, Burglary and Theft from Auto, and Other Theft*	Murder, Rape, and Felonious Assault	Total
Hollenbeck								
1965	110,246	1,517	245	2,206	1,150	303	576	5,997
1966	109,749	1,574	279	1,998	1,030	392	606	5,822
Wilshire								
1965	259,178	5,335	936	7,752	1,903	659	851	17,436
1966	214,750	4,487	707	6,584	1,520	325	778	14,701

*The 1965 and 1966 LAPD Statistical Digests do not reveal a specific crime category for Bicycle Theft, Burglary and Theft from Auto, and Other Theft. However, the digests reveal a category both in juvenile and adult arrests labeled "Other," and it is these figures that were used for this column.

Table 2

AREA CRIME RATES AND POLICE PER POPULATION

Division	Total Selected Crimes	Total Crimes as Percentage of Population	Number of Police per Population (in thousands)
Hollenbeck			
1965	5,997	5.4	1/1,070
1966	5,822	5.3	1/1,086
1969	7,932	7.3	1/1,016
Wilshire			
1965	17,436	6.7	1/1,200
1966	14,701	6.7	1/1,256
1969	18,453	8.2	1/1,118

jectives of the deployment scheme. How does one measure the police deployment *outcome?* Is crime actually prevented?

The President's Commission on Law Enforcement and the Administration of Justice found that policemen spend half of their time on "preventive patrol," but that no police chief can obtain even a rough estimate of how much crime is thereby "prevented." The Commission also discovered that the ratios of policemen per 1,000 residents in cities of over 500,000, ranging from 1.07 to 4.04, showed no differences in the incidence of reported crime in those cities. Although it might be difficult to measure the crime preventive outcomes of police patrol, it would be possible to measure what James Q. Wilson calls "Police-Invoked Order Maintenance." The most common police-initiated intervention (Police-Invoked Order Maintenance) occurs in situations dealing with offenses related to drinking.

Drunkenness arrests vary from place to place—some police departments strictly enforce drunkenness statutes, while other departments are known to be more tolerant. The President's Commission concluded that

the number of arrests in a city may be related less to the amount of drunkenness than to *police policy.* To prove its point, the Commission compared drunkenness arrests in three cities and found that the Washington, D.C. (51.8 percent drunk arrests) and Atlanta, Georgia (52.5 percent drunk arrests) police departments were guided by stricter enforcement policies than the more tolerant St. Louis, Missouri, police department (5.5 percent drunk arrests). Undoubtedly, there are many complex variables to consider when different cities in different states are compared as to drinking arrests. It would be possible, however, to consider these arrest patterns as they affect a specific Mexican American ethnic minority community in East Los Angeles, as data are available for careful analysis. Drunk and drunk driving arrests account for a little over 50 percent of all arrests in East Los Angeles—a significantly higher ratio than other communities. Table 3 compares the East Los Angeles and West Valley populations with regard to numbers of police and frequency of drunk and drunk driving arrests.

Table 3 reflects dramatic differences in

Table 3

DRUNK AND DRUNK DRIVING ARRESTS PER AREA AND POPULATION (1968)

	LAPD Hollenbeck Area and ELA Sheriff's Station*	LAPD West Valley Area**
Total population	259,275	260,832
Square miles	26.44	54.81
Ethnicity	50–60% white, Spanish-surname	95% white, non-Spanish-surname
Median family income	$5,680	$8,440
Number of alcoholics per 100,000 pop.	8,143	8,143
Drunk and drunk driving arrests		
per month:	800	125
per year:	9,676	1,552
per sq. mi.:	372	28.5
Police agencies	CHP†, LAPD, Sheriff	LAPD‡
Total number of officers	375	151
Number of officers per square mile	13.5	3.5
Major crime as percentage of pop.	4.9	4.8

* "Total Population" and "Square Miles" includes Bell Gardens (29,491 people, 2.40 square miles) and City of Commerce (10,763 people, 6.56 square miles). Bell Gardens and Commerce accounted for 1,168 of the drunk and drunk driving arrests.
** As defined by LAPD.
† California Highway Patrol.

‡ CHP statistics in the West Valley area were not available, but even when CHP arrests are subtracted from the East Los Angeles area (approximately 3,000 arrests), there still is a significantly higher ratio of arrests for those offenses in the ELA area as compared to the West Valley area. The LAPD made 2,954 ELA arrests, and the Sheriff's office produced 3,722 ELA arrests.

arrests related to drinking. From its information, one must conclude that more police are present to observe drinking infractions of the law in the East Los Angeles area, and that drunk and drunk driving arrests increase as the number of police per population and square mile increase. It is not that Mexican Americans are drinking more than their affluent neighbors, as the Division of Alcoholic Rehabilitation of the California Department of Public Health reports an identical ratio of alcoholism per population. Rather, affluent users of alcohol seem to be very much underrepresented in criminal statistics. Jack W. Bishop, Director of the USC Research Project on the Drinking Driver and Traffic Safety, found that most convicted drunk drivers are between 31 and 40 years of age, and that most of those convicted are laborers or unskilled workers. He remarked: "If we say that drunken drivers are only from lower economic groups or minorities, we are fooling ourselves. Drunk drivers come from every social stratum and occupation."

The head administrator of the Los Angeles County Jail, Chief Kramer, informed the writer on August 2, 1968, that they did not keep racial or ethnic statistical data on prisoners. There are 12,000 prisoners in the county jail. During 1967, 153,221 persons were booked into the county jail, with a third of these being arrested for offenses related to drinking. Since Mexican Americans comprise 20 percent of state adult inmates and parolees, and 25 percent of California Youth Authority wards, there would be reason to believe that Mexican Americans represent 20 percent (2,400) to 25 percent (3,000) of the county jail inmates in Los Angeles. This is not difficult to conclude when one considers the large numbers of people in East Los Angeles being arrested for drunk and drunk driving offenses. Better statistics regarding ethnic arrest patterns are needed in this area for exact documentation.

How should the police administrator deal with the "police-invoked order maintenance" phenomenon such as was presented in Table 3? Patrol deployment policies and theories do not seem to take this kind of self-generated outcome into consideration in patrol deployment planning. Might there not be too much emphasis placed on "police hazards" and the "police problem," which may lead to many intangibles, assumptions, and variables that in the end require arbitrary, subjective decisions? Rather than considering a certain category of serious crimes to assist one in defining the "police problem," the "police problem" might be those very activities, such as "revolving door" drinking offenses, that critically cut into police manpower. In 1965, one of every three arrests in America was for the offense of drunkenness (two million arrests). The great volume of these arrests places an extremely heavy load on the operations of the entire criminal justice system. Not only does it burden police, but it clogs lower criminal courts and crowds penal institutions throughout the country.

Perhaps police administrators should deliberate beyond the traditional criminal justice system (courts, police, and corrections) in comprehensive planning. Other systems that should be part of the criminal justice system, particularly as it pertains to drinking-related offenses, are mental health and public health agencies. While over 50 percent of all arrests for law enforcement agencies in East Los Angeles are for offenses related to drinking, only 2 percent of all the patients seen at the county East Los Angeles Mental Health Regional Service were there for drinking problems. With the exception of three or four Alcoholics Anonymous groups in East Los Angeles and a very modest, recently established out-patient public health satellite service, there are no detoxification or professional services available to Mexican Americans with drinking problems. In other words, it is not just a police problem, it is a bio-psycho-social problem—it is a community problem. Involving the criminal justice system with these agencies and the community system in comprehensive planning could result in a more totally efficient system for processing drinking behavior—thereby reducing law enforcement's most time-consuming burden. Shouldn't police be concerned only with enforcing the law and seeing to it that a person is taken before the judge and then punished for his drinking offense? Law enforcement cannot afford not to be concerned with the outcome of the patrol deployment scheme if it wishes to keep pace with the growing crime problem in America.

A Policeman's Journal

T. MIKE WALKER

MARCH 24

Night on Baldwin Mountain: I arrived at Northern Station in the Fillmore District at four in the afternoon and was assigned a beat alone for the last few hours of daylight because the station was short of men. The wagon driver gave me a ride down to McAllister and Fillmore, the heart of the Negro ghetto, and dropped me on the corner across from Dinny's Barrel House #2 where ragged black lettering over a fading flaming orange wall read:

> THIS IS THE PLACE.
> THERE ISN'T ANYPLACE LIKE THIS
>   PLACE
> ANYWHERE NEAR THIS PLACE
> SO THIS MUST BE THE PLACE.

I agreed with this infallible logic of the streets and followed the insidious intent of the dirty gray sidewalk past a flock of pigeons pecking in the gutter for grain, past beautiful black children in rags riding skateboards or roller-skating on one skate or playing hopscotch, who stopped laughing when I passed and watched me with wondering eyes: The Man.

And thus I began my walk on the shady side of the street with the sun sinking in the west, laced with a film of white clouds which smeared the slanting light. Above the streets

a tangle of wires crossed each other in a patchwork pattern of cables which seemed to fuse like fists of trapped power into the small squat structure of the powerhouse across the street. Six ragged black men sat on the tile steps and passed paper bags shaped like bottles back and forth, raising them to their lips, sipping and laughing, their voices as rough as their thick calloused hands. They too turned to stone for an instant as my shadow slid over their faces.

The signs in store windows seem to be saying something to me about this transient scene:

> NEWMAN'S SMOKED MEATS
> E. FRAZER BAPTIST CHURCH:
>   HEALING NIGHTLY EXCEPT
>   MONDAY, 7–11 P.M.
> JOE'S BARBECUE, RIBS TO GO
> AMERICAN THEATER
> GLAD TIDINGS TEMPLE
> NO PARKING ANYTIME
> 24 HOTEL
> HRS CHICAGO
> WILL REMODEL TO SUIT TENANT
> CARS WILL BE TOWED

But there are other signs, too. Two young Negro boys in brown leather jackets walked casually down the Fillmore hill shaking the handles of car doors and glancing inside for keys left in the ignition or packages left on seats, and saw me watching them and nodded to each other wisely and turned with great ease into Tiny's Pool Hall: NO DANCING where smoke and smuggled voices and sharp laughter covered the auto boosters like smoke. This is a watchcop watching a Negro. This is a watchcop watching you. Are *you* a Negro? Then watch out!

Invisible eyes were watching me, too. I could feel them gouging into me like hooks and knives thrown sideways from the strained white corners of passing eyes, or flung like razors through slitted, tautly pulled window shades. I felt naked and wished that I were harmless, unarmed, a Peace Officer, instead of what I was.

"Good even', Officer." A wrinkled little old Negro woman carrying a bag of groceries and wearing an old yellow straw hat with a red plastic flower stuck on top smiled a toothless greeting as she nodded and passed. I tipped my hat and grunted in surprise, to which she said, "God bless you, son."

Suddenly I felt so good that when I got to the next corner and saw five kids crowded into a doorway, hiding roaches behind their backs and holding their breaths as they watched me, I only smiled. I could smell the odor of grass hanging like heavy Chinese incense over their swept-up combs of black hair, and I knew that I could interrupt their lives and book them for possession—such a fine arrest, five (5, count them) juvenile delinquents caught red-handed: DOPE RING SMASHED BY ROOKIE COP!—but would it be worth it, after all? After hooky, petty theft, and T, to make a bust of these lives? And if one, venturing to run or punch me out or plead, should cry, "That is not fair, That is no fair shit at all," should I squeeze their universe into a smaller cell, to roll toward some overwhelming ending! No! I'm not 007, nor was I meant to be. I flipped my club in my hand as I passed and tapped the brim of my hat with it and nodded to them and said: "Good evening, gentlemen," just that, and wandered on, wading waist high through whispered comments flung at me like garbage from doorways or open windows:

"Muthafucka . . ."

"White son of a . . ."

"Get me a gun and shoot those pigs . . ."

"Just you let one of them lay hands on me, I'll . . ."

"Don't blow your cool, man. Charley ain't gonna fuck with you if you *cool* . . ."

"Got me one down in Houston in an alley, cut his thro . . ."

"Ain't he cute with that club in his ha . . ."

"Hush, he be gone soon . . ."

"Hold him back there, Richard, hold . . ."

"Be gone soon, easy . . ."

"Sheeeeee*it!*"

I stopped before a row of wooden vegetable stands in front of a market and watched flies buzz over fruit which sweated in the sun. There was a City Ordinance issued by the Board of Health prohibiting the display of foodstuff on the street. But I liked the smooth fleshy sensual texture of the fruit and fingered a green pepper curved at the top like a child's vagina. I wondered, Do I dare to steal a pear? I picked a plump yellow one and walked inside to pay, scuffling my feet on the damp wooden floor covered with sawdust. And the signs in there: DAY OLD FRENCH BREAD 10¢; WE CASH NO CHECKS; CHICKENS KILLED AND CUT WHILE YOU WAIT. Right next to a sign which said WELFARE ORDERS ACCEPTED HERE was a cage of roosters and hens packed so tightly together that they clawed and pecked and scrambled over and over each other, their red combs and white feathers molting and covered with blood as they stuck out blindly in the cramped heat of the store, exploding in crowded futility and terror. Near the checkout counter, a short shriveled bespectacled old Chinaman in a business suit and tie squinted at me carefully, keeping his eyes on the pear. A long wooden table covered with ice held row after row of glistening dark fish that stared wisely at the web- and dust-covered ceiling of the store, which smelled like a country market in a peasant village.

"Why you no catch thieves? All the time these goddamn kids steal stuff. How come you no catch?" the old man demanded as I stepped up to the counter.

"I'm new on the beat this evening, sir. I haven't seen any thieves around yet tonight. How much is this pear?" He weighed it and squinted at the scale.

"Sixteen cents," he said. "How come all the time I complain and you guys don't do anything about?" I could see he was serious and disturbed, so I put on my deluxe please-the-people police-type smile, strong sturdy young teeth.

"I don't know why we don't do anything about it," I said, pushing the pear back toward him, "but that's an outrageous price." I looked around the store as if preparing to go. "I'll tell you what part of your trouble might be, if you really want to know. Those stands out there are a temptation, and you're just asking for trouble. Did you know there was a City Ordinance prohibiting sidewalk displays?"

"Ten cents, fresh today," he said, pushing the pear back to me. "So how come you no catch?"

"I'll tell you what I'll do, I'll make a personal note of it and turn in a report requesting the day man and the prowl car to make passing calls here for the next week or two around the time you usually get clipped, how's that? What time do you think?"

"In the morning. Eight o'clock, before school. And three o'clock too, all the kids come home, hang around in front, throw things around. You catch?" He was grinning, and took out a pipe and thumbed tobacco into the clay bowl.

"I'll see what we can do," I promised vaguely, knowing that the day man and the prowl car driver would probably be out having coffee at about those times. I wrote down the address and the name of the store and the name of the owner, closed my notebook, and stuffed it back into my uniform as I started toward the door.

"Five cents," he said. "You forgot the pear."

"Oh, thanks, it slipped my mind," I said as I handed him a nickel and walked out the door, tossing and catching the pear as I stepped into the evening and bit into the white flesh of the suddenly yielding skin and met the white taste of crunching meat. The juice leaked over my mouth and chin and dripped down my wrist as I continued up the street past an abandoned lot where the cracked cement foundations of demolished houses crouched like Aztec ruins, covered with weeds and a mosaic of broken wine and Coke bottles. A flight of stairs rose majestically into nowhere, into the empty air of the sunset which seemed to illuminate the red painted words on the side of the stairs: RATTLERS RULE. And I passed, all on one block, two poolhalls, three liquor stores, two music stores, four shoeshine stands, one pawnshop, a grocery store and an all-night coffee shop, closed, with a steel folding grille door locked tight across the entranceway. And the signs continued, in a weird kind of meaningful dance before my eyes:

BEAUTY CABIN SALON
DO NOT ENTER
FOR RENT
ONE WAY
TO LET
NEGRO CULTURAL FESTIVAL:
   Hall of Flowers
SHABAZZ BOOK STORE:
      The House of Common Sense
      Where Proper Propaganda Begins

Without Struggle There Is no Freedom
PROCESS CENTER
TREE'S SECOND HAND: ANYTHING
    BOUGHT AND SOLD
THIS STORE PROTECTED BY SPECIAL
    POLICE BURGLAR ALARM

And finally a doorway near a bus stop, mottled with hastily scrawled words:

eatme fuckyou wildbunch rules turks
RULE TURKS EAT SHIT eddy loves liz
eddy loves burton martin luther king is
a facist mohammed eats shit eats raw
cock cunt would you want your sister to
marry gov. wallace
                    ?
white trash if you want a fu cal mary at

All this and more written in pencil or ink or
gouged into the wood of the doorway or
slashed into the wall with knives or scribbled
and smudged in lipstick or ashes as high as
these children could reach. I wondered for a
moment what walls so violent might contain.

Everything seemed slow, dreamlike, unreal. The dark shadows of men lurked innocently in cars parked all along the street, and tips of cigarettes and cigars began to glow in the falling light. The street lights suddenly illuminated the whole length of the street and made me feel brighter inside. I passed a little black girl with a shoulder-length pigtail, eating a purple Popsicle as she whirled a pink hula hoop around her hips while she walked. I tipped my hat to her, too, and she giggled and started to run, flirting, not out of fear. When I reached my callbox and reaffirmed my presence on earth to my station, the night was still warm in spite of the breeze from the ocean.

The Desk Sergeant's voice was like a thin tin squeak in my ear. "Get your ass over to the Morocco Inn on Webster. Cutting. There's a car on the way."

My stomach fluttered slightly as I hung up the phone. I turned off Fillmore to Webster and found the club in the downstairs garage of an old frame apartment house which had been converted into a bar. A cardboard sign, lettered in fading red paint, was thumbtacked to the wall beside the swinging doors, which I pushed through and tumbled down four stairs into a sea of surprised black faces staring at me, all except the bartender who was pounding on a long mahogany bar with the handle of an ice pick, shouting "...now I'm *tired* warning you, Booker T., you get your black ass *out* of here. I mean that now!"

A big barrel of a man with white woolly hair hunched huge and black at the far end of the counter, bleeding at the forehead. Four men were sprawled on the floor at his feet like broken toys, and the barrel was singing joyfully in a deep whiskey baritone "Every-where . . . I go . . . Sun-shine fol-lows meeee. . . ." while the bartender continued to shout:

"God*damn* you, Booker T.! Looky here, here come the Law to haul your ass to *jail* and *good riddance,* now what you say to that?" and Booker sang:

"Every-where . . . I . . . go . . ." as I walked over to him and pulled him by his sleeve until he turned on the stool and stared me full in the face almost without seeing. He focused his eyes, then put on a pair of spectacles and focused again, adjusting them meticulously with an enormous hand while blood dripped down his cheeks and nose. "Good even' *Off*icer," he said, "old Booker just havin' a little fun. Just sittin' here mindin' my business when they *pickin'* on me, I don't know why. Just got off work and sittin' here *singing.*" He inhaled deeply, doubling the size of his chest, and sang joyfully, *"Ev*-ry-*where* I . . . *go.* . . ." I looked around wildly for help, but the bartender merely looked amused, and I remembered the men on the floor.

"What's going on here, anyhow? Look, call an ambulance for these men on the floor," I told the bartender, but his face set like stone against me, perhaps against my tone, which was defensive and harsh and abrupt. But I was also scared, alone in there with all those cold faces.

"No, *sir.* I ain't going to get mixed in this. Ain't none of *my* affair. They walked in here by themselves, they can damn well walk *out* by themselves, ain't giving them no free ride," the bartender said.

"Listen, I'm serious. Call an ambulance. These men might be seriously hurt. What happened, anyhow?" I pulled at Booker's arm again, but he brushed me aside and gulped from a glass of gin which he held in his hand. "That's an *order,*" I said sharply when the bartender refused to move, and his eyebrows darted up suddenly.

"What's that? What you say, white boy?" His voice was hard, thin.

I felt my stomach shrink again, and modified my tone. "Don't you understand that these men need *help?* That they might *die?*"

"Don't look like they need no help to me. They just sleeping it off."

". . . *Sun*-shine *fol*-low *me* . . ." Booker sang, leaning back against the bar and closing his eyes.

"But you called the police in the first place, didn't you? What the hell is going on? Be reasonable, call an ambulance . . . here, give me the phone."

"Phone out of order," he said, moving in front of it and folding his arms. "You come into *my* place and order *me?*"

"For Chrissake," I shouted, "*you* called for help and I *came* here to help and all you're doing is giving me shit! Now come on, Booker, be a nice guy and step outside with me, will you?" My hand was sticky with Booker's blood which oozed from the right sleeve of his thick coat.

The bartender prodded Booker with the ice pick. "You go on with the officer, now, Booker. Go along."

"I was just minding my business," Booker explained to the air. He heaved himself to his feet and grabbed my arm for support, this monster of a man with hands like steel bands gripping my arm as he led me stumbling over the groaning figures of the men, who were now beginning to stir and sit up, rubbing their arms and heads. Booker toppled with me into the night on the sidewalk just as a prowl car pulled up.

"Whoa-up, Booker. We'll wait right here," I hauled him to a stop.

"I just *live* up the street. You can walk old Booker home can't you, Officer?"

"You've been cut. . . ." I felt like I had to explain, since I was going to book him for assault.

"But Officer, you *cain't* put Booker in jail. He got to work tomorrow, man, he got work to do. I got a whole yard full of cars just waiting for me to take them apart for Mr. Evans in the morning, and then I got burning in the afternoon. What you want to fuck up Booker's life for, Officer, he ain't hurt no one?" His voice was deep, trembling, insistent, and I suddenly realized he was fifty or sixty years old.

"What about those guys on the floor in there?"

"Those boys on the floor in there? *Those* boys? Sheeeit, Officer, we were just shucking around, you know, just talking, just minding our own business. . . . Say, you got a bandage, Officer? I got a little cut here. . . ." He pawed at his wound for a moment, examined it closely, peering through the hole in his sleeve, then ignored it. "That's okay, it's stopping, and I just live a block up the street. I think I can make it, Officer. Old Booker, ha! he making it every day for sixty-seven year, he can make it now."

He started to walk away, but the Sergeant climbed out of the prowl car and shouted, "Don't let that man get away," just as I was grabbing for Booker's arm anyhow, and Booker waved back.

"Evening, Sergeant! You remember old Booker? Tell this young officer Booker only live up the street."

"Jesus Christ, is that Booker T. you got there, kid?" the Sergeant said as he came up to us. "How's your voice, Booker? You still in the choir?"

"*Ev*-ry-*where*-I-*go, sun*-shine . . .*" Booker began while the Sergeant examined his wounded arm and glanced at the wound on his head, then turned to me.

"What happened, kid? Booker getting into a little shit again? I been booking Booker for maybe ten years now regular, every Friday night, ain't that right, Booker? How long since I last booked you?"

"Just a little fight from what I could make out, sir. Nobody seems to be badly hurt, and I don't think anyone wants to press charges," I said over Booker as he took a deep breath, preparing to explain again that which he probably couldn't even remember happening.

"Okay, Booker. On your way. Take care of that arm when you get home, and wash that cut on your forehead," the Sergeant said

solicitously as he pushed Booker up the street. We watched him lumbering from side to side, a six-foot black walking wedge of stone singing ". . . *sun*-shine *follows meee* . . ." into the darkness where he lived.

"These apes," the Sergeant sighed. "You never know what they're going to do next, always something. Send them back to the jungle where they belong, that's what I say."

"That's where they're at," I said. "They want to get out."

"What's that, kid?" The Sergeant frowned and nodded toward the car and followed me over.

"That's where they have to live down here, in a jungle. That's what this place is. A huge cage where everyone hunts and hurts. It's terrible and sad."

"Fucking *apes,* that's what they are," the Sergeant agreed. "Come on back to the station and make out a report on this, kid. And then I think you can go out to supper. You got station duty the next half the watch, so you can sit on your can and enjoy yourself. We got all kinds of characters back at the station tonight waiting for transfer. Here, get in the back, we got the shotgun bolted up front now. Just put them in a week ago."

And Booker slipped out of my mind like melting tar as we passed the zig-zag rows of neon lights. But those eyes in the Morocco Bar hating me followed me all the way home and haunt me now as I write this, chilled and half nude, in the living room waiting for the baby bottle to heat in the pan on the stove, watching the blankets fall soft over Ann's body stretched thin on the bed as she breathes the warmth of this room and sleeps with a smile which only slowly blunts those eyes. That walk. This night.

Detective Ernie Cox, Southside Chicago

L. H. WHITTEMORE

The seventeen-year-old boy was wanted for five shootings. His apartment was four steps down from the sidewalk, on the ground floor of a dilapidated Victorian building. I stood behind Detective Ernie Cox as he knocked on the door and stepped to one side, his hand rubbing the edge of the gun beneath his sports jacket. An elderly Negro woman answered. Behind her, in the dark, damp living room, the television was on. Dressed in a faded pink bathrobe and with a large towel wrapped about her head, the woman stared at the black detective without expression.

"Police officer, ma'am. Is Donald Baggot here?"

"No. He's not here."

"Well, I'd like to speak with you, ma'am. I'm Officer Cox."

"I'd like to know what it's about," she said, letting Ernie and me into the drab room.

"I'd like to talk to your son."

"Mmmm."

"May we sit down?"

"Mmmm."

"Where is Donald now, ma'am?"

"Donnie went over to his father's place. He stayed there last night. He never gave me no trouble. He's been picked up one or two times for questioning, that's all."

"Is he with his father now?"

"I said, he went over to his father's last night."

From *Cop!* by L. H. Whittemore, pp. 109–125. Copyright © 1969 by L. H. Whittemore. Reprinted by permission of Holt, Rinehart and Winston, Inc.

"Where does his father live?"

"I don't really know . . ."

"Well . . ."

"Look, mister man, my son never be out after eight o'clock at night, he's always at home or inside, causing no trouble."

"Well, ma'am, can you call him at his father's? Do you have a phone number there?"

"No. His father got no phone. But I can call Donnie's brother and tell him to relay a message to his father that y'all are lookin' for Donnie."

"Maybe you can give me the brother's address and phone number."

"No, I'll make a phone call."

"Never mind that, ma'am."

"No trouble." The woman went to the telephone and dialed, while Ernie squirmed in his chair. "Hello, Georgie? It's me. The po-leece are lookin' for Donnie. . . . No, they won't tell me what the trouble is. Now, you see if he's at his father's house, all right? 'Cause the po-leece are here, right with me, you hear?"

When she returned, Ernie stood up and said, "Now, who were you just talking to, ma'am?"

"I was talking to Donnie's brother Georgie. His oldest brother."

"Is he your son?"

"No, he's my *husband's* son. Donnie is *my* son. Donnie's my baby. And he never got in with no trouble."

"Now, ma'am—"

"See, I can give an *account* of him. I

really can do that! And then I have proof!"

"Yes, ma'am. Now, can you call Georgie back and have him give you your husband's address?"

"Yeah, I can do that."

"Thank you."

The woman picked herself up again, suddenly looking weary and alone, and went to the telephone. "Hello, Georgie? Now, the po-leece are *still* here, and they want you to give me your father's address . . . Mmmm . . . Mmmm . . . Okay, Georgie, thank you. Now, you *call* your father, hear? And tell him that the *po-leece* are lookin' for Donnie. . . . Thank you, Georgie."

She set down the receiver slowly and shuffled back into the room. She handed a slip of paper to Ernie. He copied down the address in his note book and then politely said, "I thought your husband had no phone, ma'am."

"He *don't* have no phone."

"Well, ma'am, you just told Georgie to *call* him."

"No, I did not. I told him to *get in touch* with his father."

"But—"

"Don't you tell me what I did with my mouth, boy!"

"Yes, ma'am. If you see Donald, give me a call at police headquarters. I just want to talk with him and straighten a few things out, that's all. Here's my card, and thank you."

"You're thanked as well."

"Good day."

Waiting for us outside were several young black men. One of them, apparently the leader, cocked his elbow, making a clenched fist in the air. Then he said, "Who runs it?"

Ernie raised his own black fist and asked, "How're you doing, brother?"

"Who runs it?" Ernie smiled but made no reply. The entire group chanted, "Stones run it!" The statement meant that the Blackstone Rangers, the leading street gang in Chicago, had control of this neighborhood in the South Side. Ernie maintained his stoical smile as the leader stepped forward. His hair was cut short on the sides and an orange cloth was tied around his head, knotted in front, making a headband.

"You know," the young man said, grinning, "you is in the middle of a revolution."

"Yeah, I know that."

"Well, uh, you're an Uncle Tom. You know that, too?"

"What you mean I'm an Uncle Tom, man?"

"You're a dick, ain't you? You're working for the honkies."

"Well. . . . Would you rather it be *all* white policemen? I mean, wouldn't you like to see somebody on your side?"

"Sure." Smiling again, with a glance at me, the young man added softly, "But you ain't *on* my side, man."

"But why you say I'm an Uncle Tom? I mean, you don't even know how I feel 'bout that particular subject. You just throwing all the apples in the same barrel."

"That's right, same barrel!"

"Don't you think I have *any* of your interests at all?"

"You're a dick, right?"

"That's right. You want to have all white cops instead?"

"Well, for the good you colored ones do, they might as well all be white."

"But just honestly, would you rather there be *no* black policemen? I mean, then you'd be crying that we had a segregated police department."

"Well. . . . Maybe some colored. But we don't have no black cops come to our meetings or nothing, except when they're spying on us. We don't see you around, except like now, when you're trying to bust one of your own black brothers. You in another world, man."

"How do you know what world I'm in?"

"Look, man. . . ." Turning to his friends, the leader began to laugh. As the group started to move away, he pointed his finger at Ernie and shouted, "I'll tell you one thing, man! We got the names and addresses of all the black policemen in Chicago, and when the Big Thing comes, y'all are gonna be some of the first to go!"

"Who runs it?"

"Stones run it!"

Later in the afternoon, I went with Ernie to his brownstone apartment. For half an hour he worked out with barbells, stretching and pulling the muscles of his solid, black body, which was soon drenched in sweat. I watched, drinking coffee. Before ducking into the shower Ernie turned on his favorite Tchaikovsky record for me.

We sat talking, flipping through magazines. I asked him about the encounter with the young militant, wondering how he felt when he was called an Uncle Tom.

"That boy was right," Ernie said, smiling. "I *have* spied during riots. I put on clothes to infiltrate the arsonists and the snipers, to find out who and where they were. A black cop can get closer to the action, so to speak, before being detected."

For a moment I was distracted by the sounds of children outside Ernie's window, but he continued, "I can't speak for all Negro policemen—and maybe I'm too police-oriented—but I personally feel that arson and sniping and looting are no good. I *sympathize* with what supposedly they're doing this *for*. I mean, they're protesting the injustices and so forth. I sympathize with that 100

percent! But I don't believe that you can accomplish anything by burning your own neighborhood down."

Ernie poured me some more coffee. He spoke freely and sincerely, yet he seemed to be the sort of person who enjoys solitude. At thirty-nine, Detective Ernie Cox is one of thirty-three homicide men who cover a twelve-square-mile area bordering Lake Michigan. The unit, one of six in the Chicago Police Department, handles cases in parts of the Loop, the Near South Side, and the South Side. Ernie had asked to work in the latter section.

"That's where I was born and raised," he told me. "Hell, I was a gang leader myself. I wanted to work as a detective among my own people, because I just know it better. I know my way about over there better, because it's where I come up at."

Ernie thought a moment and said, "Some of these extremely militant cats believe that the black man's world should be owned, operated, and controlled by the black people and that there should be no white people around, period. They should leave. To me, this is the extreme. And these cats wear sandals and robes and all those things, they let their hair grow out a foot long, and they say, 'We're seeking our identification.' Well, to me, I don't *want* to be identified in that way. I want to be identified as American, rather than as African."

Ernie stood up and paced about the room. "I mean," he continued thoughtfully, "I'm *proud* of my African heritage, but where I am *now* and where I've been all my life, here in Chicago, it isn't a good thing. I want to merge into Wall Street or Madison Avenue, in a manner of speaking."

As he paced the room, I could see that he had dressed for duty in black, newly shined shoes with tassles; long, black socks; neatly pressed gray pants; gold-rimmed green cufflinks on a pale-blue shirt; and dark-green tie. He also wore a navy-blue jacket with silver buttons. Two guns were concealed on his belt.

"I want to walk around without people saying I'm an oddity or an oddball," he said. "In other words, I want to merge into the mainstream of the American scene. I don't want people looking at me and saying, 'Look at him, he comes from Africa.' To me, this is not my bag. So some guys can call me an Uncle Tom, but I don't *feel* like no Uncle Tom. I'm as militant as anybody else, as any other Negro, when it comes to getting what I'm rightfully due. I want everything I have coming to me and I don't want to be obstructed from it—but *not* because I'm colored. I'll be militant, but I don't want to wear travel garb. I don't want to be an oddity one way or another, unless it comes to my profession. There, I *like* to stand out—you know, in my work, being a real good detective."

I asked if there were many Negro policemen who would be considered militant. "Sure," said Ernie. "You're looking at one. But I don't know of any black cops who preach race hatred. If a guy who's a police officer is very extreme *that* way, he's in trouble. There are many who want more identity with their African heritage, but if a cop hates whites he'd better not broadcast it so people can hear it. We're supposed to be impartial and so forth. They'll fire a white racist in short order, and they'd do the same thing if they found a black racist on the force."

Ernie interrupted himself here, laughing. "One thing, after every riot there's a rash of resignations from white cops. At least a dozen or so resign each time. And that's not too logical, because the perpetrators of a riot don't particularly care what color the policeman is. When they see that uniform, it's just like raising a red flag in front of a bull. Color don't mean too much in a riot. They'll shoot me just as quickly as they'll shoot a white cop—if we're in uniform. The badge and the uniform represent what they're rioting about. We're the enemy, and even if I *am* black, I'm the enemy along with the white cop. Of course, I don't wear a uniform, so that helps. . . ."

Sitting down again, the detective folded his hands and spoke thoughtfully. "On the other hand, without a doubt, being colored is an advantage on this job. Yes, sir. And now, at this particular time, with this turmoil and social change, we have situations where it's almost impossible for a white policeman to function effectively—because all the doors are closed when he comes in. Before all this change started taking place, a white policeman, just by the advantage of *fear*, could go in and do something or get information, because the people were *afraid* of him. Now, he's afraid of *them*. Also, we colored cops know the people's habits and everything better. We understand 'em better. We know how they think, and the Negro people figure that we're harder to fool than a white detective, say. That's why so many of the ultramilitants hate us so much.

"To me, though, I figure that the sooner the riot is over with, the less likelihood that more of my people will be killed. So I do it with dispatch, if possible. One time in a riot a colored man with a whole lot of loot said to me, 'Hey, man, you're black like we are —so what are you doing? You're grabbing people and all this, but you ought to be laying back. You're out here making a big deal, but we're all the same color!' And I looked at him and thought to myself, 'My mother worked for seven years like a slave and I'm gonna let him burn her building down?'

"I feel like a riot in a ghetto neighborhood would be a difficult thing without colored policemen, because I *know* that they're hurting my own people, in my own neighborhood. Without colored policemen, there'd be no one to put in there who could move with any amount of safety. If there were just all white policemen, the man downtown would be in a hell of a fix.

"Personally, I advocate the NAACP-type movement. I like that, because they're not extreme one way or the other. They just give a steady push for an equal-rights bag. And the Urban League, too. This is the practical way of going about the thing.

"One of my suggestions to the Police Department once was that courses in urban sociology be taught to the police recruits. Because many times, white and black alike are unfamiliar with the reasons for the problems that we have here. They need an insight into the possible reasons and a crash course in psychology. Then they would know better how to deal with the people they come in contact with, and to understand how criminals got that way, as well as helping them to understand themselves. Older policemen say they've been getting along without it, but have they really been getting along? I don't know what happened to the suggestion. I never heard anything about it."

At three o'clock Ernie was ready to leave his apartment again. We walked to his three-year-old Cadillac and in a minute we were swerving past the University of Chicago and heading for his office.

"To me," Ernie remarked, "the man's got to have a little old-fashioned mother wit, a little street savvy or common sense, mixed in with some education. You learn alleywise, and on the street you sometimes have to improvise as you go along. I know some cops with lots of college, but they can't put a patch on a good policeman's behind. That's because they haven't come from the ghetto. But if the man with street savvy has an edu-

cation as well, he's operating with the best of both worlds."

I learned later that for the past three years Ernie had been attending criminology courses every Monday evening. As the leader of a three-man detective squad, he is known to perform very well. Ernie and his partners act as a follow-up team, working on homicides, serious stabbings, shootings, beatings, rapes, sex crimes, crimes against children, incest, and anything else that falls within the category of "Homicide—Sex and Aggravated Assault."

The detectives operate from an office in an ivy-covered building surrounded by grass, trees, and shrubs. The park serves as a temporary shelter from the 300,000 people among whom the detectives work, and the office is laden with files and records that further depersonalize the population. The most important file cabinet includes all homicide cases, 90 percent of which have been solved. Some of these files have red tags attached to them, signifying that the offender is "known but flown." The unsolved cases have become part of each detective's total routine workload. A few nights before, Ernie had worked from four in the afternoon until nine the following morning, on a murder case several months old. He had worked on it piecemeal, when he was not involved in something else, and "moved in on it" when enough information had been obtained to make an arrest.

This afternoon he had tried to pick up the seventeen-year-old boy, Donald, who was wanted for five shootings, hoping to "make the grab" on his own time. "The boy hadn't *killed* anybody yet," Ernie said, "but he did an awful good job of *wounding* five people."

"What happened, Ernie?" asked another detective.

"Ah, the usual thing. Parents protecting their children. His mother probably thought

I was going to frame him or something. Next time, I'll probably be looking for him on a murder charge." To me he added, "I'm sure she knew where he was. By the time we could have gotten to his father's house, he would have been over the hill and gone. Cat-and-mouse bullshit! He'll convince his mother that he's innocent. He's been accused of five shootings—at least five that I know of. But it'll never occur to his mother that maybe she should let the law take its course. She'll probably send him away, believing she's doing the right thing. Man, I don't think I've ever met a parent who thinks the kid is guilty."

The backlog of cases in this office continues to grow faster than the unit can dispose of them. By July 4 there had been 75 murders in the unit's area this year, whereas it had taken until September the previous year for that many homicides to occur. The detectives constantly check with the hospitals to see if patients on the "critical board" have died, in which case they become victims of homicide. Some of the men work only from the "sex board," a thick catalog of the most perverted activities imaginable. "It makes good reading," one detective informed me. Also, there is a huge backlog of minor assault and sex crimes to be solved, and these are apportioned to members of the unit as "spare-time" work.

However, as the boss put it to Ernie, "Dead people take precedence in this office," so that only a select portion of the new reports—which are stacked high from each preceding day—is acted upon with immediacy. Added to the rise of violent crimes is the current unrest in the ghetto, which has depleted manpower. "Some of the dicks are back in uniform," Ernie said. "They're still detectives, but they're back in the hole for civil disorders. We're the survivors, so to speak. We have two teams going out tonight,

but there should be four. The boss wants us to keep below 75 hours of overtime, but it's hard. I've got 200 hours stockpiled, so if I spend only 2 or 3 hours extra, I don't even bother to put in a slip."

The two men who work on Ernie's team, Roy Jackson and John Brice, are also Negroes. Jackson is tall and lean, wears a thin mustache, and occasionally quotes from Freud and Descartes. Originally from Birmingham, Alabama, Roy appeared sensitive about life in general and his work in particular. He accumulated ninety semester hours in education, the fruits of three years spent at Illinois Teachers College, and his wife was studying for her master's degree in psychology at Roosevelt University.

Brice is a powerfully built man, overweight, in fact, who seems constantly on the verge of laughter. "He has no guile, no trickery in him," Ernie said of his smiling partner. "I keep him in the background sometimes, because he's such a bad liar. He's so damned straightforward! He loves to eat, read, and laugh. Can you imagine a cop with an *account* at a bookstore? He's always reading. And he looks less like a cop than anyone I know. He and I went to school together, but John was a good little boy."

When I later met him, John explained to me, "I never figured that I was tough enough or smart enough to be a cop. Then I saw some of the idiots that were *on* there and I said, 'Well, damn, I *know* I can do *that* well.' I walked into the police school and saw Ernie sitting there and I said, 'What is this? I thought this guy was in the penitentiary! This guy's gonna be a *cop?* Damn, they're letting *everybody* in here!' It turned out Ernie was suited for the job real well."

"John was one of the little boys I used to pounce on," Ernie said.

"That's right," John agreed, laughing again. "I remember one time when me and this guy Frank—we were strictly school-boys, he was on the order of me—saw Ernie and got scared. Frank and me avoided all trouble. So one day during high school we were walking down the street and we start to go into a housing-project playground and he says, 'Hey, wait a minute! That's some of the 13 Cats over there! Man, those guys'll rob you in a minute!' I looked and I said, 'Hey, I *know* that shorter fella there!' He says, 'You *know* him?' and I says, 'Yeah, that's Ernie Cox.' And so we walked past them, and Ernie and his friends were glaring at us, and I waved and shouted, 'Hi, there, Ernie! How're you doing, Ernie? Hi there, it's *me,* John Brice! Hi, Ernie!' You might say that Ernie sort of protected me."

I learned that John had worked a great deal in order to buy his mother and father a home outside the ghetto. However, almost as soon as they moved in, his father and then his mother died. John, who had been divorced, remarried and brought his new wife, with her four children, into the house.

"John always wanted a family," Ernie told me privately. "He used to teach Sunday school. He's no popsicle, though. He's fearless, actually; more so than me. He would go after a guy without calling for help—that is, even if he *could* call for help. I'm responsible for his and Roy's conduct, and the boss don't want us to take chances. But John would work the average man to death. He'll konk off after twenty-four hours, but he won't complain. While other guys are ducking work, he'll volunteer. He's got a memory like an elephant, too. The only trouble with him is he can't act, can't play a part. He starts laughing or something. He's useful for squares—old folks, children, or church women. Straights. I use certain guys for certain situations. Myself, I handle hoodlums, thugs, slickers. A detective needs a cast of characters available to play different roles, to get certain people to open up and talk. Roy is good for the young ladies."

Roy wears colorful sports jackets, occasionally with a pink shirt and black tie. Unlike Ernie and John, he wears only one gun; and a small one at that, in order to diminish the bulge in his clothing. Ernie is fond of kidding him by saying, "Hey, brother, when are you gonna get a *man*-sized gun?" From behind dark glasses, Roy's eyes usually smile in response, although his lips remain unchanged. Alluding to a certain craftiness about himself, he said, "I used to run a gambling concession in high school, over on the West Side. It was my 'thing.' You know —dice, poker, and so on."

Ernie, Roy, and John maintain a schedule whereby two of them are always working together. This particular Wednesday was John's holiday, but he had come in to do some paper work. Roy was also there, typing some reports.

"I've got about five things for us to do," Ernie told him.

"Don't count on it," Roy replied. "We've got to get over to the hospital. I got a call from a guy named Wilton James who says his brother was murdered. The body might still be at the hospital. Also, there's been a drowning that we'd better check on. And if we have time, I want to stop in and see the young boy who lost his kidney in that shooting."

Outside one ground-floor window of the office, a family softball game was under way. Out another window, I could see an unusual scene. A Negro man in a bathing suit hung by his feet from the limb of a tree. A white detective had been sitting on the window sill, watching him periodically and shaking his head. "Hey," the detective shouted, "can't we go out and arrest that guy?"

"What for?" the commander asked.

"For hanging upside down!"

"What's wrong with that? There's no law against it."

"That's the possum," Ernie explained. "If you walk up to him he'll get embarrassed and hang blankets around himself so you can't see him."

"He makes me nervous," the first man said.

"I've talked with him," Ernie briefed me. "He hangs there for eight hours at a time—says it's healthy."

"Here's what I have on this James murder, so far," Roy interrupted, handing Ernie a brief report.

The information was, indeed, scanty. On Tuesday morning two radio-car patrolmen had been called to the Acco Hotel in the heart of the South Side ghetto. There they found Rudolph James on the floor of his tiny, third-floor room: "Officers found victim unconscious and unable to talk. Victim had multiple contusions on face, arms, and legs, abrasions on right elbow and a possible skull fracture. Victim was brought to hospital, remained in deep coma until death in hospital Wednesday. Location of murder: unknown. Offender(s): unknown. Motive and manner: unknown."

In the unmarked car on our way to the hospital, Ernie and Roy expressed their thoughts to me about an unsavory aspect of the detectives' job: the handling of dead bodies.

"You know something that has happened to me?" Roy said. "I can't remember the guy's face. Can't ever remember the faces of the bodies. I really can't. That may be a psychological factor on my part, but I block out the face. Anything about the *body* I remember, but already I begin to forget the face. It might be healthy, psychologically, because I sleep better at night."

Ernie added, "When I first started on homicide, I got a kind of quickening feeling —a lump, you know? Smelling the bodies and all that kind of thing. I was kind of apprehensive about handling them. I mean, if I didn't have to handle them I wouldn't do it. If I could get around it somehow, I did. But now, I don't feel nothing, or at least it doesn't bother me as much. Now they're just a problem, a professional problem. Now I'm anxious to get to handling it, to get the clothes off and see where the wounds are, to get to positioning where the missile went in the body, to find out how many times he was cut and so on—because many times, there are a lot of wounds under the clothes that you don't see. . . .

"So now, I don't even get bothered. When I'm handling a dead person—after they're dead and then it's just a large piece of flesh—I try to see *how* it happened, rather than think about *what* actually occurred. I mean, I just don't say that I'm dealing with something valuable. I don't feel that this is a dead man or a dead woman or a dead child. I feel like I can help him if I find out why he *got* this way. A lot of times you find out why he got this way and when you *do* find out, you feel like, well he asked for it. Personally, you feel that. To me, though, I'm going to try and, at this point, and when we first get on any homicide, try to get the most expeditious answer. I mean, the truest, quickest, most accurate account as to how the dead man got this way. You just, I mean you just . . . . Once they're dead, as I say, you just don't feel like it's . . . . You don't have any compassion any more. It's just a cold thing, a job, and I want to get through with it, without missing anything."

At the hospital a nurse said that the body of Rudolph James had already been taken to the morgue. A doctor added, "The guy was just beaten up all over. No bullets, no knife cuts, or anything like that—just a terrible beating."

"Did he say anything?" Ernie asked.

"No. He never regained consciousness."

The emergency section of the hospital was crowded as usual, and I stood with Ernie and Roy a few moments while they looked in various rooms for the body of the drowning victim. At least 200 people lined the hallway, packed together in grief. Nearly all of them were black. Some were unconscious or bleeding profusely, and others were weeping softly—for themselves or their friends or loved ones—and still others were yelling and banging on the walls. It was almost impossible for the interns to wheel a dying patient through the crowd. The nurses and doctors appeared so far behind that several times they seemed out of control.

"It's like all the horror of the city bunched in one place," Ernie commented. "And each one of 'em has a story. There's some background music behind each of them wounded people."

"There's never a slack," Roy added. "It sometimes takes from one to twelve hours to get to someone, because so many of them are really bad off."

Two young, white patrolmen were sitting in the corner of a crowded room where a nurse was trying to bring about a semblance of order. The officers were waiting for detectives to arrive so that they could complete their "dead-on-arrival" report. Trying to make themselves heard above the sounds of wailing and moaning, Ernie and Roy exchanged information with the patrolmen. The nurse, one of the few white people, looked up and frowned, muttering, "You guys are always taking up room." Then in a loud voice she said to Ernie, "Will you please get out of the way?"

We stepped aside as a sheet-covered body was wheeled slowly through the confusion. "That's ours," Roy said. We followed the body down the hall and into a small room, where it was wheeled behind a pair of white curtains. To the intern, Ernie asked, "Is this the boy who drowned?" The young man nodded and hurried away.

The detectives rolled back the sheet, revealing the body of a sixteen-year-old boy. Ernie lifted one arm, Roy the other, and like two rubbery eels the arms fell dangling lifeless over the floor. The boy's body was large for its age, making it difficult to inspect. The boy was wearing only a small pair of black, elastic swimming trunks.

"He's in here."

"Oh, no! No!"

"Bobby! Bobby!"

The detectives stepped aside as members of the boy's family rushed into the small room. Ernie quickly covered the body again, but the boy's brother ripped the sheet back. Seeing the familiar face, he screamed, "Bobby!" Others surged inside—a sister, a friend, a girlfriend, another sister, the father. The brother began kicking the wall. The sister dropped to the floor, unconscious. For at least five minutes the room swirled with the moans and screams of the boy's family and friends. The two detectives stood by, waiting to get back to the body. Several times the girlfriend dropped to the floor and Ernie had to pick her up. "Please," he said, "you can't do anything now. . . ." Meanwhile, Roy tried to hold the brother back from damaging the wall. A nurse came in with a long needle and told Ernie to hold the sister who had collapsed. Now she was flaying her arms about. The nurse approached with the needle, the girl struggled but Ernie held on. She screamed, louder and louder, another nurse came in and helped to hold her down, she pleaded with her last surge of strength and the needle went in. . . .

At last, the room was cleared and the

detectives went back to their examination of the body, rolling it over and back, looking for any sign of suspicious injury. Satisfied that it had been an accident, the detectives walked outside, through the crowd, to another room in order to wash their hands. Then Ernie interviewed members of the family about the drowning. Had they been drinking? No, they said, although Ernie had smelled alcohol on the dead boy's body. Finally, we boarded the hospital elevator.

"That was a nice clean body," Ernie told me.

"I don't think there was any foul play," Roy said. "Just routine—although to the family, I don't imagine it was routine."

"I thought that wailing would go on all night," Ernie commented.

On the third floor of the hospital, there was none of the frantic activity we had just left. We walked through the dimly lit, quiet corridor, checking the room numbers. In one of the rooms lay a Negro boy, his body curled up and shaking.

"This is him," Roy said. "He was shot twice. Had his kidney removed. Now he's getting telephone threats—right here in the hospital—that if he brings charges they'll finish him off."

"How're you doing, man?" Ernie asked him.

Realizing that the boy was still frightened and worried, the detectives merely assured him that he would be taken care of. The boy, although constantly shaking, managed to smile.

"And don't worry 'bout them phone calls," Ernie advised as we left the room.

Rape Squad

GRACE LICHTENSTEIN

Sally Maxwell, her hands and feet bound with heavy twine, hobbled through the open door and pressed her neighbor's bell with her nose. "Help me!" she shouted. "I've just been robbed by two guys. And they raped me too!"

It was near quitting time on the 3-to-midnight tour at the Manhattan Sex Crimes Squad office Monday night when the call

From *The New York Times Magazine* (March 3, 1974), pp. 10, 61, 63, 65. Copyright © 1974 by The New York Times Company. Reprinted by permission.

came through. "West 74th Street," Detective Bill Carreras said, turning to his partner, Detective Ingeborg Wagner. "Off we go."

By the time the two detectives reached the Maxwell* apartment, Sally, a 25-year-old secretary whose dark brown hair fell almost to her waist, had already told her story once to a patrolman whose radio car had answered the neighbor's call to 911, the police emer-

*The names of the complainants and the circumstances of their cases have been altered at the request of the New York City Police Department.

gency number. The patrol car had taken her to a nearby hospital, where she was examined and vaginal smears taken. Now, two hours after the crime, she sat in her ransacked apartment with two friends who had come to take care of her.

While Bill Carreras dusted for fingerprints, Ingie Wagner, as everyone calls her, led Sally into the kitchen, alone, and gently began to ask questions, taking notes on a sheet of paper. "When did you first see them? . . ."

Sally had entered her building alone that evening without noticing the two men lurking in the hallway. Knives flashing in their hands, they had forced her into the elevator and demanded to be taken to her apartment. After searching fruitlessly for cash, they had settled on a television, some jewelry and several appliances. Almost as an afterthought, the older of the two pushed her into the bedroom, made her disrobe and raped her. Then he insisted the younger man do the same.

Sally smoked incessantly as she related the story, her voice quick, her movements jumpy. "I'm really very calm," she kept insisting to Ingie. "I'm just glad I'm not dead or cut up."

Ingie, a slim blond woman of 40 with a sympathetic air about her, nodded. "Did either man say anything to you? That's very important to us, because guys who do this more than once often repeat themselves. Any phrase?"

"Yeah," Sally replied. "The younger one really was pushed into it. He kept saying, 'Hurry up so we can get this over with.' When they left, he said to the other guy, 'Maybe we should leave the stuff and take her'."

Ingie quietly pressed Sally for a full description of both men—scars, height, weight, age, clothing, accents. She and Bill interviewed the neighbor to corroborate that the woman had been tied up and disheveled. They collected evidence—a possible fingerprint, and the twine used to tie Sally. As they prepared to leave, so did Sally, to spend the night at her friends' house. She appeared as composed as any New York career woman wise in the ways of the city's violence could be, under the circumstances. But as she left she remarked, "The first thing I'm going to do is take a shower. If I could wash myself down the drain I would."

"Opportunists. The guys were opportunists. They saw the shot so they took it. Basically, they're stickup men," declared Bill the next day as he prepared to follow up the Maxwell case. It was the kind of case he, Ingie and the 21 other investigators on the Sex Crimes Squad were growing all too familiar with. Together with more than 55 additional investigators assigned to the four other boroughs, they are the Police Department's field specialists in rape.

The concept of the Sex Crimes Squad is a new one, with borough units having been set up for the first time last fall as part of the New York Police Department's heightened concern with the crime of rape. The department's work was spearheaded by Lieutenant Julia Tucker, a dynamic 34-year-old administrator who was chief of the central Sex Crimes Analysis Unit created in December, 1972. Lieutenant Tucker gained national recognition for her work in developing a department of female rape investigators. Then, in late November, 1973, she was abruptly transferred to patrol duty in Brooklyn on less than 24 hours' notice. Her removal from the central unit left her many supporters among women's rights groups bitter. Despite demonstrations at Police Headquarters and City Hall demanding Lieutenant Tucker's reinstatement, however, the Police Department installed a new chief, Lieutenant Mary Keefe, in her place.

For two-and-a-half months, a curtain of silence surrounded the Tucker case. Her supporters felt she had been removed because she had become too vocal, too militant and too popular for the department's comfort. Her colleagues in the rape squad spoke of her in the warmly admiring way students recall inspirational teachers, yet they insisted they knew nothing about her transfer. Her successor, Lieutenant Keefe, acknowledged Lieutenant Tucker's pioneering work but shrugged off her removal by saying, "In a semimilitary operation like the police force this happens all the time."

Lieutenant Tucker, on patrol in the tough Fort Greene section of Brooklyn, maintained a low, almost invisible profile. The Police Department said she had been put there to gain experience for promotion to captain.

Then, last month, news stories reported that Lieutenant Tucker had been questioned in November by a grand jury investigating police corruption in an élite narcotics unit she had worked in several years ago. The stories implied she herself was involved.

Lieutenant Tucker vociferously disputed the reports, acknowledging she had appeared before the grand jury with a waiver of immunity but denying that she gave any testimony about illegal activities, "because I didn't know about any." The reports, she told me, seemed like another attempt on someone's part to discredit her. "Now I know why they transferred me," she said, "but I'm not going to be silent any more, because then it looks as if I'm guilty and I'm not. What more could they do to me?"

The news of the grand jury testimony shook the women's groups which had campaigned for Lieutenant Tucker. A few members, noting that she had been elected to the National Organization for Women's New York advisory board, wondered why she had not told them about the investigation. Lieutenant Tucker said she had no reason to believe her brief testimony was relevant or would make headlines.

When the rape unit was first organized, sex crimes were routinely investigated by detectives whose primary work was in burglaries, robberies or homicide. "Everyone did a half-baked job," admitted Sergeant Harry O'Reilly, the only man on the rape squad.

Rape victims occasionally complained that the police were insensitive to their plight, that they were rude during interrogation, that they indicated skepticism about the victim's story. There was no special training for dealing with rape victims, and a high percentage of them dropped out of the investigations of their cases before the police caught suspects. No statistics were kept on patterns of rape. Furthermore, a New York State law—repealed by the Legislature only last month—required that evidence, or a witness, corroborate the crime (even though no corroboration was required in robberies or assaults), which made it difficult for district attorneys to get enough evidence that would stand up in court. In the first half of 1972 the conviction rate on rape cases was an astoundingly minuscule 1.8 percent.

Starting with a staff of just three investigators, Lieutenant Tucker campaigned for the creation of a squad of detectives who specialized in sex crimes alone. She also inaugurated a special central number—577–RAPE (now discontinued)—that women could call to report rapes to policewomen, rather than men. She set up a computer system so investigators could cross–check a newly reported rapist's physical characteristics and *modus operandi* against those in unsolved cases, hoping to discover a link among them. (Lieutenant Tucker says many rapists are recidivists who commit the crime the same way each time.) She arranged "sensitivity" seminars at which psychologists advised detectives how to cope with victims' defense mechanisms, their families, their fears.

Many of Lieutenant Tucker's innovations were put into practice by the time she was transferred. The rape squad specialty was inaugurated in each borough, and squads included a few women. A second sensitivity seminar was held in December. The computer program is now installed.

Rape is considered by experts to be the least reported major crime, so any figures available on it are open to different interpretations. The number of rapes reported in New York in 1973 rose to 4,421, compared with 3,830 reported in 1972. How much of the increase can be attributed to women's more liberated attitude in telling about rape, how much to the public's knowledge of the rape analysis unit's existence and how much to an actual upsurge in rapes is not known. In any case, arrests on rape charges also rose during 1973, to 2,206 from 1,731 in 1972. Only the conviction rate did not show a similar increase.

The 577–RAPE number was never publicized enough for it to become the main line for reporting rapes. The special number was also plagued by hundreds of crank and obscene calls. It was discontinued in early December. Most reports of rape today are not called in to 233–3000 (the rape analysis unit) but rather to 911, which refers the case to the local precinct. The precinct then notifies the detective borough office, which notifies the borough sex crimes squad, which ultimately sends out either male or female detectives to interview the woman. Thus, it is still a man who usually has the first contact with a rape victim. (The borough squads had a total of 58 men and only 21 women in early January, 1974.) The rape analysis unit,

with its complement of 14 women and one man, has become primarily a statistics-gathering operation.

If a woman who has just been raped demands to talk to another woman, a female investigator will be sent to see her. But the option is not offered to her by the male detectives when they arrive on the scene; she must ask. Thus, Julia Tucker's dream of a strong central office staffed with women who could interview, counsel and sometimes simply "rap" with victims remains unfulfilled.

The Manhattan Sex Crimes Squad consists of a few nondescript rooms in the 13th Precinct on East 21st Street. Newspaper clippings, interoffice memos and retirement party announcements adorn the walls. One clipping headlines a police union officer's demeaning comments about women on the force; next to it a Xeroxed poster says, " 'Too much of a good thing is wonderful: Mae West'." Most of the detectives recite the full title of the squad and their own name when they pick up the phone, but one woman simply announces: "Sex!"

It was here, Tuesday afternoon, that Detectives Wagner and Carreras met Sally Maxwell and another complainant, Maria Perez, before heading out with them to do some identification work. (The squad is kept busy; during one week in January, traditionally a low–caseload month, it logged 16 new cases of rape or sodomy, several involving robbery as well.)

Maria, a bright–eyed, nervous 18-year-old, had told her story to Ingie Wagner the week before. She had been visiting a neighborhood bar in East Harlem when six men had surrounded her, stuck a gun in her side and forced her outside into a car. They had brought her to someone's apartment, where they took turns raping and sodomizing her.

(Forced anal, oral or any other nongenital intercourse is considered sodomy under the law.)

After they let her go, Maria had gone to a hospital, but she had also told her husband. The next night, he burst into the back room of the bar looking for the men. A fight erupted, a shot rang out and one of Maria's alleged abductors lay dead. Her husband was now in the Tombs, charged with homicide.

Maria, even more than Sally, seemed to have recovered from the initial trauma. Earlier, she had led the detectives to the apartment, where they had collected some immigration papers belonging to one man. This allowed Ingie to trace his photo, and Maria had unhesitatingly picked it out among those of other men in a "photo lineup." They were on the man's trail. In addition, Maria thought she might see the other men hanging out on the neighborhood streets.

"You know what I'm gonna do when this is all over?" Maria, a tough–talking street kid, was saying as the four of them drove uptown. "I'm gonna rent a hall and throw a party for all my friends. Even if it costs $400!" The two detectives laughed.

Sally simply stared at her, transfixed. The two of them lived 30 blocks apart but they were worlds apart in lifestyles and upbringing. Suddenly, a crime had made the Puerto Rican street kid and the Scarsdale–born secretary sisters.

At first Sally talked only to Ingie, whom she complimented by saying, "You don't look like a policewoman." (With 10 years' experience in catching con men, looking for missing persons and setting traps for illegal butcher–shop abortionists, Ingie still could pass, as Sally remarked, for a department–store buyer.) Sally continued to insist that she was not "uptight" about the rape, but

she kept mulling it over aloud, driven by the need to talk it out of her system. It was a defense mechanism that psychologists had told the rape investigators about: Give the victim a chance to "ventilate."

"Three days, that's all I had been in the apartment," she was saying. "All those fancy locks I bought—some good they did. I'm never going to tell my parents. They'd only start with the questions again. 'Why are you living alone? The neighborhood. . . .' They really cleaned me out, those guys. They were very honest about it. They told me they made their living that way. Funny. They were surprised when I told them I knew karate. . . ."

Maria perked up. Why hadn't Sally chopped the guys down? Sally threw her an ironic look. "With two knives facing me? In my next life, maybe. When I'm reincarnated as a gun I'll use karate."

Maria puffed furiously on her cigarette. "I wish I were a guy so I could've hit 'em," she said of her own experience. "With a gun pointed at you?" Sally said wryly.

"A guy would've hit 'em, gun or no gun," Maria insisted. "They don't care, guys don't. My father, if he ever gets his hands on those guys, there ain't gonna be no trial. . . ."

"Listen, Sally did the right thing," Ingie told Maria in the voice of a stern schoolteacher. "When a guy's standing with a weapon on you, you don't take chances." Maria didn't seem convinced. Her eyes gleamed with the thought of revenge. But beneath the surface, the hurt left by the rapes remained, even if only an alert observer like Ingie could recognize it. When Ingie, in the first interview, had asked Maria to describe the actual crime, the girl had burst into tears. Now, apropos of nothing, she said casually, "I haven't slept since last week. I keep getting bad dreams."

The two detectives drove the women first to East Harlem, where they slowly cruised the streets looking for men who might have been in the bar with Maria. "What about that dude in the hat? How about that fancy one talking to the woman?" Bill kept asking as Maria peered out the window at the men clustered on street corners and in front of bodegas. No luck.

Bill turned onto the F.D.R. Drive and headed downtown to a musty old building on Broome Street in which the Bureau of Criminal Identification is located. There, he and Ingie picked out boxes of mug shots for them to look through—Latin robbers under 30 years old in the right height range for Sally (the older man had mentioned to her that he had a record), Latin rapists for Maria.

As she started flipping through the photos, Sally wondered aloud whether she'd be sure of recognizing either man. "Don't worry," Ingie said reassuringly. "You'll know him. The minute you see him, you'll say, 'That's it!'"

After an hour of searching, Maria had come up with one possible suspect and Sally with two. "Watchya think?" Bill asked Sally, holding the two photos one on top of the other. "Is this them?"

"I couldn't swear to it," she said candidly. "I'm 95 percent sure of the younger one. Maybe if I saw them in person. . . ."

"Fine," replied Bill, a smartly dressed young man with a mustache and a brisk, confident manner. "We're not gonna lock him up. But we can pick him up on suspicion, put him through a lineup and take it from there."

Bill and Ingie took the photos to another office in order to have a clerk pull out the "yellow sheets"—prior arrest records—of the suspects. When Bill filled out his request slip, the clerk took it without a word. Ingie, however, was asked to show her shield be-

fore she was given the files. (When asked if the clerks were suspicious of policewomen, Ingie shrugged the incident off, explaining that Bill was probably better known to them.)

The yellow sheets showed that one of Sally's suspects had a long history of stickups in the city, while the other had been arrested on a robbery charge and later cleared. Bill and Ingie made plans to find the two men as well as to find Maria's suspect. The two detectives were in good spirits; the investigations seemed to be making progress.

By the time they drove the two women home, the streets were dark. "Bring me to my father's house again," said Maria. "I ain't goin' back home tonight." Neither was Sally. "I can't stay there," she said, her arms wrapped around her chest as if she were protecting herself. "What if they come back?"

Ingie put an extra ounce of assurance into her voice as she addressed Sally. "That's exactly the way every woman feels. She's sure they're going to come back. Well, don't worry about that. They'd have to be pretty dumb."

Sally still wasn't sure. "Don't they ever come back?" "One in a million," Bill said, a little too easily. The detectives were fibbing; only recently a brutal rapist had smashed through the bedroom window of a woman he had attacked a month earlier and raped her a second time. "You can't make them feel too dependent or too fearful," Ingie explained later. "It's almost like you're their psychoanalyst, or priest, or doctor."

Bill made arrangements to have Sally return to the station house the next day if they had picked up one man for a lineup. Over and over again, she relived the crime, becoming more and more insistent that it was the older man's fault.

Finally she said of the younger one, "He

was really nice about it. You know what? I won't charge him with rape. I'll just charge the older one. Can I do that?"

An outsider might have been incredulous at her attitude, but Bill's face showed nothing. "Charge both of them," he said evenly. "They both did it."

Ingie looked at her. "You think you're the first girl he's raped? You're not. And you probably won't be his last. The best thing is to get this guy locked up."

Sally's thoughts turned to the older man. "I'm worried about him. I don't care if I have to roam the streets myself, I'm going to find him."

"You let me worry about finding him, O.K.?" Bill said. "You just help me. We'll work together—a team."

Sally laughed. "Like an honest Bonnie and Clyde, huh?"

Sally and Maria were acting out a variety of the defense mechanisms the rape investigators had come to recognize, thanks to the lectures they had heard from psychologists, talks they had had with New York Women against Rape (a feminist organization that worked closely with Lieutenant Tucker) and their own experience.

"The big hangup," Lieutenant Tucker said in a recent interview, "is that the women seem to feel this is unique to them. At times they're almost losing their minds. It's a three–stage process. First, a fear of almost everything. Second, they think they're somehow responsible for what happened to them. That's where we can help. We tell them that to feel this way is normal. We have them rap about it. Sometimes parents or husbands feel guilty because they think they weren't protective enough, and they try to get the victim to stop talking. The third stage is anger: they want to get back at the guy."

Dealing with rape victims has had a pro-found psychological impact on some of the investigators themselves. "I try never to show shock when I'm interviewing even though I'm thinking, 'Oh, what a terrible thing'," said one policewoman. "I had my experiences as a kid with men in the movies, but thank God I've never been attacked. This is all so new to me."

The men have been affected too. "Before I came here," said Sergeant O'Reilly, "I was insensitive to women. I had handled some rape cases, but I made the common mistake of treating them like any other crime. I would treat a woman with the usual cordiality, but that's not enough—she needs a partner, a comrade."

Like the rest of the women, Ingie Wagner, a Brooklyn girl from Sheepshead Bay who suspects she became a police officer "because as a kid I loved Nancy Drew mysteries," feels that properly trained men can do as good an interviewing job as women can in most cases. The exceptions are real trauma cases, especially those involving older women who had lived sexually sheltered lives before they were raped.

"Only one woman out of 10 will refuse to talk to a man," Ingie said. "We live in an integrated world, and that's why I don't agree with a lot of Women's Lib. They want to keep men and women too separate. Sometimes dealing with a sensitive man right after being raped by a brutal one can really help a woman."

Police officers maintain that they "don't take the work home with them," and Ingie is no different. But there are small signs that the policewomen cannot remain entirely hard–nosed about this particular job. "It's funny," Ingie said, one night as we rode through the deserted Manhattan streets in her Volkswagen. "I never used to worry about being on the street, you know, in the dark. Never thought about it. But since I came on this squad, something's changed. When I get in my car now, alone, at night . . . I lock all the doors."

On Wednesday, Ingie concentrated on locating suspects for several other cases. Meanwhile, Bill and two other detectives drove to lower Harlem to pick up Sally's older suspect for a lineup. In the car they talked about another rape that had been reported the night before: A woman had been grabbed off a busy Lexington Avenue street corner and forced into a car. One detective remarked that there must have been 50 spectators in the immediate area. Bill snorted. "Remember Kitty Genovese," he said.

The detectives found Sally's suspect, a tall, handsome youth named Manuel, at home with his parents and brothers in a basement apartment, watching "Chase" on TV. "Your name has come up in an investigation," Bill explained as a brother translated into Spanish. "We'd like to take you downtown for a routine lineup. It won't take more than an hour, hour and a half." Only after they stepped out of the apartment, where his worried mother couldn't see, did the detectives pat the youth down for weapons.

It took some time to scare up four additional Latin men for the lineup, from neighboring precincts or the Police Academy, who were as tall as the 6-foot Manuel. While he waited for the men to report, Bill made phone calls to check the whereabouts of Sally's younger suspect, the one she was "95 percent" sure of.

"Son of a bitch," Bill said with a tight smile, putting down the phone after a call to an upstate prison. "The guy's been inside for two months."

After two full hours, with Sally waiting in one room, the suspect in another, Bill finally had four Latin policemen in street clothes ready to join the lineup. None looked even vaguely like Manuel. As he led Sally toward a one–way viewing mirror through which she could see the five men, each with a number hung around his neck, he assured her they could not see her. ("Watch the victims during a lineup," Ingie had told me. "Even if they don't say anything, you'll see the hands wringing, some will start to cry. . . .")

Bill watched Sally carefully as she scanned the lineup, almost as if he were afraid her knees would suddenly buckle. She took no more than 10 seconds. "It's none of them," she said positively.

Bill's shoulders sagged a little. "Can you tell which one you picked out in the photos?" he asked. "Number 2," she said. He glanced at her and said nothing. Manuel was Number 4.

With Sally's two main leads gone, Bill had another detective start constructing faces with her from a "Photo Fit" kit. A $123,000 grant from the Police Foundation in Washington had enabled Lieutenant Tucker to purchase kits for each squad to facilitate identification work on rape cases. The victim looks through pages of different hairlines, mouths, noses and eyes from which she may be able to compose a face that resembles that of her attacker.

But Sally had no luck with the Photo Fit. At nearly midnight, she looked at the mustached visage she had put together in the special glass frame and sighed, "It looks nothing like him."

The next day, Bill promised, he'd take her to look at a new set of photos in the robbery files. If that yielded nothing, he'd arrange for her to work with a police sketch artist. Meanwhile, he had asked the anti-crime squad of undercover men in Sally's home precinct to keep a sharp eye on her building; the rapists might make the mistake of returning. He had also fed the serial number of her stolen television into a computer, in case it might have been pawned. "Don't worry, kid," he told her in his best upbeat voice. "We'll get him." But to his fellow squad members he was less sanguine: "Who knows? Maybe we'll get lucky."

Even when a suspect has been fingered, the chances of successfully prosecuting an accused rapist are poor. "When I was first offered the command," Lieutenant Tucker said, "the chief of detectives gave me a week to think about it. I went to the library and read anything I could get my hands on about the injustices. The first thing I realized was rape. If you're not involved, you don't see how bad the law was. You wonder, 'Hey, how can this exist?' I felt embarrassed encouraging women to report rapes."

The corroboration requirement made it nearly impossible to put a rapist behind bars unless he had also committed a more easily provable robbery or assault along with a rape. According to a Police Department study, 40 percent of sex cases were dismissed even under the eased corroboration law that went into effect July 1, 1972. The main revision was that the new law did not require a witness to the act of rape itself. But it did require evidence of the attempt (torn clothing, semen present internally or externally) and of the victim's lack of consent (bruises, a neighbor who heard screams). All this, despite studies showing that the percentages of rape complaints later discovered to be unfounded was only 2 percent—the same as for all unfounded felonies.

Lieutenant Tucker, her successor, and every sex crimes specialist in the Police Department were vociferous in their demands for an end to corroboration. A strong lobbying effort by women's groups helped get a law repealing the corroboration provision passed by the State Legislature. It was signed by Gov. Malcolm Wilson in February.

While the old law was still in effect, detectives continued to collect as much evidence as they could. At the same time they battled to keep their complainants from falling through the cracks of a long–drawn-out criminal justice procedure that forces them to retell their rape story to prosecutors, lawyers, judges and juries, over and over, as months and sometimes years go by.

On Thursday night, Ingie got something of a break in Maria's case. One of the six alleged attackers, the immigrant in whose room the rapes took place, surrendered to a Harlem homicide squad after word got out that he was wanted for questioning in both Maria's case and her husband's homicide case.

At the spanking–clean homicide office on 126th Street, Ingie spent almost her entire nine–hour tour typing out papers and doing the busywork required for the "collar." (She was the only female detective on duty that night, so when other rape reports came into the squad, male detectives went out to handle the initial interviews.) Bernardo, the suspect, a small fellow of 24 with hangdog eyes, spent most of the time staring at his stacked–heel purple shoes. He looked neither deranged, sexually violent nor dangerous. ("Don't ask me what a rapist looks like," Ingie said. "They come in every shape and size and type.")

As she pressed Bernardo's inked fingers one by one onto an official print sheet, she smiled at him. "I hope you're not as nervous as I am," she said, chuckling. Then, to the homicide detectives: "It's only the second time I've done prints."

The homicide detectives were friendly and helpful. But at least one was concerned about many aspects of Maria's story. After being raped by six men, how come her hospital tests indicated she had suffered no internal or external bruises? How had she been able to "run for a taxi" afterwards? Ingie, who as a policewoman must be just as careful about every fact in a case, noted that the purely physical toll a rape takes on a victim varies depending on the woman's state of mind, her physique, her sexual experience.

While Ingie prepared to escort her prisoner to the desk sergeant, where Bernardo would be officially booked for kidnapping, rape and sodomy, another homicide detective was telling the story of the night he was assigned to ride a prowl car with a pretty young policewoman who had just been put on active street duty.

" 'Barbara,' I told her, 'I don't care whether you're behind a desk or behind the wheel—to me you're still a sex symbol!'

She turned red as a beet and transferred out two days later!" The rest of the detectives howled. Ingie didn't seem to hear. She was too busy thinking over the shaky facts in the Maria Perez case.

It was close to midnight when Ingie got back to the 13th Precinct after making sure Bernardo had been safely deposited in a lodging (overnight cell). Bill, his eyes half–closed, reported that Sally hadn't been able to find a face that evening in the new set of photos. "She moved back to West 74th Street tonight," he added. "Lotsa guts, that kid."

The phone rang, Bill listened for a few minutes, jotted something down on a scrap of paper and hung up. "Get your coat back on, Wagner," he said, winking at her. "We've got one on East 10th Street."

6

POLICE AND YOUTH

California troopers confronting members of a cruising motorcycle gang.

Youth connotes innocence, recklessness, danger and yet the possibility of character change. For the police, youth crimes may appear more threatening than those committed by adults because they are motivated less by rational, individual interests and more by group pressures and impulsiveness. Criminal law of most states provides for a special set of procedures for the processing of youth criminals. To the working policeman, however, an armed robbery may seem no less heinous because it has been committed by a fifteen-year-old person.

The motion picture *American Graffiti* nicely demonstrated society's dual vision of youth. The movie portrays graduation night in a small to middle-sized California town of the 1960s. The hero is a young man who has been awarded the Rotary Club scholarship to attend an Eastern college. He is threatened by, and becomes involved with, a gang called "The Pharaohs" who are involved in a variety of petty crimes that sometimes can result in serious consequences. The gang puts the hero up to loosening the rear axle of a police car so that when the police car gives chase, the rear end collapses. The movie finds the audience rooting for the youth who has successfully pulled off what is both a daring prank and a serious criminal act.

Suppose he were caught, which he isn't in the movie. Should he be given special treatment because of his age, his lack of a prior criminal record? Suppose it had been one of the gang members who had pulled off the prank. Should he have been given different treatment? There is a high correlation between gang membership and poverty, and also between social class and color. Should these factors be taken into consideration, and how?

The articles in this chapter reflect four different approaches to youth. One is that of the police in a black ghetto. They deal with minority youth who see the street as their turf and who develop a series of antagonistic compromises with the police. The second is that of police who perceive criminality in terms of the penal code and care little about the age of the offender. The third is that of the social service worker and the probation officer who may be more concerned about the individual character of the youthful offender than the act he or she has committed. The fourth is that of a police department attempting to deal directly with the problem of police relations with youth through a program in the San Diego high schools. This last article suggests that a greater understanding between youths and police may help curtail juvenile delinquency. Yet high school dropouts, disaffected minorities, and juvenile members of marginal associations—such as motorcycle clubs, car clubs, and street corner gangs—

are the least affected by the San Diego Police Department's program, and the most likely to be the objects of police inquiry. In light of this, it is useful to consider what other kinds of programs for police suggest themselves and what assumptions should underlie these programs.

A more general question is whether the criminal law is useful as a method, or at least the main method, for preventing the criminal misconduct of youths. When the criminal law is used, what kinds of processes should distinguish between youths and adults? To what extent does involvement with the criminal law inadvertently perpetuate delinquent behavior, that is, to what extent does policing itself cause juvenile delinquency? These are fundamental questions that have been dealt with by a variety of thoughtful scholars and officials. In response to them, society has over the years developed programs, institutions, and special procedures of varying kinds relating to youths, including the latest "diversion" from correctional institutions. Do these pay off, or are there other, better, methods available to police and other agents of law enforcement for dealing with the ever-present challenge of the youthful offender?

Gang Members and the Police

CARL WERTHMAN
IRVING PILIAVIN

From the front seat of a moving patrol car, street life in a typical Negro ghetto is perceived as an uninterrupted sequence of suspicious scenes. Every well-dressed man or woman standing aimlessly on the street during hours when most people are at work is carefully scrutinized for signs of an illegal source of income; every boy wearing boots, black pants, long hair, and a club jacket is viewed as potentially responsible for some item on the list of muggings, broken windows, and petty thefts that still remain to be cleared; and every hostile glance directed at the passing patrolman is read as a sign of possible guilt.

The residents of these neighborhoods regard this kind of surveillance as the deepest of insults. As soon as a patrolman begins to interrogate, the suspect can easily see that his

From *The Police: Six Sociological Essays* edited by David Bordua, pp. 57–75. Copyright © 1967. Reprinted by permission of John Wiley and Sons, Inc. This paper is based on data gathered during two separate research projects. The study of the police was supported by Grant MH–06328 from the National Institute of Mental Health at the United States Public Health Service and administered by the Survey Research Center at the University of California, Berkeley. The study of delinquent street gangs was initiated by the Survey Research Center on a grant from the Ford Foundation and was later moved to the Center for the Study of Law and Society on the Berkeley campus, where funds were made available under a generous grant from the Office of Juvenile Delinquency and Youth Development, Welfare Administration, U.S. Department of Health, Education, and Welfare in cooperation with the President's Committee on Juvenile Delinquency and Youth Crime.

moral identity is being challenged because of his dress, his hair style, his skin color, and his presence in the ghetto itself.

Negro gang members are constantly singled out for interrogation by the police, and the boys develop their own techniques of retaliation. They taunt the police with jibes and threaten their authority with gestures of insolence, as if daring the police to become bigots and bullies in order to defend their honor. Moreover, these techniques of retaliation often do succeed in provoking this response. When suspect after suspect becomes hostile and surly, the police begin to see themselves as representing the law among a people that lack proper respect for it. They too begin to feel maligned, and they soon become defensively cynical and aggressively moralistic. From the point of view of a patrolman, night sticks are only used upon sufficient provocation, and arrests are only made with just cause.

After studying the interaction between policemen and gang members for over a year, it became clear, at least to these observers, that behind the antagonism between these two groups lie a number of problems in the sociology of law. First, although the law and local custom overlap considerably in Negro ghettos, the disjuncture that remains brings the boys into conflict with the police, a conflict that has ecological as well as legal dimensions. Second, for a set of structural reasons to be discussed, the methods used by the police to locate suspects tend to undermine their legitimacy in the eyes of many ghetto residents. These cultural and structural conditions affect the nature of expectations in face-to-face encounters as well as the way both parties perceive and evaluate each other's behavior. This article is therefore an attempt to analyze the way patrolmen and gang boys first perceive or construct their respective worlds and then respond to the situation created for them by the actions and expectations of the other.[1]

THE PERSPECTIVE
OF THE GANG MEMBER

The Meaning and Uses of Streets

It is generally agreed that the transformation of city blocks and street corners into "hangouts," "territories," or "turfs" invests the streets with a special meaning to the members of a lower-class juvenile gang. Although much has been made of the unusual patriotism associated with these places and the quasi-military fashion in which they are occasionally defended, there has been little systematic study of the way gang members actually put the streets to use.

Sherri Cavan has suggested that a house is a place where "activities which would be unlawful in public places such as poker games and nudity, and activities which would be a source of embarrassment in public places such as family arguments and lovemaking can be freely engaged in." [2] On the basis of this criterion, the plots of public land used as "hangouts" by gang members must also be considered a sort of "home" or "private place." Activities such as poker games, arguments, lovemaking, drinking wine, and serious reading of comic books and newspapers are considered uniquely appropriate in this setting. As a rule, gang members use street corners for behavior that most ordinary adolescents would confine to a house or a car.

There are even occasions in the "home life" of gang members when the streets become functionally independent of all other settings. One function of expropriating hangout space in front of a doughnut shop or candy store is the ready access to a kitchen and to food. During the periods when entire days are spent in or around private space, gang members typically purchase a doughnut and coffee every few hours. This is often supplemented at regular intervals by food and liquor obtained through extralegal channels. The boys typically know the precise time when all deliveries to grocery stores, bakeries, homes, and liquor stores are made. The unguarded truck appears to be the major source of an unconventional food supply. Goods obtained from shoplifting (a more dangerous enterprise) are also used to stave off hunger, but shoplifting seems more often reserved for luxuries such as clothes, party supplies, and an occasional sporting good. A diet provided from these sources can sustain a boy for days, with the addition of a little cheap wine and a daily ration of about ten cigarettes.

Since all routine life functions are at one time or another performed on the streets, the conventional standards of public decorum are considerably relaxed. Entrance into the private space or hangout is occasioned by a noticeable relaxation of physical posture. Shoulders slump, shirttails appear, and greetings are exchanged with an abandon that is only achieved by people who usually receive houseguests in the kitchen. A good deal of time is also spent combing hair in front of store windows and dancing to rock and roll (often without a partner and without music) as if completely absorbed in the privacy of a bedroom.

Yet as soon as the boys leave the street corner, they become self-consciously absorbed in the demands of a public role. They pay careful attention to uniform—either casually immaculate ("looking sharp") or meticulously disheveled ("looking bad")— and cover the territory in the characteristic hiking style ("walking pimp"). Most of the boys would no sooner start a poker game two blocks away from the privacy of the hangout than more respectable citizens would think of making love in their front yards. Of course there are many notable exceptions to this rule, and on an irregular basis most boys do both.

The fact that gang members make relatively relaxed and private use of public streets does pose some problems for them, particularly when it comes to controlling the entrance of outsiders. People can take liberties in houses because a house is "an area of restricted entrance," [3] and those who enter other people's houses either by accident or against the implicit consent of their occupants are potentially subject to physical assault, legal action, or, at the very least, embarrassment.

With the exception of legal action, gang members also have these sanctions at their command. They use every means at their disposal to make outsiders accept the transparent walls they construct around the hangout. In practice, however, there are limits to the defensive measures that can be taken if one's private space is defined by most people, however innocently, as a public street corner.

Since practically every category of person who uses the public pathways is very nearly forced to violate whatever "rules of trespass" the gang members might like to make, it is easily understandable why the situation itself engenders some amount of bitterness among the boys. Over and above the negative feelings associated with this situational shortcoming, however, the gang members do recognize differences among those who actually or might potentially violate the boundaries of the hangout. Moreover, the feelings of hostility directed toward the various categories of outsiders can be ranked hierarchically.

The least disliked category of persons and those most accommodating to the claims made by a gang are the "familiars," mostly residents of the local neighborhood. They walk through even the most boisterous gatherings on private space as though they were not aware of its special character. This response to a potentially difficult situation is correctly interpreted by the boys as a sign that their claims to privacy are being politely accepted. The potential conflict between those who use this physical space as a living room and those who use it as a public thoroughfare is neatly resolved by having both parties studiously pretend to ignore the presence of the other. Occasionally a "familiar" will nod or smile at members of the club. At this time both parties seem to accept a definition of the situation as neighbors whose back doors are always open to one another's unannounced appearance.

More disliked and less accommodating are the "unfamiliars." These persons are not known to gang members, and thus there is no prior mutual understanding as to how the situation of potential conflict is to be resolved. Gang members communicate their claims on the hangout by calling an abrupt halt to verbal interchange in such a way as to suggest that a legitimate setting for private conversation has been rudely intruded upon. The members then begin to stare, and out of the hostile silence may come a wisecrack or a taunt. The boys are usually willing to accept a noticeable increase in walking pace and lowered eyes as sufficient implicit apology. An "unfamiliar" who continues to behave impolitely, either by refusing to hurry out of the space or by challenging the reality offered to him by the boys, becomes eligible for sanctions otherwise appropriate to a common housebreaker.

Usually, however, these illegal sanctions are not invoked. Gang boys have other less legally problematic ways of terrorizing casual observers, and one distinct class of favorites involves riding roughshod over the numerous rules of etiquette that organize routine behavior in public places. The boys may come within short range of a stranger, for example, and ask to "borrow" whatever the person happens to possess, be it tires from a used car salesman, a bicycle from a young boy, or money from practically anyone. This tactic constitutes a dramatic demonstration to most people of how much they are dependent on mundane conventions to maintain the assumption that one is usually safe around strangers. Similarly, the simple act of refusing to move when standing directly in the path of a passerby can destroy the faith of any witness in the orderly character of their immediate social world.

Although intentional violations of etiquette are obviously not crimes, they often succeed in doing considerable psychic damage to their targets. The stranger may give a gang boy money, walk around him if he is blocking the way, or pretend to ignore his antics altogether, but he will be apprehensive because he does not know what lies immediately ahead. With the threat of violence in the air, these situations become "disorganized." [4]

Yet as far as gang members are concerned, both "familiars" and "unfamiliars" share a single redeeming trait; neither can usually avoid trespassing on the street corner. They therefore cannot really be blamed for their presence since they are also the victims of an uncontrollable geographical factor—the awkward arrangement of streets. But there are other categories of persons who, like gang members, make something special out of public space. They are not forced for material reasons to violate the boundaries of the hangout. They make their own sets of social claims on access to the street corner.

The first of these special people are the members of rival gangs. Like the "familiars," they are willing to support the reality of claims to a private use of the street corner. Given the prestige system that exists among gangs, however, they have a vested interest (although rarely consummated) in obtaining unconditional rights of access both to the hangout and to the larger "territory" of which it is a part. Next to the rumble, the "surprise attack" on a hangout is considered the ultimate declaration of all-out war. Admittedly these events are quite rare, but should a gang ever win a total victory in one of these wars, the symbol of their success would be unconditional access to the hangout. [5]

The police are the most despised and least accommodating threat to a gang's conception of a hangout. Like gang members, the police have a vested interest in imposing a set of normative claims on the people who use the streets. The very places that are defended like homes by gang members also constitute places of work or "beats" to the police, and the home-like uses to which gang members put the streets are often perceived as threats to the patrolman's task of maintaining the conventional rules that ordinarily govern behavior on them. Although the boys attempt either subtly or violently to convince outsiders that their behavior at the hangout is a strictly private affair, the police tend to insist with equal conviction that all behavior on public property is their legitimate concern. The relationship between gang members and policemen thus has its roots in an ecological conflict over claims to final authority in the same setting. The Chicago police apparently have a phrase that expresses this relationship. When they are annoyed at a gang for their behavior at a hangout, they will say "Gi'me that corner!"

In practice, the police usually do make some concessions to the boys and allow them a privileged use of the streets. Patrolmen often tolerate drinking and gambling at the hangout, activities that become suitable grounds for arrest in other parts of the neighborhood. Under no conditions, however, is the hangout ever considered a completely invulnerable shield against the authority of the police. It is typically under constant surveillance, and the police even stage periodic "shakedowns" as a reminder to the boys that final authority for their behavior on the streets rests with the public's official landlords. A gang member describes a typical shakedown:

> One time me and a couple of friends, we came down to the corner on Monday night because we was supposed to have our meeting. And we was standing there on the corner bullshitting like we always do, and there was only four of us. Then this cop on a motorcycle pulled over and walked over to us. I seen him before. He rides around the neighborhood a lot. He didn't say nothing. He just zipped down his jacket and there was his big old billy club. And then he started asking questions, identification, what were we doing, and all like that. And he searched us and got our names down on the book and everything. We wasn't doing anything except what we usually do on that corner—stand there bullshitting. They do anything to get our names on that book. You know. They want us to know they in charge.

Gang Boys and the Law

This ecological conflict thus has a legal dimension. The view of fighting held by gang boys, for example, is clearly a case in which the law and the customs conflict. The police are often called upon to break through layers of screaming girls in order to separate a pair of street-style gladiators, and one patrolman even suggested that the worst injuries he had sustained as an officer had been leg bites received from females on these occasions. Yet to gang boys, most of these fights are both honorable and necessary. They were either challenged, insulted, or hit first, and thus they are always bitter when penalized by the police:

> Like that time that me and this kid from the Sabines was having this big fight up at school. He hit me during gym class. It was sort of accidental, but, see, I said something to him, and then he said something back and so we had this fight. The girls was going crazy. Jumping up and down and screaming and everything like they do. I guess this cop thought there was a riot going on or something cause he really came busting in there. Well, he grabbed us and threw us into the car and all that old shit. We tried to tell him what we was fighting about, but he wouldn't listen. Them cops is something else, man. What he expect us to do? Have one of them duels with guns or something?

There are other situations, however, in which the formal legal status of a disorder is more ambiguous, and these situations can cause trouble when both the police and the gang boys lay claims to the benefit of the doubt. For example, when strangers or "unfamiliars" are being treated to gross violations of etiquette or to other such attacks on their faith in social order, the police quite naturally feel constrained to take action. Yet from a gang member's point of view, the legal issues involved in disorganizing a social situation are not always clear-cut. For example:

> Last Sunday we went to see about buy-

ing a car. So we went down to a shop. We were out there parked, and this friend of mine was trying to con the guy into giving him some tires. He was standing there next to this Merc saying, "Why don't you give us the tires?" So the guy says, "No, I'm gonna sell it, and who'd want to buy a car with the tires gone?" So we were trying to open the door, but the guy wouldn't give us the keys to open the door. So there were about ten of us there, and it was in the daytime, and we was just messing around. You know, laughing and everything.

So finally this cop comes by. This fat slob. He was drunk when he got out of the car cause his shirt was out, man. So the dude gets out, and he comes up to me and he say, "What's wrong?" And I go, "What do you mean, what's wrong?" I wasn't trying to get smart with him. I was just saying it. And he goes, "Don't get smart! I was just asking you what's wrong?" I say, "I'm not trying to get smart!" So then he goes, "Now you are!" I didn't say nothing. I just shut up.

So he walks over to this other friend of mine and he goes, "What seems to be the trouble?" But my friend didn't say nothing. So he pulled out this club, and he came over to me and pushed me against the car and he goes, "So you're a smart guy huh?" So I say, "No." And then I smelled him. He must have been drinking wine cause I smelled it all over his breath so I knew he was drunk. So I moved away from him. But he goes, "Come over here!" I didn't want to get next to him 'cause I knew he was going to try something.

So after that, the jerk, he stands out in the middle of the street and he says, "Well, if there's any trouble and you want it settled, I'll settle it!" And he starts slapping the club on his hands and walking around to see who he can hit. So we start telling him there ain't no trouble or nothing. And the guy's older brother, he was twenty-one, he came out and said, "What's wrong?" And the cop goes, "Who's asking

you? I'm asking the questions, not you!" Smart dude you know. We didn't want to offend him 'cause we knew he was drunk. So he walked up to me again. I don't know what was wrong with the dude! He trying to do something! He says, "I'm gonna give you three minutes to get off the street!" He can't give you three minutes to get off the street when you're not doing nothing, right? So we were laughing.

After a few minutes we got in the car and started driving around. And the first thing you knew he started following us. We went around the corner and stopped. And he throw me in the car and goes, "Now I'm taking you down to the station!" I say, "For what?" And he goes, "Because I told you to get out of here and you didn't do it!" So I tried to stick up for my rights, and I asked what he was taking me in for. I say, "Just 'cause I was on the street?" And he goes, "Yeah."

Finally, there is the issue of the role played by the police in protracted conflicts between gang boys and other segments of the community, particularly local store owners, school personnel, and Recreation Department officials. Much of the vandalism in low-income neighborhoods is directed at these targets, and the reasons for attack are often not hard to find. The following quote, for example, was taken from a Negro gang boy whose colleagues had just ransacked a local grocery store and been sent to jail.

I know why them cats did it, and I bet they ain't sorry. Even now. We used to go to this place all the time to buy Cokes and stuff, and this Chinaman who run the place, he didn't like us. He'd sometime call us "boy" and "nigger" and be hollering that we stealing stuff, and when we start talking back to him, he'd quick turn around and start calling the cops. Then the cops would come. You know, like they always do. About fifteen minutes or an hour late. And by that time we just be standing around in front of this place waiting on them. Well, one day we walked in and this Chinaman, he tell us he don't have no Cokes. But we can see them. They just sitting there behind this glass. So then he says, "Okay." He gonna sell us the Cokes. But he gonna charge us eighteen cents. So Leroy got mad and just grabbed one, and then the cops picked him up. They didn't do nothing to him. Just rode him around or something. But that made Leroy even madder so he went and wrecked the place. Man, you shoulda seen it. Glass all smashed. Cans all over the floor. They got Leroy and them. It was in the papers. But if they got out, I bet they gonna do it again.

The Situation of the Patrolman

As William Whyte observed some thirty years ago, the police and the gang boys do not always agree about *what* rules the police should enforce or about *how* they should enforce them. Whyte said:

> The policeman is subject to sharply conflicting social pressures. On one side are the "good people" of Eastern City, who have written their moral judgments into the law and demand through their newspapers that the law be enforced. On the other side are the people of Cornerville, who have different standards and have built up an organization whose perpetuation depends upon freedom to violate the law.[6]

This conflict forces patrolmen to make a decision about which set of standards to enforce, and Whyte's advice to them about this choice was unambiguous. "Under these circumstances," he said, "the smoothest course for the officer is to conform to the social organization with which he is in direct contact and at the same time to try and give the impression to the outside world that he is enforcing the law."[7]

From the point of view of a patrolman, however, this advice is not quite as helpful as it might sound, since it still leaves unanswered the question of precisely what "conforming" to local standards involves. It is clear, for example, that the residents of most low-income communities, gang members included, expect the police to stand for *something*. The boys, in fact, are exceedingly contemptuous of patrolmen who know that legal standards are being broken but who are either too frightened or too cynical to act. If a patrolman tolerates all behavior, legal and illegal alike, he is likely to be defined by gang boys either as "chicken" or as "corrupt."

> Man, you should have seen them cops out at the Point on Saturday night. Zeke, and Orville, and Percy (gang workers) and them were there. They can tell you. Five carloads of cops was there, lights flashing and everything. And everybody is just standing around after this party. Fights going on, girls screaming, everything. And then this cat pulls out a gun and starts firing. Man, he was five feet away from them cops and they stood there! Just stood there looking! Somebody coulda got killed or something. Or maybe they just didn't care. Maybe they was saying, "Why not let them niggers go kill each other anyway. They ain't got no sense."

A patrolman can therefore compromise his legitimacy while maintaining order in one of two ways, either by visibly betraying his obligation to enforce *some* rules of law or by fulfilling these obligations in ways that conflict with the moral standards of the local population. If he is too legalistic, he runs the risk of being perceived as arrogant and unjust; but if he tailors his standards to the *practices* of the neighborhood rather than to its *ideals,* he is looked down upon for abdicating his responsibilities altogether. The gang boys are not without their own standards of fairness, and it is these standards that the patrolman must attempt to enforce.

A "good cop" is thus a man who can successfully handle a subtle and narrowly defined moral challenge. He must try to order the life of an ethnic lower-class community from within by holding people such as gang boys to their own ideals, however little these ideals may be reflected in behavior. As Whyte suggested,

> Cornerville people and many of the officers themselves believe that the policeman should have the confidence of the people in his area so that he can settle many difficulties in a personal manner without making arrests. . . . The policeman who takes a strictly legalistic view of his duties cuts himself off from the personal relations necessary to enable him to serve as a mediator of disputes in his area.[8]

Whyte's emphasis on mediation certainly applies to the way gang boys expect patrolmen to handle fights. In situations involving violence, it seems that the "good cop" functions as an arbitrator. He does not turn the boys over to a local school principal for "fighting after school," nor does he cart them away to the station. He isolates them in a squad car, talks the situation over with them, and then does what he can to achieve at least a semipermanent peace. In response to the question, "Have you guys ever met any good cops?" a gang member related the following incident:

> Yeah, there was two studs out in Lakeview once, not the regular cops, who was pretty straight. Remember when he had that big fight at the playground and those guys from Hunters Point got hurt? Mr. J. [the playground director] sent for the cops only they didn't take us in. They talked to us for about an hour. They asked us what

we fighting about and why did we fight and could we use boxing gloves and did we know that fighting was against the law and all that. But they finally let us go, and they got Willie to take the Hunters Point boys home. They was *real* straight, those two. I think they must have lived out there or something, or maybe they was in a club once themselves.

Yet the task of being defined as a "good cop" in the process of handling routine "disorders" involves something more than arbitration. As we have seen, the act of badgering a used car salesmen for free tires may be sufficiently annoying to prompt a patrolman to intervene; but if a patrolman makes categorical claims to final authority in these situations, his authority is likely to be challenged.

When gang boys are apprehended for disorganizing a social situation or for behaving badly at a hangout, a "good cop" will therefore remind them of their values while also suggesting that he could claim the right to use force. He responds to formally ambiguous legal situations with an artful ambiguity of his own, and his reward for this delicate maneuver is legitimacy.

> Those two studs out in Lakeview wouldn't always be on our back for playing neither. We'd be standing on the corner pulling some kinda phoney shit, and they'd pull up to find out if we was up to something. But they talked to us nice. They wouldn't let us get away with nothing, and, I mean, them cats would bust you if they had to. But they talked to us nice.

Even with the best of intentions, then, it is not easy to be considered a "good cop." Not only must the gang boys be persuaded that a policeman understands and likes them, they must also be convinced that he shares their conception of justice and is fully prepared to enforce it. In practice, most confrontations between patrolmen and gang members thus contain the possibilities of conflict—a conflict over whose conception of proper behavior *will* prevail, a conflict over whose conception *ought* to prevail, and therefore a conflict over whose moral identity is to remain publicly intact. Furthermore, the fact that most policemen are not defined as "good cops" cannot be accounted for simply by the wide variety of social and personal defects commonly attributed to them. For example, it may be true that the behavior of policemen is affected by a class and ethnic predisposition to prejudice against Negroes and a psychological predisposition to danger, violence, and authoritarianism, not to mention inadequate education, training, and pay. Yet there are also structural and situational contingencies associated directly with the process of law enforcement itself that make it difficult for even the most enlightened and saintly of policemen to avoid being seen as pariahs by a large segment of the ethnic poor, contingencies that are part and parcel of the methods used by the police.

THE PERSPECTIVE OF THE POLICE

Stated formally, the fundamental problem of police work is the location of a set of criminals that corresponds to a set of reported crimes. The primary resource needed to accomplish this objective is knowledge, and for obvious reasons this resource is limited. With the exception of those whom the police can manage to witness in the act of breaking the law, little is generally known about the specific identities of people who have committed crimes in the past. Thus, the police are structurally predisposed to adopt research procedures that will produce this knowledge most efficiently.

In the classic detective story, the police begin the detection process with a crime. The crime itself defines a population of "suspects," and this population is then broken down into smaller and smaller subgroups as "evidence" accumulates, "evidence" being defined as information about the categories of people to eliminate as suspects. At the end of the story, the culprit is finally located by a process of deduction.

In the world of modern police work, however, this procedure is considered hopelessly inefficient. The police attempt to solve particular crimes either by going directly to a population of previously located suspects, or they first locate "suspicious" individuals and then attempt to link them with some item in the set of previously committed crimes. The first of these methods is often adopted by juvenile officers, and the second is standard practice among patrolmen. Moreover, each of these methods creates a unique situation for the various suspect populations involved.

The Situation of Detection

Most juvenile officers actually do begin their investigations by adopting the methods of their fictional colleagues in detective stories. All complaints from schools, parents, citizens, and other policemen about specific infractions believed to involve young people are referred to the juvenile detail, and work proceeds from the crime to a search for the offender.

The first step in this process is usually to exhaust the knowledge of a complainant. A woman whose car has been damaged by thrown rocks, for example, may say that the damage was done by "those boys next door," thereby eliminating in one step everyone but the guilty parties. But she might also report that the car was damaged by "a bunch of Negro boys between the ages of fourteen and sixteen"; or worse, if she has no idea who threw the rocks, she may only be able to produce the name of a school or the name of a place where the adolescent troublemakers in the neighborhood are known to congregate. This kind of information, although eliminating a great many boys, still leaves the police with a sizable number of suspects.

In practice, therefore, the juvenile officer often proceeds directly to boys who have proven themselves capable of committing the crime, and then he relies on his skills at interrogation. Although the officer may consult his files on the population of suspects and offenders located during previous investigations, these files are used largely as memory aids.[9] Most of this information is in his head.

The success of this method is suggested by the fact that over 90 percent of convicted juveniles confess, a rate that testifies both to the competence of juvenile officers at interrogation and the incompetence of gang boys at concealing information. Those boys who have unusual control over words, voice tones, facial expressions, and body muscles can sometimes manage to avoid conviction indefinitely unless they are apprehended at the scene of a crime. Yet these talents are rare. Some gangs contain no such talented members; other contain two or three. It is therefore rarely necessary for a juvenile officer to expend much time and energy collecting evidence in order to build his case against a boy.

Although the procedures used by juvenile officers are unquestionably efficient, the boys on permanent suspect lists do not appreciate the elegance of these techniques. As David Matza has pointed out, efficient enforcement systems contain agents who suspect, apprehend, and interrogate only a few possible candidates. Most of us—the happy few—are rarely if ever contacted or questioned. Thus, even in those cases in which guilt is confessed, the subcultural delinquent may sense injustice because of selective procedures inherent in any efficient system of enforcement. He feels that cognizance is unevenly exercised.[10] This sentiment is often expressed as follows: "Every time something happens in this neighborhood, them mother fuckin' cops come looking for me! I may not be doing nothing, but if somebody gets beat or something gets stole they always be coming right to my place to find out what's going on!"

Encounters

The techniques of interrogation used by juvenile officers can best be viewed as self-conscious variations in the posture adopted toward suspects. If an officer has not been able to compile a good list of suspects after interviewing a complainant, he may simply cruise the local neighborhood asking familiar boys for information. This style of interrogation is usually conducted in a casual, informal, and conspiratorial tone of voice. It is designed to suggest that nothing serious has happened, that the officer is merely curious about a particular incident, or that a "favor" from the boy being interrogated will someday be returned. As far as the boys are concerned, however, this posture is simply "sneaky."

> Some cops may be nice when you meet them, but as soon as you turn your back they be keeping full tab on you. Like this juvenile officer, Sergeant K, and his buddy. Every time I see him in school the sucker come up to me real nice and start running down his shit. "How's it going? What you been doing?" He gets to interrogating my ass, man, like I done something wrong! And all the time he be coming on nice! You know, like, "It's just between you and me." All that old shit. He sometimes say, "No, we don't expect you to squeal on your friends or nothing. We just want a little help. You do us a favor, we do you a

favor. You go on and tell me what boys was involved and I guarantee you I let you go home. Nothing gonna happen anyway. You know. It ain't really serious." All that old shit! And then they turn around and try to book you every damn chance they get! Some of them nice cops you got to watch real careful.

When a juvenile officer has compiled a more promising list of suspects, however, his approach to interrogation is likely to be decidedly less flattering. After confronting a boy with a list of acquaintances, the officer may wait for a suspicious silence to follow a particular name; or he might accuse a suspect directly in the hope that, even if innocent, the boy might get rattled enough to produce the actual offender.

Yet a juvenile officer is likely to give his most deferential and endearing performance when he thinks he has finally located the culprit. By suggesting that the suspect is regarded as a "good boy" and will not be done any harm, the officer attempts to ease him into a confession.

Although a great many gang boys are tricked into confessions, the authority of a juvenile officer is rarely rejected because of the hypocrisy involved in his techniques of interrogation. Since it strikes the boys as reasonable that a juvenile officer would attempt to catch them for the crimes they actually do commit, these defeats are often taken philosophically. As one boy put it: "If you done something and you be lying and yelling when the boys from juvy come around and they catch you lying, well, what you gonna do? You gonna complain 'cause you was caught? Hell man, you can't do that. You did something, and you was caught, and that's the way it goes."

Yet the sense of injustice created by the actions of a juvenile officer does not necessarily disappear after a confession. In many cases, the equity of a disposition also becomes an issue.

Outcomes

The juvenile officer exercises a good deal of discretion in deciding how to process offenders, a discretion that far transcends the measure of ambiguity ordinarily involved in legal assessments of motivation and intent. Although a truant may not be responsible for his behavior, he may be a touch rebellious, or he may be acting in complete and willful disregard for law; the nature and intent of this crime is not as important to a juvenile officer as what he learns about the attitude of the offender toward the idea of the law itself. For example, if an officer decides he is dealing with a boy who is "guilty but essentially good" or "guilty but sometimes weak," the probability is high that he will decide to let the boy go with a warning about the consequences of committing this crime again. He might feel that contact with the unsavory clientele of a juvenile hall would damage an otherwise positive attitude toward the law or that moral contamination in the eyes of parents and teachers as a result of being sent to jail might weaken an otherwise firm commitment to conventional behavior. On the other hand, if the officer decides that the offender is a "punk," a "persistent troublemaker," or some other version of a thoroughly bad boy, he may well decide to make an arrest.[11]

A "delinquent" is therefore not a juvenile who happens to have committed an illegal act. He is a young person whose moral character has been negatively assessed. And this fact has led some observers to conclude that the transformation of young people into official "delinquents" is best looked at as an organizational rather than a legal process since policemen, probation officers, and juvenile court judges often base their dispositions on a host of criteria that are virtually unrelated to the nature of the specific offense.[12]

The *magnitude of an offense,* of course, can become a factor in dispositions. One responsibly planned and willfully executed robbery, rape, or assault can ruin the moral status of a juvenile indefinitely. Since 90 percent of the crimes committed by juveniles are minor offenses, however, this criterion is only rarely used.

The number of *previous contacts with police* has a more important effect on dispositions. These contacts are typically recorded on easily accessible files, and these files contain everything from arrests and convictions to contacts made on the flimsiest of contingent grounds. If a boy confesses to a crime and is not known to the police, he is often released. If he is caught for a third or fourth time, however, the sum total of previous contacts may be enough to affect a judgment about his moral character adversely, regardless of the nature or magnitude of the present offense and regardless of the reasons he was previously contacted. For example:

> Like last night, man, me and Willy got busted for curfew. I mean I got busted for curfew. We was walkin' up the hill toward home, and these cops pull up. It was a Friday night, man; so we didn't want no trouble. When the cops ask us what we was doing and what about our names we was all nice. So then the cop gets on that radio and checks us out. There was a whole bunch of noise comin' over that box. I couldn't hear what they was sayin'. But then the cop comes out and says to Willy, "O.K., you can go." And I say, "What about me?" And the cop says, "You been in trouble before. We don't want you walkin' the streets at night. We going to take you down to the station for curfew." Then I got real mad. I almost ran. Lucky

thing I didn't though. I woulda been in real trouble then.

There is even some evidence to suggest that assessments about the type and quality of *parental control* are even more important factors in dispositions than *any* of the offense-related criteria. One of the main concerns of a juvenile officer is the likelihood of future offense, and this determination is often made largely on the basis of "the kinds of parents" a boy happens to possess. Thus, the moral character of parents also passes under review; and if a house appears messy, a parent is missing, or a mother is on welfare, the probability of arrest increases. Similarly, a boy with a father and two older brothers in jail is considered a different sort of person from a boy whose immediate family is not known to the police. As Cicourel points out, these judgments about family life are particularly subject to bias by attitudes related to class.[13]

> See, like you or maybe one of your brothers, say both of you, been to Y.A. [detention facilities for youth], or your sister, every time they see you they get on your back. They know all your family. If they ever pick you up and look at your records, they automatically take you in. They see where your sister been to jail, your brother, or if you ever went to jail. And they start saying, "Your whole family is rotten. Your whole family is jailbirds." Shit like that. And this is what really make you mad, when they tell you your mother don't know how to read!

Although the family situation of a boy and his record of prior police contacts both enter into dispositions, the most important factor affecting the decision of juvenile officers is the *attitude* displayed by the offender, both during and after the confession itself. Cicourel, for example, found that juvenile officers were strongly influenced by the style and speed with which the offender confessed.[14] If a boy blurts out his misdeeds immediately, this behavior is taken as a sign that the boy "trusts" authority and is therefore "under control." If the boy proves to be a "tough nut to crack," however, he is viewed with suspicion. As soon as a juvenile is defined as "hardened," he is considered no less dangerous to society than the adult criminal.

Similarly, the boys who appear frightened, humble, penitent, and ashamed are also more likely to go free. They are often defined as "weak, troubled, and the victim of circumstances" but basically "good boys," an assessment of moral character that may win them a release.

On the other hand, if a boy shows no signs of being spiritually moved by his offense, the police deal harshly with him. Not only has he sinned against a legal rule, but he has also symbolically rejected the norma-tive basis for conforming to it in the first place; and it is this double deviation that has fateful consequences for the way he is treated by the police. Once he gets himself defined as "the kind of person who doesn't respect the law," he becomes a perfect candidate for arrest, detention, and eventual incarceration. Most of the juvenile officers we interviewed felt that the attitude of the offender was the major determinant of dispositions in 50 percent of their cases, and Nathan Goldman reports that "defiance on the part of a boy will lead to juvenile court quicker than anything else." [15]

It is hardly necessary to describe the way most gang boys feel about the equity of these dispositions. One only needs to imagine the look on a boy's face when he is told that he is about to spend a year in jail for an offense committed with a friend who was sent home when he promptly confessed.

NOTES

1   The data on policemen were collected by Irving Piliavin, Scott Briar, and Roy Turner, who spent eighteen months observing and interviewing patrolmen and juvenile officers on daily patrols in Oakland and San Francisco. We are deeply indebted to Briar and Turner for the long hours they spent in the field on this project and for the many contributions they made to the analysis. The data on gang members were collected by Carl Werthman in a series of taped interviews with 56 "core" members of 11 "delinquent gangs" or "jacket clubs," plus observations and more informal conversations involving over 100 members of these 11 gangs. The boys were drawn from the clientele of a delinquency-prevention program in San Francisco called Youth For Service, and we owe particular thanks to Orville Luster, Percy Pinkney, and the rest of the staff at this agency for helping us conduct this research out of their offices for a two-year period. Of the 56 boys interviewed on tape, 37 were Negro, 11 were Mexican, and 8 were Caucasian. This article is thus based primarily on a sample of Negro gang boys.

2   Sherri Cavan, "Interaction in Home Territories," *Berkeley Journal of Sociology* **VIII:** 18.

3   Ibid.

4   For a systematic discussion of this approach to the problem of "social disorganization" see Albert K. Cohen, "The Study of Social Disorganization and Deviant Behavior," in Robert S. Merton, Leonard Broom, and Leonard S. Cottrell, Jr., eds., *Sociology Today* (New York: Basic Books, 1959), pp. 474–483.

5   No conflict of this magnitude took place while this study was being done. However, some of the boys studied tell stories about an immediately preceding period in San Francisco gang history when these raids were not uncommon. In fact, a number of boys in the same neighborhood remember seeing a machine gun hidden in a park near the hangout that was used on at least two frequently mentioned occasions to defend the private space. These boys

also claim that the machine gun was not used any place else.

6 William Foote Whyte, *Street Corner Society* (Chicago: The University of Chicago Press, 1943), p. 138.

7 Ibid.

8 Ibid., p. 136.

9 These files are often cross-examined by name, nickname, race, and previous offense. Many juvenile bureaus also keep membership lists of gangs (if available) and a picture or sample of the club jackets currently in use.

10 David Matza, *Delinquency and Drift* (New York: Wiley, 1964), p. 108.

11 For a more complete discussion of police discretion in dealing with juveniles, see Irving Piliavin and Scott Briar, "Police Encounters with Juveniles," *American Journal of Sociol-*

ogy **LXX,** No. 2 (Sept. 1964): 209–211.

12 The problem of discretion has been formulated and studied by Aaron Cicourel in these terms. See Aaron V. Cicourel, *The Social Organization of Juvenile Justice* (New York: Wiley, 1968).

13 Aaron Cicourel, "Social Class, Family Structure and the Administration of Juvenile Justice," Center for the Study of Law and Society, University of California at Berkeley, Working Paper, MS.

14 Cicourel, *The Social Organization of Juvenile Justice.*

15 Nathan Goldman, *The Differential Selection of Juvenile Offenders for Court Appearances,* National Council on Crime and Delinquency (1963), p. 106.

The Implementation of a Complex Policy

AARON V. CICOUREL

The organization of juvenile justice is complicated by different and often conflicting philosophies and policies. The police are theoretically bound by the philosophy of the juvenile court law, but changes in the law in California have come about because of abuses attributed primarily to the police. The Governor's Special Study Commission on Juvenile Justice (1960) in California led to many changes in the law, many of which were designed to protect the minor's rights.

The Commission's recommendations were not always far ahead of rapid changes in several of the more professionally oriented police departments in the state, but the reports and subsequent legislation did validate those practices and introduce innovations into administrative procedures vis-à-vis juveniles.

The different and conflicting issues here revolve around what I take to be a basic dilemma in police and probation work—the use of punishment-oriented views during encounters with "difficult-to-handle," "rough," juveniles who do not seem to respond to the essentially "clinical" orientation some juvenile police and, especially, probation officers assume should be used. Police officers appear to be least interested in adopting this "clinical" orientation even though juvenile officers do formally claim to identify with the principles of the juvenile court law. At state and regional meetings of the California State Juvenile Officers Association, there are frequent remarks acknowledging both the criticism or jokes made by other police officers and the indication of increased desirability of working in juvenile bureaus. But the clinical-control cleavage stems from juvenile officers' attempts to implement simultaneously both a "clinical" or permissive approach (where the notion of a "permissive approach" does not always imply imputations of illness) and a social control orientation practiced by their colleagues in patrol or the detective bureau. The probation department and the court, various community agencies, and the juvenile court law-created Juvenile Justice Commission of each county remind the police of the special or "civil" nature of the juvenile court law and the importance of "rehabilitating" youth who get into trouble. But the professional orientation of the police department emphasizes the repression and control of criminal activities regardless of age and relies upon typified imputations of "disorganized" or "bad" environments for seeking offenders. For the police, "robbery" or "rape" has little to do with the age of the offender or his life circumstances. The two departments studied provided both a professionally oriented organization and one more or less patterned after the model of the corrupt big city force, intimately associated with political and criminal graft and corruption, vividly illustrating the conflicting orientations the police employ. The following general statements, based upon my impressions, will give the reader a rough idea of how the administration of juvenile justice proceeds and the organizational context of police and probation activities:[1]

1. The apprehension of juveniles involves an almost immediate disregard for the procedures of criminal law; adult arrest and search and seizure rules are seldom followed.

2. There are few formal legal procedures followed, and the problem of evidence seldom poses a serious issue, inasmuch as a presumption of guilt is often an integral part of the investigative process.

3. Although the issue of advising the suspect of his constitutional rights was a controversial issue in California during the period of this study, the two departments studied did not routinely advise the juveniles accordingly. In rare and serious cases the suspects would be advised. (In a nearby large city, however, both juveniles and adults were usually advised of their rights by juvenile officers.)

4. The police utilize a rather strict social control model for juveniles they feel are guilty and repeaters; the juveniles are handcuffed and treated as adults.

5. The police investigation of a case invariably includes a meeting between the suspect, his family, and the officer, and separate interrogations with both the juvenile and his family. The mood appears "serious," and the simulated use of legal rules of procedure varies with particular cases.

6. Probation investigation also includes a meeting with the family, but here the atmosphere is clinical in orientation. Legal rules of procedure are notably absent. The conversation always revolves around "helping" the juvenile, and there is explicit interviewing concerning family problems

and the personal adjustment of the offender.

7. The court hearing always includes a (sometimes quick, unclear, or perfunctory) reference to the right to counsel by the juvenile and his family, even though the hearing itself represents a fairly cut-and-dried operation which is seldom challenged. The "hearing" (or occasionally simulated "trial") has been settled by way of unofficial communications between the probation officer, his supervisor, the offender and his family, and the court referee or judge. The hearing is sort of a ritual ceremony that provides an abstract operational validity to underscore the seriousness of the matter. The hearing enables the probation officer, the judge, or the family to underscore particular or general features of what has happened and the consequences that may follow if it happens again.

8. Neither the offender nor his family takes the suggestion of the right to counsel seriously unless there is a fear (hinted at by the probation officer beforehand) that the juvenile may be placed outside the home. In the latter case, the family is often middle- to upper-class in the socioeconomic scale. A due process format may then be introduced into the proceedings.

All parties in the administration of juvenile justice formally assume their task is to "help" the youth in question; therefore, promoting a concern with constitutional rights is difficult to enforce. One source of changes in the California juvenile court law has been motivated by legally minded partisans who felt that the police were routinely adopting a punishment-oriented view toward the suspect known to be a repeater where the presumption of guilt was common, and where the lack of due process procedures was felt to necessitate the inclusion of changes to protect the juvenile. The argument is clearly similar to the continuing debate in adult cases over arrest and search and seizure procedures. An understanding of police "rationality" requires an appreciation of their practical circumstances.

A basic dilemma of juvenile justice is the belief in individualized "treatment" so that the offender may be helped back to a "normal" life, but the professional orientation of police departments emphasizes social control and an efficient administrative operation that does not include the allocation of time for a "treatment-oriented" approach to "helping" youth. The juvenile officer is ambivalent because he seeks to embrace a semiprofessional view of juvenile activities that includes a justification of the juvenile court law, but his daily work activities are oriented by the adult penal code, so that his cases are not seen always as falling under the juvenile court law. By invoking the punitive, social control model of the police department, the juvenile officer is caught between general administrative policy and practice, and the particular, more special type of case the juvenile offender implies. The matter is complicated because the semiprofessional juvenile officers' association officially sanctions the "special treatment" approach implied in the juvenile court law.

The probation department, on the other hand, is somewhat less troubled by the same dilemma. Probation officials, when dealing with particular types of juveniles, often employ a similar solution, but for different reasons and with less severity—but with their own professional image and professional objectives. One group seems oriented toward social work, while another group seeks to avoid complete identification with social work and to develop an independent professional orientation. Inasmuch as the clinically oriented social work position is more developed, is organized professionally, and is invariably invoked as a needed set of procedures for handling delinquent youth, it is difficult for the probation officer to avoid at least a superficial usage of clinical terminology in describing a youth's problems and his family context. The case load assigned to the probation officer and the organization of the staff along professional-supervisory lines, with less hierarchy than the police, tends to force the probation department into a kind of social work organizational structure. The use of secretaries for dictating the results of interviews, a standard type of outline for writing up the interview, frequent staff meetings to discuss cases and policies that give a professional atmosphere to the department, and considerable autonomy and personal freedom in carrying out work assignments and accounting for time—all contribute to the desire on the part of the probation officer to generate professional appearances.

But the professional aspirations of both police and probation officers are dampened by the fact that salary scales are fixed, and social mobility within the organization is limited. Most police departments, regardless of whether they operate on a civil service or merit system, are slow to promote their men, and a series of tests and interviews are constant obstacles. The fact that officers are neither always motivated nor feel they have the time to study for examinations, are often "nervous" about board interviews, realize that promotions will invariably take them out of their present assignment, put them on nights more often, or work more weekends, means that the monetary rewards and added responsibility accompanying promotions are not always very attractive. Thus the daily routine of work occurs within a setting that does not offer many changes, surprises, or aspirations, except for a few who are willing to undergo the difficulties of moving up in the system. Some dissension results from younger men successfully passing examinations and interview boards and then moving up faster than the men who "broke them in." Inasmuch as seniority is a critical factor for maintaining a particular position and level of pay, it is very difficult for a police officer to change jobs and move to other departments except as a chief. The latter often is not done until he has accumulated enough years in one department so that he can later receive retirement pay at the age of 60 or 65, thereby lessening the danger of getting fired as chief. The police officer, therefore, is fairly "locked" into his job and must adjust to the circumstances of the particular department he is in. For officers who do not move "up" very far—the bulk of them—everyday police work takes on a routine character. The officer develops his theories about individuals and groups, morality and immorality, good and bad people, institutions, practices, and typifications of community settings, and such theories or conceptions are employed in routine ways according to recipes not likely to make due process features of his work problematic. An administrative organization demanding standardized reports and standardized procedures readily suggests a social control model as the central orienting ideology for everyday police activities, but where rationalities of action are fused with the problems of limited mobility and the practical circumstances of restricted ingroup relations that seldom change.

The average probation officer's college degree gives him a broader base from which to claim professional status, but the organizational structure of the probation department leaves him few possibilities for change and little difference in pay. The probation department pyramids faster than the military-like police, so that a regular deputy probation officer is restricted in his internal social mobility. The emphasis is upon professional work orientation, and there are few higher positions whose occupancy he can achieve. Civil service or merit system seniority requirements make it difficult to move to another department, except early in the game, because one must start at the bottom again, as in the police department. Therefore, within the probation department, there is little excitement generated by the cases handled, and personalized or individualized attention is difficult because of heavy case loads, court appearances, investigative interviews, or routine calls. Keeping up with bureaucratic ritual and administrative demands leaves little time for more professional activity, for example, additional training, quality control of interviews and reports, and professional discussion about theories and trends in crime and delinquency, even though the state and county organizations seek to supply some of these activities at annual or more frequent regional meetings. Those probation officers interested in professional development recognize the discrepancy between their aspirations and the practical circumstances of achieving the necessary activities. Both police and probation departments have a difficult time obtaining the necessary funds from city councils and county supervisors for the kind of in-service and outside training which they would like and which they feel is necessary for continued professional growth, as well as minimal information flow into the departments. Few officers (among the police as well) are interested in taking the time away from other activities they enjoy and from their families

for "re-tooling" periodically or regularly. The fact that professional activities do not guarantee rewards in the form of pay, promotion, or change in duties has not helped this picture. But there are demands for giving lectures or appearances before various civic groups and voluntary associations interested in "youth" or community "betterment." Success with regional or statewide organizations is not necessarily correlated with success or rank in the local organization, and participants and elected officers of both juvenile officer associations and probation, parole, and corrections officers' associations are not always of higher rank in the police or probation department.[2]

My observations suggest police and probation perspectives follow community typifications in organizing the city into areas where they expect to receive the most difficulty from deviant or "difficult" elements to areas where little trouble is expected and where more care should be taken in dealing with the populace because of socioeconomic and political influence. The partition of the city into areas of more or less anticipated crime provides both police and probation officers with additional typifications about what to expect when patrolling or making calls in the areas. Thus the officer's preconstituted typifications and stock of knowledge at hand leads him to prejudge much of what he encounters, which an independent observer does not always "see." Thus, particular ecological settings, populated by persons with "known" styles of dress and physical appearance, provide the officer with quick inferences about "what is going on," although not based upon factual material he must describe sooner or later in oral or written form.

The officer's typifications about social types, causation, and typical outcomes enable him to construct "careers" based on what different delinquent types are likely to follow, contingent upon the kinds of decisions made at given points in time. Thus, at a certain point, the officer may narrow the possible alternatives down to one: commitment to the California Youth Authority. The prior activities of the youth, his family situation, his "attitude," the kinds of resources available to him and his family, and the likelihood they will be used and prove effective narrow the possibilities of the disposition decision.

The officer's imputation of "career" (for example, "this kid is a real loser") is revealed by the oral and written remarks made about the suspect and is to be distinguished from the "career" that the sociologist constructs as a consequence of tracing the different conceptions of the same youth, revealed by official records of the police, the family, the school, and probation department. Each of the latter have their own notion of "career" or the short-run and long-run courses of action the suspect is likely to pursue. The sociologist's imputation of a composite career is intended to show how each separate career is produced, and how the composite career can be an unintended product that is independent of the various careers taken singly, or "historicized" by whoever chooses to interpret the meaning of the juvenile's actions after the fact.

Each career-generating agency maintains and selects "facts" for interpretation by means of its own ideology, theories, organizational policies, and practices. Therefore, categorization into "points of no return" or the view that "nothing more can be done" or "the right foster home will do the trick" or the "right peer group will change him," and so forth, are rooted in the kinds of structural arrangements the agency feels are possible and the particular encounters a representa-

tive of the agency maintains with the juvenile in question.

But the careers generated by different agencies are also dependent upon the particular way information is obtained and the resources available to the police, probation, the school, the family, and so on. The school information may only include an official transcript of grades, omitting relevant comments about behavior in class, truancy, and other factors, or simply stress the existence of a behavioral problem in class.

The juvenile officer is a detective armed with a variety of theories about different areas of the city, the kinds of "kids" who "get into trouble," a network of informers and sources of information, written and mental notations about possible suspects and "shady characters," various fragments of information about persons he feels are guilty of different offenses but against whom he does not have the evidence necessary to convince the probation department or the district attorney, and so forth. The policeman's network or "map" of community activities is, therefore, much more extensive than the information obtainable from observations of concrete action he undertakes for initiating, and following through with, judicial procedures designed to convict persons of law violation. His written and mental "dossiers" include persons who may be "clean" now, and with respect to whom no action is now possible, and those for whom there is insufficient evidence, but the perspective which guides the officer's actions is that at any point in time the information might be instrumental in suggesting "leads" and evidence for conviction and clearing cases.

Probation officers employ a kind of quasi-social work or psychiatric interview that—in contrast to those conducted by the police—takes into account such factors as establishing "rapport" with the subject and utilizing more abstract interrogative procedures. The probation officer's training and sources of information are more limited and do no have the aura of "inside dopesterism" that is implicit in police contacts and information. Whereas police and probation officers seldom take systematic notes, the latter follow a fairly standard outline which resembles a clinical sheet often found in social work agencies or in the files of psychiatric clinics. The language used to describe the suspect or offender's life and behavior is full of global phrases and often empty remarks that are designed to be "objective" and detached but are often based upon vague notes and impressions about the subject. The simulation of a professional interview appears more successful on paper than when it is observed or overheard, and the final product contains little documentation and many labels, clichés, and vaguely used global con-

cepts designed to "explain" the subject's predicament. But the reader must always be aware of the truncated nature of police and probation files. Thus, tables constructed from files are even more truncated abstractions of the original events leading to the assembly of the files. It is not the abstractions themselves about which I am complaining, but the lack of theories and procedures in sociological studies for moving from original events to files and then to tables. Tables derived from police and probation records, census materials, vital statistics, and other organization sources are invariably disengaged from the original events, and there is an absence of theories and procedures that would show what meanings are preserved, distorted, and transformed by the abstraction process. To ignore members' and researchers' abstraction processes is to ignore the heart of the problem.

NOTES

1   In large California cities, more attention is now given to the use of adult arrest and search and seizure procedures than was true during my study. But the practices are not always standardized.

2   The reader should note that it is difficult to show always how police and probation satisfaction or dissatisfaction with their occupational predicaments influence their day-to-day activities; daily actions vis-à-vis juveniles and parents are likely to include their occupational problems as tacit difficulties seldom revealed in their work routines. My impressionistic observations revealed the intrusion of

such problems in the form of disinterest in pursuing cases that meant working overtime, simplifying cases that required extensive paper work, taking more time when making investigations in the field, or spending more time on outside work activities, and the like. I should not hazard any generalizations about such matters, however, because my feeling was that considerable variation occurred in officers' depictions of "gripes," interest in their work, concern with organizational changes, personal changes, and the like. I should hesitate to give even impressionistic accounts of situational variations I have observed.

Secondary Schools' Task Force

RAYMOND L. HOOBLER

Due to rapidly changing social conditions, law enforcement organizations must re-evaluate their policies and operational procedures. Many duties which are performed today were unheard of fifteen years ago, particularly activities of a nonenforcement or service nature. With this change in emphasis, we must take the steps necessary to conform to the times.

The city of San Diego, California, has been as deeply affected by these changing conditions as any other area of the country. Of particular concern to the San Diego Police Department is the negative attitude of many of the young people toward police officers in uniform and also the amount of criminal activity in and around schools, especially drug-related violations.

A problem of mutual concern to school administrators and police is the disruptive influence of the nonstudent loiterer around the junior and senior high schools. In San Diego, it was found that these individuals accounted for the majority of the disturbances on or around school campuses.

In the late spring of 1971, city school officials requested the assistance of the police department in combating the loitering problem. At that time, a special Task Force, consisting of six officers and a supervising sergeant from the Patrol Division, was assigned the responsibility of enforcing the loitering laws and developing a long-term program to

From *The Police Chief* (June 1973): 28, 30. Reprinted by permission of The International Association of Chiefs of Police.

eliminate the problem. The efforts of this group, which became known as the "Secondary Schools' Task Force," were concentrated in the Central Division's area of the city, primarily around six high schools and nine junior high schools. The officers were assigned to work in two-man teams and were given the responsibility for a specified group of schools. The two-man team concept was adopted because it was felt that two officers would be more effective and safer than a single officer. The Task Force was in operation for 23 days—from May 17 through June 16, 1971, the end of the school year. During that period, loitering around the affected schools became almost nonexistent. While the officers were working this assignment, they on numerous occasions went on the school campuses and made informal contacts with school administrators and students.

While on campus, the Task Force adopted a nonenforcement posture. Their purpose was primarily to make themselves available to any student who wanted to talk to them; however, they let it be known that although they were there in a nonenforcement role, they would take police action if an obvious violation were committed in their presence. Frequently, when their visits were during school lunch periods, they ate their lunch in the patios or cafeterias with the students.

In laying the ground rules for the Task Force, it was clearly established that these officers would in no way become involved in handling the internal discipline in the schools and would not act as hall monitors or school security agents. It was felt that school administrators should take a firm stand on internal problems, as this was not a function in which a police agency should be involved. It also became apparent that the only way in which the loitering problem could be controlled would be through the cooperative efforts of school administrators on the inside and the police on the outside. Through the actions of school administrators and the Task Force officers, it was quickly established that no area in or around the schools would become a haven for loiterers or students not attending classes.

It was equally important for school administrators and the officers to make the purpose of the Task Force known to the students in order to enlist their support of the programs. It soon became apparent that there were only a small number of students involved in disruptive conduct, and the vast majority were interested in attending school and having a trouble-free campus.

The most important concept of the Task Force operation was that the students would observe the police officers, both in their enforcement role off campus and in their informal student contacts on campus. Every effort was made to eliminate the Task Force officers from "special status." The Task Force officers performed their duties in full uniform and in marked cars and were highly visible. It was found that contrary to the opinions voiced by detractors of the program at its inception, the officers were well received by the majority of the students. There were those who told us that "all of the students" in the high schools felt that policemen should not come on a school campus for any purpose; others told us that officers could not succeed in the dual role of enforcement and public relations because these activities were incompatible.

The main objective of the program was

for the students to see the uniformed officer in his enforcement role and accept that role as a very necessary part of the police function. Many police departments have utilized community relations officers or school resource officers on secondary school campuses. These officers have been divorced completely from any enforcement duties and, because of this, students look upon them as "special," not as police officers who, of necessity, must make arrests or sometimes have to overcome violence or resistance with force. In the eyes of the students, the community relations or resource officers have never been identified as being the same as the "cop on the beat."

In past years, one of the causes of problems around the schools was that officers would make an arrest which was viewed by a large number of students; then as soon as the officer left the area, some students would create highly inflammatory rumors about the incident. This is not the case of the Task Force officers because they have made it a point, after an arrest, to return to the school as soon as possible to squelch any rumors created through person-to-person contacts. This procedure has been instrumental in eliminating the disruptions which sometimes follow arrests.

After the pilot project in May and June of 1971, the Task Force was reactivated in September 1971 at the beginning of the fall semester. At this time, the staff was enlarged to eight men and a sergeant, and its activities spread out to cover all 33 secondary schools in the city of San Diego, although major emphasis was still on the schools in the Central Division area. During the fall semester, the Task Force officers made some 250 arrests around the schools, and at the same time made approximately 16,000 nonenforcement contacts with students. It was noted that generally the presence of the officers on campus was accepted, and the name calling and rock throwing that had been prevalent six months earlier whenever a policeman came near some schools no longer existed.

At the beginning of the fall semester, every effort was made to increase the number of informal rap sessions with students and participation in classrooms as guest speakers. In these classroom sessions, the officers give talks on the duties of police officers and the purpose of the Task Force. They open the class up for questions on any subject, and, from that point on, no holds are barred. These class sessions have proved to be very successful and well received by the students. While in the classroom, and in an effort to keep the presentations on an informal basis, the two Task Force officers sit with the students. They position themselves on each side of the group so they are able to field questions or respond to comments from all directions. The presence of two officers in the classroom, rather than a single officer, has proved to be far more effective in handling this type of meeting.

During the 1971–1972 school year, the Task Force made 2,012 visits to 33 secondary schools; 228 classroom presentations to a total of 6,379 students; had 2,531 enforcement and 34,380 public relations contacts, for a total of 36,911 contacts; made 146 criminal investigations; and broke up a total of 95 actual or pending gang fights. This activity covered a period of 178 school days, with the Task Force working 30 two-man units short.

Since the inception of the Task Force, praise has been received from parents, students, and school administrators for the manner in which the officers have performed, particularly for their ability to develop rapport with the students. They have also pointed out that many problems of internal discipline, some of which have existed for years, have been alleviated by the presence of the Task Force.

The program has also been a success in the eyes of the rest of the uniformed Patrol Division; they have noticed a change in the attitude of many students toward the police. A side benefit is the fact that regular beat officers do not have to spend as much time around the schools quelling disturbances as they did in the past; also, they seldom run into name calling or rock throwing in responding to calls at the schools.

The Task Force was again reactivated for the 1972–1973 school year, with an expanded unit of eighteen patrolmen and two sergeants, and was permanently assigned to the Patrol Division. The nine two-man teams will cover a total of thirty-seven secondary schools. Four of the secondary schools are administered by the Sweetwater School District, but these schools are located within the city of San Diego.

The ultimate goal of the Task Force, in addition to maintaining order around the schools, is to develop in our junior and senior high school students an understanding and acceptance of the uniformed police officer and his duties and create an atmosphere on campus that is conducive to the educational process. As a result, it is hoped that in the future, any police officer will be able to perform his duties on or around any school campus without evoking fear or hostility, and serious students will be able to pursue their education without interference.

7

MENTAL ILLNESS, DEVIANCE, AND DISSENT

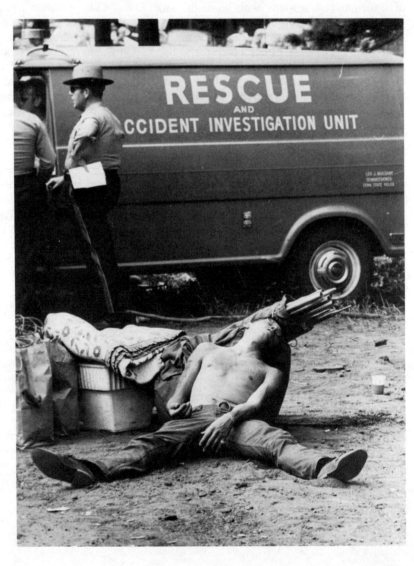

Connecticut police work with rescue units in coping
with the realities of drug abuse.

The phenomena of mental illness, deviance, and dissent dramatically illustrate the policeman's responsibilities in the area of public order and the dilemmas and choices patrolmen and police officials face. Everyone, regardless of political opinion, agrees that a certain minimum of public order is necessary and desirable for a society to function. But the agreement often stops there. Recognition of public order as a goal does not determine its character. Consider a crowd of 100,000 people on their feet shouting at the top of their lungs, some of them stamping up and down, some of them blue in the face. Is this a scene of public order? Yes, if the setting is a football field and if a favorite halfback has just returned the kickoff to win for the home team. Suppose the same crowd descends onto the field and tears down the goal posts, violating a rule banning spectators from the field. Whether those tearing down the goal posts are to be considered an "orderly" group is questionable as every police official knows. But suppose an even smaller group of enthusiasts moves to the streets and jubilantly overturns buses to celebrate home team victory. (Overturning trolley cars was a "customary" activity following Yale victories over Harvard in the early part of this century.) Obviously, the situation has moved to one likely to be defined as disorderly, and the police are likely to take action.

These examples suggest that the interpretation of public order is variable and dependent upon the setting and customary perceptions of normality and deviance. For example, military organizations typically require tight conformity in dress and demeanor. When the order of the day requires soldiers to wear gloves, then all soldiers will wear gloves. By contrast, bohemian communities tolerate, indeed encourage, individualistic expression in dress and behavior.

American society is governed by norms of constitutional democracy. Such norms imply tolerance of diversity and anticipation of social change. The typical major metropolitan area and its suburbs may encompass a diversity of conceptions of public order, plus norms of free movement from one community to another. Different values and goals engender social tensions within a pluralistic constitutional democracy. Although norms are set by the legislature through substantive criminal law, these norms may not be equally clear or equally accepted among different segments of the population. For example, rural Protestant anti-drinking norms were widely challenged and violated by many urban Catholics—as well as by many rural Protestants who subscribed to one set of norms in theory and another in practice—during the era of national Prohibition.

The substantive areas of public order discussed by the authors of the articles in this section—mental illness, deviance in the form of drug use, and protest—are among the most controversial and difficult for contemporary police. In the area of mental illness, the policeman is called upon to make judgments that are perhaps more properly, although perhaps not any better, made by a professional psychiatrist. We can question whether police should be responsible for identifying mentally ill persons on the street and for placing them in mental institutions. It is also worthwhile to inquire, along the same lines, why no objective standards understandable to both police and psychiatrist have been developed in determining the degree of mental illness serious enough to require hospitalization. Matthews' article is certainly a useful exploration of this subject.

The person who is screaming on the street may have taken an overdose of drugs or may not have. Certainly, large numbers of American citizens regularly take drugs of various kinds, including alcohol, barbiturates, amphetamines, marihuana, and opiates. Some of these drug users end up screamers and some of them don't. In the drug area, police would seem to possess a mandate, since certain forms of drug use are illegal and the sale of certain forms of drugs carries heavy penalties. Yet enforcement of drug laws is highly complicated because there's such widespread use of a variety of drugs. There is often little agreement between users and nonusers on what the laws ought to be, and the police effort is therefore necessarily selective and controversial. Jackson's article takes the view that since citizen complaints are rare and informers constitute an intrinsic link in the structure of drug law enforcement, the police who are arresting drug addicts are as marginal in American society as the addicts themselves. Is this an accurate perception, and if not, why not? In what ways does Jackson suggest that police and drug addicts tend to help each other's "careers"? Would it be possible to see both drug police and drug addicts as unintended victims of legislators who do not fully comprehend the consequences of law enforcement in the drug area? What are the benefits of drug enforcement, and are they worth the costs?

When people observe phenomena with which they are relatively unfamiliar, they tend to develop theories, not necessarily based on fact, of why these phenomena occur. Police who observe street protest have often explained it in terms of conspiracies and foreign influence. Why do police agencies make such interpretations, and what efforts might be suggested to revise police conceptions of protest along more realistic lines?

Observations on Police Policy and Procedures for Emergency Detention of the Mentally Ill

ARTHUR R. MATTHEWS, JR.

The following example related by a police chief from a suburban community north of Chicago summarizes the major problems in police handling the mentally disabled:

> The trouble with being a cop is you get all the dirty jobs no one else will touch with a ten-foot pole. Take psychos and alkies. The hospitals won't take them, the doctors don't even want to talk to them, the relatives have given up trying. We're all that's left. We try to humor a guy, talk to them nice, but sometimes they're better off in jail with three squares and a roof over their heads. Next thing you know we've got lawyers and doctors around here screaming about civil rights and us cops keeping sick people in jail. We had a case the other day. This teen-age kid about 9 o'clock at night is playing poker in the middle of Main Street without a deck and with no other players. One of my men took this kid over to the hospital. They wouldn't admit him without a lot of red tape. I'm home watching T.V. when I get the word. Wait, I'll be right down. I get the run around from the clerk so I had him call his boss—the psychiatrist who runs the hospital—at home. He was pretty mad about being called at home. I told him we would let the kid go unless they took him for the night. He said he didn't have the authority to give the go

From the *Journal of Criminal Law, Criminology and Police Science* **61** (2): 283–284, 288–295. Copyright © 1970 by Northwestern University School of Law. Reprinted by special permission of the Journal of Criminal Law, Criminology and Police Science.

ahead signal. "Okay," says I, "but I want your name and your official title so if anything happens to this kid we know where to send the reporters." The boy was admitted.

In the spring of 1963, the American Bar Foundation undertook an 18-month field study entitled "Mental Illness and Criminal Law." [1] The aim of the study was exploratory, to discover and identify the actual practices of the police and other agencies of criminal justice administration in use from state to state in dealing with the mentally disabled. This paper will discuss procedures used to move apparently mentally ill persons from the community to some place where care may be had and will explore some of the implications of these practices for professional police policy. A moment's reflection reveals that the police deal daily with all sorts of mentally disturbed persons, alcoholics, suicides, narcotic addicts, seniles, and the like. The issue of police handling of the mentally disabled is a legal one to the extent that laws specify the class of persons subject to apprehension, either for crime or for compulsory mental treatment, and establishes the procedures to be followed. It is also a medical one since much of the information legal officials act upon is based upon a medical model of mental illness and supplied by doctors. This is not to say that the police perform a ministerial function; as Egon Bittner has written:

> In real police work the provisions contained in the law represent a resource that

can be invoked to handle certain problems. Beyond that, the law contains certain guidelines about the boundaries of legality. Within these boundaries, however, there is located a vast array of activities that are in no important sense determined by considerations of legality. In fact, in cases in which invoking the law is not a foregone conclusion, as for example in many minor offenses or in the apprehension of mentally ill persons, it is only speciously true to say that the law determined the act of apprehension, and much more correct to say that the law made the action possible. The effective reasons for the action are not located in the formulas of statutes but in considerations that are related to established practices of dealing informally with problems.[2]

POLICE PROCEDURES
FOR EMERGENCY SITUATIONS

In making decisions concerning persons who are or are thought to be mentally ill, the policeman's perception is nearly identical with that of the ordinary lay person of similar age and background. Generally, the training the police receive in handling mentally ill persons is limited to cataloging major psychological symptoms that mentally ill persons display and learning to handle violently abnormal people. Two major attitudes, somewhat in conflict, color police activity in handling supposed mentally ill persons: (1) that mentally ill persons are sick persons and should receive medical attention,[3] and (2) that mentally ill persons are dangerous and the sooner someone else takes custody (and hence responsibility) the better.[4] Police perception of mental illness is shaped by these attitudes, with the result that mental illness, as perceived by the policeman, consists either of violence or of highly abnormal behavior. It tends, in other words, to parallel quite closely the substantive requirements articulated in the common law standard of emergency detention.

The initial contact of the criminal law with the mentally ill person is usually made by the policeman who is confronted daily with the behavior of persons who are or may be mentally ill. The policeman may ignore this behavior or deal with it informally short of official action, handle it as a civil matter by attempting to provide some medical or social help, or proceed according to the ordinary processes of the criminal law. All three alternatives were present in the following example, which occurred in New York City.

Looking back on what had happened, the officer, a young man with a sense of humor, wondered why he had gone to so much trouble. He had been standing on a corner observing people go about their usual activities, he recalled, when he noticed a young Negro who appeared a bit drunk, very intently talking to himself. When the man punctuated this conversation by punching his fist through the window of an empty automobile parked at the curb, the officer approached and inquired the reason for his behavior. The man acted "strangely," and either could not or would not answer, leading the officer to think he was "a psycho case." The officer led him to the hospital which was nearby and told this story to the psychiatric resident who examined the man. In response to specific questions the man said he was drinking and out of work and added that he had been hospitalized at this hospital recently for a period of two weeks; he seemed quite content to spend the night at the hospital, but the doctor said that since he was only drunk there was no basis for hospitalization. However, the doctor would take his temperature and would keep him, at least over night, if he showed a temperature. Finding that the patient did not have a temperature, the doctor informed the police officer that the man could not be admitted.

Regardless of what the man had told the doctor or what the doctor thought, he was "still crazy" in the officer's judgment, and the officer passed on these sentiments to the desk officer at the precinct when he called for instructions. The officer at the precinct told him to use his own discretion. Reasoning that although there was damage to the car, he did not know to whom the car belonged and that consequently there would be no complaining witness, the officer told the man he was free to go. After once blinking his eyes in mild disbelief, the man wasted no time in making his exit which evoked a good-natured laugh from the officer.

There are numerous situations where the policeman will ignore the behavior of persons who are apparently mentally ill or will not take any official action unless forced to do so when the behavior in question becomes threatening, violent, or criminal, or because a citizen makes a complaint. This particular officer had no desire to handle what happened as a criminal matter and called the precinct only to protect himself. If the man had not broken the window, it would have been possible for the officer to completely ignore the behavior.

Police frequently receive phone calls, sometimes on a regular basis, from persons who are under the delusion that others are trying to harm them. When a serious crime such as murder which receives publicity occurs, the police are besieged by persons ready to confess. Many of these are known to the police from past experience as harmless. The stories of other persons are checked out, and they are subsequently released. It is a common practice for the police, in order to protect against false confessions, not to release certain items of evidence to the press and in some cases to release false or ambiguous items. Although falsely confessing to a crime

could constitute interference with the police and obstruction of justice, criminal proceedings are never instituted against these people, and civil proceedings are rare.

The police may be called by a family member or by some neighbor who has perceived a disturbance. It is often the case that the family member or neighbor has called the police not because he seriously wants the person in question to be arrested but because he can no longer tolerate the sick person's behavior and is reaching for outside intervention. The police sometimes are able to mediate family and neighbor disputes and settle the problem so that no official action is taken, or the family or the neighbors decide to proceed with a civil commitment on their own without further police involvement. In these situations either there is no criminal infraction, or one is willing to sign a criminal complaint. Many police officers actively discourage persons from signing a disorderly conduct complaint pointing out that the result is a criminal arrest record and a night spent in jail, both of which the patient is likely to resent in the future. Furthermore, the police are reluctant to take the initiative themselves in these cases, feeling that the responsibility is with the family member, who should not be allowed to pass the buck by calling in the police. As a general rule, then, the police will not take official action unless the family member or neighbor agrees either to sign a criminal complaint or sign a petition for civil hospitalization, in which case the police will help to transport the person to the hospital, if no other means of transportation is available.

Workable Procedures:
New York City and San Francisco

When the policeman decides on the necessity for care, he initially apprehends the person, brings the person to some place where care may be had pending a decision whether or not to hospitalize him, and by providing information, helps the doctor to decide whether the person requires admission to a mental health facility.

It is at the hospital that most police problems arise. No matter how well defined is the policeman's authority to detain a mentally ill person in an emergency, unless he can get the person admitted, his efforts will have been futile. Typically the policeman will take no official action unless there are pressing reasons for doing so, but once a law enforcement officer has decided to take the person to a mental health facility he feels he has "assumed responsibility" by taking the person into his custody. The policeman will stay with the case and see it through— as did the officer in the example—until there has been some final resolution of the situation. A decision by a policeman to use emergency detention is influenced by a number of pragmatic considerations in addition to the seriousness of the offense and the person's potential for violence. The policeman must be concerned with whether there is room at the hospital, whether the orderly or the intern on duty at the hospital will accept this person or not, and how much of his time alternative courses of action will consume. In addition to statutory authority to act at all, the policeman needs a procedure that is workable; one that will provide an authoritative medical resolution of the situation following the initial apprehension and transporting the person to a mental health facility. The following example illustrates the procedure for emergency admission in New York City.

The policeman agreed with the store owner that stealing grapes in plain sight was odd especially when the man then dared the owner to call the police. The two had been talking only a few minutes when the man in question returned to the store. The officer suggested that the hospital was where the man belonged, and the store owner said he would not file any criminal charges if the officer thought this was best. As the officer left, he told the store owner that he would let him know what happened.

When brought to the hospital, the patient told the doctor that he did not say to the policeman that angels were going to kill him because he was the devil. Furthermore, the doctor had no right to hold him; he would call his lawyer and sue the city. He loudly and profanely protested this violation of his civil rights and the unjust treatment he was receiving. After his examination the doctor said the best thing would be for him to be admitted to the hospital, but the patient threatened the doctor and refused to go. One officer took hold of the patient from behind bringing him to the floor while another officer and an attendant took a firm grasp on his arms and legs; in this fashion they carried him into the elevator which would take him to the admitting ward.

Under the New York emergency admission procedure, the decision of the physician on duty at the Bellevue psychiatric admitting desk is sufficient legal authority to hospitalize the patient.[5] When the doctor on duty at the admitting desk admits or refuses to admit the person, he assumes the responsibility for that decision; the policeman simply tells the doctor the facts that have occurred up to the point of bringing the patient to the hospital. The admission is based less on those facts than on the psychiatric examination that takes place at the admitting desk. The point to be noticed about this procedure is its simplicity from the police point of view: no paper work, no red tape, no petition, no application, no medical certificate, and no mandatory court appearance. The doctor takes over once the policeman gets his "problem" to the hospital. The New York City procedure has proved a workable alternative to criminal arrest.

Practice in San Francisco suggests that effective police handling of the mentally disabled is more than a matter of paper work. In California emergency admission does not require a petition. Hospitalization of up to 72 hours is authorized on the "application" of a police officer under section 5050.3 of the Welfare and Institutions Code. At the end of 72 hours the patient is entitled to immediate release unless judicial commitment proceedings are initiated by filing a "petition" for court commitment. According to an official of the California Department of Mental Hygiene: "Prior to 1939, when a police officer apprehended an obviously mentally ill person trying to kill himself or others or one who was causing a serious disturbance, he took him to jail since there was no alternative; the new procedure provided they be taken to the hospital." In San Francisco, the California statute has proven workable because the doctors at the admitting desk there, like their counterparts in New York City, take responsibility for the decision to admit. A lieutenant on the San Francisco police department who served as an advisor on legal matters explained the procedure:

> The officer on the beat and the sergeant at the station level have absolute discretion whether to take to a hospital or to jail a person who may have committed a crime but is also mentally distracted. Police do not sign petitions for the commitment of mentally ill individuals. We feel this is the responsibility of the district attorney. A person obviously mentally ill but causing a disturbance would be taken into custody on the authority of section 5050.3 and taken to the hospital. No charges would be

filed. We have been successful in getting the doctors to decide who should be admitted.

> If the police officer, instead, arrests the person, no information as to mental illness or symptoms of mental illness is communicated to the court; this is on the theory that if the individual is sufficiently showing symptoms of mental illness, a decision to take him to the hospital would have been made. If the doctors think the symptoms are not enough to warrant hospitalizing him, at least for observation, we do not think there would be enough to present to a judge.

Red Tape and Paper Work

Admission to a mental health facility on an emergency basis is not always as uncomplicated as it might appear from the examples in New York and San Francisco. The New York City procedure is in fact atypical.[6] Bellevue is a large teaching hospital staffed at night by psychiatric residents who are medical school graduates, have spent one year training in general medicine, and have had two years of psychiatric internship. They are, consequently, well qualified to make the necessary judgment. Not all facilities designated for emergency admissions are staffed by people as competent or as experienced. In most cases the facility involved is either a county or municipal general hospital with a psychiatric wing. During daylight hours, when experienced doctors are available to make the decision, no serious problems seem to arise. However, at night and on weekends the authority and consequently the responsibility for admission is delegated sometimes to a medical resident, sometimes to an orderly, a nurse, or a clerk. The power of emergency detention clearly authorizes initial apprehension by the police and police custody while an emergency situation exists, including transportation to some place where care may be had. But it is equally clear, both at common law and from reading the modern statutory provisions, that the power of "emergency detention" when exercised by the police is not sufficient authority for involuntary admission to a mental hospital—the point at which the police relinquish their physical control over the person. This issue is mooted in New York City and San Francisco because the admitting facility can, and, in practice does, take full responsibility for the admission. Under the California and Illinois statutes however, the policeman is required to "apply for admission" and "petition for admission" respectively, the functional equivalent in criminal law of signing a complaint against the person. When a petition or written application is required, as it is in many jurisdictions, whoever signs it (the police or mental health official from the admitting institution) accepts the legal responsibility. The person effecting the admission must be able subsequently (as in a suit for false arrest or malicious prosecution) to establish that the conditions in fact existed that would justify admission. From the point of view of the admitting institution, the simplest and safest procedure for escaping this legal responsibility is to persuade somebody—anybody—to sign a formal petition which initiates civil commitment. This shifts the legal responsibility to the petitioner and obviates the doctor's appearance in court. If a relative will sign a petition or if the patient himself is capable and willing to complete a voluntary admission form, admission follows. The policeman, if handy, will do. But the police are generally not willing to sign a petition for civil commitment—and for good reasons. In the absence of a petition (or a court order), the responsibility for accepting the patient is squarely placed on the admitting institution.

Some institutions flatly refuse to admit a person without a signed petition. If the person making the decision for the mental health facility is inexperienced, or if he is accustomed only to limited authority and is not comfortable making the decision to admit on an emergency basis, he is unlikely to be willing to assume the responsibility, making admission difficult. Typically, an impasse develops at the mental health facility while the policeman and the orderly wait for a psychiatrist to come.

In some areas admission is complicated by the fact that psychiatric beds in the county or municipal facility are scarce and only those in serious need of treatment will be accepted; some persons will be rejected even though they may be quite disturbed and in need of treatment. Because police usually arrive at the mental health facility at night or early in the morning, they must frequently wait hours before they obtain any sort of medical advice. Since interns rotate quite frequently, the policemen find themselves dealing with different people every week. No consistent policy about admissions emerges, and almost every case comes down to a decision on its individual facts. On the other hand, the police are normally quite reluctant to take mentally ill persons, even if violent, to police lockups. In some cases where the police could not effect admission to the mental health facility, they tracked down family members and persuaded them to take the person home for the night instead of having the police take him to jail. Then in the morning the patient is brought to the same facility and admitted without difficulty.

Just how difficult admission may be when the police refuse to sign a petition and the hospital refuses to admit without a petition can be seen in the following example from Chicago.

A well-dressed man told the desk officer he was mentally ill and asked to be taken to the hospital immediately explaining: "When I am going to be sick I can feel it coming on."

The officer preferred not to argue and said he would oblige. As another officer was closing the door of the police van, the man jumped upon him from inside the van, knocking both officers to the ground. They were unable to restrain the man who now seemed to have "superhuman strength," until two nearby policemen helped.

At the hospital the four officers waited for the intern on call to be awakened by phone; the orderly on duty said he did not have authority to make an admission unless a "petition" was signed. Meanwhile the patient became docile. When the intern did arrive he concluded the man was not a fit person for emergency admission because he was not actually violent at the moment. The officers reacted with surprise and anger. One officer said: "There we were, four police officers who would usually be dressed very neatly, standing in front of him completely disheveled, dirty, cut, and bruised and here was another person whom we claimed was mentally ill who was also disheveled, dirty, dusty, and bruised." The intern's behavior violated the officers' notions of common sense.

The police, who had witnessed the violence decided they would have to take the man to the police lockup. As they were about to leave the man grabbed the intern by the throat and pulled his tie tightly around his neck. Only the quick work of the police officers saved the intern from serious injury. The intern was then convinced and admitted the man.

The police finally enjoyed the humor and poetic justice of this situation, but the problems they find in admitting people to local mental health facilities are frequently much more irritating, with the result that they stop bringing such persons to mental health facilities and take them instead to jail where procedures are available to hospitalize them—a psychiatric examination ordered by the criminal court. There were 89 such cases in one month during 1963 in Chicago.

It is evident from talking to policemen that, in addition to the reasons which the police explicitly give for not signing petitions, there are other motivations present. Policemen are sometimes afraid of mentally ill persons generally; fear of signing petitions appears to be closely connected with their fear of violence and of reprisal. The policeman who advises a family member that a disorderly conduct complaint will irritate the disturbed person and possibly result in reprisal may also be expressing his own fears. Police also feel out of their element when defining people as mentally ill. While they feel their experience does equip them to spot a "criminal," they do not feel it equips them to spot a "mental case," except where the person is obviously disturbed. The ambivalence the police show in handling mentally ill persons is reinforced by the difficulties they face in dealing with local mental health facilities. The practical effect of difficulty in securing admission to the mental health facility is that the police begin to use other, more familiar, alternatives and take the prisoner to jail instead of to the hospital or, in some cases, release him. This is not to imply that the police should decide who should be admitted; their complaint is that the doctors will not decide and will not take the responsibility. The trip to the hospital consumes time that could be devoted to other police work and may tie up not only one but several officers and police equipment as well, especially if there is violence. On the other hand, since the only alternative to the hospital is the police lockup, there is pressure to hospitalize because of the trouble such persons may cause when placed behind bars, because police officers, like citizens generally, balk when obviously sick people are denied medical care, and because the critical decision about hospitalization is merely being temporarily postponed.

IMPLICATIONS FOR POLICE POLICY

Police Training

The job of dealing on a mass scale with the mentally ill, however narrowly or broadly one defines this class, is constantly left to the police. The problem of inadequate medical facilities, inadequate public provision for the old, the destitute, the helpless, and countless other social problems receive concrete expression by a complaint to the policeman on the beat. So it is in the case of the mentally disabled, and so it is likely to remain for some time. Police need education in the principles of mental health, but the extent to which one could increase police training for handling and recognizing the mentally ill is almost without limit. While some training in this area is essential for all police officers, we cannot, nor should we, attempt to make doctors or psychiatrists out of policemen. The experience state hospitals have had in training "attendants" to be mental health workers indicates that police as well can be trained in the basics of mental health technique. Special squads for mental health problems may be helpful in some larger departments.[7] But there is no reason why all policemen should not know exactly where to take mentally disabled persons, and under what conditions and at what times people are likely to be admitted. The National Association for Mental Health booklet, "How to Recognize and Handle Abnormal People" is a start, but every city should supplement this with a catalog of the local medical facilities available. Such a booklet,

"Emergency Hospitalization for the Mentally Ill," used by the police in Cleveland, Ohio, lists the name, address, and telephone of the available community mental health facilities, together with the type of service available, any special conditions on the service, and the hours when these services are available. The police department of Winston-Salem, North Carolina, uses a similar booklet that gives detailed information about all social agencies in that area. Such manuals could easily be written with peculiar application to particular localities, except for very small police forces where existence of these facilities is a matter of common knowledge among police officers.[8]

Adequate Community Mental Health Facilities

In our experience there is less problem with the police recognizing persons who are mentally ill than in dealing with persons everyone would agree are mentally ill and in need of medical attention. There is little point to heightening police perception of mental illness unless concomitant measures give policemen some realistic hope of being able to dispose of such cases other than by the traditional method of criminal arrest. In many communities the key problem is a lack of medical facilities; either there are no medical facilities at all, or they are unwilling to take the kinds of cases the police bring in, or they are not open when business is at its peak, that is, at night and on weekends. It is the lack of such facilities that accounts for the fact that mentally ill persons are sometimes housed in local jails supervised by police departments where only inadequate facilities can be maintained despite the good will of many policemen.

What the police need most is a workable procedure that allows them to take persons they reasonably suspect to be dangerously mentally ill to some place where expert evaluation of the policeman's lay judgment can be had with reasonable dispatch. From the police point of view where the procedures are cumbersome, where they fail quickly to identify the person in question as being mentally ill, where they fail to provide doctors willing to assume responsibility for the person's care, where in short the collective police experience is one of futility, the route of mental health care for the mentally ill offender is unlikely to be followed. This must, of necessity, remain the case until the public provides community mental health facilities consistent with the recognition that mentally ill persons should be handled by civil rather than criminal process and provides workable procedures to that end.

Legal Authority for Emergency Detention and Emergency Admission

Despite the fact that most state laws appear to give policemen adequate legal protection when apprehending persons they reasonably suppose to be dangerously mentally ill and in need of medical attention, some emergency detention statutes are unnecessarily complicated and confusing. Whether we should hold the policemen to the standard of "probable cause" or the standard of "good faith" in detaining the mentally ill depends on whether one wants to encourage the police to take mentally ill persons to mental hospitals. In the case of the genuine emergency when doctors and judges are not available, the police, acting in good faith, should have clear statutory authorization to take persons thought mentally ill and dangerous at the moment to local mental health facilities or state hospitals for a preliminary examination without fear of civil liability. Many policemen say

they fear the possibility of a civil suit for damages. Insurance protection, if necessary, should be provided policemen. If, as we think, such suits are seldom successful, coverage should be available at a modest cost.

Some statutes, such as that in New York, are substantively defective. Hawaii, for example, recently copied the New York definition of persons mentally ill and "disorderly" that, as we saw, does not include the non-disorderly but dangerous mentally ill person. It was, in fact, just such a gap that led to the New York decision that the broader common law power survived enactment of the New York emergency detention statutes. But substantive coverage should not have to wait on appellate decisions. Emergency detention statutes should be as broad as the common law power.

Our findings indicate that the problem is less substantive than procedural. Moreover, our observations indicate that no *emergency detention procedure* will be effective unless there is also a workable *emergency admission procedure*. So far as we can discover, the difficulties of the police are not precipitated by a failure of the emergency detention power but by the practical failure of the emergency admission procedures, a failure due to medical unwillingness to accept the responsibility for who will be admitted. This finding has been confirmed in a 1968 study of rural areas in Illinois that concluded as follows:

> Emergency situations are usually not handled by the emergency detention and admission procedures of Article VII of the Mental Health Code which authorizes admission for as long as 24 hours upon presentation of an emergency petition without more. This is so despite the fact that the 24 hour admission on petition alone, first enacted in 1952, has undergone several revisions in recent years designed, according

to statements of those who drafted the revisions, to informalize the procedure and encourage its use. The major reason for this seems to be that the 24 hour emergency procedure requires the presence of hospital and judicial personnel at mandatory court hearings held in the county in which the hospital is located. Judges in counties in which hospitals are located must hear cases for all the counties in the zone served by the hospital. These judges have pressured the hospitals to reduce the number of emergency admissions. Hospital administrators comply not only to preserve good relations with the judge but also because they too consider mandatory hearings at best a burden and often unnecessary. Who is to pay the cost of these hearings—the state, the county in which the hospital is located, or the county in which the patient resides—is also an issue of considerable importance.

Voluntary admissions are preferred to emergency admissions because they require less paper work and "red tape." On the operational level, this preference becomes a reluctance to admit persons on an emergency basis. While other studies of urban areas have indicated police are reluctant to execute emergency petitions when called upon to do so, this does not seem to be the case in the areas we studied. Hospital officials interviewed were unaware of any such reluctance. Police and sheriffs said they have no objection to executing emergency petitions. In fact, they do execute a few in practice, but infrequently for several reasons: 1. Executing an emergency petition is a futile gesture if the hospital will not accept an admission. 2. Relatives or others are typically available for that purpose. 3. In one of the counties studied, the states attorney signs them instead. The hospital will refuse emergency admission under Article VII but grant "voluntary" admission if the police can "persuade" the prospective patient to execute a voluntary application. Some police officers second-

guess the hospital by having a friendly local doctor examine the psychiatric emergency in the local jail and execute a physician's certificate, in which event the hospital automatically admits the person.

Despite the hospitals' systematic avoidance of Article VII procedures, difficulties from the law enforcement point of view are minimal since nearly every police referral of a mentally ill person results in admission to the hospital. Police expressed neither reluctance about bringing disturbed persons to the hospital nor doubt about whether they are legally authorized to do so. We have found no evidence that obviously mentally ill persons are being criminally charged prior to referral to the state hospital. Moreover, the only time they spend in local jails is waiting to be examined by a local doctor pending medical certification, a period that may be as short as an hour or as long as overnight.[9]

The police do not want—nor should they have—the authority or the responsibility for effecting admission to the hospital; this is a medical responsibility, which is what the debate over signing petitions is all about. The emergency detention power is sufficient for getting the person to the hospital pending medical examination. State law might take a cue from the policeman in our first example and fasten responsibility for what happens thereafter onto the medical institution when the police present the person at the admitting desk. Doctors should be as responsible for mistakenly refusing a person admittance as they are for mistakenly admitting a person.

Responsibility for who is admitted to a mental hospital is not, need not, and should not be a police responsibility. The law should require that the critical decision—whether to admit the person—be made by the doctor (without the formalities of a petition, an application, or a medical certificate).

Appropriate procedural protections against unwarranted admission are inapposite in an emergency; they can wait until the next day. Experience has shown that, when the law in its attempt to protect the civil rights of its citizens has sought to impose its procedural protections at the point of initial decision, the emergency admission procedure will not be efficacious. Such procedures protect all the citizens rights save one—his right to prompt medical attention.

NOTES

1   This paper was presented as a lecture to police executives who attended the Law Enforcement Policy Development Seminar held by the Law Enforcement Study Center of the Social Science Institute of Washington University, St. Louis at Bromwoods, Missouri, March 7, 1968, sponsored by the National Institute of Mental Health, the International Association of Chiefs of Police, the St. Louis Metropolitan Police Department, and the School of Continuing Education of Washington University. It also reflects the final draft of portions of the final report of the American Bar Foundation project, "Mental Illness and Criminal Law" (P.H.S. Grant MH 302–02, National Institute of Mental Health).

2   Egon Bittner, "Police Discretion in Emergency Apprehension of Mentally Ill Persons," *Social Problems* 15, No. 278 (1967): 291. For the medical approach to these questions generally, see Glasscote, et al., *The Psychiatric Emergency* (1966), a publication of the Joint Information Service of the American Psychiatric Association and the National Association for Mental Health; Silbert, "Psychiatric Patients in the Admitting Emergency Room," *Arch. Gen. Psych.* 11, No. 24 (1964); Ungerleider, "The Psychiatric Emergency," *Arch. Gen. Psych.* 3, No. 593 (1960); *Psychiatric Emergencies and the General Hospital* (1965), a publication of the American Hospital Association.

3   See "Handling Abnormal People," Chicago Police Department Training Bulletin II–S (1962): "Your job, as a police officer, is to get the disturbed persons safely to a hospital where successful ways of treating and curing mental cases are available."

4   See ibid: "The quiet and unassuming behavior of a mentally ill person is not an absolute guide to his degree of probable dangerousness. Atrocious crimes have been committed by the mentally ill. On the whole, however, only a very small portion of the mentally ill are a menace to others."

5   New York Mental Hygiene Law §81 (1962).

6   The procedure is not even typical of New York State. Outside the City of New York different procedures apply.

7   See Rock, *Hospitalization and Discharge of the Mentally Ill*, 97–105, for a discussion of the special squad in Los Angeles. One of the many complications of this complicated problem is the difference in police practices within a single state. In Los Angeles, (not included in this study), Rock, Ibid., 103–104, reports:

> The willingness of the Los Angeles Hospital detail officers to act as commitment petitioners deserves special attention since it represents a departure from the police reluctance or refusal observed elsewhere. . . . Later, if continued hospitalization seems necessary, the officer is willing once again to supply the necessary act of executing a petition for commitment. He does not feel that he is committing the person; the doctors of the court do that — he merely supplies a necessary formality. The police hospital detail — if its officers take any note of the legal implications of petitioning at all — is apparently content to continue to rely on the medical judgment that the person needs hospitalization. . . .
>
> In the Los Angeles arrangement the doctors provide the medical judgment and the police through a specialized unit supply the person willing to assume responsibility as a petitioner.

Yet the San Francisco Police (included in this study but not in Rock's study) never sign commitment petitions and are reluctant to execute even the 72 hour emergency admission "application." The Los Angeles experience suggest, again, that the key problem is getting the person to a doctor who will assume

responsibility for the judgment whether hospitalization is indicated.

8   This assumption has been drawn into question
by a 1968 American Bar Foundation study,
"Rural Criminal Justice," in which 7 of 8
law enforcement officers interviewed did not

know of the existence of ongoing local community mental health centers; see note 9.

9   Brakel, South, and Matthews, "Diversion from
the Criminal Process in the Rural Community," *American Criminal Law Review,* Vol.
7, No. 3, 1969: 122.

Exiles from the American Dream: The Junkie and the Cop

BRUCE JACKSON

In the summer of 1966 I traveled around
the country for a Cambridge research organization that had contracted with the President's Commission on Law Enforcement
and Administration of Justice to study certain problems having to do with drug abuse
and control in this country. The main part
of my job was talking with and observing at
work a spectrum of participants: police,
judges, doctors, administrators, addicts,
pushers, ex-addicts, rehabilitation personnel,
and so on. We found early in the study that
none of the sets of figures purporting to tell
the numbers of drug abusers and their relationship to the economy were much good,
and that almost everyone had The Answer.
We spent the summer getting as many points
of view as we could, then tried to make sense
of those that were sufficiently rational and
to evaluate those that seemed worth it.

After the report was written, I realized
that many of my blacks and whites had gone

to problematical gray, the burden of increased knowledge. I realized also that part
of that knowledge was of a kind outside the
numbers and specifics that fill government
reports and sociological journal articles; it is
composed of pieces of information that do
not array themselves in nice neat patterns;
they do not form pretty theses or admit nice
tabular or verbal conclusions—but somehow
I cannot help feeling that they are in many
ways more important, more germane, than
the figures and the charts. Art and science
go around constructing and projecting coherences; the street does not think in
coherences, it is just there.

An example: Unlike police who deal
with homicide or other major crimes, who
have onetime or rare contact with their cus-
tomers, the police who handle problems of
morality rather than injury, crimes like prostitution and drug addiction, tend to develop
a peculiar rapport with the people with
whom they war. They do not deal in terms
of single events, but in continuing relationships, some of which they must maintain in
order to obtain information, others because

From *The Atlantic Monthly* **219** (January 1967):
44–51. Copyright © 1966 by The Atlantic Monthly
Company, Boston, Mass. Reprinted by permission.

there is no reason not to. This varies from city to city, but there is a clear level of consistency. The narcotics detective must live in the junkie's world, know his language, appreciate his pain; he may be—and often is—antagonistic to all of these, but he is rarely independent of them.

The sections that follow are from notes scribbled in police cars, in bars, on planes, on a beach, sitting in a park; they are some of those other pieces.

NEW YORK

Ray Viera is the larger, more volatile of the two. His hair is wavy with streaks of gray, and he tends to tap your shoulder when he is involved in a statement. Burt Alvins is smaller, wiry; most of his head is a short gray-flecked crew cut. Burt negotiates the green Lark around some construction on F.D.R. Drive; it doesn't feel much like a police car.

"Everybody lives outside the city now," one of them says.

"Not everybody," I say.

"I mean all the cops and firemen I know. Except for a couple of young single guys. Everybody else is out on the Island or up in Westchester. It's going to be just the poor and the illegal left in New York. People are moving out in droves. They're not doing it to escape the taxes. Taxes are just as high out there. They're doing it to keep their children together."

They complain about court decisions. "We've become robots. We can't think, we're mechanical men."

"Everybody I know quits at twenty years to the day. It's not the job he dislikes, it's the handcuffing."

"A thing a normal person would consider suspicious a policeman can't consider suspicious because we're robots."

"I'd give a month's pay to bring Earl

Warren here and give him the tour I'm giving you."

"There's legitimate people here. They're suffering, they're in jail."

I ask how to break through the hostility, what you do about the reputation for brutality.

"You just count the days you have left."

We drive along 118th Street. The area crawls with big-city specialties: numbers, junk, whores. Garbage piles up in back, between the houses. The garbage men can't get in there because the backs are locked, so the stuff mounts and mounts, and every once in a while they make an assault and get some of it out, chasing away rats as big and careless as dogs.

"We have to go see somebody."

"One of our informers," Ray says. "This guy's not stupid. He's intelligent. He's a nice guy. Wait till you see him though."

We enter a building just above Central Park. Someone lives on the first floor. The second, up the narrow dark stairway that is even darker after the bright sun, is vacant. All the doors are open; one is unhinged and lies flat in the room, as if something walked right in without bothering to stop. Another door hangs at a grotesque angle, the top hinge ripped off. More rubbish in there. A few empty bottles. We go up another flight, and Ray goes to Elmer's door. It is unlocked, and he eases it open slowly. Elmer is sitting on the bed, a blanket over his knees. "Anybody here?" Ray asks.

"No. I'm alone."

Ray waves us in. The room is about twelve by twelve. A big, old TV is on a bureau by the wall. A new Sony is on another bureau, turned on to a talk show. Elmer tells us a prostitute friend bought it for him as a present.

"How are your legs, Elmer?" Ray asks.

Elmer moves the blanket from his thighs.

On both are long running sores, about four or five inches long and a half inch or so wide; they look deep; something oozes.

"Jesus Christ," Burt says. "Why don't you let us get you in the hospital for a while?"

"Maybe next week."

"Those sores don't look so good."

"I can't go in this week. You know."

"How are your arms?"

"Feel a little better." He holds his forearms out and moves the fingers. A Popeye caricature: from the elbows up, the arms are the thin sticks of an old man; below the elbow, they are swollen like thighs. The fingers all look like oversize thumbs. Like his thighs, Elmer's arms are covered with scars that look like strip photos of the surface of the moon. There are too many of the dime- and quarter-size craters to count.

"This is Bruce, Elmer. He's a new man, and we're breaking him in."

Elmer looks up, noticing or acknowledging me for the first time. He nods and shrugs. They make a date to meet somewhere later in the week.

"You sure you don't want us to get you in a hospital, Elmer?" Ray asks.

Elmer says no.

For me, Ray asks, "Elmer, what you shooting now?"

"About eight bags."

"When did you start?"

"1955."

"And how old are you now?"

"Forty-eight."

"There's a silence, directed to me. Elmer looks sixty-five or seventy, and they all know I'd thought him an old man. He folds the blanket over his thighs, and we go out. On the way, Burt gives Elmer a few bucks and says get some cigarettes.

Going down the stairs, Ray says, "If he tells you he's shooting eight bags, that means he's shooting twelve. That's sixty bucks a day. Seven days a week. Four hundred and twenty dollars a week. Almost what I make a month." Elmer, obviously, is in some business activities about which the police prefer not to ask.

Most New York addicts, I know, spend less than twenty dollars a day for narcotics. Few look as grim as Elmer. But enough do. And enough wind up dead because of infection or accidental overdose; many have TB. The physiological debilitation and destruction result from concomitants of drug taking: the junkie spends his money for drugs instead of food, his drugs are cut with quinine and other chemicals that often do him considerable damage, and worst of all, the material he injects and the instruments he uses are so unsanitary that he constantly risks the kinds of infection that have scarred Elmer. The junk itself, so long as it does not exceed the addict's tolerance, is not really as physiologically harmful as cigarettes or alcohol, but the life style is vicious.

"Some of these guys," Burt says, "they get worse than Elmer. Ruin all the veins in the arms and legs, burn them out, and they shoot in the mouth. And when that goes, in the penis. Hurts like hell, they say, but they can find the vein."

I ask them if their visiting Elmer's apartment in daylight might not get him into trouble with other addicts. They say no, they spend a lot of time questioning addicts, most of whom are not informers, standard procedure.

"These people around here—they know who you are?"

"Sure, they know us. Even if they'd never seen us before, they'd know us. If you're white around here, you're either a bill collector or the Man. They maybe don't know which Man you are, but you're one of them."

"Or a trick looking for a whore," Burt says.

"You still get white tricks coming up here?"

"They'll always be coming up here."

We drive past a crap game. There are about fifty men standing around. Some of them yell.

They talk about Elmer. "I'm worried about him, Burt. Can't we get him into some hospital?"

"He doesn't want to go. We can't force him."

"Well, how about we get him some antibiotics for those sores? They're just awful."

"You have to have a prescription for that stuff."

"Maybe I can get somebody to let me have some."

"Heroin you can get; for penicillin you need a prescription."

We stop for a traffic light. A kid about five years old looks in the car, at me, says, "Fuck you, cop," and walks away.

We sit in the car by the 125th Street New York Central station. Two junkies they know hustle down 125th, counting money. We know where they are going, but there isn't sufficient cause to follow and arrest.

"I know what the courts are trying to do—protect the honest citizens. But you know something: in all the years we've been in this business, we've never hit one guy that was a square."

"The trouble with this job," Burt says, "is you take it home with you. We get together, and our wives say, why don't you talk about something else. They don't understand."

"You can't put it off at night," Ray says.

I look through their report book. They get two days off per week, but I notice that they work at least one, and sometimes both

of them, either going out with an undercover agent or appearing in court. Many of the workdays run twelve to sixteen hours. I ask why they stick with it.

"I think it's a challenge," Burt says. "I like the work. But as my partner and I have told you a number of times, our hands are tied. To do this kind of a job I guess you have to have some dedication in you. It's a losing battle: for every one you arrest, there's five to take their place. But when you do make a good arrest, it can make the whole thing worthwhile."

I say something about Elmer.

"They ought to put a picture of him in the papers," Ray said. "Show some of these people."

"You could show them a picture of Elmer," Ray says. "Tomorrow they pick up a paper to see what the Giants did. That's it. As far as it goes."

Driving downtown we pass through Central Park. "It's like reverse shock treatment," Ray says. We see a spreading plume of black smoke over on the East side, somewhere in the Eighties.

Burt: "Probably a junkie cooking up."

Ray: "Good-sized cooker."

And Burt: "You come back after a day off and hope maybe things are going to be a little different. Then it's not. There's still glass in the street. The same people."

HOUSTON

Morning in the Narcotics Squad room. Captain Jack Renois and Don McMannes are the only ones in. Hooker, the secretary, does things and fetches coffee. The detectives come in around 11:00 or 11:30 and wait for the phone calls from informers. Things come alive around noon, after the addicts get up. One of the detectives is selling a shotgun; it is passed around and admired.

A phone rings. An addict snitching on another addict. For money, for a break on a case. Or maybe just talking for a while. I begin to appreciate the odd symbiosis. The addicts and the cops move in the same world, live the same hours, wait for deals to happen on the same streets. One addict had said something to me the week before, complaining about the hassles he was always in, and one police official had complained to me this morning about the difficulty he had getting adequate funds and equipment. Both used exactly the same sentence: "We got to scuffle for every fucking thing."

Don comes back into the room; he had been on the phone for about thirty minutes. "He just wanted to talk for a while," he tells me. "Somebody I arrested once." The addicts sometimes call up officers, not to snitch or bitch, but just to talk to someone who understands. For them, no one appreciates their hassles and their world better than the cop, who is so close they don't even consider him a square.

On Lieutenant Kennedy's desk: *"FIAT JUSTITIA, RUAT CAELUM."* And under it, in small letters, "Let justice be done, though the heavens may fall." "I saw it a long time ago and I liked it and it's been on my desk ever since," he says. "A reminder, I guess."

With one of the detectives, I go out to visit an informer. She is a slight, pretty girl with dark eyes. Two children are in the house, and she says she can't stay in the car talking for very long. She talks about Joey, with whom she lives, currently in jail needing bond. "They say that county farm's a bad place. I don't know. Maybe I'll get him out."

She used to be a good booster but no more. Shoplifting has become too dangerous: "I got too many children now. Nobody to take care of them if I go to the joint." A new connection had come by a few days ago and given her fifty dollars' worth of narcotics without asking for money.

"How come?" asks the detective. "He want some trim?"

"I don't know. Maybe. If Joey wasn't there." She tells us where the connection lives and who is with him, and the phone number.

"You hooked again?"

"No. I can't afford it. I shoot all the dope I can get, though."

"You high now?"

"No. I had two caps this morning. That's all."

Later the same day: riding with Mike Chavez and his partner, Charley. While Mike is at a phone booth, Charley tells me he has just been transferred into Narcotics from Vice. He says about every whore he knows is on some kind of drugs, that whenever they broke into a prostitute's apartment they found narcotics or pills.

"Did you ever file?"

"No."

"Why not?"

"Wouldn't stand up. Almost everything we would do is illegal. They know it, and we know it. Our job was mainly harassment. Make them uncomfortable enough to move on." Later he tells me it is as hard to make a prostitution case as a narcotics case. A few weeks earlier in Harlem, a New York policeman had told me the same thing.

Mike comes back. "Anything?" Charley asks.

"No."

Chavez has never taken the test for sergeant. Only one sergeant is permitted in the Narcotics unit, and if Chavez were promoted, he would be forced to change assignments. He likes the work and is very good at it.

He tells me that the talk and newspaper

articles about violent addicts are nonsense; what bothers him is the crime associated with addiction. I mention the six million or so alcoholics, and all the damage they do. Chavez pulls up to a booth to make another call. While he is gone, Charley tells me what I said is irrelevant. Chavez comes back and says, "Funny, what you were saying. They have a bar in that store, and I could see that every stool was occupied." He says he would like to find some other way of handling the problem, but he doesn't know one that would work. He shrugs and says it bothers him sometimes. "But I'm a policeman, you know." He turns to Charley, sitting in the back, and says, "You got your gun?"

"Yeah."

I turn and see on the seat a .38 automatic. He tells me you need a holster for a revolver and everything bulges, but an automatic can be just tucked in the belt. I ask Mike if he has his.

"In the trunk."

Later that night, Donny tells me they almost never need weapons. No Houston addict would draw on a detective because the addicts know the detectives aren't going to shoot without a good reason. "Only time any of them ever does anything with a gun is to say, 'I got a gun.' I say, 'Where?' and he points, and I say, 'Put it on the table,' and he does. Or if he has one in his hand when we bust in, he just swings it around and hands it over. We all know each other."

AUSTIN

I was in the homicide room of the police station waiting for Lieutenant Harvey Gann, the detective in charge of the Vice and Narcotics Squad. According to friends of mine in Houston and Huntsville, he is a very good policeman. Gann came in, laughing. He and his partner had just been out on a narcotics watch that didn't work out. They were using an old pickup truck and had stopped for a red light when two women walked over, and one said, "You want to have a good time?"

"How much?"

"Ten and three."

"What's the three for?"

"The room, baby."

Gann asked if the same applied for her friend and his friend. The other woman said yes. Gann noticed a tall Negro standing in a nearby doorway, and said, "Who's he?"

"Just an old nothing sonofabitch that hangs around."

Gann and his partner got out of the truck, took off their LBJ hats and lensless glasses.

"Goddamn, Lieutenant! It's you again!" The woman began laughing.

"You see," he told me, "I had arrested her four times before. And I put those hat and glasses right back on because we couldn't all fit in the front, and I had to ride with them in the back of the pickup, and I'd be damned if I'd have anybody I know see me riding around town in a pickup truck with two old whores like that."

NEW YORK

The undercover man is late.

The two detectives, Al Koch and Ray Imp, lean against the phone booth they use for an office. The phone has an "Out of Order" sign on it that is phony. The two men are easily identifiable (one is about 6 feet 3 inches and has shocking red hair; the other is about 5 feet 10 inches and is shaped like a triangle but gives the feeling of a tank), and when they appear on the street, the dealers disappear, so they hover outside the Village perimeter, wait for a call from someone telling them a person they want to arrest is at a specific location, then go in and come out quickly.

The undercover man arrives at eight, an hour late. His name is Sam, and even though I know he is a police officer, I can't quite believe it—the first qualification of an undercover agent.

Al tells me it will be boring waiting with them. He suggests I go with Sam.

"But I know people in the Village."

"Do they know what you're doing in town?"

"No."

"OK. You go with him. They'll think he's just some beatnik friend of yours. We'll just be standing here until he calls anyhow. But take that notebook and cigar and pen out of your pocket."

I hand over my things and go away with Sam.

We walk to the Rienzi, where we are to meet someone named Wilson, his informer. Wilson isn't there, and Sam curses him, saying he can't stand an unpunctual man. He tells me the statistics reporting 60,000 addicts in the United States are all wrong, there are hundreds of thousands of them. I must have looked incredulous because he says, "Yeah, man, I'm serious. Look around you. Half these people smoke weed."

"You don't get addicted to marijuana. They're not addicts."

"Goddamn right they are."

We walk down the street. Someone says hello to me, and I nod. Sam says, "I'll tell you who uses weed all the time: those folk singers. Bunch of addicts."

"Oh."

"You know any of those folk singers?"

"A few."

"They use weed."

We pass one place just as a four-man singing group is going in with their guitars. They pass in front of us. One of them sees me and waves; another says, "Hi, Bruce." I wave back. Sam looks at me queerly, then shrugs it off.

We go back to the Rienzi and talk about court decisions.

"Those bastards. What this country needs is a Hitler for a while. Get these people off the streets. Should have elected Goldwater; he'd have straightened that court out. You know why I hate addicts?" I shake my head. "I'll tell you why: I got a nice wife, over on Staten Island. She never heard a dirty word in her life. A nice girl." He says it with finality. I don't make the connection, but I decide to let it ride; it is too early in the evening to reveal my opacity.

We watch the teen-age girls in their carefully considered outfits.

We go into a bar, and over a beer he talks about his work. "Shouldn't we talk about something else? Someone might be listening."

"Nah. Nobody's listening. Nobody listens here." I don't tell him that when I go into bars like this, I always eavesdrop. Constitutional.

We go up the street to get something to eat but on the way meet Wilson, the informer. With him is another man, who wears khakis, a white T-shirt, and a yellow sport shirt open all the way except for the bottom button. Wilson, the informer, goes off to talk with Sam.

The man in the yellow shirt says to me, "Who you with?"

"Huh?"

"I said who you with?"

"What are you talking about?"

"It's OK, man, I'm undercover too."

"A city cop?"

"No," he says, shaking his head.

"FBN?"

"No."

"Who?"

"FDA." He pauses, maybe to see if I'm going to make a wisecrack. When I don't, he says, "You city?"

I shake my head.

"Federal?"

I shake my head.

"Then who are you undercover for?"

"I'm not a cop."

"Come *on,* man."

A thin effeminate man in his twenties lopes up the street, walking sine waves. "My consciousness has expanded, expanded!"

"Man, is he drunk," the FDA man says.

"It might be something else." The thin guy weaves back. "What you on, man?" I ask.

"Five days on, five days off."

"Off and on what?"

"LSD, psilocybin off days. Little junk to keep the heebies away." He bumps into the FDA man and pats the shoulder of his yellow shirt. "Ain't it a bitch when your family's square?"

"Your family square?"

"You don't *know.* My father is——[he names someone in city government whose name we know], and he is *square.*"

On an off chance there's another celebrity with the same name, I ask, "Which ——?"

"You know which one."

"Come on."

He pulls out his wallet and shows us his collection of identification cards, credit cards, and licenses; they all say ——, Jr. Sam joins us. I look for Wilson, the informer, but he has disappeared. Thin says his family is down on him because he uses drugs.

"What else?"

"Drugs and because of the homosexual business."

"Are you queer?"

"Maybe a little."

He says he can get, in quantity, marijuana and pills. Sam and the FDA man try to stare one another down: if Thin produces grass, he is Sam's; if he produces pills, he is FDA's. Thin weaves in and out of the street. He goes to peer in a car window.

"I thought he'd pat my gun when he was tapping my shoulder just now," FDA says.

"You wearing a gun?" Sam says.

"Yeah. You?"

"I got a little .25."

"Ah. I got my .38 service."

"That cannon. You're crazy. If you ask me, you're better off with nothing."

Thin swings back to the sidewalk. Wilson, the informer, returns and points at someone, and Sam says, "Oh, oh, there's my man," and goes off down Bleeker. FDA wanders away with Thin, talking hippy.

"Come on," Wilson, the informer, says. "We got to stick with Sam."

"Where is he?"

"I don't know. Maybe he went into the park." We walk toward the park. "You new on the squad?"

"I'm not on the squad."

"Oho. A fed, huh?"

"What makes you think I'm a cop?"

"C'mon, man, it's OK. I'm an informer. We're all in this together. It's like I'm a half-cop, you know."

"Oh, all right, I'm working for the feds. But I'm not a cop. I'm a schoolteacher, and I'm doing a study."

"Hey, that's good. Say, what's your undercover name?"

"Bruce."

"What's your real name?"

"Bruce."

"You can't do that. You got to have an undercover name."

"I always use Bruce."

"OK, man, it's your *schtik.* We might meet someone, and I might have to introduce you or something. Where do you say you come from?"

"Cambridge."

"Come on, man, the Village is crawling with people from Cambridge."

"I *am* from Cambridge."

"Jesus Christ, man!"

We walk into Washington Square Park. (Wilson stopped and talked with some characters he knew, and I stayed out of the light, which he seemed to appreciate. I knew several undercover agents had been exposed, "burned" in the argot, and badly beaten recently. I wondered what this nut was leading me into. I wondered what they were all leading themselves into. These people were so different from the cops uptown, the serious and competent Alvins and Viera, with whom I'd sat that afternoon in a car in the west Eighties, talking with an informer while pretty polished women and expensive fat ladies passed us by, seeing only four men in a car; that informer knew he was dead if he should be seen with us, and the conversation was serious. Here it seemed they'd adjusted to the madcap crowd, not only in appearance but in procedure, in thought. A crazy game world on both sides again, like Houston. But different.)

We walk on toward the arch. Wilson tells me he'd like to work for the FBI as an undercover man in the Communist Party. "They ever use people for anything like that?"

"I believe they have, on occasion."

"You think they'd hire me? It's not like I'm inexperienced. And I hate this amateur crap."

"I don't know."

"They wouldn't take me in the army. I would have been good in the army, but they wouldn't take me."

"Why not?"

" 'Cause I'm an addict. Got a record. All that crap." He shrugs. "But I'd sure like to be an undercover man working on Commies. Man, I'm a natural. Who'd ever suspect."

We spot Sam. Wilson and I sit next to him on the bench. Sam tells us where the suspect is sitting. Wilson gets up, grabs my arm, and say, "Come on, man."

"Where we going?"

We walk behind the public toilets to a phone booth, and I wonder again about the setups. If even the police, who should know better, want to think I'm a cop, surely the other side would be willing to make the assumption. He calls the phone booth where Al and Ray wait. Wilson describes the suspect. "In the park, man, on Junkies' Row. Junkies' Row, I said." He hangs up, and we go back to watch the bust go down, but neither Sam nor the suspect is there. We rush out of the park, but see neither of them.

"You sit on that rail over there, and when Al comes by, you say, 'I don't know where the sonofabitch is.' Keep your head turned away. That way, if anyone is nearby, they'll think he asked you about someone and you wouldn't tell him anything; if no one is near, it won't look like you're talking to him at all. Everybody in the Village knows Al and Ray."

I sit on the rail, watching out of the corner of my eye for the two detectives to appear. I see them coming. As they near, I cooly turn away, waiting subtly to deliver my code message.

Several shoes stop in front of me, toes pointing my way. "Hey, Bruce," Al says. "Where'd they all go?"

"Shhh! We'll be spotted."

"Ah. Where'd they go?"

"Down McDougal."

They go down McDougal. I wait a tactful time, then follow. I see Al standing on the sidewalk across the street from Minetta's. I sit on a stoop about four doors away. Al comes over and sits next to me.

"Go away, Al. We'll be seen together." I feel as paranoid as a pusher.

"Ah, it's just the school kids. Nobody will notice."

A policeman with a walkie-talkie strapped to his body tells us to move on.

"In just a minute, officer," Al says. The policeman says make sure it's just a minute, and Al says we certainly will and thank you officer.

We watch the girls in their carefully considered outfits and the boys in their page-boys. "Bunch of kids," Al says. "Let's go back to the car."

"What if I get noticed walking with you?"

"Nah. Don't worry about it."

We walk back to the car.

After a while Ray comes with another detective, and we go back to the phone booth. It rings, and Ray answers. He listens for a moment, then sticks his head out. "Hey, Bruce: you're burned."

"I'm what?"

"You're burned. They saw you with Al, and they all know you're a cop."

"I'm not a cop."

"Tell *them*."

They all laugh. "Way it goes," one of them says.

It is almost 1 A.M., and the street is thinning as the action moves indoors and only the desperate are left. No business here. They adjust the "Out of Order" sign and decide to quit early for a change.

LOS ANGELES

Bill Sanderson and Jack White look like TV actors who are supposed to look like L.A. detectives: both are good-looking, young, bright detective sergeants; both have been attending college part-time and expect a degree this year; both have been on the police force for eight years, in narcotics for less than one year.

Like police everywhere, they complain about some of the Supreme Court decisions, but they do not seem to feel as hamstrung. It takes more work and more men, but still the jobs seem to get done. "I think the Supreme Court is trying to force the problems back on the community that created the problems," one of them says.

"I can see why some people go to heroin," the other says. "It is the ultimate: it puts you to sleep and keeps you awake."

In Watts, we stop at the intersection of Central and Vernon. Where a large drug-store used to be there is now a tremendous tent and a hand-painted sign: *You must see and hear Rev. Eugene Lewis. Evangelist who ministers like Christ.* Like the topless joints in San Francisco, Watts is one of those places visitors must see; one gets the same feeling of futility in both. White and Sanderson point out locations where they made interesting drug arrests, locations where they hope to make others, places where they were during the riot. We are supposed to be discussing narcotics, but during the early part of the afternoon it is the riot. They still do not understand it; no one seems to. The houses are a surprise to me: in the East it would be a lower-middle-class neighborhood in a residential town. Parks, lawns, some cars. If you don't have a car, I find out, it takes an impossible amount of time to get around out here. Still, it is so unlike Harlem. Had so overwhelming a riot occurred first in swelling and wretched Harlem, we might have dismissed what Watts said: a man could want and need more than a house.

Later, we have dinner in a Mexican restaurant around the corner from the temple

Aimee Semple McPherson built; then we ride over to Hollywood. The radio gives Jack White a woman's phone number. The first phone booth cheats him out of two dimes, the second booth works.

White makes a date to meet her, and we race back to headquarters to pick up another car and some buy money. A lieutenant comes with us. We follow Jack to the bar, then drive down half a block and park in the shadows of a closed garage.

The lieutenant, just off vacation, says, "It gets harder and harder to generate enthusiasm for this kind of mess."

"Vacations do that," Bill says.

"It's not the vacation. Just getting a little tired of it."

After a while, Jack comes out of the bar with two women. One of them gets into the car with him, the other goes away. He U-turns and goes up the street, and we follow him at a distance.

Jack parks in front of an apartment house, and we park under a streetlamp fifty yards behind. There are three cars between us. With the light directly overhead, our car is not so suspicious: you can't see anyone inside unless you are quite close. I can't see anything in the other car, but Bill says Jack and the woman are still in it. He tells me they are probably arguing about whether or not Jack will be allowed to go inside with her. Jack isn't going to give her a chance to go out a back door with the money, and he wants to find out what apartment the man with the stash is in so we can move in later— if there is a man inside; it might be a phony deal.

It gets tense. If there is someone inside, there may be trouble: if Jack is recognized, he is unarmed and might not be near enough a window to call for help. We wait, nothing moves in the car ahead, and after a while Bill wonders too. He gets out of our car,

strolls down the block away from both cars, crosses in the dark somewhere below, walks up a side street, comes back down the opposite side, then retraces his steps. He gets back in. "They're still there."

Footsteps from down the block. A man approaches, reading a magazine in the dark. He slows down when he's under streetlamps, speeds up in the dark places between. He crosses directly in front of our car, his face buried in the magazine. "Now isn't that something," the lieutenant says. The man is reading *Startling Detective*.

More time passes. Jack's car lights up and U-turns, going back toward the bar. We duck, let it go a little bit, then do the same, going pretty fast. We come out of the U-turn, run a red light, and zip past a patrol car.

"Uh," I say.

"I guess they recognized me. Or the car," Bill says.

Jack is stopped at a red light a block ahead. He turns right, then stops in front of the bar. After a while the woman gets out and Jack drives away. We follow him and park both cars in a dark place.

He tells us the woman wouldn't let him come inside, and he refused to trust her with the money. "C'mon baby, take a chance," she said. "Everybody gets screwed sometimes in this business."

"Not me," he told her.

They tell me they've been having trouble nailing a couple of Cuban traffickers. The lieutenant says he liked the old days better. "I'd rather work a nice clean old Mexican dope peddler. You go boot his door in, take him down, and that's all there is to it."

I'll tell you something: it is not *just* a nitty-gritty world out there; it is a thing more unreal sometimes than the one we academics are usually accused of maintaining. You discover after a while that no one wears a white hat except the man who is talking to you right now; everyone spouts dogma except that single voice under that single white Stetson. Little Pavlovian mechanisms set junkies and cops in the same motions, day after day after day. The élan varies with the jurisdiction: in New York it is cold and faithless antagonism with exceptions, part of the general *Weltanschauung;* in Texas, where everyone has a gun, the policeman and criminal feel closer to one another.

It is little people, little, little people, playing out an ugly little game among themselves and taking it with precious and desperate seriousness, positing some lovely and fragile élan because both sides know that no one else in the world is willing to love them. Exiled from our American dream where everyman has his soporific and his weapon, the junkie and the cop find themselves bound to one another in one agonizing coil, and like Burton and Taylor in *Virginia Woolf,* they've learned the visceral lesson: people who bleed each other need each other.

The Police View of Protesters

JEROME H. SKOLNICK

Faced with the mounting pressures inherent in their job, the police have naturally sought to understand why things are as they are. Explanations which the police, with a few exceptions, have adopted constitute a relatively coherent view of current protests and their causes. The various propositions making up this view have nowhere been set out and made explicit, but they do permeate the police literature.

As will be seen, this view functions to justify—indeed, it suggests—a strategy for dealing with protest and protesters. Like any coherent view of events, it helps the police plan what they should do and understand

From *Politics of Protest* by Jerome H. Skolnick, New York, Simon and Schuster, 1969, pp. 258–268.

what they have done. But it must also be said that the police view makes it more difficult to keep the peace and increases the potential for violence. Furthermore, police attitudes toward protest and protesters often lead to conduct at odds with democratic ideals of freedom of speech and political expression. Thus the police often view protest as an intrusion on, rather than as a contribution to, our political processes. In its extreme case, this may result in treating the fundamental political right of dissent as merely an unnecessary inconvenience to traffic, as subversive activity, or both.

THE "ROTTEN APPLE" VIEW OF MAN

What is the foundation of the police view? On the basis of our interviews with police and a systematic study of police publications,[1] we have found that a significant underpinning is what can best be described as a "rotten apple" theory of human nature. Such a theory of human nature is hardly confined to the police, of course. It is widely shared in our society. Many of those to whom the police are responsible hold the "rotten apple" theory, and this complicates the problem in many ways.

Under this doctrine, crime and disorder are attributable mainly to the intentions of evil individuals; human behavior transcends past experience, culture, society, and other external forces and should be understood in terms of wrong choices, deliberately made. Significantly—and contrary to the teachings of all the behavioral sciences—social factors such as poverty, discrimination, inadequate housing, and the like are excluded from the analysis. As one policeman put it simply, "Poverty doesn't cause crime; people do."

The "rotten apple" view of human nature puts the policeman at odds with the goals and aspirations of many of the groups he is called upon to police. For example, police often relegate social reforms to the category of "coddling criminals" or, in the case of recent ghetto programs, to "selling out" to troublemakers. Moreover, while denying that social factors may contribute to the causes of criminal behavior, police and police publications, somewhat inconsistently, denounce welfare programs not as irrelevant *but as harmful* because they destroy human initiative. This negative view of the goals of policed communities can only make the situation of both police and policed more difficult and explosive. Thus, the black community sees the police not only as representing an alien white society but also as advocating positions fundamentally at odds with its own aspirations.

*   *   *

A similar tension sometimes exists between the police and both higher civic officials and representatives of the media. To the extent that such persons recognize the role of social factors in crime and approve of social reforms, they are viewed by the police as "selling out" and not "supporting the police."

Several less central theories often accompany the "rotten apple" view. These theories, too, are widely shared in our society. First, the police widely blame the current rise in crime on a turning away from traditional religion and they fear an impending moral breakdown.[2] Yet the best recent evidence shows that people's religious beliefs and attendance neither reduce nor increase their propensity toward crime.[3]

But perhaps the main target of current police thinking is permissive child-rearing, which many policemen interviewed by our task force view as having led to a generation "that thinks it can get what it yells for." Indeed, one officer interviewed justified the use of physical force on offenders as a corrective for lack of childhood discipline. "If their folks had beat 'em when they were kids, they'd be straight now. As it is, we have to shape 'em up." While much recent evidence has shown that students most concerned with social issues and most active in protest movements have been reared in homes more "permissive," according to police standards, than those who are uninvolved in these matters, it does not follow that such "permissiveness" leads to criminality. In fact, the evidence strongly suggests that persons who receive heavy corporal punishment as children are more likely to act aggressively in ensuing years.[4]

The police also tend to view perfectly legal social deviance, such as long hair worn by men, not only with extreme distaste but as a ladder to potential criminality. At a luncheon meeting of the International Conference of Police Associations, for example, Los Angeles patrolman George Suber said:

> You know, the way it is today, women will be women—and so will men! I got in trouble with one of them. I stopped him on a freeway after a chase—95, 100 miles an hour. . . . He had that hair down to the shoulders.
>
> I said to him, "I have a son about your age, and if you were my son, I'd do two things." "Oh," he said, "what?" "I'd knock him on his ass, and I'd tell him to get a haircut."
>
> "Oh, you don't like my hair?" "No," I said, "you look like a fruit." At that he got very angry. I had to fight him to get him under control.[5]

Nonconformity comes to be viewed with nearly as much suspicion as actual law violation; correspondingly, the police value the familiar, the ordinary, the status quo, rather than social change. These views both put the police at odds with the dissident communities with whom they have frequent contact and detract from their capacity to appreciate the reasons for dissent, change, or any form of innovative social behavior.

EXPLAINING MASS PROTEST

It is difficult to find police literature which recognizes that the imperfection of social institutions provides some basis for the discontent of large segments of American society. In addition, organized protest tends to be viewed as the conspiratorial product of authoritarian agitators—usually "Communists"—who mislead otherwise contented people. From a systematic sampling of police literature and statements by law enforcement authorities—ranging from the Director of the Federal Bureau of Investigation to the patrolman on the beat—a common theme

emerges in police analyses of mass protest: the search for such "leaders." Again, this is a view, and a search, that is widespread in our society.

Such an approach has serious consequences. The police are led to view protest as illegitimate misbehavior, rather than as legitimate dissent against policies and practices that might be wrong. The police are bound to be hostile to illegitimate misbehavior, and the reduction of protest tends to be seen as their principal goal. Such an attitude leads to more rather than less violence; and a cycle of greater and greater hostility continues.

The "agitational" theory of protest leads to certain characteristic consequences. The police are prone to underestimate both the protesters' numbers and depth of feeling. Again, this increases the likelihood of violence. Yet it is not only the police who believe in the "agitational" theory. Many authorities do when challenged. For example, the Cox Commission found that one reason for the amount of violence when police cleared the buildings at Columbia was the inaccurate estimate of the number of demonstrators in the buildings:

> It seems to us, however, that the administration's low estimate largely resulted from its inability to see that the seizure of the building was not simply the work of a few radicals but, by the end of the week, involved a significant portion of the student body who had become disenchanted with the operation of the university.[6]

In line with the "agitational" theory of protest, particular significance is attached by police intelligence estimates to the detection of leftists or outsiders of various sorts, as well as to indications of organization and prior planning and preparation. Moreover, similarities in tactics and expressed grievances in a number of scattered places and situations are seen as indicative of common leadership.

Thus the late J. Edgar Hoover stated on September 18, 1968:

> Communists are in the forefront of civil rights, anti-war, and student demonstrations, many of which ultimately become disorderly and erupt into violence. As an example, Bettina Aptheker Kurzweil, twenty-four year old member of the Communist National Committee, was a leading organizer of the "Free Speech" demonstrations on the campus of the University of California at Berkeley in the fall of 1964.
>
> These protests, culminating in the arrest of more than 800 demonstrators during a massive sit-in, on December 3, 1964, were the forerunner of the current campus upheaval.
>
> In a press conference on July 4, 1968, the opening day of the Communist Party's Special National Convention, Gus Hall, the Party's General Secretary, stated that there were communists on most of the major college campuses in the country and that they had been involved in the student protests.[7]

Mr. Hoover's statement is significant not only because he was at the time our nation's highest and most renowned law enforcement official but also because his views were reflected and disseminated throughout the nation—by publicity in the news media and by FBI seminars, briefings, and training for local policemen.

Not surprisingly, then, views similar to Mr. Hoover's dominate the most influential police literature. For instance, a lengthy article in the April 1965 issue of *The Police Chief,* the official publication of the International Association of Chiefs of Police, concludes, referring to the Berkeley "Free Speech Movement": "One of the more alarming aspects of these student demonstra-tions is the ever-present evidence that the guiding hand of communists and extreme leftists was involved." [8]

By contrast, a "blue-ribbon" investigating committee appointed by the Regents of the University of California concluded:

> We found no evidence that the FSM was organized by the Communist Party, the Progressive Labor Movement, or any other outside group. Despite a number of suggestive coincidences, the evidence which we accumulated left us with no doubt that the Free Speech Movement was a response to the September 14th change in rules regarding political activity at Bancroft and Telegraph, not a pre-planned effort to embarrass or destroy the University on whatever pretext arose.[9]

And more recently, the prestigious Cox Commission, which was headed by the former Solicitor General of the United States and investigated the Columbia disturbances, reported:

> We reject the view that ascribes the April and May disturbances primarily to a conspiracy of student revolutionaries. That demonology is no less false than the naive radical doctrine that attributes all wars, racial injustices, and poverty to the machinations of a capitalist and militarist "Establishment." [10]

One reason police analysis so often finds "leftists" is that its criteria for characterizing persons as "leftists" is so broad as to be misleading. In practice, the police may not distinguish "dissent" from "subversion." For example, listed in *The Police Chief* article as a "Communist-linked" person is a "former U.S. government employee who, while so employed, participated in picketing the House Committee on Un-American Activities in 1960." [11] Guilt by association is a central analytical tool, and information is culled from such ultraright publications as *Tocsin* and *Washington Report*. Hostility and suspicion toward the civil rights movement also serve as a major impetus for seeing Communist involvement and leadership. *The Police Chief* found it significant that black civil rights leaders such as James Farmer, Bayard Rustin, John Lewis, James Baldwin, and William McAdoo were among "the swarm of sympathizers" who sent messages of support to the FSM.[12]

Some indication of how wide the "Communist" net stretches is given by a December 1968 story in the *Chicago Tribune*. The reporter asked police to comment on the Walker Report to the Violence Commission. He writes: "While most district commanders spoke freely, many policemen declined to comment unless their names were withheld. The majority of these said the Walker report appeared to have been written by members of the United States Supreme Court or Communists." [13]

Supplementing the problem of police definition and identification of leftists is a special vision of the role that such persons play. Just as the presence of police and newsmen at the scene of a protest does not mean they are leaders, so the presence of a handful of radicals should not necessarily cause one to conclude that they are leading the protest movement. Moreover, studies of student protest—including the Byrne Report on the Free Speech Movement and the Cox Report on the Columbia disturbances—indicate that "the leadership," leaving aside for the moment whether or not it is radical leadership, is able to lead only when events such as administration responses unite significant numbers of students or faculty. For example, the FSM extended over a number of months, and the leaders conducted a long conflict with the university administration and proposed many mass meetings and protests, but their appeals to "sit-in" were heeded by students only intermittently. Sometimes the students rallied by the thousands; at other times the leadership found its base shrunken to no more than several hundred. At these nadir points the leaders were unable to accomplish anything significant; on their own they were powerless. Renewal of mass support for the FSM after each of these pauses was not the work of the leadership but only occurred when the school administration took actions that aroused mass student feelings of betrayal or inequity. The "leadership" remained relatively constant in its calls for support—and even then had serious internal disputes—but the students gave, withdrew, and renewed their support independently, based on events. Clearly, the leaders did not foment student protest on their own; and whatever the intentions or political designs of many FSM leaders, they never had the power to manufacture the protest movement.

One special reason for this kind of police analysis of student protest may derive from police unfamiliarity with the student culture in which such protests occur. When this culture is taken into account, one need not fall back upon theories of sinister outside organizers to explain the ability of students to organize, plan, and produce sophisticated leaders and techniques. Even at the time of the Free Speech Movement in 1964, many of the students, including campus leaders, had spent at least one summer in the South taking part in the civil rights struggles. Moreover, everyone had read about or seen on television the "sit-ins" and other nonviolent tactics of the civil rights movement. Also, while the police in Berkeley saw the use of loudspeakers and walkie-talkies as evidence of outside leadership, the former had long been standard equipment at student rallies and meetings, and the latter were available in nearby children's toy stores (and were largely a "put-on," anyway). Finally, with the intellectual and human resources of thousands of undergraduates, graduate students, and faculty at one of the most honored universities in the world, one would hardly expect less competent organization and planning.

A similar analysis may be made of conspiracy arguments relying on similarities in issues and tactics in student protests throughout the nation; explanations more simple than an external organizing force can be found. There is no question that there has been considerable contact among student protesters from many campuses. For example, students who are undergraduates at one university often do graduate work at another. And television news coverage of protest, student newspapers, and books popular in the student culture have long articulated the grievances and tactics around which much unrest revolves. Thus, when it is also considered that students throughout the country do face similar circumstances, it is hardly surprising that similar events occur widely and follow a recognizable pattern. Interestingly, collective actions, such as panty raids, have spread through the student subculture in the past without producing sinister conspiracy theories.

A related problem for police is sorting among certain types of claims from and statements about radical movements. Chicago prior to and during the Democratic National Convention is a case in point. To quote from the Walker Report:

> The threats to the City were varied. Provocative and inflammatory statements, made in connection with activities planned for convention week, were published and widely disseminated. There were also intelligence reports from informants.
> Some of this information was *absurd*, like the reported plan to contaminate the city's water supply with LSD. But some were *serious;* and both were strengthened by the authorities' *lack of any mechanism for distinguishing one from the other.*
> The second factor—*the city's response*—*matched in numbers and logistics, at least, the demonstrators' threats.*[14]

Surely it is unsatisfactory not to distinguish the absurd from the serious.[15] And just as surely, the incapacity to distinguish can only result in inadequate protection against real dangers, as well as an increased likelihood of unnecessary suppression and violence. Again, this illustrates some of the problems of the police view when confronted with modern mass protest. The police are more likely to believe that "anarchist" leaders are going to contaminate a city's water supply with LSD than they are to believe that a student antiwar or black protest is an expression of genuine, widespread dissatisfaction. Moreover, some radicals have increasingly learned to utilize and exploit the power of the media in order to stage events and create scenes, to provoke police into attacking peaceful protesters, and the police have played an important role in assuring their success.

As an interesting footnote to this discussion of police ideas about protest, we might note that, if the standards used by leading police spokesmen to identify a conspiracy were applied to the police themselves, one would conclude that police in the United States constitute an ultra-right-wing conspiracy. For example, one would note the growing police militancy with its similar rhetoric and tactics throughout the nation and the presence of such outside "agitators" as John Harrington, president of the Fraternal Order of Police, at the scene of particular outbursts of militancy. We hasten to add that we do not feel that this is an adequate analysis of the situation. Police, like students, share a common culture and are subject to similar pressures, problems, and inequities; the police across the country respond sim-ilarly to similar situations because they share common interests, not because they are a "fascist-led" conspiracy.

NOTES

1 Among numerous other publications *Law and Order* and *The Police Chief* magazines for the past eighteen months were reviewed. We read them both for an understanding of the police perspective of their world and for their theories of appropriate response to social problems. Interviews and other reports augmented this study.
2 See, e.g., J. Edgar Hoover, quoted in John Edward Coogan, "Religion, a Preventive of Delinquency," *Federal Probation,* **18** (December 1954): 29.
3 Travis Hirschi and Rodney Stark, "Hellfire and Delinquency," publication A–96, Survey Research Center, University of California at Berkeley.
4 See, e.g., R. R. Sears, et al., "Some Child-rearing Antecedents of Aggression and Dependency in Young Children," *Genetic Psychology Monograph* (1953), pp. 135–234; E. Hollenberg and M. Sperry, "Some Antecedents of Aggression and Effects of Frustration in Doll Play," *Personality* (1951), pp. 32–43; W. C. Becker, et al., "Relations of Factors Derived from Parent Interview Ratings to Behavior Problems of Five Year Olds," *Child Development,* **33** (1962), pp. 509–35; and M. L. Hoffman, "Power Assertion by the Parent and Its Impact on the Child," *Child Development,* **31** (1960), pp. 129–43.
5 *Washington Post,* December 15, 1969, p. B3.
6 Cox Commission, p. 164.
7 *Proceedings,* p. 56.
8 *The Police Chief* (April 1965): 10.
9 The Byrne Commission Report submitted to the Special Committee of the Regents of the University of California on May 7, 1965; most easily available in *Los Angeles Times,* May 12, 1965, Part IV, pp. 1–6. Quoted section, p. 5.
10 Cox Commission, p. 189.
11 *The Police Chief* (April 1965): 36.
12 Ibid., pp. 42–44.
13 Donald Yabush, *Chicago Tribune,* December 3, 1968, p. 1.
14 Chicago Study Team, pp. vii–viii, emphasis added.
15 The variety of intelligence received by law enforcement officials is indicated by this listing of Yippie threats published in the mass media: "There were reports of proposals to dynamite natural gas lines; to dump hallucinating drugs into the city's water system; to print forged credentials so that demonstrators could slip into the convention hall; to stage a mass stall-in of old jalopies on the expressways and thereby disrupt traffic; to take over gas stations, flood sewers with gasoline, then burn the city; to fornicate in the parks and on Lake Michigan's beaches; to release greased pigs throughout Chicago, at the Federal Building and at the Amphitheatre; to slash tires along the city's freeways and tie up traffic in all directions; to scatter razor sharp three-inch nails along the city's highways; to place underground agents in hotels, restaurants, and kitchens where food was prepared for delegates, and drug food and drink; to paint cars like independent taxicabs and forcibly take delegates to Wisconsin or some other place far from the convention; to engage Yippie girls as 'hookers' to attract delegates and dose their drinks with LSD; to bombard the Amphitheatre with mortars from several miles away; to jam communication lines from mobile units; to disrupt the operations of airport control towers, hotel elevators and railway switching yards; to gather 230 'hyper-potent' hippie males into a special battalion to seduce the wives, daughters and girlfriends of convention delegates; to assemble 100,000 people to burn draft cards with the fires spelling out 'Beat Army'; to turn on fire hydrants, set off false fire and police alarms, and string wire between trees in Grant Park and Lincoln Park to trip up three-wheeled vehicles of the Chicago police; to dress Yippies like Viet Cong and walk the streets shaking hands or passing out rice; to infiltrate the right wing with short haired Yippies and at the right moment exclaim: 'You know, these Yippies have something to say!'; to have ten thousand nude bodies floating on Lake Michigan — the list could go on." Chicago Study Team, p. 49.

Labor representative presenting the bargaining position
of policemen at a news conference.

IV

Organization and Control of the Police

THE ORGANIZATION OF POLICEMEN

Policemen picketing the Massachusetts State House
for changes in the capital punishment law.

Ordinarily, when we think of protest we might envision a public rally of predominantly young people, followed by a march, perhaps followed by a sit-in. But protest can take other forms. During the 1960s many police came to believe that other officials and the courts did not accept their prescriptions for social action, let alone their demands for adequate compensation and equipment. Rank-and-file police became more militant in their views and demands and began to act out this militancy, occasionally by violence, but more often by threatening illegal strikes, lobbying, and through political organization. In their own way, police joined the ranks of protest.

The militancy and political organization of police was built upon an already available framework: guild, fraternal, and social organizations. These organizations, especially the guilds, which were originally devoted to fellowship and then to increasing police pay and benefits, have grown stronger in the past decade. They have begun to challenge and sometimes disobey the authority of police commanders, the civic government, and the courts and have entered the political arenas as an organized and sometimes militant constituency.

Political involvement of the police, suggests the Skolnick Report to the National Commission on the Causes and Prevention of Violence, raises serious problems:

> First, aside from the military, the police have a practical monopoly on the legal use of force in our society. For just such a reason our country has a tradition of wariness toward politicization of its armed forces, and thus both law and custom restrict the political activities of members of the military. Similar considerations obviously apply to the police.
>
> In some senses the police are an even greater source of potential concern than the armed forces because of their closeness to the day-to-day workings of the political process and their frequent interaction with the population. These factors make police abuse of the political process a more immediate prospect. For example, bumper stickers on squad cars, political buttons on uniforms, selective ticketing, and similar contacts with citizens quickly impart a political message.
>
> A second factor which has led to restrictions on members of the armed forces is the fear that unfettered political expression, if adopted as a principle, might in practice lead to political coercion *within* the military. Control over promotions and disciplinary action could make coercion possible, and pressure might be exerted on

lower-ranking members to adopt, contribute to, or work for a particular political cause. Thus, again, regulation (and sometimes prohibition) of certain political activities has been undertaken. For example, superiors are prohibited from soliciting funds from inferiors, and many political activities are prohibited while in uniform or on duty. Such considerations, again, apply to the police.

Even where coercion of the populace (or fellow force members) does not exist in fact, politicization of the police may create the appearance of such abuses. This can affect the political process and create both hostility toward the police and disrespect for the legal and political system.

Moreover, lobbying, campaigning, and the like, in and of themselves, tend to make the policing function itself appear politically motivated and nonneutral. Since the policing function is for so many people so central and important a part of our legal mechanisms, the actual or apparent politicization of policing would carry over to perceptions of the entire legal system. Such perceptions of politicization would be contrary to society's view that the system should be neutral and nonpolitical. And such a situation would, of course, have adverse consequences for confidence in and thus reliance on its legal system to resolve disputes peacefully. And this is most true of those groups—students, antiwar protesters, and blacks—who perceive the police political position as most hostile to their own aspirations and who are also among the most heavily policed. Moreover, the legal system would in turn be exposed to even greater political pressures than is presently the case.

So, while the police may be analogous to other government employees or to members of the armed forces, they are also, and perhaps more importantly, analogous to the judiciary. Each interprets the legal order to, and imposes the laws on, the population, and thus the actions of each are expected to be neutral and nonpolitical. In the case of the judiciary, there is a strong tradition of removing them from the partisan political arena lest their involvement impede the functioning of the system.

It may be useful in this connection to illustrate just how strong are our societal norms concerning judicial behavior and to note that these norms often demand standards of conduct higher than what is legally required. For example, even when judges run for re-election, it is widely understood that the election should not be political in the usual sense. Moreover, at various times in our history there has been public uneasiness about justices of the Supreme Court advising Presidents of the United States. Perhaps even more to the point, however, is the fact that whereas justices have from time to time informally advised Presidents, it is unthinkable that they would take to the stump or engage in overt political activity in their behalf.[1]

The article by William J. Bopp describes one form of organized police militancy, and the article by Juris on police unions describes a longer-range development growing out of police frustration—the unionization of police. Police unionization poses many issues. One hardly needs to be reminded of the strikes of transit workers, sanitation workers, teachers, and so forth, to realize that the right of government employees to strike is a disputed issue and an action that has become commonplace only in the last decade or so. Whatever the merits of the argument on the right of government employees to strike, it is clear that a police strike is among the most serious, since continued police services are not only necessary in the public interest but also required for public safety.

And even within the class of government employees the policeman is different; we have already observed that his role as a law enforcement officer is peculiarly important and sensitive. Thus, when police demands for higher material benefits are expressed in a manner that defies law, such as illegal strikes, unique problems arise. First, the law enforcement apparatus is placed in the incongruous position of one part having to enforce a law against another part.

Second, police are generally engaged in the effort to encourage public respect for law, and such efforts are seriously undermined by police violations of law. To more people than ever, the law comes to be seen as arbitrary concept subject to the policeman's whim and lacking in moral force. So a general question that is raised is the extent to which police unions create difficulties with the policemen's image of themselves and with the image they present to others. Another serious question concerns the degree to which such development and imagery is compatible with police goals or professionalization. Are the material benefits worth the costs in esteem? Should the police association perform the same role for police that labor unions perform for factory workers? Or should it be different, and if so, how? For example, for police, is binding arbitration preferable to negotiation of a contract through the normal expression of power involved in a strike? Do police occupy an emergency role that exceeds in responsibility that of other service personnel, such as ambulance drivers and firemen? And do they hold a moral obligation that exceeds those of such health service personnel as doctors, nurses, and other hospital staff? Or do restrictions on the police regarding striking place them in the category of second-class citizens?

Finally, police unions, according to Juris, may reduce the authority of the police administrator. Is such a reduction in authority to regulate the internal workings of the police department necessary? Is it desirable? Should police unions ultimately dominate the actual administration of police departments? If so, how should this control be achieved, and how should it be exercised?

NOTE

1 *The Politics of Protest,* a report submitted by Jerome H. Skolnick, Director, Task Force on Violent Aspects of Protest and Confrontation of the National Commission on the Causes and Prevention of Violence (New York: Ballantine Books, 1969), pp. 286–288.

The Detroit Police Revolt

WILLIAM J. BOPP

The troubles that occurred in 1967 between Mayor Jerome Cavanagh and his Detroit Police Department were predictable. Cavanagh, a liberal, was a man deeply concerned with the plight of the Negro in his city, a concern which consistently led to the establishment of extraordinary community relations programs. The police were often asked to enforce the law diligently and uniformly while exercising restraint in their dealings with minority groups, a request many line officers felt was contradictory. Among policemen, the mayor had a reputation for being soft on crime and unsympathetic to the needs of the police. One could go on chronicling the differences between the mayor and his police department; however, suffice it to say that the relationship was not unlike police-liberal relations in a score of core cities nationwide. There was mutual distrust, hostility, and bitterness.

Mayor Cavanagh was a reformer who had earned his liberal credentials through hard work, innovative programs, and a creative mind. By 1967, Detroit was rapidly becoming a model community to which students of urban government came to learn their craft. Articles were published, scholarly papers were written, and studies were conducted on the renaissance of Detroit, a city that was being rebuilt, both physically and philosophically. Crime was a major concern of the mayor, but in the true liberal tradition,

he planned to lower the crime rate by providing jobs, better housing, medical services, improved transportation systems, and education. To the mayor, strict enforcement of the law was not the answer to a spiraling crime rate; it did nothing to attack the root causes of crime, and Mayor Cavanagh was not a man to ignore the root causes of any evil. He committed his administration to strenuous programs of social and economic importance in a sincere attempt to uplift the status of minority groups in Detroit. It appears that, with the weapons at his disposal and with limited resources, he did an admirable job. This concern for the plight of minority citizens won him plaudits nationwide. But there was one minority group in Detroit which did not benefit from the enlightened leadership of City Hall, a group which experienced few economic gains. It was a minority group which was all but ignored by the mayor and one that fairly cried out for help: the Detroit Police Department.

The social status of policemen in Detroit had deteriorated badly over the years. Disrespect for the law and its agents had led to a breakdown in relations between the police and the citizenry they had sworn to serve. Student unrest and militant Negro activity also served to downgrade the police craft in the eyes of many. Rising tensions in the community greatly affected the policeman's job. Fewer people now wanted to be a policeman in Detroit, and positions remained unfilled even though the city had a high rate of unemployment. The status of policemen was low in the eyes of citizens and the police. But

From *The Police Rebellion* by William J. Bopp, pp. 162–172. Copyright © 1971 by Charles C Thomas Publishers. Reprinted by permission.

if the social status of the police had fallen, the economic status of officers had plummeted dramatically. In 1950, the maximum salary for Michigan state troopers was almost $900 below the Detroit patrolman's maximum. In 1966, however, the state trooper maximum was $1,100 higher than the Detroit police maximum, even though it was generally conceded that the job of the state trooper was significantly less demanding. By 1966, the Detroit Police Department consisted of some 4,500 persons, 3,300 of whom were unhappy patrolmen. And therein lies the tale of the "The Detroit Police Revolt."

On January 18, 1966, the Detroit Police Officers Association (DPOA) was recognized by the City of Detroit as the representative of all patrolmen in the department. The DPOA, under its president, Patrolman Carl Parsell, immediately began a strenuous campaign to improve officers' pay and working conditions, and as a result, a series of collective bargaining problems arose between the city and the police union. The following is an official synopsis of some of the early interplay between labor and management:

> ... (The) DPOA submitted its bargaining requests for fiscal year 1966–1967, which included a $1,665 across-the-board salary increase, which would have raised the maximum base salary to $9,000. DPOA claims that, although "negotiations" commenced in March 1966, and although there were meetings between DPOA and City Representatives in March, April, and May, "no progress was made," in part because the City took the position that certain of the economic issues were not subject to negotiation. City Labor Relations Director Leggat, in a communication dated March 28, 1966, to Mayor Cavanagh made certain budget recommendations. He included in his letter the following paragraph: "Perhaps the most critical need is that of a very

substantial adjustment in pay rates for the Police and Fire Fighting ranks. Current demands for adequate public security make this a necessity. I concur in the Police Commissioner's observation that the greater part of their $1,665 increase be absorbed this year, if possible." The City budget, as adopted for 1966–1967, included, however, an across-the-board annual salary increase for all City employees of a minimum of $312, and policemen and firemen were granted an additional special increase of $688, making a total increase for them of $1,000. Meetings between DPOA and City Representatives were resumed in September 1966. DPOA requested that the parties negotiate an additional wage increase and fringe benefits for the then current fiscal year, and that maximum base salaries be increased to $10,000 beginning with the 1967–1968 fiscal year. The City Representatives took the position that the budget was closed for 1966–1967 and, according to the Union (DPOA), that there would be no negotiations relating to the 1967–1968 budget until it was determined how much money would be available for salary increases. On October 14, 1966, DPOA filed unfair labor practice charges of refusal to bargain against the City with the State Labor Mediation Board. There were no further negotiating meetings until after January 1, 1967. In the interim, the Police Department took certain unilateral action with respect to overtime pay and other fringe benefits. Negotiating sessions were held between January 1 and July 1, 1967, resulting in agreement on a number of matters. Meanwhile, there had been no negotiations on such demands prior to the completion and adoption by the Common Council of the budget for the current (1967–1968) fiscal year, which provided *no* increases in base pay for any City employees.[1]

The $10,000 figure was extremely important to officers who considered it more than just a pay boost. It had symbolic meaning, too. It represented a step into a new pay classification, a five-figure classification, and a giant step toward that long-sought goal: professionalization. It meant a boost in pay, a rise in status, and a partial fulfillment of a dream. The police did not get their pay raise that year, and an embittered rank and file met to plan action, extreme action, aimed at pressuring the city into meeting their demands.

Complicating the situation was the lingering bitterness over an unpleasant incident which had occurred during early negotiations. At a State Labor Mediation Board hearing, it was reported that Tom Gallagher, an Assistant Corporation Counsel, had lashed out at Carl Parsell, referring to the patrolman as, "this dolt, this police officer." Parsell, a veteran of twenty years of distinguished service and an immensely popular and talented leader, was highly respected by his constituency, and his abuse by a *city official* angered not only the membership of the DPOA, but police administrators as well. Up to that time Gallagher had been handling negotiations for the city. After his outburst he was reassigned to other duties. The damage, however, had been done.

On May 15, 1967, a closed meeting of the Detroit Police Officers Association was held. A ticket strike was among the suggestions offered by the patrolmen as a means to enforce economic demands on the city. It was also suggested that members halt the practice of taking leave days when they were sick and entitled to paid sick leave. The practice, initiated by the police to ease the manpower shortage, put more officers on the job because patrolmen were sick on their own off-duty time instead of having the paid sick day off to which they were entitled. Following the meeting, President Parsell stated that he would oppose any ticket strike; however, the uncompromising mood of his membership was to become apparent within forty-eight hours.

On May 17, after a series of spot-checks by Police Commissioner Ray Girardin, it became clear that Detroit's patrolmen were engaged in a ticket slowdown. Issuance of tickets for minor violations was down approximately 50 percent in all parts of the city. Rumors that policemen were also calling in sick to press their demands proved unfounded. At first Commissioner Girardin and Mayor Cavanagh took a restrained attitude in dealing with the ticket slowdown. It was, after all, an extremely sensitive situation. While traffic enforcement is a critical part of a patrolman's activities, any directive from higher authority ordering line officers to issue a specific number of citations smacks of a quota system, an unpopular policy among the public and the police. Realizing this, the mayor and his commissioner simply warned officers that neglect of duty was the worst possible approach to seek a pay raise, hoping that the slowdown would ease without a need for drastic administrative action. It did not.

Three days passed and the slowdown showed no sign of waning. In fact, the situation appeared to be worsening, with ticket writing down more than 60 percent. While police administrators claimed that the slowdown was having little effect on the day-to-day operations of the city, it was hitting officials where it hurt most—in the pocketbook. Court revenue was down significantly. In another effort to end the affair, Commissioner Girardin, who had publicly sympathized with officers' pay demands, told his men that, as much as the city would like to grant their raise, it was impossible; there simply was no money available. The rank and file, however, were not buying excuses. The slowdown continued in earnest.

As the first week of the slowdown drew to a close, city administrators sought to convince the citizenry that the internal problems of the police department were not as bad as they appeared. A recent survey had been conducted by a private advertising agency at the behest of the Greater Detroit Board of Commerce. The results of the survey, which indicated that morale on the police department was "high," were released to the news media. The rank and file immediately challenged the validity of the survey, stating through their leaders that the original survey sample included only one hundred policemen, that the questions themselves were slanted, and that the method of interviewing was faulty. To emphasize their point, the DPOA threw a two-hundred-man picket line of off-duty officers around the building housing the offices of the advertising agency. Carl Parsell then submitted a survey of his own on duplicate questionnaires, these completed by 3,300 patrolmen, which refuted the results of the original poll. The placards carried by the picketing officers underscored their argument. The signs read: "It's Too Late To Survey The 230 Men Who Quit." The controversy over the poll did little more than illustrate the growing hostility that existed between the patrolmen and their bosses.

On May 19, the city council approved Mayor Cavanagh's budget for fiscal year 1967–1968. The budget did not include pay increases for city employees. However, instead of ending the ticket slowdown, the action appeared to motivate patrolmen to fight even harder for their economic demands. Pledges of support for their position began pouring in from the metropolitan Detroit area, and by the 21st of May unions representing more than 200,000 workers had

agreed to assist the DPOA in pressing the city for a raise. Unions who said they would back the police included the powerful United Auto Workers Union, the Teamsters, the Hotel, Restaurant Employees and Bartenders International Union, Local 38 of the Brewery Workers Union, and the Detroit Chapter of the American Federation of State, County and Municipal Employees.

Traffic ticket writing had fallen 66 percent during the first week of the strike, yet accidents and traffic fatalities remained normal during that period. One precinct dropped from an average of 323 tickets a day to 6. The patrolmen claimed that they were not ignoring traffic violations—motorists were still being stopped; but officers were giving warnings, a form of traffic enforcement, in lieu of citations. This protested the mayor's hold-the-line budget and the "quota system" that the DPOA claimed existed on the Detroit Police Department. As the slowdown entered its second week, Mayor Cavanagh decided to switch to hard-line tactics. He ordered Commissioner Girardin to use disciplinary action, if necessary, to end the slowdown immediately. Assailing the DPOA for resorting to "totally irresponsible actions," he declared angrily:

As mayor I have rejected the demands of the police organization for pay raises when no other city employee has gotten a pay raise. This is not an employee group asking for more money. This has become a special interest group that is going to bludgeon the city officials into giving them what they want. Their conduct borders on insubordination and, in the real sense of the Police Manual, conduct unbecoming a police officer. I have told Police Commissioner Girardin to end the slowdown of writing tickets. How can the policeman ignore a violation of the law just to prove that he should get more money.

Mayor Cavanagh's charge that the police were ignoring violations of the law was not true. They simply were not issuing tickets for many of them, an exercise in discretion which most police administrators feel is valid. In further action, Commissioner Girardin hinted that the slowdown could affect the standing of men on promotional eligibility lists.

Instead of shaking the DPOA's position, Mayor Cavanagh's threats prompted an equally hard-line stance by the patrolmen. Within twenty-four hours, the following statement was released by DPOA officials:

> If the mayor wants war, war he will get. . . . The DPOA is shocked that the mayor has taken the position that there is no raise for the policemen in view of recent events. The policemen of this city are clearly demonstrating their discontent. The mayor cannot sweep the issue of public safety under the rug and pretend a problem doesn't exist. We will move forward with our protests and continue to take our fight to the citizens.

Part of that fight consisted of an all-out effort to convince the citizenry that the Detroit Police Department did indeed have a ticket writing quota. President Parsell asserted that supervisors consistently exerted pressure on their subordinates to issue citations because of the revenue they generate for the general fund ($7 million the previous year). Officers who fell behind the norm were often transferred to less desirable beats. Parsell said that traffic officers were even encouraged to take their motorcycles home so that they could write tickets to and from work. Mayor Cavanagh denied the charge but, in a curious statement, acknowledged that ticket revenue does go into the general fund and that, when policemen ask for pay raises, the raises must come out of the general fund. Anything that reduced the general

fund, said the mayor, reduced the ability to give pay raises. Cavanagh, in his desire to get the patrolmen to end their slowdown, had all but confessed to Parsell's charges. The police, it seemed, had to write revenue-producing tickets in order to get a pay raise. The more tickets, the better the chance for a raise.

By the third week of the slowdown, ticket writing had fallen 75 to 80 percent, costing the city upwards of $15,000 a day in lost revenue. Commissioner Girardin gave officers "a direct written order" to cease their slowdown. In it he tried to refute their charges of a "quota system." It read: "There is no quota on traffic tickets. But there is a norm. The norm will be based on your current assignment and on the approximate number issued seasonally by you prior to mid-May, 1967.

The patrolmen ignored Commissioner Girardin's order, and, taking the offensive, they filed unfair labor practices against the city with the State Labor Mediation Board. The suit alleged that the mayor "has bypassed and subverted the entire collective bargaining process by using the public media to make disparaging remarks about the DPOA." In a further slap at the city, members of the DPOA voted to halt voluntary overtime work on weekends.

As the fourth week of the slowdown drew to a close, the city made good on its threat to invoke disciplinary action against patrolmen involved in the ticket strike when it reassigned twenty-nine men, fifteen officers from the Motor Traffic Bureau and fourteen from the Accident Prevention Bureau, from scout cars and motorcycles to walking beats. The change of duties were termed "assignments" and, unlike "transfers," which were considered permanent, they could be rescinded at any time. Commissioner Girardin stated that the changes were made because the events of the past month had made it unnecessary to assign traffic specialists throughout the city who were not practicing their specialty. According to the Commissioner:

> While these men in the traffic bureau were performing their function on motorcycles and in cars to protect against injuries and deaths on the streets, they could not be taken off this important job. However, they have shown they are not doing the job—over a prolonged period, and what I would call a patient waiting period by the administration.

On June 13, Girardin suspended 61 patrolmen for failure to enforce traffic laws. While the reactions of the disciplined officers were subdued, the reaction of the DPOA was not. Two days later the membership retaliated with its most feared weapon: the strike.

On June 15, 323 policemen called in sick, and the city was faced with the first police strike against a major United States city since 1919. The DPOA predicted that within seventy-two hours the number would climb to 1,000 if city officials did not become more responsive to the demands of their patrolmen. The city was quick to act. Commissioner Girardin canceled leaves and days off and assigned all men to twelve-hour shifts. The state police were notified and put on standby alert should they be needed. The men who had called in sick were ordered to undergo physical examinations at the police doctor's office; those thought to be malingering were ordered back to duty under threat of suspension if they refused. In addition, the city obtained a temporary injunction from Wayne County Circuit Judge Thomas J. Foley, which restrained union members from further sick calls. The injunction directed the DPOA to "desist and refrain" from the following:

1. Counseling, advising, or threatening employees of the police department to cease or remain away from work.
2. Participating in the strike or engaging in the work stoppage.
3. Failing to fulfill assigned duties.
4. Interfering with and obstructing the operations of the police department.
5. Voluntarily claiming to be sick and deliberately refusing to report for duty.

In its suit, the city asked the court to require the DPOA to pay $1 million in punitive damages and $50,000 a day for the duration of the sick strike. It was the city's belief that the best way to resolve the issue at this point was through a legal and administrative blitzkrieg aimed at crushing, once and for all, the resistance of rebellious officers. By the second day of the strike, it looked as though the tack was working as the rhetoric of the DPOA became more conciliatory and the number of officers calling in sick fell. Some officers, however, switched their tactics by asking for emergency leaves, claiming that members of their families were sick. The city could not order family members to submit to medical examinations.

Although the strike was not over, the next day it appeared that the city's action had taken some of the steam out of the strikers, who now seemed to be less enthusiastic about their sick call tactics. The wave of sickness appeared to be subsiding as 212 men called in sick, 111 less than the preceding day. Carl Parsell, concerned over the temporary injunction issued by the circuit court, denied the strike was a planned operation of the DPOA. He asserted that the sick calls were individual actions and that the DPOA had "lost control of the membership." The association posted picket lines around police headquarters and all precinct stations.

Just as it seemed that the court would have to settle the strike, the city and the DPOA agreed to sit down at the bargaining table and talk out their differences.

By the fifth day of the sick-in, it appeared that the strike was collapsing: the commissioner had suspended 193 officers for failing to report to work after having been ordered to do so; the Police Lieutenants and Sergeants Association had broken with the DPOA because of the strike; the area newspapers were roundly criticizing the striking patrolmen for resorting to unlawful tactics to press their demands. Only 41 day-shift patrolmen called in sick on Sunday, compared to 131 on the preceding day shift. While there had been little progress in the mediation sessions, at least both sides were talking to each other. Just as the situation began to improve, Mayor Cavanagh committed a horrible blunder. Cavanagh was president of the United States Conference of Mayors, which was holding its annual meeting in Hawaii. The mayor had planned to address the conference earlier that week; however, the strike had forced him to cancel his plans. Now, after receiving assurances from Commissioner Girardin that the crisis was abating, Mayor Cavanagh, during the most sensitive part of the negotiations, decided to join his colleagues in Hawaii. On Sunday morning, the 18th, the mayor left by plane for Honolulu. The result of Mayor Cavanagh's ill-advised journey was predictable.

On June 19, angered over their mayor's "junket" to Hawaii, policemen again began calling in sick in large numbers. By the following day, more than one-third of Detroit's patrolmen were off the job. Officers and their families walked picket lines around police buildings. Mayor Cavanagh, notified of the new crisis, rushed back to Detroit. Just as

conditions seemed hopeless, a third party entered the scene in the person of the Right Reverend Richard S. Emrich, Episcopal Bishop of Michigan. Bishop Emrich, heading an ad hoc citizen's committee of prominent Detroiters, offered to mediate the dispute. Both labor and management, obviously weary of the controversy, accepted the offer, and a truce was arranged on the evening of June 20. The DPOA agreed to order its membership to return to work and resume normal operation, including ticket writing, while the city promised to lift the suspensions of officers who had been disciplined and drop the lawsuits against the DPOA. Both sides agreed to submit the unresolved issues to a panel of persons mutually acceptable to labor and management. By the morning of June 21, Detroit's officers returned to work. The strike was over.

Negotiations between the city and the DPOA began almost immediately, and on July 11, they reached agreement on all the "noneconomic issues." The settlement dealt with such issues as seniority, grievance procedures, management rights, vacations, and leaves. The most important part of the agreement, however, was union recognition. The city for the first time agreed to recognize the DPOA as the exclusive bargaining agent for policemen. Mayor Cavanagh hailed the contract as "the first agreement of its kind ever made between a municipal government and its local police officers." A panel of three citizens was chosen to settle the "economic issues." Before the panel could reach a decision, though, racial riots broke out in Detroit, and policemen were again assigned to twelve-hour shifts in order to meet the emergency. Although the riots were bloody and costly, they did nothing to hurt the officers' chances of getting their raise. On February 27, 1968, the Detroit police dispute panel recommended that the city raise the pay of patrolmen to a maximum of $10,000 per annum. The policemen were to get their

pay raise after all. The revolt of Detroit policemen had been successful.

NOTE

1 *Findings and Recommendations on Unresolved Economic and Other Issues,* a report to the City of Detroit by the Police Dispute Panel, Feb. 27, 1968, pp. 10–11.

The Implications of Police Unionism

HERVEY A. JURIS

Virtually unstudied and largely unobserved, the police employee organization has evolved over the last fifty years into a strong economic and political institution. The rapid growth of militant police unionism as a new political and economic force in the society has raised serious problems for the police agency administrator in the exercise of his professional responsibilities in the area of law enforcement and his executive responsibilities in the area of personnel management. It has also raised serious public policy questions as to whether the protected right to organize and to bargain collectively, which is being extended to all other public employees, ought to be extended to the police without limitations. Underlying all these questions is the basic issue of whether official sanction should be extended to another entrant in the competition for control of local police operations.

This paper will argue that police unionism is an established institution in the society, and that there is a need for both police executives and public officials to consider how they intend to approach this new power center. It will be suggested that there now exists a sufficiently large body of experience which should be examined before legislative bodies adopt guidelines for institutionalizing the relationship.

Police employee organizations can be traced back to the end of the last century.[1] Early attempts at unionization (in the sense of affiliation with organized labor and a desire for collective bargaining) ended, with scattered exceptions, with the 1919 Boston strike. However, from that time until the 1960s police employees remained highly organized. Local independent police-only

From *Law and Society Review* **6,** No. 2 (November 1971): 231–232, 235–242. Reprinted by permission of the author and *Law and Society Review,* the official publication of the Law and Society Association.

Hervey A. Juris is associated with the Graduate School of Management, Northwestern University.

organizations pursued their wage and benefit goals through legislative lobbying at the municipal and state levels. With the beginning of extensive public employee bargaining at the municipal level in 1961, police employee organizations began to assert themselves as economic organizations, pursuing collective bargaining where possible and occasionally engaging in job actions (such as slowdowns, working to rules, sick calls) or strikes.

Civil rights demonstrations, student unrest, and antiwar protests have put tremendous pressures on police agencies and police officers. Amid a conflict between pressure group concerns, and a general concern for law and order, public officials and police agency executives have attempted to define a response to crises consistent with the needs of society. Police employee organizations, however, have in some instances taken policy positions which have conflicted with those of the hierarchy or of elected officials. It is this competition for authority on the part of the union as a political and economic institution which has caused a great deal of concern among police executives and others. This concern with the potential role of the union has led some police agency executives to oppose police employee organizations, although recognizing that the reasons behind the militancy might reflect shortcomings in the agency itself. Usually this opposition is couched in terms of police employee organizations being incompatible with professionalism and the movement toward professionalism in the police service.

THE POTENTIAL IMPACT
OF POLICE UNIONS ON THE OPERATION
OF THE POLICE AGENCY

The police agency administrator has long enjoyed *carte blanche* with respect to the internal operations of his agency, especially as they relate to personnel management. Furthermore, as the head of a quasi-military organization highly dependent on discipline and loyalty for its efficient operation, he looks askance at any challenge to his traditional authority. Balanced against this, however, is the realization on the part of many police officers that just cause and due process are the rule rather than the exception in personnel actions by managers, not only in the private sector but also in segments of the public sector as well.

Given the ability to bargain collectively, it is to these needs that most police unions have addressed themselves. The most obvious challenge to traditional personnel management practices is the negotiation of grievance procedures whereby superior officer implementation of regulations can be effectively subjected to review by an employee who believes his rights have been violated.

Contracts have also abridged management flexibility in other ways. The 1969 New York City agreement provided portal-to-portal pay for officers assigned to another section of the city on temporary special duty, revised overtime provisions, and prohibited the rescheduling of off-days in order to avoid payment of overtime in a given week. While managerial flexibility was curtailed, these provisions also served to bring working conditions in the police service into equilibrium with working conditions in other occupations to which the patrolman might look as alternatives, an important labor market consideration.

Other bargaining demands by police unions which have been considered more threatening in their implications are often cited as self-evident reasons why police unions must be constrained. A careful review of these situations has led this author to conclude that the fault may lie less in the concept of collective bargaining than in the implementation of that concept by police agencies and the institutional and administrative environment which these agencies have created over time.

An example of how the parties may handle a policy disagreement within the context of a bargaining relationship is seen in the issue of one-man squad cars and the assignment of investigative duties to patrolmen in New York City. Both proposals were made by management in the interest of better manpower utilization. The union objected to each and wanted to discuss them within the context of the collective bargaining process. The city refused on the grounds that these were management prerogatives not subject to bargaining. The impasse was presented to an arbitrator who ruled that manning requirements and job duties were not bargainable issues.

An example of an issue handled outside the total context of bargaining can be seen in the question of tenure for detectives in New York City. Detectives serve at the pleasure of the chief of detectives and may be returned to the patrolman rank at any time in their career. Management argues that this is necessary for incentive reasons and also because the nature of the duties of the detective bureau is such that they must be able to demote for misfeasance and malfeasance. The union argues that an individual suitable for promotion to detective should, after a probationary period, be able to obtain some measure of job security. The issue was not resolved in the bargaining process and was taken by the detectives' association to the city council in the form of a bill which would require just cause and due process before a detective could be demoted. The

bill passed the council but was vetoed by the mayor. The policy issue raised is whether the union should have had access to the council, after being turned down by management with respect to a personnel issue of this type.

Herman Goldstein, in his "Administrative Problems in Controlling the Exercise of Police Authority," [2] applies to the police agency the generally accepted management principle that an individual or organization with responsibility should be given the authority to carry out that responsibility and then be reviewed by higher authorities for the quality of execution. While he was discussing possible cases of police malfeasance, the principle is equally applicable here.

Largely because of earlier reform movements and concern from time to time with the issue of keeping the police out of politics, there exists a variety of models for the control of police agencies. As a result, police unions find they often have wide latitude with respect to avenues of appeal from the bargaining process. Among these are personnel commissions, city councils, mayor or manager's offices, and, in some cases, the state legislature.

The problem then is to limit undesirable egress from the bargaining process so that management may deal with authority in personnel matters—a principle central to the success of a bargaining system. While recognizing that for political reasons little can be done with respect to instituting a rational administrative structure, still with respect to *personnel* policies it should be possible to allow the agency to establish its own bargaining posture and to hold the executive responsible for the ramifications of that posture. Where the council by law must retain these powers, it can still limit changes to the bargaining process, rather than lobbying, and be sure to include the chief or his representative as a consultant to, or member of, the bargaining committee.

Many of the threatening implications referred to previously can be viewed in this perspective. For example, in the city of Boston the police union objected to name tags on uniforms, the assignment of traffic personnel to patrol duty, changes in the color of squad cars and uniform shirts, and the consolidation of precincts and streamlining of operations in general. In each case, the union went outside the bargaining process to accomplish its goals. The city council outlawed name tags. Appeal to the council delayed, but did not prevent, the redeployment of traffic personnel. The council approved a change in the color of squad cars but backed the union on the question of shirt color. On the question of precinct consolidation, the union was able to block the city in the state legislature. Had there been some agreement among these agencies to limit the discussion of these issues to the bargaining proces, management would have been in a better overall position to cope with the potential impact of police unions on the operation of this agency.

THE POTENTIAL IMPACT
OF POLICE UNIONS ON LAW
ENFORCEMENT POLICY FORMULATION

The impact of the discretionary power of individual police officers on the formulation of law enforcement policy at the street level is already well documented.[3] In this paper, however, we will be concerned with the more overt efforts on the part of police employee organizations to influence the law enforcement policy of the community through participation in elective and legislative politics and through attempts at generating a set of signals distinct from those issued by city and agency officials to guide the exercise of discretion by individual members.

Public policy with respect to these issues is unclear. For years, the celebrated dictum of Mr. Justice Holmes had been predominant: "The petitioner may have a constitutional right to talk politics, but he has no constitutional right to be a policeman."[4] This has been interpreted as limiting the rights of police officers to make critical public statements on policy issues and as limiting their participation in elective politics—the latter because of possible misuse of their unique power and station in the society. However, as we shall see, this position has recently been substantially modified with respect to public policy statements.

The ambivalence of public policy with respect to political participation is best seen in the sometimes tacit, sometimes overt encouragement by police executives of participation by employee organizations in legislative political activity directed at larger appropriations for police agencies—especially as these appropriations relate to salary items, retirement systems, and welfare benefits. Given this official sanction and a functioning political organization, and given the leverage inherent in the public concern with law and order, it is not surprising that police employee organizations took advantage of their new constituencies to move into elective political action and public statements on issues of law enforcement policy, even though local regulations may have prohibited both.

This expanded activity with respect to public statements was reinforced by the changing Constitutional climate during the 1960s. In a line of cases from *New York Times Co.* v. *Sullivan* (1964) through *Pickering* v. *Board of Education* (1968), the

Court moved from a virtual prohibition of public employee rights to the exercise of critical speech to a standard which has been interpreted as allowing critical statements so long as they do not include knowing falsity, disclosure of confidential information, or falsehoods which would impair the operation of the agency, destroy an effective superior-subordinate relationship, or adversely affect work relationships in the agency.[5]

An example of the extent to which we have moved from Holmes's statement can be seen in a Maryland case, *Eugene C. Bru-kiewa* v. *Police Commissioner of Baltimore City* (1970). Brukiewa, the president of the Baltimore police union, had made comments critical of the department and the commissioner on a local television program. He was suspended by the department's disciplinary board which ruled that he had violated two departmental regulations relating to discussion of departmental business in public and criticism of superiors. A Baltimore city court upheld the suspension on the grounds that the regulations cited were clear and unambiguous. The Appeals Court overruled the city court on the grounds that the city did not show that the appellant's statements hurt or imperiled the discipline or operation of the police department and were, therefore, within his right to make under the First Amendment and the decisions of the Supreme Court.

The Police Benevolent Association in New York City, from time to time in recent years, has, among other things, charged political interference with the operation of the department, warned of gaps in police protection, called for 100 percent enforcement of the law by officers regardless of signals from the commissioner and the mayor, and warned the public about changes in hiring standards for officers. At one point, police pickets paraded in front of city hall chanting, "We want Daley; Lindsay must go." Of course the most famous New York City case is the role of the PBA in the defeat of the civilian review board referendum. More recently they have been debating the implementation of the mayor's campaign to eliminate graft and corruption.

The police unions in Chicago, Newark, Syracuse, Cleveland, and elsewhere have spoken out on similar issues. The national Fraternal Order of Police from time to time issues statements on civil unrest and at one time called for the removal from the Kerner Commission of Herbert Jenkins, chief of police in Atlanta.

A case more directly related to collective bargaining occurred in the fall of 1970 in Waukegan, Illinois, where a group of officers, fired by the city for participating in a recognition strike, accused the mayor and chief of various indiscretions, from ticket-fixing to the coddling of vice activities. Perhaps even more significant than the process of accusation is the fact that several of the discharged officers ran for city council.

These examples might be termed the center of police political commentary. From the right come the voices of associations such as the Law Enforcement Group in New York City, and from the left come the voices of groups such as the Afro patrolmen's associations. This spectrum of political activity serves to point up a basic issue: Is society better served by more or less participation by police employee organizations in the public debate on law enforcement policy?

Police management views political activism as a challenge to its authority when issues of policy are raised but endorses it when legislative political activity results in large appropriations. Of the employee organizations of the left, center, and right, each feels it has a legitimate analysis and solution, an obligation to publicize it, and a protected right to do so. On the other hand, each is intolerant of political activity by the other two. Within the society the constituency of each group is tolerant of political activity by those with whom it agrees and intolerant of similar activity by its opponents. I would suggest that the policy most consistent with our pluralistic society and representative democracy would be to increase rather than decrease the number of voices contributing to the debate. While there are costs inherent in such a position, there are many who feel that the long-run benefits have historically outweighed the short-run costs.

A natural extension of free speech and participation in legislative politics in participation in elective politics. Regardless of local prohibitions, many police employee organizations have backed candidates for public office. Notable successes (from the point of view of the employee organizations) have included Yorty in Los Angeles, Stenvig in Minneapolis, and Gribbs in Detroit. Notable failures (again from the point of view of the employee organizations) have been the election of Lindsay in New York and Stokes in Cleveland.

No one questions the policeman's right to vote. Can he as an individual, however, make a contribution to an individual campaign? Can he distribute leaflets, canvass, or collect money for a candidate if he does so off duty and out of uniform? Can an officer ever be considered "out of uniform" if he is known by the merchants and citizens on his beat? If he is not prohibited from these activities as an individual, can he be prohibited from them as a member of an organization? These are some issues which must be considered in adopting a policy with respect to elective politics.

Another aspect of participation in elective politics is participation in the election campaigns of those most intimately concerned with the administration of criminal justice in the community—the prosecutors and judges.[6] In the theoretical construct of the criminal justice system, each level is expected to function independently: the policeman makes arrests, the prosecutor decides if a formal charge is warranted and prosecutes the case, the judge presides over the trial and passes sentence. While in practice these are not independent events, still the question arises as to whether we want to make the interdependence overt through police union endorsements and campaigns for candidates. The same issue arises in campaigns for mayor and governor where the candidate states a position on the types of individuals he will appoint to civilian review boards, civil service commissions, parole boards, and other agencies which might have jurisdiction in the criminal justice area. These are raised as issues for discussion which must be considered within the context of free speech, political activity, and law enforcement policy formulation. There are no easy answers.

NOTES

1 Kay B. Hutchison, "Municipal Police Employee Organizations: A Study in Functional Unionism" (Master's thesis, University of Wisconsin, 1969).
2 Herman Goldstein, "Administrative Problems in Controlling the Exercise of Police Authority," *Journal of Criminal Law, Criminology and Police Science* **58** (1967): 160.
3 See Kenneth Culp Davis, *Discretionary Justice* (Baton Rouge: LSU Press, 1969); Jerome H.

Skolnick, *Justice Without Trial* (New York: John Wiley, 1966); and James Q. Wilson, *Varieties of Police Behavior* (Cambridge: Harvard University Press, 1968).

4 *McAuliffe* v. *City of New Bedford,* 1892: 220.

5 From a legal point of view: Georgetown Law Review (1968); from an operational point of view: Mondello (1970).

6 I am indebted to Herman Goldstein for his pointing out the need to highlight this issue within the context of elective politics.

POLICE MALPRACTICE

The Denver Police Chief discharges an officer who has been indicted for robbery.

Police malpractice refers to a broader spectrum of behavior than police corruption. Corruption normally suggests the sale of official authority for personal gain, whereas malpractice includes not only corruption but also mistreatment of prisoners, discrimination, illegal searches, perjury, planting evidence, and other misconduct committed under the authority of law enforcement.

Various forms of police malpractice are doubtless attributable to different causes. For example, it might be useful to distinguish between the overzealous narcotics officer who engages in illegal investigatory tactics and the corrupt narcotics officer who takes bribes to deter him from enforcing the law. Still, whatever the difference in motivations, whenever police violate their professional responsibility to uphold the law they create problems both within the department and in the public mind. Honest cops come to be lumped together with the dishonest, the overzealous, and the incompetent. Police malpractice affects the public image of police everywhere, undermining public confidence in the police enterprise and making a difficult job more difficult.

The articles in this section offer several views of police malpractice: from the perspectives of a patrolman, a police chief, and observers of the police. The articles raise fundamental questions about the problem and its solutions: How are we to define police malpractice? What causes different aspects of it? How is it continued from one generation of police to the next? Do certain norms inhere in the job of policing, for example, the idea that police should protect each other and should be secretive with respect to the outside world? Do these norms encourage or at least cover up police misconduct? If so, are there ways to make police organizations less secretive?

Such questions raise other kinds of issues which also need to be explored: Is the problem of police malpractice primarily the responsibility of the chief? Suppose an honest police officer learns of outright corruption. How should he respond, and should his response be the same for every department? How should the dishonesty of policemen be interpreted by other officers and administrators, that is, should a dishonest policeman be viewed as a crook in uniform or an unfortunate victim of job circumstances? Should poor or indifferent services to one segment of the community be considered any more excusable than taking gifts or money to invoke differential service on the part of police officers? Why?

One fact is clear. Police malpractice is an important reality of policing in America and has consequences for law enforcement officers far beyond the immediate time or police department or community where they work. It is hoped that the articles in this chapter will help to define police malpractice as a real and potentially solvable problem.

Police Corruption in New York

KNAPP COMMISSION

THE EXTENT OF POLICE CORRUPTION

We found corruption to be widespread. It took various forms depending upon the activity involved, appearing at its most sophisticated among plainclothesmen assigned to enforcing gambling laws. In the five plainclothes divisions where our investigations were concentrated we found a strikingly standardized pattern of corruption. Plainclothesmen, participating in what is known in police parlance as a "pad," collected regular biweekly or monthly payments amounting to as much as $3,500 from each of the gambling establishments in the area under their jurisdiction and divided the take in equal shares. The monthly share per man (called the "nut") ranged from $300 and $400 in midtown Manhattan to $1,500 in Harlem. When supervisors were involved they received a share and a half. A newly assigned plainclothesman was not entitled to his share for about two months, while he was checked out for reliability, but the earnings lost by the delay were made up to him in the form of two months' severance pay when he left the division.

Evidence before us led us to the conclusion that the same pattern existed in the remaining divisions which we did not investigate in depth. This conclusion was confirmed by events occurring before and after the pe-

From a report by the Commission to Investigate Allegations of Police Corruption in New York City, Whitman Knapp, Chairman (August 3, 1972).

riod of our investigation. Prior to the Commission's existence, exposures by former plainclothesman Frank Serpico had led to indictments or departmental charges against nineteen plainclothesmen in a Bronx division for involvement in a pad where the nut was $800. After our public hearings had been completed, an investigation conducted by the Kings County District Attorney and the Department's Internal Affairs Division—which investigation neither the Commission nor its staff had even known about—resulted in indictments and charges against 37 Brooklyn plainclothesmen who had participated in a pad with a nut of $1,200. The manner of operation of the pad involved in each of these situations was in every detail identical to that described at the Commission hearings, and in each almost every plainclothesman in the division, including supervisory lieutenants, was implicated.

Corruption in narcotics enforcement lacked the organization of the gambling pads, but individual payments—known as "scores" —were commonly received and could be staggering in amount. Our investigation, a concurrent probe by the State Investigation Commission, and prosecutions by federal and local authorities all revealed a pattern whereby corrupt officers customarily collected scores in substantial amounts from narcotics violators. These scores were either kept by the individual officer or shared with a partner and, perhaps, a superior officer. They ranged from minor shakedowns to payments of many thousands of dollars, the largest narcotics payoff uncovered in our investigation having been $80,000. According to information developed by the SIC and in recent federal investigations, the size of this score was by no means unique.

Corruption among detectives assigned to general investigative duties also took the form of shakedowns of individual targets of opportunity. Although these scores were not in the huge amounts found in narcotics, they not infrequently came to several thousand dollars.

Uniformed patrolmen assigned to street duties were not found to receive money on nearly so grand or organized a scale, but the large number of small payments they received present an equally serious if less dramatic problem. Uniformed patrolmen, particularly those assigned to radio patrol cars, participated in gambling pads more modest in size than those received by plainclothes units and received regular payments from construction sites, bars, grocery stores, and other business establishments. These payments were usually made on a regular basis to sector car patrolmen and on a haphazard basis to others. While individual payments to uniformed men were small, mostly under $20, they were often so numerous as to add substantially to a patrolman's income. Other less regular payments to uniformed patrolmen included those made by after-hours bars, bottle clubs, tow trucks, motorists, cab drivers, parking lots, prostitutes, and defendants wanting to fix their cases in court. Another practice found to be widespread was the payment of gratuities by policemen to other policemen to expedite normal police procedures or to gain favorable assignments.

Sergeants and lieutenants who were so inclined participated in the same kind of corruption as the men they supervised. In addition, some sergeants had their own pads from which patrolmen were excluded.

Although the Commission was unable to develop hard evidence establishing that officers above the rank of lieutenant received payoffs, considerable circumstantial evidence and some testimony so indicated. Most often when a superior officer is corrupt, he uses a patrolman as his "bagman" who collects for him and keeps a percentage of the take. Because the bagman may keep the money for himself, although he claims to be collecting for his superior, it is extremely difficult to determine with any accuracy when the superior actually is involved.

Of course, not all policemen are corrupt. If we are to exclude such petty infractions as free meals, an appreciable number do not engage in any corrupt activities. Yet, with extremely rare exceptions, even those who themselves engage in no corrupt activities are involved in corruption in the sense that they take no steps to prevent what they know or suspect to be going on about them.

It must be made clear that—in a little over a year with a staff having as few as two and never more than twelve field investigators—we did not examine every precinct in the department. Our conclusion that corruption is widespread throughout the department is based on the fact that information supplied to us by hundreds of sources within and without the department was consistently borne out by specific observations made in areas we were able to investigate in detail.

THE NATURE AND SIGNIFICANCE
OF POLICE CORRUPTION

Corruption, although widespread, is by no means uniform in degree. Corrupt policemen have been described as falling into two basic categories: "meat-eaters" and "grass-eaters." As the names might suggest, the meat-eaters are those policemen who, like Patrolman William Phillips who testified at our hearings, aggressively misuse their police powers for personal gain. The grass-eaters simply accept the payoffs that the happenstances of police work throw their way. Although the meat-eaters get the huge payoffs that make the headlines, they represent a small percentage of all corrupt policemen. The truth is, the vast majority of policemen on the take don't deal in huge amounts of graft.

And yet, grass-eaters are the heart of the problem. Their great numbers tend to make corruption "respectable." They also tend to encourage the code of silence that brands anyone who exposes corruption a traitor. At the time our investigation began, any policeman violating the code did so at his peril. The result was described in our interim report: "The rookie who comes into the department is faced with the situation where it is easier for him to become corrupt than to remain honest."

More importantly, although meat-eaters can and have been individually induced to make their peace with society, the grass-eaters may be more easily reformed. We believe that, given proper leadership and support, many police who have slipped into corruption would exchange their illicit income for the satisfaction of belonging to a corruption-free department in which they could take genuine pride.

The problem of corruption is neither new nor confined to the police. Reports of prior investigations into police corruption, testimony taken by the Commission, and opinions of informed persons both within and without the department make it abundantly clear that police corruption has been a problem for many years. Investigations have occurred on the average of once in twenty years since before the turn of the century, and yet conditions exposed by one investigation seem substantially unchanged when the next one makes its report. This

doesn't mean that the police have a monopoly on corruption. On the contrary, in every area where police corruption exists it is paralleled by corruption in other agencies of government, in industry and labor, and in the professions.

Our own mandate was limited solely to the police. There are sound reasons for such a special concern with police corruption. The police have a unique place in our society. The policeman is expected to "uphold the law" and "keep the peace." He is charged with everything from traffic control to riot control. He is expected to protect our lives and our property. As a result, society gives him special powers and prerogatives, which include the right and obligation to bear arms, along with the authority to take away our liberty by arresting us.

Symbolically, his role is even greater. For most people, the policeman is the law. To them, the law is administered by the patrolman on the beat and the captain in the station house. Little wonder that the public becomes aroused and alarmed when the police are charged with corruption or are shown to be corrupt.

DEPARTMENTAL ATTITUDES
TOWARD POLICE CORRUPTION

Although this special concern is justified, public preoccupation with police corruption as opposed to corruption in other agencies of government inevitably seems unfair to the policeman. He believes that he is unjustly blamed for the results of corruption in other parts of the criminal justice system. This sense of unfairness intensifies the sense of isolation and hostility to which the nature of police work inevitably gives rise.

Feelings of isolation and hostility are experienced by policemen not just in New York but everywhere. To understand these feelings one must appreciate an important characteristic of any metropolitan police department, namely, an extremely intense group loyalty. When properly understood, this group loyalty can be used in the fight against corruption. If misunderstood or ignored, it can undermine anticorruption activities.

Pressures that give rise to this group loyalty include the danger to which policemen are constantly exposed and the hostility they encounter from society at large. Everyone agrees that a policeman's life is a dangerous one, and that his safety, not to mention his life, can depend on his ability to rely on a fellow officer in a moment of crisis. It is less generally realized that the policeman works in a sea of hostility. This is true not only in high crime areas but throughout the city. Nobody, whether a burglar or a Sunday motorist, likes to have his activities interfered with. As a result, most citizens, at one time or another, regard the police with varying degrees of hostility. The policeman feels, and naturally often returns, this hostility.

Two principal characteristics emerge from this group loyalty: suspicion and hostility directed at any outside interference with the department and an intense desire to be proud of the department. This mixture of hostility and pride has created what the Commission has found to be the most serious roadblock to a rational attack upon police corruption: a stubborn refusal at all levels of the department to acknowledge that a serious problem exists.

The interaction of stubbornness, hostility, and pride has given rise to the so-called "rotten-apple" theory. According to this theory, which bordered on official department doctrine, any policeman found to be corrupt must promptly be denounced as a rotten apple in an otherwise clean barrel. It must never be admitted that his individual corruption may be symptomatic of underlying disease.

This doctrine was grounded on two basic premises: First, the morale of the department requires that there be no official recognition of corruption, even though practically all members of the department know it is in truth extensive; second, the department's public image and effectiveness require official denial of this truth.

The rotten-apple doctrine has in many ways been a basic obstacle to meaningful reform. To begin with, it reinforced and gave respectability to the code of silence. The official view that the department's image and morale forbade public disclosure of the extent of corruption inhibited any officer who wished to disclose corruption and justified any who preferred to remain silent. The doctrine also made difficult, if not impossible, any meaningful attempt at managerial reform. A high command unwilling to acknowledge that the problem of corruption is extensive cannot very well argue that drastic changes are necessary to deal with that problem. Thus neither the Mayor's Office nor the Police Department took adequate steps to see that such changes were made when the need for them was indicated by the charges made by Officers Frank Serpico and David Durk in 1968. This was demonstrated in the Commission's second set of public hearings in December 1971.

Finally, the doctrine made impossible the use of one of the most effective techniques for dealing with any entrenched criminal activity, namely, persuading a participant to help provide evidence against his partners in crime. If a corrupt policeman is merely an isolated rotten apple, no reason can be given for not exposing him the minute he is discovered. If, on the other hand, it is acknowledged that a corrupt officer is only one part of an apparatus of corruption, common sense dictates that every effort should be made to enlist the offender's aid in providing the evidence to destroy the apparatus.

THE COMMISSION'S ACTIONS

The Commission examined and rejected the premises upon which the rotten-apple doctrine rested. We concluded that there was no justification for fearing that public acknowledgment of the extent of corruption would damage the image and effectiveness of the department. We are convinced that instead of damaging its image a realistic attitude toward corruption could only enhance the department's credibility. The conditions described in the Commission's public hearings came as no surprise to the large numbers of city residents who had experienced them for years. If, then, the department makes it a point to acknowledge corrupt conditions the public already knows to exist, it can hardly damage its image. On the contrary, it can only promote confidence in the department's good-faith desire to deal with those conditions.

The Commission looked at the question of morale in much the same way. We did not—and do not—believe that the morale of the average policeman is enhanced by a commanding officer who insists on denying facts that the policeman knows to be true. We believed—and continue to believe—that such false denials can only undercut the policeman's confidence in his commander. If a policeman listens to his commander solemnly deny the existence of an obvious corrupt situation, the policeman can draw only one of two conclusions: either the commander is hopelessly naive or he is content to let the corruption continue.

Once we had rejected the premises of the rotten-apple doctrine, the Commission determined to employ one of the techniques that adherence to the doctrine had made impossible, namely, to persuade formerly corrupt police officers to work with us in providing evidence of continuing corruption.

The mere decision to use the technique did not automatically produce a body of officers able and eager to assist us in this manner. Indeed, knowledgeable persons assured us that the code of silence was so strong that we would never find a corrupt officer who could be persuaded to assist in exposing corruption. We ultimately did persuade four officers, including Detective Robert L. Leuci and Patrolmen William Phillips, Edward Droge, and Alfonso Jannotta to undertake undercover work. Of these, all but Detective Leuci did so under the compulsion of having been caught by Commission investigators. Patrolmen Phillips and Droge testified at public hearings held in October 1971. Patrolman Jannotta was unavailable due to illness at the time of the hearings. The information disclosed by Detective Leuci was so vital that we did not, since our time was limited, feel justified in keeping it to ourselves. Leuci and the Commission staff members who had debriefed him and worked with him on his initial undercover operations were turned over to the federal government for the long-term investigation which was required. Leuci's work as a federal undercover agent is now resulting in the series of important narcotics-related indictments being obtained by United States Attorney Whitney North Seymour, Jr.

Success in persuading these officers to assist in the investigation was a first step in demonstrating that the rotten-apple doctrine was invalid. Patrolman Phillips' three days of testimony about systematic corruption in various parts of the department, corroborated by tape-recorded conversations with many police officers and others, was in itself enough to make the doctrine seem untenable. Patrolman Droge described how departmental pressures gradually converted an idealistic rookie into an increasingly bold finder of bribes and payoffs. Former Patrolman Waverly Logan, who volunteered to testify about corruption in which he had been involved, corroborated Droge's testimony and went on to tell about policemen in Harlem who received monthly as much as $3,000 each in narcotics graft. Patrolman Logan also introduced the Commission to two addicts who were willing to work with us in obtaining evidence to corroborate these assertions. The Commission's work with these addicts produced movies and recorded conversations of policemen selling narcotics. Some of the narcotics were paid for with merchandise the policemen believed to be stolen. Captain Daniel McGowan, a police officer of unquestioned integrity and experienced in anticorruption work, testified that the picture of corruption presented by Patrolmen Phillips, Droge, and Logan was an accurate one. In addition, there was testimony from, among others, a Harlem gambler, Commission agents describing their investigations, and witnesses in the business community revealing corrupt police dealings with the hotel and construction industries. Recorded conversations and movies documented instances of police corruption, including gambling and narcotics payoffs, fixing court cases, and shaking down a tow-truck operator. The cumulative effect of these two weeks of testimony made it not only unrealistic but absurd for anyone thereafter to adhere to the rotten-apple doctrine, either publicly or privately.

The doctrine did not die easily. Institutional pressures within the department seemed to force the high command to continue giving lip service to the doctrine even when speaking out against corruption. Commissioner Murphy in his early statements about corruption regularly included a pointed statement indicating that the corruption in the department was limited to a few officers. On one occasion he went so far as to imply that there were no more than about 300 corrupt police officers in the entire department. After Patrolman Phillips had completed two of his three days of testimony at our public hearings, Commissioner Murphy found it necessary to discount his testimony of widespread corruption, referring to him as a "rogue cop."

However, one week later, after Phillips had completed his testimony and had been followed by Patrolmen Logan and Droge and others, the department, speaking through First Deputy Commissioner William H. T. Smith, forthrightly rejected the rotten-apple doctrine by name. Smith defined it as standing for the proposition that "police departments are essentially free of corruption except for the presence of a few corrupt officers who have managed to slip into police service and also into key assignments such as gambling investigations, despite rigorously applied screening procedures designed to keep them out." He said that traditional police strategy had been to react defensively whenever a scandal arose by "promising to crack down on graft, to go after the 'rogue cops,' to get rid of 'rotten apples.' " Smith said the department now rejected this approach "not just on principle, but because as a way of controlling corruption it had utterly failed." He acknowledged that the result of adherence to the theory had been a breakdown in public confidence: ". . . they [the public] are sick of 'bobbing for rotten apples' in the police barrel. They want an entirely new barrel that will never again become contaminated."

CHANGING DEPARTMENTAL ATTITUDES

The public hearings, in addition to helping bring about official abandonment of the rotten-apple doctrine, have had dramatic effect on the way members of the department discuss corruption. This change was graphically described shortly after our hearings by former Assistant Chief Inspector Sidney C. Cooper in colorful language: "Not very long ago we talked about corruption with all the enthusiasm of a group of little old ladies talking about venereal disease. Now there is a little more open discussion about combatting graft as if it were a public health problem." In short, the first barrier to a realistic look at corruption has been overcome: the problem has been officially, and unofficially, acknowledged.

Some time after the public hearings were over, it was revealed that Detective Leuci had been doing undercover work for the federal government for over a year and a half, and that he had been doing it with both the knowledge and protection of the department's high command. News also began to spread throughout the department that other formerly corrupt policemen were doing undercover work for the department's Internal Affairs Division and for at least one district attorney's office. These revelations had considerable impact, both direct and indirect, upon attitudes toward corruption within the department.

To put the direct impact in proper perspective, it should be pointed out that any criminal activity, within a police department or elsewhere, cannot thrive unless all of its participants are able to maintain confidence in each other. Patrolman Phillips' testimony made this very clear. In testifying about his own corrupt activities, he described how he could, by making a few telephone calls within five or ten minutes, "check out" the reliability of any other officer whose assistance he might require in a corrupt enterprise. By way of illustration, he described instances where he had been similarly checked out while doing undercover work for the Commission. This ability to check out, and rely upon, an officer with whom one has had no previous contact rested on the assumption—unchallenged before the advent of our Commission—that no police officer who had once become involved in corruption could ever be persuaded to disclose the corruption of others. The actions of Detective Leuci and Patrolmen Phillips and Droge and of others as yet unnamed who are presently working undercover have undermined this assumption.

Even more important was the indirect effect produced by general knowledge that the undercover activities of these formerly corrupt policemen had been known to—and protected by—the department's high command. Traditionally, the rank and file have shown a deep cynicism, well justified by history, concerning pronouncements of new police commissioners. They carefully examine the new commissioner's every word and action, searching for "messages": Does he mean business? Can he stand up against institutional pressures?

The initial lack of clarity in Commissioner Murphy's statements on the rotten-apple theory and his "rogue cop" reaction to the first widely publicized defiance of the code of silence were interpreted by some as suggesting a lack of commitment to total war on corruption. However, the department's final repudiation of the doctrine and the general knowledge that the department was using and protecting policemen who had agreed to do undercover work gave reassurance to the doubters.

In short, we believe that the department's recent reactions to the Commission's activities have promoted realistic self-criticism within the department. This spirit of self-criticism is an encouraging sign. For one thing, it is becoming less unusual for police officers to report evidence of police corruption. If this tendency continues, the day may be approaching when the rookie coming into the department will not be pressured toward corruption, but can count on finding support for his desire to remain honest.

The present situation is quite like that existing at the close of previous investigations. A considerable momentum for reform has been generated, but not enough time has elapsed to reverse attitudes that have been solidifying for many years in the minds of both the public and the police.

After previous investigations, the momentum was allowed to evaporate.

The question now is: Will history repeat itself? Or does society finally realize that police corruption is a problem that must be dealt with and not just talked about once every twenty years?

Both immediate and long-term actions are mandatory. The reforms already initiated within the department must be completed and expanded; there must be changes, both legislative and administrative, to curb pressures toward police corruption and to facilitate its control; and the momentum generated by the events before and during the life of this Commission must be maintained.

Serpico: The Cop Who Defied the System

PETER MAAS

In January 1969 the grand jury had completed its hearings and was preparing its report. Grand jury proceedings are theoretically secret, but just before Serpico's transfer to plainclothes duty in Manhattan North came through he bumped into an old friend, a cop he had worked with in Brooklyn, now

From *Serpico: The Cop Who Defied the System* by Peter Maas, pp. 89–93, 227–229, 234–244. Copyright © 1973 by Peter Maas and Tsampa Company, Inc. Reprinted by permission of the Viking Press, Inc.

a plainclothesman, who seemed to know all about them. "Gee, Frank," he said, "the word is you went in there and didn't hold back anything."

"What was I supposed to do," Serpico countered, "stick my neck out for those fucks?"

"Well, everybody is saying that if you got hurt, you would've been taken care of."

"How?"

"Uh, you know, fifty Gs for keeping your mouth shut. Now nobody's going to get near you. Nobody wants to disturb the system."

Serpico was even less enchanted about being assigned to Manhattan North when he learned that his new commander was Philip Sheridan, who had become a full-fledged inspector—undoubtedly promoted, Serpico jeeringly imagined, because of his ace detective work in uncovering corruption in the 7th Division. When Serpico reported for duty, his reception was exactly as his friend had predicted. It was as if he were a nonperson. There were perhaps a dozen men in the Manhattan North borough plainclothes office, sitting and standing around, drinking coffee and gossiping among themselves. Serpico was elaborately ignored. No one said anything to him or even looked at him.

And then it happened.

As Serpico stood alone, a plainclothesman, Irish, with black curly hair and watery blue eyes, walked up to him. He stopped about three feet from Serpico, and reached into his pocket and took out a knife. He cradled the knife, unopened, in his hand. The others in the room fell silent. Out of the corner of his eye Serpico could see some of them smirking. The plainclothesman with the knife said, "We know how to handle guys like you." He extended his right hand, the one with the knife in it, pressed a button in the handle with his thumb, and five inches of steel blade leaped out, pointing up. "I ought to cut your tongue out," the plainclothesman said.

Serpico tensed. He looked at the plainclothesman, at the knife, at the watching, smirking faces in the room. It was incredible that this was actually happening inside a police station and he remembered thinking, They're trying to put me down. He knew he had to do something, but he didn't know quite what.

Serpico saw the knife move. He did not wait to find out what the movement was, where it was going. All his reflexes sprang into action. His left forearm swung up savagely and chopped against the man's wrist. The knife clattered to the floor.

In one fluid motion Serpico gripped the man's right hand across the palm with his own right hand, and twisted it back and down. The plainclothesman cried out. Serpico kept twisting his hand back and down, and the man had to turn and follow it, or his wrist would have snapped.

The plainclothesman was now completely helpless, doubled over toward the floor, still moaning in pain and surprise, when Serpico let go of his hand and shoved him forward with his knee. He landed heavily on the floor, face down. The knife was a few inches away from his outstretched hand. Serpico was over him at once. He whipped out his Browning automatic, cocked it, and pressed it against the base of the plainclothesman's skull. "Move, you motherfucker," Serpico said, "and I'll blow your brains out."

The man's body went limp, his face was jammed so tightly against the floor that he could not speak. Serpico kept the gun on him and looked around the room. Everyone was frozen in place, and no one was smirking any more.

Perhaps thirty seconds passed before one of the other cops in the room coughed nervously and said, "Jesus Christ, is that a forty-five?"

"No, nine-millimeter," Serpico said.

"Oh, so that's the new Browning, huh? How many rounds does it hold?"

"Fourteen."

"Fourteen? What do you need fourteen rounds for?"

"How many guys you got in this office?"

"Hey, look, we were just joking."

"Yeah, so was I," Serpico said. He stepped back from the plainclothesman on the floor.

The man swiveled his head cautiously and looked up at Serpico and gasped, "I was only kidding. Mother of God, I was only kidding!" Then, as Serpico put the Browning back in its holster, he scrambled to his feet and darted out of the room.

"Um, I guess I better show you where the coffee is," another plainclothesman said.

Inspector Sheridan immediately detached Serpico from Manhattan North for temporary duty in the "pussy posse," the midtown prostitution detail that operated out of the 18th Precinct on West Fifty-fourth Street. That night in a diary he kept from time to time Serpico wrote, "I finally got my big reward for being a good guy. Times Square and the whore patrol!"

Serpico worked on the pussy posse for about five weeks when he went on vacation. Before he left, the grand jury returned indictments against eight plainclothesmen in the 7th Division, among them Stanard, Zumatto, and Paretti, and on his return Serpico would find out why an honest cop who dared cross the crooked ones had to watch his step constantly.

He traveled through Switzerland, Austria, and Italy, visiting relatives of his parents in the town of Caserta outside Naples, and continued on to Spain. In Madrid he happened to pass a shop with a display of knives and went in to look them over. One particularly intrigued him. It was a pushbutton knife, but instead of the blade snapping open, it thrust directly out. Knives like this were against the law in New York for police and civilians alike, though many cops carried them anyway. With all the thinly veiled threats Serpico had been receiving, he

thought it might come in handy, so he told the shopkeeper that he would probably return the next day to buy it. He overslept the next morning, however, and did not have enough time to get back to the shop before catching a plane to London on the last leg of his trip.

After London he flew straight to New York. At the customs booth in Kennedy Airport, Serpico handed over his passport, health certificate, and declaration of purchases. The man checked a list of names on a counter, and Serpico remembered how he suddenly looked a little nervous. He told Serpico to wait, disappeared behind an office door, and returned perhaps a minute later. "Anything wrong?" Serpico asked.

"Oh, no," the man replied.

On the baggage line a second customs man asked Serpico to open his two bags and started going through them. "Maybe I can save you some time," Serpico said. "I'm on the job."

The man appeared astonished. "Where?"

"NYPD," Serpico said, producing his shield.

"Just a minute," the customs man said, "let me check something."

Serpico watched him walk away and consult with two supervisors. One of the supervisors followed him back and said, "Bring your bags and come with me."

Serpico was led into a small room where two other customs agents stood waiting. He was ordered to strip. He was about to protest, but he suddenly realized what was happening and decided to keep quiet. It was almost an article of faith among other cops that since he lived in Greenwich Village, he must be smoking marijuana or hashish, and that must be what the customs people were looking for. Somehow this had been arranged, but nothing in the customs regulations said a cop could not be stopped, and

Serpico figured there was no point in stirring up trouble that might wind up on his record.

So he submitted to a humiliating body search, and his baggage was gone over inch by inch. There was a flurry of excitement when a five-ounce package of Ty-Phoo tea he had bought in London was discovered. The package was emptied, but all it contained was tea. Finally one of the men turned to the supervisor and shrugged his shoulders, and the supervisor glared at Serpico and stormed from the room.

On his way out of the customs area Serpico spotted the agent who had initially poked into his bag on the inspection line. "What was that all about?" Serpico asked.

"Honest to God, I don't know. I told them you were a cop, and they just said they knew it."

Serpico told him about the push-button knife he had almost purchased in Madrid, and the customs man said, "It's a good thing you didn't. If they were looking to hang you, and I guess they were, that'd be plenty."

Serpico had to admire the subtlety of it all. He could have been thrown off the force if somebody had wanted it badly enough, to say nothing of how it would have discredited him as a witness against the 7th Division cops facing trial.

He returned to the Times Square prostitution detail for about a week and then was transferred back to the Manhattan North borough plainclothes office. After the confrontation with the plainclothesman who had pulled the switchblade, everyone figuratively tiptoed around him, but he remained completely ostracized.

He had nearly reached the breaking point. He felt he had been denigrated by his assignment on the pussy posse, and the customs incident did not improve his mood. But more than anything he was depressed be-

yond measure by the grand jury indictments. After all the promises of a thorough investigation by the Police Department and all the reassurances that the Bronx District Attorney's office had given him, only eight plainclothesmen, eight lowly cops, had been indicted. There was nothing said or done about superior officers or about the system. After all he had gone through, eight cops were ticketed to take the rap, and the systematic corruption would go on as if they had never existed; and as far as other policemen were concerned now, he might as well be wearing a leper's bell.

Then Serpico met Inspector Paul Delise.

Philip Sheridan had resigned from the department—probably because his nerves couldn't take me being around, Serpico thought when he heard about it—and Delise was the new commander of the Manhattan North plainclothesmen. He was a short, powerfully built man with a soft voice and hard brown eyes. The first time he saw Serpico in the office, standing apart from the rest of the men, with his beard and shaggy hair, army shirt, dungarees and sandals, an old army gas-mask bag over his shoulder to carry his .38 service revolver since he had his Browning automatic in his belt, Delise thought he must be an informant and made a mental note to tell his men not to display their informants so openly.

The next day, when Delise saw Serpico again, dressed the same way, still apart from the others, he asked one of the men who he was. "Oh, that's Serpico. He's in 'clothes.' He's been down on the pussy posse."

Delise went over to Serpico and introduced himself and asked him to come into his office. When they were alone, Delise said, "Are you by any chance related to the Frank Serpico in the 7th Division?"

Serpico stared guardedly at Delise, wondering what this was all about, what new indignity was coming. Finally, defiantly, he replied, "That's me. I'm Frank Serpico."

Inspector Delise got up, walked around his desk, and reached for Serpico. "I want to shake your hand," he said. "You know, you did a wonderful thing for the department. You're a credit to it, and you've got a hell of a lot of guts. I'm lucky to have you in my command, somebody that I can rely on. You're like a breath of fresh air for me."

For a moment Serpico thought this was a crude putdown, but he looked at Delise more closely and realized that he was absolutely in earnest. Serpico felt a surge of exuberance. No superior officer had ever spoken to him like this before. He had never heard of Delise, but he would subsequently learn that he had a reputation of being so straightforward and honest that other policemen sneeringly referred to him behind his back as "Saint Paul."

Delise asked Serpico if there was any one man in the command that he wanted to work with, someone he would feel comfortable having as a partner.

Serpico laughed wryly and said, "It's not a matter of who I want to work with. It's who wants to work with me."

"Well, if we can't find anybody," Delise said, "I'll work with you myself."

He was as good as his word. It was almost unheard of for an officer of Delise's rank and age—fifty—to be traipsing on roofs, creeping down alleys, climbing over backyard fences, but Delise did it with Serpico, and he seemed to enjoy it. Serpico would worry about him sometimes, and Delise would say, "I'm fine. I feel like a cop all over again."

They worked together throughout much of the spring and summer of 1969. Delise was the first superior he had ever respected enough to call "boss," and Serpico always remembered this period as his best time as a police officer. He let his beard and hair grow even more unkempt, and to reinforce his appearance as a junkie on the street, he often smoked a black Italian cheroot on an empty stomach—which actually gave him a dazed high, as if he were coming off a narcotics fix. The usual procedure he followed was to spot a policy operation, observe its activity from a rooftop with binoculars, and then have Delise back him up when he hit it, swooping down through a skylight, charging up a flight of cellar stairs, blocking off an alley. Another of Serpico's stratagems to avoid attention as he went from neighborhood to neighborhood in Manhattan North was to munch on oranges and grapefruit, like a vagabond on the move, and all Delise had to do for a rooftop rendezvous was to follow the rinds that Serpico left in his wake.

Delise and Serpico discussed the possibility of corruption existing in Manhattan North similar to that in the 7th Division, but their reputations so completely cut them off from the rest of the men that they were unable to pin anything down.

Then one day Serpico reported to Delise that he had zeroed in on what looked to be a major numbers location. It was in a store, the windows painted over so no one could look inside, on the ground floor of a six-story building off Lenox Avenue in Harlem, and it was important enough to have a lookout posted on each end of the block equipped with walkie-talkies, and a third man, also with a walkie-talkie, directly in front of the store. The street was completely inhabited by blacks, and even with his disreputable appearance Serpico doubted if he could get by the lookouts without being noticed. From the roof where he had been observing the operation, he had seen a cellar door. It was in an alley next to the store, but the lookout in front of it often walked by the alley and could easily spot anyone coming along it. Serpico told Delise that the best way to bust the location was to come down from the roof through the building and out the entrance. From there it was only about twenty feet to the door of the store, and they could take it by surprise.

Delise agreed. The two men climbed to the top of a tenement on a parallel street and laboriously made their way across the rooftops until they reached the building where the store was. Serpico peered over the edge of the roof and saw that the situation was still the same, the posted lookouts, people streaming in and out of the store to make their bets.

The plan was for Serpico to proceed down the stairs first, with Delise following in case of any trouble. But when Serpico came out of the entrance of the building, the startled lookout was staring right at him and recognized him from another numbers arrest he had made not two weeks before. The lookout shouted, "Close up!" and dashed into the store, and by the time Serpico got to the door it was bolted. In his haste Serpico had dropped his police walkie-talkie, and it lay in pieces on the sidewalk. He surveyed it and the bolted store door and, in a sudden rush of anger and frustration, picked up an ashcan and hurled it through the store window and went in after it.

Inside some men were already beginning to burn records, "Police, hold it!" Serpico said. He had his hand in the gas-mask bag where he carried his .38 service revolver, gripping it, but not drawing it. Several startled numbers players huddled back against the wall.

A moment later Delise joined him. The man in charge of the location was what the police termed a "big" collector. He had three assistants writing up the betting slips, and he looked on sullenly while Serpico gathered up the slips for evidence. Very little cash was found, but this was not unusual; in a large operation the money was moved out as fast as it came in.

Almost at once the collector's controller arrived in the store. "Man, what's going here?" he said. "Where you from?"

"The borough," Serpico said.

"The borough!" the controller said, his voice rising in an indignant shriek. "I don't believe it. I just paid the borough." The controller demanded to see Serpico's shield number, and when he was shown it, he muttered again, "But I paid the borough. What kind of shakedown is this?"

"Who'd you pay in the borough?" Delise quietly asked.

The controller started to answer, then stopped and looked curiously at Delise, and said, "Nobody. I didn't pay nobody."

"OK, let's go," Serpico said to the collector.

"Wait a minute," the controller protested. "He's my man. You got to take somebody, take me."

"You want to go, you can go," Serpico replied, "but he's going too."

"I ain't going nowhere, then," the collector said. "You want us, you got to drag us through them people out there."

Delise tried his own walkie-talkie to get help, but it wouldn't work inside the store. "Listen, boss," Serpico said. "I think I can get out through the cellar." So while Delise held the men in the store at bay with his gun, Serpico ducked through the cellar door to the alley, made his way across a courtyard to the street, and called for assistance from a phone booth.

The crowd dispersed as soon as it heard the radio-car sirens, and Serpico and Delise took their prisoners out. But they could extract nothing further from them about police payoffs. Still, with this first direct indication that there was a pad in Manhattan North,

Delise and Serpico did some additional probing and concluded that it was far more
sophisticated than the one in the 7th Division. The best Serpico could glean from
some of his informants was that a "collection agency" of retired cops made the actual
pickups, so that none of the plainclothesmen
were physically involved. Beyond this, isolated in his own command, Delise could do
little, and finally he called Supervising Assistant Chief Inspector McGovern for investigative help. McGovern was away at the
time, and Delise got one of his top assistants
on the line. Delise explained his problem and
was told that he would have to go through
the Manhattan North chain of command for
a request like this.

"Maybe I should just broadcast it over
the radio," Delise shot back.

"What's the matter," McGovern's assistant said, "don't you trust your bosses?"

Delise did not reply. A few days later,
however, he decided to see what would happen if he went through channels. He spoke to
the acting borough commander, a deputy
chief inspector named Fred Catalano, and repeated his suspicions of corruption among
the Manhattan North plainclothesmen. Catalano told Delise that if he needed any investigative help, he could requisition some
recruits from the Police Academy.

"Recruits?" Serpico said when he heard
this. "You're kidding."

"That's what he said," Delise replied.
"We'll just have to go on the way we were."

Serpico kept knocking off numbers locations as fast as he could find them, and, as
had happened in the South Bronx, one of
his black informants asked him if he was
only after blacks, or would he also arrest
white policy operators? Serpico said, "Try
me," and the next time the informant gave
him a name and location Serpico knew he
was being tested. The collector the informant
had supplied was an Italian, Peter Tancredi,
and the address was at Second Avenue and
116th Street in East Harlem, where the rem-
nants of a once huge Italian community,
which had spawned such famous Mafiosi as
Thomas (Three-Finger Brown) Lucchese,
Frank Costello, and Joseph Valachi, still
held sway and was left virtually untouched
by the police.

Serpico immediately put Tancredi under
observation, saw him station himself openly
on the sidewalk in front of an Italian social
club, and watched as people regularly came
up to him, whispered a few words, and continued on. Each time this happened, Tancredi would disappear inside the club and
show up on the sidewalk a minute or so
later. Satisfied that he was taking numbers
bets, Serpico was ready to arrest him. The
day he picked for the arrest, however, Delise
was unavailable, so Serpico brought along
a black policewoman to back him up. In a
way, he thought, she would be less noticeable on the street if there were any lookouts
that Serpico had not spotted. He himself had
trimmed back his beard, and was wearing
slacks and a sports coat to fit more into the
neighborhood pattern. He was so leery of a
leak about what he was planning that he did
not even tell the policewoman about it until
they were half a block from the social club.
He instructed her to remain in the doorway
of a bank on the corner and to follow him
wherever he went.

He waited until a player came up to
Tancredi. The moment Tancredi turned to
go into the club, Serpico was after him. He
entered the club just as Tancredi was going
into a kitchen in the rear. All around Serpico
as he walked through the club were elderly
Italians playing cards and drinking coffee;
none of them looked up, at either Tancredi
or him.

At the kitchen doorway Serpico saw

Tancredi take a slip of paper out of the oven and start to write on it. Serpico stepped forward, grabbed the slip, took more of them out of the oven, and said, "You're under arrest." Tancredi looked at him, speechless.

Serpico brought him back into the front room. The old men playing cards were still paying no attention to either of them. The policewoman was waiting by the door, and Serpico told her to lock it. This finally caused a stir among the cardplayers and coffee drinkers. The man behind the coffee counter suddenly announced that he wanted to leave. "Stay where you are," Serpico said. "I want to look around a little more."

The counterman said, "You can't keep me here."

"Don't pull Philadelphia lawyer on me," Serpico replied, "or I'll break your chops. There's gambling going on in here, and what's that guy over there doing with a beer? You got a license to sell beer?" The man shut up and started polishing the counter.

Just then there was a tap on the glass street door. Two men were standing there, one taller than the other, both expensively dressed and sporting wide-brimmed hats. Serpico told the policewoman to open the door. Both men started to enter, the shorter man first. "Just you," Serpico said.

The shorter man nodded to his companion and came inside, and all the old men in the club became very quiet. "What can I do for you?" Serpico said.

"Well, why don't we have a soda or something?"

"I'm not thirsty."

"Hey, relax," the man said. "Don't you know who I am?"

"No."

"Think about it. I got the same name as you."

Then Serpico knew who the man was—Frank Serpico, alias Farbi, a known gambler in the New York police files and listed by the FBI as a lieutenant in what at the time was the most powerful Mafia clan in the country, the Vito Genovese family. Frank had never encountered a Mafioso of such rank face to face, and he wondered how the racketeer had learned about the arrest in the social club. Had the news spread that rapidly? Even more fascinating was the fact that the other Serpico knew who *he* was.

"Can we go back and talk?" the other Serpico said.

"All right." He told the policewoman to keep the door locked and not to let anyone in or out.

In the kitchen, Serpico the racketeer said, "Look, what's the problem with you, kid? Everybody's OK, and then you come along. What's the matter, huh? I tell you what. I'll take care of you out of my own pocket."

"I'm not interested in what's in your pocket. If I was, I wouldn't be here."

"Listen," the racketeer continued, "you take that guy out of here and you're going to be sorry. He's just trying to make a living. It's bad. It's bad for the whole neighborhood. A thing like this gets everybody upset. I know about you. I mean I know about you and the Bronx and all that, and I don't get it. What the hell, we're the same blood. I know where you grew up. I know the car you drive. I know you live in the Village." He paused, and said, "I even know where your family lives. How are they, your mom and pop?"

There were two ways, Frank Serpico thought, that he could interpret this. His namesake had chosen his words very carefully. Ostensibly he was simply pointing out that they ought to be friends, but there was an implicit threat in everything he had said.

Serpico decided to take it the wrong way. He suddenly drew his Browning and pointed it at the racketeer's stomach. "I'm through listening to all this bullshit," he said. "I made an arrest and the guy's going."

The Mafia lieutenant flushed. "Hey, come on. Can't we talk to you? What kind of a guy are you? There're other honest cops, but at least they honor the contracts."

"Either I walk out with him now," Serpico said, "or the whole bunch goes. It doesn't make any difference to me."

"OK, have it your way, but I don't think that's the way to do things. It's not nice."

"You got anything else to say?"

"No," the gangster said. "I'll see you around."

It was not long after this that another white numbers operator Serpico had arrested, Vincent Sausto, alias Mickey McGuire, turned to him in court and said, "Hey, you know they're going to do a job on you," and when Serpico asked him who he had in mind, Sausto said, "Your own kind," and Serpico asked, "What do you mean my own kind, the Italians?" and Sausto replied, "No, cops!"

*   *   *

The second "condolence" card arrived at Brooklyn Jewish Hospital on February 10, 1971, seven days after Frank Serpico had been shot in the head. It was the kind that someone, lacking words of his own, might send to a bereaved friend or acquaintance. The printed message read:

WITH
SINCERE
SYMPATHY

Except this particular card contained an additional handwritten note of regret *"That you didn't get your brains blown out, you rat bastard. Happy relapse."*

The drainage from his ear continued, but it had slowed somewhat. The heavy doses of antibiotics had thus far warded off any infection, and there was every hope that the rip in his cerebral membrane was beginning to mend. If it did not, the alternative was surgery, a possibility that had not yet been ruled out. The operation was a delicate one in which the neurosurgeon would have to go into the side of his head at the base of the brain, and, like any surgery of this sort, it carried with it great risk, especially unpredictable and uncontrollable swelling of the brain.

The left side of Serpico's face remained paralyzed, and his mouth was still twisted, but he could open the right corner of it enough to communicate fairly well and to down the diet of baby food he was on, now that he was no longer being fed intravenously. The worst part was the blinding headaches that came on him without warning.

He had asked for a mirror and saw the clotted bullet hole on the left side of his nose. It seemed to him to be absurdly innocuous compared to the rest of his battered face. He looked as if he had been in a really good fight. While the swelling was nearly gone, there was still considerable discoloration. His left eye was blackened and still partly closed. With his beard, the overall effect, he thought, gave him a piratical air. One of his nurses tried to talk him into getting rid of the beard, but he refused; he rather liked the buccaneer image he presented.

The afternoon that he received the second anonymous card he was wheeled out of his room on a stretcher for a new series of X rays called a tomogram. This involved a lengthy process in which consecutive exposures were taken almost centimeter by centimeter around his head so that the neurosurgeons would have a more accurate, three-dimensional picture of the bullet fragments inside. It confirmed that the fragments were all in the area of the ear bone, and that one of them was very near the carotid artery. This fragment, and the possibility that it might move, caused the gravest concern. But the tomogram showed that so far it appeared to have stayed in its original position.

Serpico was under the direct care of the chief of neurosurgery at Brooklyn Jewish, Dr. Aaron J. Berman, and the associate chief, Dr. Zeki Ugar, a former medical officer in the Turkish navy who had been sent to the United States to study and who had decided to return here after his naval service was over. Dr. Ugar had never met an American policeman, much less one who looked like Serpico, and, fascinated by his patient, had taken an interest in him beyond his medical condition, making it a point to drop in every afternoon to chat with him for a few minutes in an effort to boost his morale.

He came in after the tomogram had been taken to tell Serpico how encouraging the results were. But Serpico had something else on his mind. During most of his first week in the hospital, he had lain on his right side, oblivious to his surroundings. For the last two days, however, he had been more aware of what was going on, and his bed had been raised for brief periods. He noticed that whenever someone spoke to him, he had to turn the right side of his head toward the speaker to hear anything. He thought that it was caused perhaps by the blood clogging his left ear, and he now asked Dr. Ugar how soon it would be before he started getting his hearing back.

The problem had already been noted in Serpico's records, and Dr. Ugar knew that it was a post-traumatic condition caused by the indirect impact, the concussive effect,

of the bullet on the ear bone, and that the chances of recovery were practically nil. But he just replied that it would take a while. With everything Serpico was undergoing at the time, Dr. Ugar felt there was nothing to be gained by telling him that in all likelihood, regardless of what else happened, he would be permanently deaf in the ear.

Serpico was still so woozy when the first card had come, the one calling him a "scumbag," that he really had not reacted to it. But the second card, with its vicious "rat bastard" accusation, left him hurt and depressed. When he had embarked on his lonely fight against corruption in the Police Department, he had believed that the blame lay with the system, not individual cops, and he had to ask himself now what kind of people could have sent him cards like that. Were they truly examples of how much he was hated?

He never ceased to be amazed at the idea that he was a "rat," a fink, an informer. It would have been different, he supposed, if he had sworn fealty to, say, even the Mafia, and then spilled its secrets. He could see that, in all of its variations. But the only oath he had taken as a cop was to uphold the law, and there was nothing in it that said that policemen had some special immunity. If anything, he thought, the opposite was true, that it was incumbent upon a cop to adhere to a stricter standard of conduct than the average citizen, to exemplify what society should be rather than reflect what it was. Perhaps that was asking too much, perhaps not; in this regard he could only answer for himself.

A few days later the door to his room opened, and a nurse started to enter. He saw her pause and turn to speak to someone outside. Then she came in, shaking her head. "What was that all about?" he asked. The nurse said that the cop on guard wanted to know what Serpico looked like, and she had told him he could come in and see for himself, and that he had said, Oh, no, he couldn't, that he had been told that he couldn't. Then Serpico suddenly realized that the hospital was in the 80th Precinct, and that the patrolman guarding him must be from there. It was the same precinct where he had caught two cops shaking down his brother's grocery store and he could imagine what they were saying in the station house.

Eventually some of the younger officers did come into his room to chat with him. When the first of them walked hesitantly in and said, "Hi, how you feeling?" Serpico said, "What's the matter with you? Didn't you get the word?"

"Sure I did, but *fuck* them. I'm supposed to be a troublemaker too." He told Serpico that during a police "action" for higher wages that had taken place in the city a few months before, he had insisted on going to work anyway. As a result, he was transferred from a pleasant precinct in Queens to the less desirable 80th, which included a large chunk of the Bedford-Stuyvesant ghetto.

Their conversation inevitably turned to corruption among policemen, and Serpico was saying something about it when a nurse came in. He continued to talk, and the cop reddened and put a warning finger to his lips. Serpico ignored the signal and went on talking. The cop got up and abruptly walked out of the room. Only after the nurse had left did he return.

"You shouldn't say things like that in front of people," he said. "They'll get the wrong idea."

"Are you kidding?" Serpico said. "You think people don't know, she doesn't know, what the hell's going on? The trouble with you is you listen to the bullshit these guys

hand out. It's about time we started admitting what it's really like and do something about it. That way we'll get the people's confidence."

The cop was unconvinced. "I don't know," he said. "We have to think of our image. We can't wash our dirty laundry in public."

That was the crux of the problem; even this young, somewhat rebellious officer clung to the idea that it was a question of "us" versus "them." Cops didn't seem to think of themselves as part of the community. Too many of them, Serpico thought, had isolated themselves not only professionally but socially. They believed they were misunderstood by the "outside world," that there was a general public antagonism toward them, and this notion had fed on itself back and forth, until in fact there *were* "sides" and neither side could relate to the other. If cops talked to people more, instead of just other cops, if they took the initiative in reaching out to them, Serpico was certain they could break down some of these barriers. But they tended to withdraw more and more into themselves and became contemptuous of the public. Cops, after all, saw the seamy side of life every day; they knew what the public was capable of. It colored their whole outlook. If a kid had long hair, he was a sure bet to have dope on him. If a girl happened to have birth-control pills in her purse, she was promiscuous. "Oh boy," Serpico recalled hearing a cop say on one such occasion, "she puts out."

He was willing to grant that in a nation where, despite all the rhetoric, the ordinary white man couldn't relate to a black man, it was demanding a great deal to ask a white cop to assume the burden. But, he thought, there had to be a bottom line somewhere; and a cop had a social responsibility that he could not ignore. Serpico saw policemen forgetting what their job was all about, beginning to exist just for themselves, developing what amounted to their own subculture. He was sitting around with some cops in a bar once when one of them declared, "I got my gun and I'll protect me and mine," and the others nodded in agreement. "Me and mine" meant his family, and Serpico remembered him now, wryly imagining him stashing away weapons and ammunition in his home, waiting for the revolution to sweep down.

The subculture made up its own rules. If a cop was, say, a Catholic, he went to mass every Sunday because if he didn't he was liable to go to hell. But taking money did not seem to mean anything. When Serpico was first exposed to bribery and graft in the Police Department, there was talk of "clean" money and "dirty" money. Clean money meant things like traffic bribes or payoffs to overlook gambling and prostitution. Dirty money was in narcotics. Gradually, however, the distinction blurred, and finally it was just money.

A Candid Analysis of Police Corruption

JAMES C. PARSONS

The remarks contained in this paper result from some eighteen years of experience in the law enforcement field. From the various assignments I was privileged to perform, from patrolman to administrative assistant to the chief of a department of over 600 sworn personnel, comes the basis of this report. Since I have set the stage for a subjective analysis of a law enforcement problem, some additional information about myself should enlighten the reader.

I was born the third of five sons of a white coal miner in rural Alabama in 1933. To state that my family was in the upper portion of the lowest socioeconomic class might border on exaggeration. My father was highly vocal about his prejudice toward anyone not a coal miner. His close associates were also prejudiced.

After sixteen years in coal mining communities, living in company-owned housing, and subjected to an inferior educational process, I dropped out of high school and entered the U.S. Navy. Four years later, I was discharged and sought employment in the law enforcement field. I was employed by a police department in a city with a population of 350,000. Among the 400 officers comprising the force, there were no Negroes, only two Italians, and no Jews.

From this background base, I will now discuss one of the main problems I have encountered in improving relations between law enforcement personnel and the citizens they serve.

From *The Police Chief* (March 1973): pp. 20–22, 67. Reprinted by permission of The International Association of Chiefs of Police.

DEEP-SEATED HOSTILITY

It has often been said, and I agree, that nothing is wrong with law enforcement that is not wrong with the entire society. Law enforcement does not operate in a vacuum. It represents and is a cross section of the community. In communities where the majority of the citizens are not prejudiced, you find very little prejudice in law enforcement. The officers in highly prejudiced communities are rewarded for their prejudicial attitude by the general public. This is noticeable particularly by the high esteem in which citizens hold those officers who have a reputation for brutal behavior toward minorities.

Actually, there are several major causes for the problems encountered in police-community relations. However, two in my experience stand out. One is obvious; the other is much more subtle and seldom discussed in law enforcement circles. The obvious problem is the frustration experienced by the officer and by some of the citizens he serves. At this point, let us focus on the black minority in the low-income areas of our cities.

THE BLACK MINORITY

The black person is frustrated by life in general and government in particular. He views life as a cynic and is overwhelmed in a free enterprise system with few or no talents to sell. There is no hope, and he feels that his government has forsaken him. As Dr. Kenneth B. Clark testified before the National Advisory Commission on Civil Disorders:

> This society knows . . . that if human beings are confined in ghetto compounds of our cities and are subjected to criminally inferior education, pervasive economic and job discrimination, committed to houses unfit for human habitation, subjected to unspeakable conditions of municipal services, such as sanitation, that such human beings are not likely to be responsive to appeals to be lawful, to be respectful, to be concerned with property of others.[1]

Law enforcement officers are the visible symbols of government and therefore a ready target for frustration venting. As frustrations are vented, violations of law occur and law enforcement reacts. The cycle goes on and on. The prejudiced officer sees conclusive evidence that his preconceived notions of the black minority are correct and valid.

THE OFFICER'S FRUSTRATION

The American law enforcement officer, unlike his British counterpart, does not enjoy the prestige, pay, dignity, or esteem which he believes are worthy of his responsibilities. He faces complex situations daily that perplex him to no end. His education and training have not equipped him to face his responsibilities with confidence. It is a rare department in America that provides enlightened leadership and clearly enunciated policy. The officer is left to make his own decisions, often without even minimum guidance. He seldom hears about his "good" decisions but is quickly brought to task for his "bad" ones.

Officers seldom can retaliate against their superiors or middle- and upper-class citizens. This leaves only the low-income and black minority to use as a frustration vent. These groups serve well as scapegoats since they seldom have the ear of influential officials. Low-income groups and black minorities seldom have the will to complain or retaliate.

CORRUPTION: A SUBTLE ISSUE

There have been several national reports concerning crime, civil disorders, and police-community relations; however, the issue of police corruption has been summarily treated, if mentioned at all. *The Challenge of Crime in a Free Society* (1967)[2] devoted one page to the general topic of police misconduct and made one self-evident recommendation. I recently participated in a conference with several nationally noted police chiefs, and during a dinner discussion the conversation turned to police corruption. As expected, the chiefs were reluctant even to discuss the issue. One chief in a very large resort city stated that he would be surprised if 5 percent of his force were "on the take." I do not believe the chief was naive, nor do I believe he was unintelligent. In many private conversations I have had with officers from lower ranks, most will admit to a much higher percentage. In a recent study, Albert Reiss, Jr., the noted sociologist, largely exploded the myth that there are occasional "rotten apples" which give a bad reputation to the whole lot. Not counting contracts with organized crime, illegal assaults on citizens, or the general acceptance of free food, 20 percent of the policemen observed by the teams of observers he utilized were in violation of the criminal laws. The crimes included taking money and property from defendants, stealing merchandise from previously burglarized stores, taking bribes in lieu of issuing traffic citations, and accepting money to alter testimony.[3]

PERFECT SETTING FOR CORRUPTION

A crime-ridden community suffering from all the social ills possible—minority groups, matriarchal homes, poor education, insufficient jobs, poor housing, and little political representation—serves well to set the plot. The police in the role of enforcer is generally underpaid, poorly trained, and ineptly led in most cases. Is there any wonder that corrup-

tion is widespread in many departments?

Once integrity is compromised, the path to total corruption is easy. In fact, peer group pressure tends to pull the neophyte officer into the web of corruption. After all, it appears that "everybody is doing it." Compromised supervisors are no threat, and corruption succeeds unhindered—sometimes with unofficial acceptance by police officials.

Economic gain is a prime motivator in our society, and underpaid officers are only human in their desires for expensive automobiles and homes on the lake. However, once they become indebted for such luxuries, turning back becomes virtually impossible.

The black minority poses no security risk to the corrupted officer. Who will listen to him? Who will believe him when the officer denies wrongdoing? After all, if the officer wants to book him, he is also suspected of a criminal offense. Many officers will arrest the offender the first time he observes a violation and then form an unholy alliance. As some officers state, "If he complains later, it will appear that he is trying to cause me trouble for the first arrest."

Once compromised, the officer has problems with his conscience and projects his guilt feelings to the scapegoat, the minority member. This is obvious as one listens to and observes corrupt officers. The corrupt officer fears change and the granting of equal rights to minority groups. The problems in police-community relations created by corruption may be subtle, but they are real and are cause for concern on the part of today's police administrators and government officials.

MIDDLE-CLASS WHITES

Generally, the police enjoy much support from the middle-class white population. Two reasons for this support are plainly visible. The first and most important is the fear of crime. Citizens in the middle class see the officer as protector of their safety, property, and the status quo. This group has most recently escaped the conditions now experienced by minority groups.

Police departments are now recruiting from the middle class, and the value systems of the two groups are more compatible. Again we see the problem in police-community relations as being the same as in society in general.

As for corruption, the middle-class white hesitates to accept this fact, which is a misconception on his part because he rarely experiences it. Statistics published in the President's Crime Commission Report indicate that whites have a much better attitude toward police integrity than do blacks. I feel it is due to the different experiences of the two groups.

Like educators, many police administrators assign their best personnel to the most desirable neighborhoods and their worst to the minority community. The corrupt officer seeks out these minority area assignments and does whatever is necessary to obtain them.

The middle-class neighborhood demands extra police protection and gets it. The ghetto resident takes what is assigned him and works with it. I have heard many supervisors in our department say, "I am assigning Officer X to a minority community because he can keep those people in line. Officer X puts the 'fear of God' in those people."

DISCRETIONARY DECISIONS

The complex nature of law enforcement and the myriad of problems the officer faces require a tremendous number of discretionary decisions. As noted previously, for the most part, police organizations in America today are staffed with officers who possess a modicum of education and were exposed to faulty training. Very few departments have clear policy guidelines or enlightened supervision. Discretionary decision making is not at its best under such circumstances, especially when other variables such as prejudice and/or corruption are present.

Another victim of such circumstances is the police officer himself. The National Advisory Commission on Civil Disorders explained the plight of the policeman in its report to the President:

> Alone, the policeman in the ghetto cannot solve these problems. His role is already one of the most difficult in our society. He must deal daily with a range of problems and people that test his patience, ingenuity, character and courage in ways that few of us are ever tested. Without positive leadership, goals, operational guidance and public support, the individual policeman can only feel victimized. Nor are these problems the responsibility only of police administrators; they are deep enough to tax the courage, intelligence and leadership of mayors, city officials and community leaders.

Although it may appear that I am trying to confuse the reader by pointing out problems on both sides of the issue, this is not the case. I started out with the premise that nothing is wrong with law enforcement and police-community relations that is not wrong with society in general. This is still the case, and I hope the issue begins to clear a little as we view the problem as a system and not as an isolated and conscious pattern of behavior.

GOVERNMENTAL RESPONSIBILITY

Many police administrators have stated, "The public gets the kind of law enforcement they want." I personally feel this is a negative attitude and a shirking of ethical responsibility. The professional police administrator must accept the responsibility of community leadership and point out problems to other agencies and political representatives for solution. He must inform the citizens of threats to their peace, safety, and welfare. After all, police organizations should have leadership and maintain a certain amount of discipline.

The public is an amorphous conglomerate lacking the discipline and direction of police organizations. It is most unlikely that the public will or can enunciate clear policy which will serve the needs of all its segmented groups. In a democracy where justice is the end product of balancing the needs of society with the needs of the individual, some disciplined ethical group must provide the safeguards.

LONG-RANGE IMPROVEMENTS

Not enough is known about police organizations, policy, procedures, attitudes, or behavior. The role of the law enforcement officer is too important to society to make assumptions based on intuition. Basic research is sorely needed in law enforcement. Questions need answering from an analytical point of view based on empirical evidence. All facets of law enforcement need scrutiny in an effort to determine if they serve society and, if so, are they worth the price. For example, is aggressive patrol effective and, if it is, does the cost in effecting poor community relations offset its value?

Another important question needing an answer is whether there is a personality type suitable for law enforcement and, if there is, how it can be detected. After all, does not the officer serve as the conscience of the community? Do those persons who have un-

derlying need to dominate other human beings seek law enforcement for employment? Is this good or bad? Is crime increasing as fast as the FBI crime statistics and the news media indicate? What is the so-called Negro crime? Can it be explained? Only after intelligent answers to these questions are available can we plan meaningfully for the correction of our problems.

Can the police accept responsibility for the ills of society? I seriously doubt that we can or that we should. However, I do believe we in law enforcement have the responsibility to cooperate with other agencies of government and outside groups whose assistance is needed and who share in the law enforcement responsibility.

As David Bordua commented in 1968:

> The police should make every effort to avoid being placed in the position of hired "bully boys" by other social agencies—public or private—that operate in the ghetto. Thus if, for example, schools wish to avail themselves of police service they should be required to have representatives present and participating at every stage of the case so that it is clear that both agencies share in the imposition of authority. Too often in slum areas the police are visibly despised by social agency personnel and used as a "bogey man" with which to frighten people, especially adolescents. The maintenance of order is a necessary accompaniment of the provision of services.

Recently, while engaged in an operation to eliminate illegal drinking establishments, I enlisted assistance from the health department and local realtors. The realtors were requested to evict those convicted of liquor violations in an effort to improve community life. Some realtors, however, seized the opportunity to evict other tenants who were delinquent in paying rent. Of course, the culprits were identified as the police.

CHANGING THE POLICE VIEWPOINT

During the last decade, law enforcement as an institution has developed a defensive posture and drawn an imaginary line separating itself from the rest of society. The two basic reasons for this position are: (1) frustration and (2) many years of inattention. Frustration is a concomitant manifestation of a lack of self-confidence which results from facing complex problems one does not understand. Since the late 1920s and early 1930s, which was a time of police spoils reform, politicians have vowed noninterference in police matters. As a result, law enforcement administrators enjoyed complete autonomy. Responsiveness to public needs and demands suffered in the interim. When public recognition of this fact finally came, law enforcement was ill prepared to accept the ensuing criticism and necessity for change.

Since law enforcement problems have centered in the low-income black communities and the officer has the resident stereotyped, the logical place to start with a solution is with the police. As mentioned before, law enforcement is more organized and disciplined than the community. The officer must consider himself a community manager and the welfare of the ghetto residents his objective. He must align himself with the victim of a faulty system and rally other community agencies as allies. For the officer to change his perspective, it will require a knowledge of crime prevention in its broadest sense. Empathy can be developed by subjecting officers to ghetto conditions as part of their training. Close contacts with minority people in an academic and social setting can and will dispel many of his misconceptions. A complete reorientation is required in many police agencies.

In the interest of efficiency, many police organizations have ceased to perform many services which were nonpolice in nature. This shredding out of the "nonessential" has left police with a coercive role to play. Supportive-type services, such as performing ambulance duties, supervising playgrounds, conducting traffic schools and furnishing crossing guards build goodwill and public support. To perform these and additional functions, I must admit police organizations would need restructuring.

A redefinition of the role of the police seems inevitable. Already police serve somewhat as community managers. It is the police who receive nearly all calls for assistance during emergencies. It behooves those of us in law enforcement to prepare the police to fill this new role which would be comparable to that of a generalized *ombudsman*. It would involve working as crime control teams and forming alliance with neighborhood leaders in the community.

Again, in the interest of economy and efficiency, police administrators have closed many community precincts and motorized the officer on the beat. These moves were desirable in a strictly economic sense, but I wonder at what cost to community-police relations. I would now recommend that some modifications of these approaches are in order. Storefront precincts are having some success, and the police officer with his walkie-talkie is not confined to his cruiser.

Another reason frequently given for centralization of operations is to exercise control. Again Bordua comments to the Crime Commission:

> Problems of control are central and complex. Area team concepts presuppose a police controllable largely through training, commitment to mission, and involvement in local teams that change personnel slowly enough to maintain an esprit de corps. Present control techniques such as crime clearance rates, response time mea-

sures, arrest quotas, presuppose law commitment and lack of sub-group morale.

Is Bordua telling us that poor training has caused law enforcement officials to repress the legitimate initiative of the patrolman because the department has been derelict in its training responsibilities?

IMMEDIATE ACTION

Law enforcement as an institution is a long way from the goals set forth in the previous section. The problems mentioned in the first portion of this article must be resolved prior to attempting the long-range goals. The most critical variable in the initial stages is strong and uncompromised leadership. A planned program of improvement can be accomplished under skilled guidance. The program must include:

1. Improved selection techniques for personnel entering police service and those selected for leadership.
2. Increasingly stringent personnel requirements, such as advanced education and formal training.

3. Basic research and development in police organizations, goal setting, policies, techniques, and community attitudes.
4. Policy guideline formulation and training in its application and practice.
5. More control over discretionary decisions.
6. Change in the perspective of their citizen clientele by law enforcement personnel, accompanied by more supportive services to offset problems created by the coercive role inherent in police work.

It might first appear that the goals of the immediate plan are in conflict with those of the long-range plan. This is not the case. Control must first be obtained to shape and reorient the institution of law enforcement where frustration and corruption exist; extreme and harsh measures must be utilized to first get attention. It is most difficult to mold an undisciplined and fragmented group. Human nature does not accept innovation readily, and attitudes will remain the same until behavior is compelled to change.

NOTES

1 *Report of the National Advisory Commission on Civil Disorders* (New York: Bantam Books, 1968).
2 The President's Commission on Law Enforcement and Administration of Justice,

Challenge of Crime in a Free Society (Washington, D.C.: U.S. Government Printing Office, 1967).
3 Albert J. Reiss, *The Police and the Public* (New Haven: Yale University Press, 1971).

The Informal "Code" of Police Deviancy:

A Group Approach to "Blue-Coat Crime"

ELLWYN R. STODDARD

It has been asserted by various writers of criminology, deviant behavior, and police science that unlawful activity by a policeman is a manifestation of personal moral weakness, a symptom of personality defects, or the result of recruitment of individuals unqualified for police work. In contrast to the traditional orientation, this paper is a sociological examination of "blue-coat crime" [1] as a functioning informal social system whose norms and practices are at variance with legal statutes. Within the police group itself, this pattern of illicit behavior is referred to as the "code."

Following an examination of these contrasting viewpoints, this case study will provide data to ascertain the existence of the "code," its limitations and range of deviancy, and the processes through which it is maintained and sanctioned within the group. The guiding hypothesis of this study is that illegal practices of police personnel are socially prescribed and patterned through the informal "code" rather than being a function of in-

dividual aberration or personal inadequacies of the policeman himself.

THE INDIVIDUALISTIC APPROACH

Almost four decades ago August Vollmer emphasized that the individual being suited to police work was the factor responsible for subsequent deviancy among officers. This approach implicitly assumes inherent personality characteristics to be the determinant which makes a police recruit into a good officer or a bad one. [2] A current text of police personnel management by German reaffirms the individualistic orientation of Vollmer and suggests that the quality of police service is ultimately dependent upon the individual police officer. There is no evidence of an awareness of group pressures within his analysis. [3]

A modified version of this individualistic approach is the view that perhaps the individual chosen had already become "contaminated" prior to being hired as a member of the force, and when presented with chances for bribery or favoritism, the "hard core guy, the one who is a thief already, steps in." [4]

A third factor, stressed by Tappan, [5] is the poor screening method at the recruitment stage. Such an officer might have had inadequate training, insufficient supervision, and poor pay and is ripe for any opportunity to participate in lucrative illicit enterprises.

From the *Journal of Criminal Law, Criminology and Police Science* **59** (2): 201–213. Copyright © 1968 by Northwestern University School of Law. Reprinted by special permission of the Journal of Criminal Law, Criminology and Police Science.

Revision of a paper presented at the Rocky Mountain Social Science Association, Air Force Academy, April 1967. It was supported in part by a grant from the University Research Institute, University of Texas at El Paso.

This author then goes into great detail to show the low intelligence and educational level of police officers. Another author adds that improved selection and personality evaluation have improved the quality of the police considerably over the past 20 years,[6] thereby attacking this problem directly. One recent author wrote that low salaries make more difficult the attraction of applicants with the moral strength to withstand temptations of "handouts" and eventual corruption.[7] Sutherland and Cressey, although aware that graft is a characteristic of the entire police system rather than of isolated patrolman,[8] stress the unqualified appointments of police officials by corrupt politicians as the source of police deviancy. They state:

> Another consequence of the fact that police departments often are organized for the welfare of corrupt politicians, rather than of society, is inefficient and unqualified personnel. This is unquestionably linked with police dishonesty, since only police officers who are "right" can be employed by those in political control. Persons of low intelligence and with criminal records sometimes are employed.[9]

THE GROUP APPROACH

In contrast to the individualistic approach of the foregoing authors, the emphasis on the social context in which police deviancy flourishes has preoccupied the sociological criminologists. The present case study would clearly reflect this latter orientation.

Barnes and Teeters mention police deviancy in conjunction with organized syndicated crime.[10] Korn and McCorkle,[11] Cloward,[12] and Merton[13] see political and police corruption as a natural consequence of societal demands for illegal services. When these desired services are not provided through legal structures, they are attained through illegal means. However, documentation in support of these theoretical explanations is sketchy and limited in scope. Bell suggests that "crime is an American way of life." In the American temper there exists a feeling that "somewhere, somebody is pulling all the complicated strings to which this jumbled world dances." Stereotypes of big crime syndicates project the feeling that laws are just for "the little guys." Consequently, while "Americans have made such things as gambling illegal, they don't really in their hearts think of it as wicked."[14] Likewise, the routine discovery of an average citizen in overt unlawful activity rarely inflames the public conscience to the degree that it does when this same deviant behavior is exhibited by a police officer. Thus, the societal double standard demands that those in positions of trust must exhibit an artificially high standard of morality which is not required of the average citizen.

A measure of role ambivalence is an inevitable part of the policeman occupation in a democratic society. While he is responsible to protect the members of his society from those who would do them harm, the corresponding powers for carrying out this mandate are not delegated.[15] To perform his designated duties, the conscientious policeman often must violate the very laws he is trying to enforce. This poses a serious dilemma for the police officer since his attempt to effectively discourage violation of the law among the general public is often hinged to extra-legal short-cut techniques which are in common practice by his law enforcement cohorts.[16] For example, the use of "illegal" violence by policemen is justified by them as a necessary means to locate and harass the most vicious criminals and the organized syndicates.[17] These procedures are reinforced through coordinated group action.

> The officer needs the support of his fellow officers in dangerous situations and when he resorts to practices of questionable legality. Therefore, the rookie must pass the test of loyalty to the code of secrecy. Sometimes this loyalty of colleagues has the effect of protecting the law-violating, unethical officer.[18]

Such illegal practices which are traditionally used to carry out a policeman's assigned tasks might well be readily converted to the aims of personal gain.

In these tight informal cliques within the larger police force, certain "exploratory gestures"[19] involving the acceptance of small bribes and favors can occur. There is a hazy boundary between grateful citizens paying their respects to a proud profession and "good" citizens involved in corruption wishing to buy future favors. Once begun, however, these practices can become "norms" or informal standards of cliques of policemen. A new recruit can be socialized into accepting these illegal practices by mild, informal negative sanctions such as the withholding of group acceptance. If these unlawful practices are embraced, the recruit's membership group—the police force—and his reference group—the clique involved in illegal behavior—are no longer one and the same. In such circumstances the norms of the reference group (the illegal-oriented clique) would clearly take precedence over either the formal requisites of the membership group (police department regulations) or the formalized norms (legal statutes) of the larger society.[20] When such conflicts are apparent a person can "(1) conform to one, take the consequences of non-conformity to the other [or] (2) he can seek a compromise position by which he attempts to conform in part, though not wholly, to one or more sets of role expectations, in the hope that sanctions applied will be minimal."[21]

If these reference group norms involving illegal activity become routinized with use they become an identifiable informal "code" such as that found in the present study. Such codes are not unique to the police profession. A fully documented case study of training at a military academy in which an informal pattern of behavior was assimilated along with the formal standards clearly outlined the function of the informal norms, their dominance when in conflict with formal regulations, and the secretive nature of their existence to facilitate their effectiveness and subsequent preservation.[22] The revelation of their existence to those outside the cadet group would destroy their integrative force and neutralize their utility.

This same secrecy would be demanded of a police "code" to ensure its preservation. Although within the clique the "code" must be well defined, the ignorance of the lay public of even its existence would be a requisite to its continuous and effective use.[23] Through participation in activity regimented by the "code" an increased group identity and cohesion among "code" practitioners would emerge. As Johnson puts its,

> Group identity requires winning of acceptance as a member of the inner group and, thereby, gaining access to the secrets of the occupation which are acquired through informal contacts with colleagues.[24]

Lack of this acceptance not only bars the neophyte from the inner secrets of the profession but may isolate him socially and professionally from his colleagues and even his superiors. There is the added fear that, in some circumstance in which he would need their support, they would avoid becoming involved, forcing him to face personal danger or public ridicule alone.

The social structure in which law enforcement is maintained has a definite bearing on what is considered normal and what is deviant behavior. The pattern of "bluecoat crime" (that is the "code") seems far more deviant when compared to the dominant middle-class norms of our society than when compared to lower-class values. Whyte maintains that in the Italian Slum of Cornerville, the primary function of the police department is not the enforcement of the law, but the regulation of illegal activities.

> ...An outbreak of violence arouses the "good people" to make demands for law enforcement...even when they disturb police racketeer relations. Therefore, it is in the interest of the departments to help maintain a peaceful racket organization. ...By regulating the racket and keeping peace, the officer can satisfy the demands for law enforcement with a number of token arrests and be free to make his adjustment to the local situation.[25]

Since an adjustment to the local situation might well involve adopting some of the "code" practices, the successful police rookie is he who can delicately temper three sets of uncomplementary standards: (1) the "code" practices adopted for group acceptance, (2) the societal standards regulating the duties and responsibilities of the police profession, and (3) his own system of morality gained from prior socialization in family, religious, educational, and peer-group interaction.

Methodological Considerations

The difficulties connected with any intensive investigation into the "code" are self evident. The binding secrecy which provides the source of its power would be disrupted if the "code" were revealed to an "outsider." Thus, standard sociological research methods were ineffective in this type of investigation. The traditional ethnographic technique of using an informant familiar with the "code" and its related practices made available the empirical data within this study. Obviously, data from a single informant do not begin to meet the stringent scientific criteria of reliability for the purpose of applying the conclusions from this case to police agencies in general. It is assumed that subsequent research will establish whether this is a unique episode or more of a universal phenomenon. However, the decision to enrich the literature with this present study in spite of its methodological deficiencies was felt to be justified inasmuch as an intensive search through the professional literature revealed no empirical accounts dealing directly with deviant policemen.[26]

Because of the explosive nature of such materials on the social, political, and economic life of the persons involved, the use of pseudonyms to maintain complete anonymity is a precaution not without precedent and was a guarantee given by the director of this study in return for complete cooperation of the informant.[27] The informant was a police officer for 3½ years before he was implicated in charges of robbery and grand larceny. He was subsequently tried and convicted, serving the better part of a year in prison. At the time of these interviews, he had been released from prison about three years.

The initial design of this study attempted to correlate these empirical data with two journalistic accounts,[28] but the subjective handling of those stories neutralized any advantage gained from an increased number of informants. The present design is based exclusively on the single informant.

The Code and Its Practices

Some of these terms used to describe police deviancy are widely used, but because of possible variations in meaning they are defined below.[29] These practices are ordered so that those listed first would generally elicit the least fear of legal prosecution and those listed last would invoke major legal sanctions for their perpetration.

Mooching: an act of receiving free coffee, cigarettes, meals, liquor, groceries, or other items either as a consequence of being in an underpaid, undercompensated profession *or* for the possible future acts of favoritism which might be received by the donor.

Chiseling: an activity involving police demands for free admission to entertainment whether connected to police duty or not, such as price discounts, etc.

Favoritism: the practice of using license tabs, window stickers, or courtesy cards to gain immunity from traffic arrest or citation (sometimes extended to wives, families, and friends of recipient).

Prejudice: situations in which minority groups receive less than impartial, neutral, objective attention, especially those who are less likely to have "influence" in City Hall to cause the arresting officer trouble.

Shopping: the practice of picking up small items such as candy bars, gum, or cigarettes at a store where the door has been accidentally unlocked after business hours.

Extortion: the demands made for advertisements in police magazines or purchase of tickets to police functions or the "street courts" where minor traffic tickets can be avoided by the payment of cash bail to the arresting officer with no receipt required.

Bribery: the payments of cash or "gifts" for past or future assistance to avoid prosecution; such reciprocity might be made in terms of being unable to make a positive identification of a criminal or being in the wrong place at a given time when a crime is to occur, both of which might be excused as carelessness but no proof as to deliberate miscarriage of justice. Differs from mooching in the higher value of a gift and in the mutual *understanding* regarding services to be performed upon the acceptance of the gift.

Shakedown: the practice of appropriating expensive items for personal use and attributing it to criminal activity when investigating a break in, burglary, or an unlocked door. Differs from shopping in the cost of the items and the ease by which former ownership of items can be determined if the officer is "caught" in the act of procurement.

Perjury: the sanction of the "code" which demands that officers lie to provide an alibi for fellow officers apprehended in unlawful activity covered by the "code."

Premeditated theft: planned burglary, involving the use of tools, keys, etc., to gain forced entry or a prearranged plan of unlawful acquisition of property which cannot be explained as a "spur of the moment" theft. Differs from shakedown only in the previous arrangements surrounding the theft, not in the value of the items taken.

Mooching, chiseling, favoritism, and *prejudice* do not have rigid interpretations in the "code." Their presence appears to be accepted by the general public as a real fact of life. Since the employment of one of these practices can be done while in the normal routine of one's duties, such practices are often not considered to be "deviant" in any way. Ex-Officer Smith sees it in this light:

> . . . the policeman having a free cup of coffee? I have never thought of this as being corrupt or illegal because this thing is just a courtesy thing. A cup of coffee or the old one—the cop on the beat grabbing the apple off the cart—these things I don't think shock too many people because they know that they're pretty well accepted.

But when the practice of *mooching* was brought up by name, it assumed a different character of increased importance to Smith!

> I think mooching is accepted by the police and the public is aware of it. My opinion now, as an ex-policeman, is that mooching is one of the underlying factors in the larger problems that come. . . . It is one of the most basic things. It's the easiest thing to accept and to take in stride because it's so petty. I think that it is the turning point a lot of times.

The "Sunday Comics" stereotype of the policeman initiating mooching, bribery, and favoritism is incorrect according to Smith's experience:

> Generally, the policeman doesn't have to ask for things, he just finds out about them. Take for example the theaters. I know the Roxy theaters would let the policeman in on his badge, just about any-

time. It's good business because it puts the owner in a closer relationship with the policeman, and the policeman is obligated to him. If they had a break-in, a fire, or a little favor such as double parking out front to unload something, they'd expect special consideration from the policeman.

> When I walked the east side beat the normal thing was for bartenders to greet me and offer me a pack of cigarettes or a drink. When I walked the beat I was pretty straight-laced, there were a few bartenders that I felt were just trying to get along with me, and I loosened up a little with those people. One bartender gave me cigars when he found out that I didn't smoke cigarettes. I always accepted them; he always pointed out there wasn't any obligation. Some of the beat men accepted cigarettes, some cigars, some took cash, and these men know when they're dealing with bootleggers, and why they're being paid. Different businessmen in the loop area give policemen Christmas presents every year.

Shopping and *shakedown, extortion* and *bribery* are all clearly unlawful, but in these practices the manner in which they are carried out contains a measure of safety to the policeman should his presence or behavior be questioned. A policeman's investigative powers allow him entry into an open building in which a "suspected robbery" has occurred, and various types of articles such as cigarettes and the like cannot be traced to any given retail outlet. Hence, his presence on such occasions is not *suspected;* rather, it is *expected!* Also, should a clumsy job of *shopping* or *shakedown* result in witnesses reporting these unlawful practices, the "code" requires that participating officers must commit *perjury* to furnish an alibi for those colleagues observed in illegal activities. This is both for the protection of the deviant officer and to preclude public disclosure of the widespread involvement of fellow officers in "code" practices. How extensive is *shopping* and *shakedown* as practiced by a department?

> As far as the Mid-City department is concerned I would say that 10 percent of the department would go along with anything, including deliberate forced entries or felonies. But about 50 percent of them would openly go along with just about anything. If they found a place open or if there had been a break-in or if they found anything they could use and it was laying there, they'd help themselves to it.
>
> Whenever there's an open door or window, they call for all the cars and they shake the whole building down—loot it!

Would those policemen involved in shopping and shakedown participate in something more serious? According to ex-officer Smith, they would.

> Most of the policemen who shop or go along with shopping would go along with major theft, if it just happened. I think where you've got to draw the line is when you get into premeditated, deliberate thefts. I think this is where the big division comes.
>
> In shopping, the theft just happens. Premeditated theft is a cold, deliberate, planned thing.

Here Smith points out the limits of the "code" which, though condoning any level of theft that "just happens," cannot fully support *premeditated theft*.

> I think in premeditated theft that the general police attitude is against it, if for no other reason just for the matter of self-preservation and survival. When you get to a premeditated, deliberate thing, then I think your police backing becomes pretty thin.

At the time Smith was engaged in the practice of *premeditated theft* in Mid-City, it looked somewhat different to him than it did later. When he took an objective look, he was aware of just how little this extreme deviancy *actually was practiced*.

> When I was involved in it, it seemed like all the people around me were involved in it and participating in it. It looked more to me like the generally accepted thing then than it does now, because actually the clique that I was in that did this sort of thing was a small one. I'm not discounting the fact that there may have been a lot of other small cliques just like this.

Looking at his behavior as an outsider, after his expulsion, Smith saw it in this light:

> After taking a long, hard look at my case and being real honest about it, I'd have to say that this [premeditated theft like mine] is the exception. The longer I'm away from this thing the more it looks like this.

In Mid-City, *extortion* was not generally practiced and the "code" prescribed "street courts" (that is, bribery for minor traffic offenses) as outside the acceptable pattern.

> [Extortion is] something that I would classify as completely outside the law [here in Mid-City], something that in certain areas has been accepted well on the side of both the public and the police. There's a long-standing practice that in Chicago if you are stopped for a traffic violation if you had a five dollar bill slipped in your plastic holder, or your billfold, the patrolman then asks for your license, and if that's in there you'll very rarely be issued a summons. Now this thing was something that was well known by truck-drivers and people who travel through that area.

Smith maintains that the "code" is widespread, although from the preceding analysis of extortion it can be clearly seen that specific practices have been traditionally practiced and accepted in certain areas, yet not found acceptable in another community. Would this mean that the bulk of these "code" practices occur in police departments other than the one in which Smith served his "apprenticeship" in "blue-coat crime"? Our informant says "yes" and offers the following to substantiate his answer:

> I think generally the Mid-City police department is like every police department in the world. I think the exceptions are probably in small towns or in a few cities that have never been touched by corrupt politics, if there are any. But I think that generally they are the same everywhere,[30] because I have talked to policemen from other cities. I know policemen in other cities that I've had contact with that were in those things. I've discussed open things, or out and out felonies, with policemen from Kansas City on. And I know that at least in that city that it happens, and it's a matter of record that it happens in Denver and Chicago. And I think that this happens in all cities.

From a scientific point of view, other than the incidence of police scandals from time to time, there is no evidence to confirm or deny this one ex-officer's opinion regarding the universal existence of the "code."

The Recruit's Initiation into the "Code" Clique

Bucher describes a profession as a relatively homogeneous community whose members share identity, values, definitions of role, and interest. Socialization of recruits consists of inducting them into the "common core." [31] This occurs on two levels: the formal, or membership group, and the informal, or the reference group.

In the Mid-City police department the failure to socialize most of the new recruits into the "code" would constitute a threat to those who presently practice it. Thus, all "code" practitioners have the responsibility

of screening new recruits at various times to determine whether they are "alright guys" and to teach by example and mutual involvement the limitations of "code" practices. If the recruit accepts such training, he is welcomed into the group and given the rights and privileges commensurate with his new status. If he does not, he is classified as a "goof" and avoided by the rest.

In a journalistic account of police deviancy, it was argued that if corruption exists in the political structures controlling police department appointments, this "socialization" into deviancy begins at the point of paying for the privilege of making an application or of buying an appointment.[32] Although Smith did not "buy" his appointment, he cited the existence of factions having influence in recruit appointments, even within the structure of a Civil Service Commission.

> There are four different requirements to the whole thing. One is your written test, one is your agility, one is your physical examination, and the fourth is the oral examination which is given by the civil service commission. I really crammed before I took the test. When I took the test it was a natural for me, it was a snap. I scored a 94 on my test for the police department. With my soldiers preference, which gives you 5 points, I scored a 99.[33] I passed my agility test and my physical. I could have had a 100 score, I could have been a gymnast, gone through the agility test and made everyone else look silly and still I could have failed in the oral exam. And this is the kicker where politics comes in.
>
> There are three old men that are aligned with different factions, different people on and off the department, different businessmen that have power, different groups, different lodges and organizations, and all these things influence these men, these three people that make up the civil service board.

The existence of the "code" had hurt the level of morale generally in the Mid-City department. In fact, the breakdown of each new recruit's morale is an important step in gaining his acceptance of the "code."[34]

> The thing that hurt the morale was the fact that a large percentage of the people on the department were involved in illegal practices to some degree. And actually you take a man that has just joined the department, has good intentions[35] and is basically honest, and in this, to a man that's never been dishonest and hasn't stepped over the line, there aren't degrees. It's all either black or white. And the illegal activity I know shocks a lot of these young men . . . because it was the thing to do. It's a way to be accepted by the other people. It's a terrible thing the way one policeman will talk about another. Say an old timer will have a new man working with him and he'll tell you, "You've got to watch him, because *he's honest!*"

For a recruit to be accepted in the Mid-City police department he must accept the informal practices occurring in the department. Illegal activity is pursued within the police force as the dominant "norm" or standard.

> To illustrate the group pressure on each policemen who dares to enforce the law as prescribed in the legal statutes, the following account is typical.

> We'll take a classic example—Mr. Sam Paisano. Now when I was on the force I knew that whenever I worked in the downtown area, I could go into Sam's restaurant and order my meal and never have to pay a dime. I think that just about every patrolman on the force knew that. If I had run across Sam doing anything short of murder, I think I would have treaded very lightly. Even if I hadn't accepted his free meals. Say I had turned it down; still, if I stopped this man for a minor traffic viola-

tion, say I caught him dead to rights, I'd be very reluctant to write this man a ticket because I'd suffer the wrath of the other men on the force. I'd be goofing up their meal ticket. Now he in turn knows this. The rest of the officers wouldn't waste any words about it, they'd tell you right off— "You sure fouled up our meal ticket." The old timers would give you a cold shoulder. If it came to the attention of the gold braid, your immediate superiors, they'd make sure you had a little extra duty or something. In most cases if you did this just to be honest, just to be right, it would go badly for you.

> This special treatment of Mr. Paisano wasn't something that you concealed, or that you were ashamed of because it was the normal accepted thing to do. I'd have been more ashamed, and I'd have kept it quiet if I'd stopped such a man as this, because I'd have felt like some kind of an oddball. I would have been bucking the tide, I'd have been out of step.

Yet, such general practices must be converted to individual participation at some point, and to be effective this involvement must be on a primary group relationship basis. Smith's account of his introduction to the "code" follows the first steps of the assimilating process.

> The first thing that I can recall seeing done [which was illegal] was on the night shift when I first went on patrol. The old timers were shaking buildings down and helping themselves to whatever was in the building. The first time I saw it happen I remember filing through the check-out counter at a supermarket, seeing all the officers grabbing their cigarettes or candy bars, or whatever they wanted and I passed through without anything.

> I got in the car and this old timer had, of all the petty things, two of these 25- or 30-cent candy bars and he sat them down in the seat and told me to have some. I

told him I really didn't want any. And he asked me if "that shook me up" or something. And I told him, "Well, it sort of surprised me." He said that everybody did it and that I should get used to that.

And as it went on it progressed more. Well, in fact, he justified it at the time by telling me he had seen the same market one time, when there had been a legitimate break-in and one particular detective had been so busy loading the back seat of his car full of hams and big pieces of beef that he was stumbling and falling down back and from the cooler to the alley, and he didn't even know who was around him he was so busy carrying things out. And he named this officer and I don't doubt it because I've seen the same officer do things in that same nature.

And this was the first direct contact I had with anything like this.

The old timers would test the new recruits with activities which could be laughed off if they were reported, such as the 30-cent candy bar taken from the supermarket in the preceding account.

> The old timers would nose around 'til they found out whether a young guy was going to work with them and "be right" as far as they were concerned, or whether he was going to resist it and be straight as far as the rest of the world was concerned.

If the recruit cooperated, the practices were extended and the rookie became involved. Once he was involved there was no "squealing" on fellow policemen breaking the law. Then he could have some personal choice as to how far he personally wished to go. However, those who were straight-laced and wanted to stay honest had their problems too. Social isolation appears to be a powerful sanction as can be seen from Smith's information.

> There are a few policemen that are

straight-laced all the way. I can remember one policeman who might have made an issue of another policeman taking something. He had that attitude for the first six months that he was on the force but by that time, he had been browbeaten so bad, he saw the writing on the wall. He knew better than to tell anything. In addition to browbeating, this man in very short order was put in a position where they had him on the information desk, or kicked around from one department to another, 'cause nobody wanted to work with him. This kind of a man they called "wormy," because anything that would happen he'd run to the braid.

> This fellow, I knew, wanted to be one of the boys, but he wanted to be honest, too. As it turned out, this guy was finally dismissed from the force for having an affair with a woman in his squad car. Just a couple of years before that he would have had a fit if he thought that somebody was going to take a drink on duty, or fool around with a woman, or steal anything. For this reason this man spent a lot of time on the information desk, working inside, and by himself in the squad car.

Negative sanctions were applied against "goofs" who advocated following the legitimate police ethic. Group acceptance by senior officers was the reward to a recruit accepting the "code," and the "code" was presented to the recruit as the police way of life having precedence over legal responsibilities.

> This small fraction that . . . are honest and would report illegal activity are ostracized. Nobody will work with them. They look at them like they're freaks, talk about them like they're freaks, and they are freaks.

> The goofs that would talk about doing things the way they should be done, they had to be ignored or put down. There were older policemen that as they found out I

would go along with certain things, pressed to see how much further I would go. And showed me that they went farther, whether I cared to or not. So naturally I went along quite a ways with some of them. And I don't really remember how we first became aware of how far the other person would go. I think this is just a gradual thing.

The existence of a social system of an informal nature working quietly under the facade of the formal police department regulations has been clearly demonstrated in Mid-City. One further note in explaining the motivations of policemen toward illegal activities involves the condition of low salaries. Smith's department pay scale and working conditions would suggest that economic pressures were a factor in condoning or rationalizing "code" practices.

> The pay wasn't good. I went on the department and earned $292 a month. The morale of the force was as low as that of any group that I've ever been around. There was constant complaining from all of them about everything.
> The training programs were set up so that you would have to come in on your own time and weren't compensated for it. ...They dictated to you how you lived your whole life, not only what you did during the eight hours you were a policeman but how you'd live your whole life. This as much as anything hurt the morale.

But when Smith was asked directly, "With the policeman's low salary, do illegal activities become necessary to keep up financially?" he discounted it as a major factor.[36]

> I don't think this is the case. I don't think there are very many policemen that I knew, and I knew all of them, that were social climbers or that tried to keep up with the Joneses, by illegal activities anyway.
> Actually most of the police officers

think that they are even above those people that have money, because they have power. Those people with money are pretty well forced to cater to a policeman. And you'll find that very few people ever tell a policeman what they think of him, whether they like him or not. They know that a policeman will do them harm. The businessmen, especially the bigger businessmen, pamper the policemen. They will treat them with respect when they face them.

Sanctions for Preservation of the "Code"

Normally, practitioners of the "code" would consist of a united group working to protect all fellow patrolmen from prosecution. However, Smith had exceeded the "code" limits[37] by committing *premediated theft,* and in order to protect the "code" from being exposed during the scandal involving Smith and two accomplices, the "clique" socially and spatially isolated themselves from the three accused policemen.

> Everybody ran for cover, when the thing hit the front page of the newspapers. I've never seen panic like there was at that time. These people were all ready to sell out their mothers to save their own butts. They knew there was no holding back, that it was a tidal wave. They were grabbing just anything to hang on. The other policemen were ordered to stay away from us, myself and the other men involved. They were ordered to stay away from the trials. They were told to keep their noses out of this thing, that it would be handled.
> There were a few policemen who came around during this time. Strangely the ones who came around were the ones who didn't go in for any of the illegal activity. They didn't have anything to worry about. Everybody else ran and hid.

During a time like this, group consensus is

required to preserve the "code." A certain amount of rationalization is necessary to mollify past illicit activity in light of present public exposure. Smith continues:

> I think if they had really gone by the book during the police scandal, that 25 percent of the policemen would have lost their jobs. I've talked to some of them since, and the worst violators all now have themseves convinced that they weren't guilty of a thing.
>
> I've never referred to myself as this before, but I was their goat, their scapegoat. The others stuck together and had support. I got what I deserved, but if I compare myself with the others, I got a real raw deal.

Preservation of the "code" occurs when policemen work with another person who has similar intentions and begin to "trust" one another in illegal activities without fear of the authorities being informed. A suggestion of rotating young officers from shift to shift to weaken the "code" had been given public discussion. To this, Smith reacted thusly:

> I think that the practice of rotating young officers will serve a purpose. It will eliminate a lot of things because you just can't take a chance with somebody that you don't know. If you don't know but what the next person they throw you with might be a CID ... short for Criminal Investigation Department. They're spies! Say there are just 10 percent of the men on the department that wouldn't go along with anything, and they are switching around with the new system, you don't know when you're going to catch one of them, and if you do you're a cooked goose. The old system you were 90 percent sure of the people you were with.

This same process used to preserve the illegal "code" as a group phenomenon is also the same process used to develop and promote the acceptable professional ethics of the police. A situation in which it is "normal" for a policeman to "squeal on his fellow patrolmen" would undermine professional ethics. Personal insecurity would mount with the constant fear of just being accused with or without supporting evidence. Such an anarchical system lends itself to intrigue, suspicion, and an increased possibility of each officer being "framed." Thus, these same procedures which would effectively reduce the continuation of the "code" would also prove dysfunctional to the maintenance of the ethics which are the core of the police profession itself. These concurrent processes reflect the dual standards extant in society at large.

Difficulties Involved in Breaking the "Code"

If a "code" does exist in a law enforcement agency, one of the major factors which protects it from attack is secrecy. This factor is compounded by public acceptance of the traditional view of illegal behavior as only an individualistic, moral problem.

Another factor that shields the "code" from attack is the apathy resulting from the myriad of complex demands and responsibilities placed upon the average citizen. So many things touch him with which he *must* become involved that he does not pursue problems which do not directly concern him. Inextricably connected with this is the realistic fear of retaliation, either through direct harassment by the police or indirectly through informal censures.[38]

Smith says that only a really big issue will provoke an apathetic public to action.

> Everybody's looking out for number one. And the policeman can do you harm. It's

such a complex thing, there are so many ways, so many different people are affected by the police—most people will back off. Most people are afraid to do anything, if it looks like it's going to affect them adversely.

If the police have carefully practiced *prejudice,* in their day-to-day operations, the chances are slim that the persons against whom these illegal practices were committed possess either the social or political power to break the "code" before the system could retaliate. Knowing this fact keeps most of the persons with any knowledge of the "code's" operation silent indeed.

The rigid procedures of obtaining legal evidence and the dangers of committing a *false arrest* are gigantic deterrents to bringing accusations against any suspicious person, especially a policeman. Ex-Officer Smith discusses the realistic problems involved in attempting to enforce legal statutes against *shopping* or other aspects of the "code":

> I think that any law against *shopping* would be hard to enforce against a police officer. You'd really have to have the evidence against him and really make it public, cause it would be soft-pedalled all the way otherwise. Let's say you see a police officer in a restaurant taking a pack of cigarettes or let's say it's something other than a pack of cigarettes, something that you can prove came from the restaurant. And along comes a radio news unit and you stop the unit and say you just saw a policeman steal a pack of cigarettes or something bigger. When other police arrive on the scene the newsman would probably pull the other policemen off to the side and tell them that their buddy just took a pack of cigarettes and that goofball [the informer] wants to make trouble about it. You insist that they shake down the policeman and they find the item. Here you're in

pretty good shape. In this case you'd have a policeman in a little bit of trouble. I don't think he'd lose his job or do any time over it, but I'd say there would be some scandal about it. Unless you were real hard-headed they'd soft-pedal it.

> Let's back up a little and say the policeman threw the item back into the restaurant and then you made your accusation. Then you're in trouble, 'cause when they shake him down he doesn't have a thing. Now you're a marked man, because every policeman in town will know that you tried to foul up one of their boys. Even the honest policemen aren't going to like what you did. In other words, they are tightly knit, and they police this city by fear to a certain extent.

In Mid-City only those who are involved in practicing the "code" are equipped with the necessary information to expose its operations. Whether one *can* inform on his fellow officers is directly connected with the degree of his illegal involvement prior to the situation involving the unlawful event.

> It all depends upon how deeply you are involved. If you've been a guy who has gone along with a free cup of coffee, the gratuities, the real petty things and you'd happen to drive up on a major theft, drive up on another policeman with his shoulder against the door, then you might take action. However, if you had gone a little farther, say you'd done some shopping, then you're forced to look the other way. It's like a spider spinning a web, you're drawn in toward the center.

It appears obvious that those who are involved in the "code" will be the least useful instruments for alleviating the problem. Only the professionally naive would expect a "code" practitioner to disclose the "code's" existence, much less reveal its method of operation, since his own position is so vulnerable.

SUMMARY OF FINDINGS

From data furnished by a participant informant, an informal "code" of illegal activities within one police department was documented. The group processes which encouraged and maintained the "code" were identified. It was found that the new recruits were socialized into "code" participation by "old timers," and group acceptance was withheld from those who attempted to remain completely honest and not be implicated. When formal police regulations were in conflict with "code" demands among its practitioners, the latter took precedence. Since the "code" operates under conditions of secrecy, only those who participate in it have access to evidence sufficient to reveal its method of operation. By their very participation they are implicated, and this binds them to secrecy as well. In this study the public indignation of a police scandal temporarily suspended the "code," but it flourished again when public apathy returned.

Although some individual factors must be considered in explaining police deviancy, in the present study the sanction of group acceptance was paramount. This study

clearly demonstrates the social genesis of the "code," the breeding ground for individual unlawful behavior. From evidence contained herein, an individualistic orientation to police deviancy may discover the "spoiled fruit," but only when the "code" is rooted out can the "seedbed" of deviancy be destroyed.

From related research in group deviancy, it can be stated that the social organization of a given community (including its respectable citizens) is the milieu in which a "code" flourishes. Thus, a police department is an integral element of that complex community structure, and deviancy found in an enforcement agency is a reflection of values which are habitually practiced and accepted within that community. This was found to be true in the present study.

The findings of this case study should not be interpreted as applicable to all police departments, nor should they be considered as a rationalization for the existence of an illicit "code" anywhere. Rather, this case study represents a very limited effort to probe the very sensitive area of "blue-coat crime" and describe its operation and method of perpetuation in one enforcement agency.

NOTES

1 This concept is a restricted modification of Sutherland's term "White Collar Crime"; see Edwin H. Sutherland, "White Collar Crime," *Amer. Soc. Review* **5** (1940): 1–12. However, the stress of Sutherland's thesis is the lowering of social morale *of the larger society* by the violation of trust by those holding these social positions. The present emphasis is upon the group participating in those violations and *their* reactions, morale, and behavior, rather than the consequences accruing to the larger society as a result of these illegal actions. The same violation of trust might produce a degree of disorganization and lowering of morale among nonparticipants, while producing a

heightened morale and cohesion among all of those in the norm-violating clique.

2 August Vollmer, *The Police and Modern Society* (1936), pp. 3–4.

3 A. C. German, *Police Personnel Management* (1958), pp. 3–4.

4 Mort Stern, "What Makes a Policeman Go Wrong? An Ex-Member of the Force Traces the Steps on Way from Law Enforcement to Violating," by a former Denver Police Officer as told to Mort Stern, *Denver Post,* October 1, 1961. Reprinted in *J. Crim. L., C. & P.S.* **53** (1962): 97–101.

   A similar reaction is given by James F. Johnson, a former state trooper, Secret Service

Agent, security officer, and private investigator in *World Telegram and Sun,* March 10, 1953, quoted in Tappan, *Crime, Justice and Correction* (1960), p. 290.

5 Tappan, *Crime,* pp. 309ff.

6 Wilson, "Progress in Police Administration," *J. Crim. L., C. & P.S.* **42** (1951): 141.

7 Johnson, *Crime, Correction and Society* (1964), p. 452.

8 The Lexow Committee in New York (1894–1895), and the Seabury Committee a generation later found the same situation of *departmental* corruption quoted in Sutherland and Cressey, *Principles of Criminology* (6th ed., 1960), p. 338.

9 Sutherland and Cressey, *Principles.*

10 Barnes and Teeters, *New Horizons in Criminology* (2d ed., 1958), pp. 245–247.

11 Korn and McCorkle, *Criminology and Penology* (1959), pp. 85–86, 125–136.

12 Richard A. Cloward, "Illegitimate Means, Anomie, and Deviant Behavior," *Amer. Soc. Rev.* **24** (1959): 167.

13 Merton, *Social Theory and Social Structure* (Revised and enlarged ed., 1958), Chaps. 1, 4, 5.

14 Bell, "Crime as an American Way of Life," *Antioch Rev.* **13** (1953): 140–141.

15 Sutherland and Cressey, *Principles,* p. 331.

16 This dilemma is presently being compounded by recent Supreme Court decisions involving police powers and personal civil rights. The fear of an emergent police state (which may or may not be valid) leads the present Justices to feel that freedom of the individual will result when police powers no longer encroach upon individual rights. The paradox is that the police are required to fulfill their traditional protection duties in spite of these new formal procedures designed to limit their investigative activities. To fulfill the social expectations of "catching criminals, dope peddlers, etc.," the policeman must adopt certain extra-legal procedures strictly on an informal basis, while appearing on the surface to be adhering to the formal limitations imposed upon him. See Arthur Niederhoffer's recent monograph *Behind the Shield: The Police in Urban Society* (1967).

17 Westley, "Violence and the Police," *Amer. J. Soc.* **59** (1953): 34–41.

18 Westley, "Secrecy and the Police," *Social Forces* **34** (1956): 254–257.

19 This concept was taken from Cohen, *Delinquent Boys: The Culture of the Gang* (1955), p. 60.

20 Sherif and Sherif, *An Outline of Social Psychology* (revised ed., 1956), pp. 630–631, 638. For a sophisticated treatment of reference group theory, see ibid., Chapters 4, 16, and 18.

21 Stouffer, "An Analysis of Conflicting Social Norms," *Amer. Soc. Rev.* **14** (1949): 707.

22 Dornbush, "The Military Academy as an Assimilating Institution," *Social Forces* **33** (1955): 316–321.

23 Moore and Tumin, "Some Social Functions of Ignorance," *Amer. Soc. Rev.* **14** (1949): 791.

24 Johnson, *Crime,* pp. 445–446.

25 Whyte, *Street Corner Society* (1955 ed.), pp. 138–139. Another author conceptualized this problem by delineating it as two separate police functions. "Law enforcement" has specific formal legal procedures whereas "keeping the peace" is vague and without a clear-cut mandate. This study updates by three decades the classic work of Whyte. See Egon Bittner, "The Police on Skid-Row: A Study of Peace Keeping," *Amer. Soc. Rev.* **32** (1967): 699–715.

26 Many authors have written of police deviancy as tangential to their central theme. However, persistent search failed to reveal recent empirical studies focusing directly on the deviant policeman himself. Most applicable were Westley's, "Violence and the Police" and "Secrecy and the Police" although even here the data were gained from policemen still "in favor," who might well have reservations about revealing the full extent to which the "Code" was practiced.

27 A graduate assistant from the Department of Sociology, Mr. Ivy L. Gilbert approached ex-officer "Smith" as a friend, and under guidance of the present author was able to gain "Smith's" cooperation for a scientific study. Taped interviews over a period of several months were recorded and transcribed by Gilbert. Many of these materials were used in Gilbert's Master's Thesis, "A Case Study of Police Scandal: An Investigation into Illegitimate Norms of a Legitimate Enforcement Agency" (June 1965).

28 One article is a composite of personal experience as a police reporter: David G. Wittels, "Why Cops Turn Crooked," *Saturday Evening Post,* April 23, 1949, pp. 26ff; the other is an

account of a former Denver policeman as re-told by a news editor, Mort Stern, "What Makes a Policeman Go Wrong?"

29   The majority of these terms and definitions are modified from those listed by Gilbert, "A Case Study," pp. 3–4, and discussed by German, *Police Personnel Management,* p. 173.

30   Smith's evaluations are heavily influenced by his experience. He was a patrolman in a police department totaling about 250 personnel, serving a metropolitan area of a quarter of a million persons.

However, other sources have suggested that when a community gets larger than 80,000 people, political corruption and graft are inevitable; see Wittels, "Why Cops Turn Crooked," p. 26.

31   Rue Bucher and Anselm Strauss, "Professions in Progress," *Amer. J. Soc.* **64** (1961): 325–326.

32   One policeman reported having paid $300.00 to take the police examination. He also was required to pledge his family's vote to the "right" party. After some wait, he took a "special exam," then more waiting lists, and a final $300.00 to the party fund was required before he was hired. Then he had to purchase his own uniform on contract at the "right" store. Before this man became a member of the department, by his participation in the recruitment process, he was an involved member practicing the "code". Wittels, "Why Cops Turn Crooked," pp. 105–107, 111.

33   In spite of Smith's remarkable test level, he was left off a list of the highest 10 eligible applicants, and some three months later was put on the list through the influence of his father, a respected member of the police department with many years of unblemished service. Otherwise, he may never have been placed on the appointment list.

34   This is not unlike the planned removal of old civilian standards and values when a new soldier recruit is given basic training. The formal regulations are presented to him, but in company with "old salts" he learns how

the system can be worked and what a person must do to participate in it.

35   One writer corroborates this by stating that young recruits who show traits of being ambitious, as well as those with family responsibilities, are the most susceptible to graft. The pressures toward success and achievement are clearly indicated by either or both of these factors. Wittels, "Why Cops Turn Crooked," p. 27.

36   To evaluate Smith's statement on economic pressures, an additional personal datum is relevant. Smith used most of his money from *premeditated theft* for his "habit"—a racing car. He later declared he probably wouldn't have participated in this crime *so much* had it not been for the "habit." His response did not seem to indicate that he *began* theft for racing money, but that he *continued* it to counter the economic drain created by owning and driving the racing machine.

37   One officer reports that he wondered why he was not promoted—perhaps they thought he was lazy. He was tagging cars of all violators and even reported a broken sidewalk belonging to an "organization" man. He couldn't get ahead. He made a couple of outstanding arrests and was made a detective. Later, he ran a "vice" raid against a "protected" place, and was back as a rookie on a beat in "Siberia." He finally took some payoffs and cooperated and eventually became a police captain but, exceeding the "Code" limits, was caught and prosecuted. Either not accepting the "Code" or exceeding its limits had negative effects. Wittels, "Why Cops Turn Crooked," pp. 111–112.

38   The campaigning attack on the "untouchable" image of J. Edgar Hoover and the FBI has made political news. The very act of exposing methods used by Hoover's organization, which though admittedly effective were clearly unlawful, caused the political downfall of an otherwise popular politician in the November 1966 Nevada election.

CONTROL OF THE POLICE

Member of the Boston Police Speakers Bureau presenting a
Crime Prevention program to neighborhood citizens group.

It is difficult to overestimate the importance of police to American legal processes. The police are the everyday interpreters of the legal order to the population; indeed, for many people, the police are the sole source of contact with the legal system. Moreover, the police are given legal authority to administer force, at times deadly force. As we have already indicated, police decisions often do not take place in public; they are "low-visibility" decisions. The nature of the job often allows for the exercise of discretion in behavior beyond review by higher authorities. Styles of police enforcement have been observed by a number of scholars to vary from place to place, and a good deal of informality and individual initiative prevails. So what the policeman does is often perceived by the citizen as what the law is, and this is not an inaccurate perception.

At the same time, precisely because police are law enforcement officers, they are expected to exhibit neutrality in the enforcement of criminal law, to abide by standards of due process of law, and to be responsible to higher officials. In practice, observers of police have also noted that these expectations are not always met. What sorts of mechanisms are appropriate for ensuring, or at least enhancing the possibility, that high standards of policing will prevail?

The articles in this section comment upon and analyze several different alternatives. James R. Hudson studied the Operating Civilian Review Board of Philadelphia and compares its functions with the Internal Police Board of Inquiry. He concludes that both methods of reviewing and functions were markedly different as performed by these two boards of inquiry.

Jerome H. Skolnick's article on neighborhood police is an analysis of a proposal brought before the Berkeley, California, voters in the spring of 1971 to break up the presently constituted Berkeley Police Department and to substitute five smaller departments whose policies and practices would be governed by the neighborhoods they served. The article was written before the election, and, in fact, the proposal was defeated overwhelmingly in the city of Berkeley. Interestingly, it received its greatest support from the area of the city predominantly occupied by students and did not carry the predominantly black sections of the community. Nevertheless, a couple of years later, in the spring of 1973, a more moderate proposal to establish a Police Review and Policy Board was carried. That Board, composed of nine persons selected by each of the members of the City Council, had its first meeting on October 5, 1973, too recently to allow us to assess it in this volume. It is worth noting, however, that among those attending the meeting was an influential high-ranking official of the Berkeley Police Department. A general feeling of optimism and cooperation prevailed. Whether these high hopes will be realized remains to be seen.

The last selection is from the American Bar Association's Project on Standards for Criminal Justice. Its Advisory Committee on the Police Function, headed by Frank J. Remington, rejects the use of an independent police review board as a desirable method for handling grievances and clearing tensions between police and the public, although it acknowledges that the system used in Philadelphia possessed certain virtues. In general, the committee prefers to rely upon strong internal controls by a chief administrator as the main instrument for controlling police misconduct and for answering citizen grievances. Yet the committee seems far more sure of the critical *need* for an answer to the problem of police review than of its own suggestions. It states that "The continuing failure to devise and implement necessary procedures and sanctions to deal with police abuses is one of the most critical problems now confronting our society."

In considering how to remedy the problem of police abuses we should consider what kinds of assumptions lie behind notions of how much control the internal police organizations ought to have over themselves and how much control ought to be allocated to the larger community. We should also consider whether the notion of neighborhood control is the same for every urban place or whether it varies depending upon the size of the area. For example, would smaller police departments be a more viable possibility in such large metropolitan areas as New York, Chicago, and Los Angeles? Would it be possible to have certain kinds of policies implemented at the neighborhood level and responsive to smaller groups of people, with other sorts of police facilities and arrangements coordinated at a regional level?

Finally, in any discussion of "controlling the police," we must consider the phenomenon we wish to control and the degree of control we wish to exert. To what extent do we want to control the policies of police departments, the behavior of individual officers, the attitudes of individual officers? And whatever instruments for control we may develop, what sort of research might be undertaken to determine the usefulness of certain controls within a specific area and the generalizability of the results of research to other areas?

Organizational Aspects of Internal and External Review of the Police

The issue of civilian complaint review boards for incidents involving citizen grievances against the police has continued unresolved for over a decade. While most of the acrimonious debate has been carried on at the municipal level, presidential commissions, the FBI, and many national organizations have contributed arguments and recommendations at one time or another.[1] Nevertheless, the debate has had to thrive mainly on ideology, rhetoric, and opinion, for few cities have experimented with civilian review boards, making data difficult to obtain.

There is one city, however, that did have an operating civilian review board for a sufficient length of time to permit an analysis of its activities. For about ten years (1958–1969), the mayors of Philadelphia appointed a group of prominent citizens to the Philadelphia Police Advisory Board (PAB) that had a mandate to accept citizen complaints about alleged police misconduct.[2] At the same time, the Philadelphia Police Department's Police Board of Inquiry (PBI) continued to hear cases that involved citizen complaints, although the bulk of its activity centered on internally generated disciplinary

From the *Journal of Criminal Law, Criminology and Police Science* **63** (3): 427–433. Copyright © 1972 by Northwestern University School of Law. Reprinted by special permission of the Journal of Criminal Law, Criminology and Police Science.

cases. Data on both these agencies have been obtained, permitting comparison of the organization and functions of the two.

This is especially pertinent because some critics of civilian review have argued that such agencies are redundant, performing functions that the police organization already effectively handles.[3] The data presented here suggest that, in Philadelphia at least, the civilian review board was able to provide services that the internal review board of the police department did not. (Some of these functions may be performed elsewhere in city government or elsewhere within the police department, but that is not at issue here. The purpose of this article is to compare two organizations that had as a major activity the handling of complaints against policemen brought by citizens.)

The structure of these two agencies will be examined, beginning with the mandate each received. Data on civilian complaints will indicate the kind of complaints received and the methods of resolving them. The analysis shows that differences in mandate, staffing, organizational environment, and ideological commitment produced two rather distinct types of procedures that ostensibly dealt with the same problem. The comparison raises some important questions about the handling of citizen complaints and the consequences these complaints have for the police department and the community.

MANDATES AND PROCEDURES

Most cases that come to the Police Board of Inquiry originate on the precinct level, where a superior officer determines that a violation of the Disciplinary Code may have occurred. The alleged violation can come to his attention through a complaint by a citizen or a fellow officer, by observation or inspection. An investigation is then conducted, and a report is forwarded through channels until it reaches the police commissioner's desk. Although the report passes through a number of command levels after leaving the precinct, these officers can not adjudicate the case; only the commissioner can make a decision. Based upon this report, the commissioner takes direct disciplinary action or he refers the case to the PBI for hearing. Most disciplinary cases, in fact, do come to the attention of the PBI. It has two distinct functions —one administrative and the other judicial.

PBI hearings are held before a panel of officers whom the administrative staff selects from outside the accused policeman's district. These panels usually include a captain, a lieutenant, and a patrolman who sit for a number of cases. The officer against whom the complaint has been made may request that one member of the panel be of his own rank. It is the responsibility of the permanent staff of the PBI to set a time for the hearing, inform the concerned parties, and bring together all relevant information and files, including the policeman's complete departmental dossier.

Hearings are open to the public, and evening hearings have been instituted to accommodate civilian witnesses who might otherwise have to miss work in order to appear. The accused policeman has the right to counsel, and he is most often represented by a lawyer provided by the Fraternal Order of Police, a benevolent association of police officers.

The charges upon which a policeman can be brought before the PBI are carefully detailed in the Duty Manual of the Police Department which forms the Disciplinary Code of the department. There are five broad categories of offense: Conduct Unbecoming an Officer, Intoxication, Insubordination, Neglect of Duty, and Disobedience of Orders. Within each of these articles are a number of sections that specify various infractions. Each carries a recommended disciplinary action. For example, under Disobedience of Orders there is the specific infraction: "Soliciting money or any valuable thing without proper authorization." The first offense carries a recommended five-to-ten-day suspension without pay. In addition, each charge carries a reckoning period for repeated offenses, essentially a statute of limitation. When the PBI panel finds against an officer, it recommends to the commissioner a penalty based upon the offense, the officer's previous record, and other mitigating circumstances that might guide a disciplinary decision. The commissioner then makes a determination, which is duly transmitted to the officer and recorded in his dossier.

The Philadelphia Police Advisory Board, originally the Philadelphia Police Review Board, was established in 1958 by Mayor J. Richardson Dilworth and was "charged with the responsibility of considering citizens' complaints against police where the charge involved brutality, false arrest, discrimination based upon race, religion, or national origin, or other wrongful conduct of police personnel towards citizens." [4] It came into existence after hearings before the City Council where, among other police issues, the internal review procedures came under sharp attack. The case against that system was summarized in an article by Spencer Coxe, Executive Director of the Greater Philadelphia Branch of the ACLU, who wrote: "When the Commissioner's office ordered an investigation, complainants found that the matter was likely to peter out; they were usually not notified of any conclusion unless they pressed for a report, when they were told that the investigation showed that the complaint was without justification." [5]

Philadelphians filed their complaints directly with the PAB. Initially, the only staff were the volunteer panel of prominent citizens. In 1960 an executive secretary was appointed on a part-time basis and in 1963 on a full-time basis. The executive secretary interviewed each complainant personally, reviewed with him the substance of the complaint, and discussed the kind of action the complainant desired. For the PAB records, complaints were classified as: brutality, illegal search and seizure, harassment, and other.

Over time, the PAB worked out different strategies for dealing with citizen complaints. Two of these were conciliatory or mediating procedures. In some cases, the citizen merely wanted an explanation of police behavior—was the police action legal or not? did the police have jurisdiction? and so on. In such cases an explanation of the police actions often resolved the complaint. In other cases, the executive secretary arranged for a conference between the complainant and the accused officer or another member of the police department. Again, whenever this informal arrangement resolved the dispute to the satisfaction of the citizen, his case was closed without a formal hearing.

The third type of settlement involved a public hearing before the appointed board of the PAB. Prior to a hearing, the PAB requested from the police department an investigation of the incident, which was essentially a statement from the police officer, along with copies of pertinent official documents and sometimes statements of witnesses. The complainant's statement to the PAB served as his written account of the incident. For the greater part of the PAB's history, the Community Relations Office of the police department carried out these investigations. Both the citizen and the officer were permitted counsel at hearings. Usually, citizens did not have legal representation and policemen were represented by the Fraternal Order of Police. At the conclusion of the hearing, the board would meet privately and make a determination. There were no standardized penalties for any offenses, nor was there an attempt to institute a reckoning period.

If the PAB found the officer at fault, it would send a recommendation for disciplinary action to the office of the Managing Director of the City of Philadelphia, who in turn passed it along to the police commissioner. The intermediate step, sending the recommendation to the Managing Director's office, reflected the status of the PAB as an advisory body to the mayor. The PAB's recommendation was in no way binding on the police commissioner. As a matter of fact, however, the PAB's recommendations were almost always accepted and implemented by the commissioner.

Since the PBI is an administrative adjunct to the commissioner, his orientation affected its operations directly. The commissioner's authority to send cases to the PBI and act upon its recommendations give him a good deal of administrative power over the PBI. All disciplinary cases cross the commissioner's desk before going to the PBI. While the writer has no data on the kinds of cases that did not reach the PBI, the fact remains that the commissioners in Philadelphia could make such decisions and these, in turn, would influence the role played by the PBI. By the same token, the commissioners could either accept or reject the recommendations from the PBI hearing panels. Again without data it is difficult to document the consequences of this discretionary power. Nonetheless, it would seem apparent that the commissioner's actions on cases would become part of the orientation of the PBI staff.

Of course, the commissioner could also accept or reject PAB recommendations. But the PAB was more autonomous in its operations. Even though it was administratively responsible to the mayor of Philadelphia, it did not have the same kind of organizational relations with the mayor's office as the PBI did with the commissioner's. The citizen brought the case directly to the PAB and there was no intermediate screening. Under these conditions the PAB received a wider range of cases than those processed by the PBI, which resulted in developing the strategies of settlement that have already been mentioned.

THE PROBLEMATIC STATUS
OF CITIZEN COMPLAINTS

Although both the PAB and the PBI received complaints from civilians, the problem these complaints posed is fundamentally different for the two organizations. One difference is the constituency each serves and the legitimation their constituencies give to the agencies. The constituency for the PAB is the citizen-complainant on one level and the wider community on a more general level. The PBI, by contrast, is concerned with the officer-offender most immediately and the general discipline of the department more abstractly.

The PAB was primarily concerned with the citizen who believed he had been abused

and with what that meant to the community at large as well as to the individual citizen. This orientation stems, in part, from the underlying assumption that unresolved police-citizen conflicts increase community tensions. The day-to-day objective was less to document police misconduct or recommend disciplinary action than to reach a satisfactory accord between the parties involved. The PAB's interest was more in the citizen and his allegation than in the policeman's action. This orientation toward the citizen is further underscored in the PAB's use of simple complaint categories adopted from the language citizens employed during the early years of its existence.

The Police Board of Inquiry is directed inward toward the police organization, not outward toward the community. The analogy between police departments and military organizations is often made. As with the military, police departments often regard certain violations as much more serious than similar incidents would be in civilian life, for example, disregard for dress regulations or personal grooming. At the core of these regulations and adherence to them is the issue of discipline. Even in those cases with civilian complainants, the main issue is not police-community relations, but discipline. The charges against the policeman that the PBI can hear are listed in the Duty Manual of the Philadelphia Police Department under its Disciplinary Code. They are stated in formal language and reflect a concern with breaches in technical competence.[8] Violations in the code indicate a failure on the part of the policeman to carry out his duties in the prescribed manner.

The difference in orientation between the PAB and the PBI is further reflected in the criteria for accepting or rejecting complaints. The PBI's emphasis on discipline focuses on the policeman's alleged violation of the Disciplinary Code. The precinct officer's decision to accept and process an allegation is dependent upon his being reasonably sure that a violation has taken place. No doubt there are organizational pressures within the department not to forward any complaint where a violation cannot be established. By contrast, the PAB was under no such organizational constraint; it was willing to accept and hear almost any citizen complaint. Regardless of the investigation report received from the police department, the PAB would pursue the case and, if the complainant wished, would hold a public hearing. The PAB was concerned with giving the citizen the opportunity to file a complaint and to engage in the process of gaining redress. The process itself was regarded as important because it involved the citizen.

This difference in intake philosophy is reflected in Table 1. The probability of a policeman being disciplined was far greater if the PBI held a hearing than if the PAB did. The PBI recommended suspensions, that is, days off without pay, in over half of all cases it heard, about three times as often as the PAB. Recommendations for dismissal were also much more frequent for the PBI (14 percent) as compared to the PAB (1 percent). Unlike the PBI, the PAB used other methods of settling a case after a hearing, such as requesting that the complainant's arrest record be expunged or that a letter of apology be sent to the citizen either from the policemen involved in the incident or from officers in the Community Relations Office. The PAB made no recommendation either against the officer or for the citizen in two-fifths of all the cases it heard. The PBI found 28 percent of the policemen not guilty in its hearings involving civilians.

While these data are far from conclusive, it appears that if a citizen's complaint enters into police channels, there is a very high

Table 1

COMPARISON OF PAB AND PBI HEARING RECOMMENDATIONS (IN PERCENTAGES)

| | | PBI (1960–1968) | |
Recommendations	PAB* (1958–1968) (N = 145)	Civilian Complaints (N = 458)	Non-civilian Complaints (N = 2214)
Suspensions	14	52	76
Dismissals	1	14	5
Reprimands	16	6	9
Other negative action	6	**	**
Other action (letter of apology, expungement of record, etc.)	20	**	**
Not guilty	**	28	10
No recommendation	40	**	**
Not ascertained	3	—	—
Totals	100	100	100

* Includes only principal complainants to eliminate double counting on recommendations.
** No comparable category.

likelihood that some disciplinary action will be taken against the police officer. What is not known is how many times citizens tried to complain or did complain, but their cases were not forwarded from the precinct so that the PBI got them. In addition, it is not known for what allegations the police officer was found at fault. About 65 percent of all cases involved multiple allegations, and it could not be determined which allegation produced what disciplinary action. On the other hand, the few negative recommendations by the PAB do not necessarily mean that it was less effective in dealing with citizen complaints. The PAB, it should be recalled, was more interested in giving the citizen an opportunity to pursue an alleged grievance than it was in sanctioning police officers.

The PAB's orientation to the problem of community tensions and its role as an advisory board to the mayor produced another difference between the two agencies. While both processed a number of cases, the PAB was more conscious that the cases themselves represented only a part of the whole picture of police-community relations. It acted on the premise that these cases were a selection from a larger but unknown number of incidents. In annual reports the board not only listed the number of cases, how they were settled, and the allegations involved but used these data as the basis for making more general recommendations to the mayor. For example, a number of incidents involving the use of handcuffs came to the attention of the PAB, and its report made specific recommendations that the policy governing handcuffs be reviewed.[7] This kind of advice was not a part of the PBI's mission. The PAB was interested in changing police practices and policies that contributed to community tensions; the PBI is not involved in policy formation.

IMPACT ON CITIZEN COMPLAINANTS POLICEMEN, AND THE COMMUNITY

Because the PAB developed alternative strategies for settling complaints, strategies that rested, in part, with the citizen, the consequences for the policeman involved were much less predictable than if charges against him were heard by the PBI. If the citizen decided that an apology or an explanation satisfied his grievance, the case could be settled without a hearing and therefore without the possibility of an adverse recommen-

dation from the PAB. On the other hand, if the citizen did push for a hearing, another policeman could face disciplinary action for an offense similar to the first. The issue, then, is whether the function of civilian review is to satisfy a civilian with a complaint or to assist the police department in monitoring the behavior of its men. If it were the latter, then the focus of civilian review would be on whether or not the policeman was at fault. In Philadelphia, because of the emphasis on the reduction of community tensions, the citizen's satisfaction was the central concern. In practice, the PAB would not pursue a case in which the citizen lost interest, withdrew the complaint, or accepted a settlement without a hearing.

The PBI is not as dependent upon the citizen as the PAB. If a citizen brings a complaint and subsequent investigation suggests that the policeman has violated some article of the Disciplinary Code, the PBI may no longer need the citizen nor does it care what action the citizen desires because it becomes a matter of internal discipline. For example, a citizen could accuse a policeman of illegally entering his home. If the investigation supports the allegation and additional violations of the Disciplinary Code are un-

Table 2

ALLEGATIONS AGAINST POLICE OFFICERS BASED UPON CIVILIAN COMPLAINTS SENT TO THE PBI (IN PERCENTAGES; N = 1029)

Conduct unbecoming an officer	51
Intoxication	3
Insubordination	2
Neglect of duty	29
Disobedience of orders	16
Totals	100*

* This total reflects multiple allegations against the 458 officers involved.

covered, the police department acts independently from the citizen in pursuing the case leading to disciplinary action on the part of the commissioner or the PBI. Even if the citizen were to withdraw his allegation against a policeman, other evidence gathered in the investigation could serve as a basis for a hearing.[8]

As a matter of fact, complaints involving citizen witnesses or complainants form a minority of the cases coming to the PBI. In a review of over 2700 cases from 1960 to 1968, not quite one out of five (19 percent) was based upon a citizen complaint. Even in those cases with civilian complainants, the main issue is not police-community relations but discipline. Thus a citizen's complaint is translated into this perspective. For example, a citizen complaint of brutality or excessive use of force becomes in official language "repeated violations of department rules and regulations or any other course of conduct indicating that a member has little or no regard for his responsibility as a member of the Police Department." It is the official departmental position about the officer's act that is at the core of departmental discipline, not the citizen's interpretation of the act.

It should also be noted that the sheer number of hearings reflects a difference between the two agencies. During its history the PAB received and processed about 677 cases. Some of these had multiple complainants, so that about 1000 individuals made use of the PAB, although only a small proportion of the incidents reached a hearing (about 21 percent). This indicates the alternative routes open to the PAB for settling citizen complaints. Such options simply are not available to the PBI.

The comparison within the PBI between complaints initiated by civilians and those by noncivilians is also of interest. Complaints originating in the police department are far more likely to result in disciplinary recommendations than those that come from outside the department. About three times as many hearings are settled with a "not guilty" for cases with a citizen complainant than for cases coming from members of the department itself. It would be useful in future research to investigate the allegations made by civilians to see what kinds of cases result in "not guilty" recommendations. In particular, it would be important if these cases come from the more controversial allegations, such as brutality.

While those data are not available for this study, there are data on the allegations each agency received that suggest some of the organizational and functional differences between them. In Table 2 the total number of allegations involved in the 458 hearings held by the PBI with civilian complaints is listed. Fifty-one percent of all allegations fell within the category of Conduct Unbecoming an Officer (CUAO). Within that category no single charge accounts for more than 12 percent, and this is the title category itself. Within CUAO the charge of "using rude or insulting language or conduct offensive to the public" was made in 9 percent of the cases, followed by the charge of "knowingly and willfully making a false entry into any departmental report or record" (7 percent). The charge under which brutality would be subsumed was next with just under 5 percent of all allegations. Under Neglect of Duty, the two major charges were "failure to comply with any Commissioner's orders, directives, regulations, etc., oral or written; and those of superiors and supervisors" and "failure to take police action when necessary, at any time, in or out of uniform, and/or failure to make a written report of same to commanding officer." The proportions were 9 and 7 percent, respectively. All other charges never exceeded 4 percent.

In Table 3 it can be seen that brutality, either alone or in combination with some other allegation, comprised 45 percent of all complaints the PAB received. Harassment was the next most frequent allegation (21 percent), followed by illegal search and seizure (15 percent).

Table 3

ALLEGATIONS AGAINST POLICE OFFICERS OF PRINCIPLE COMPLAINANTS TO THE PAB (IN PERCENTAGES; N = 868)

Brutality alone and in combination with other allegations	45
Illegal search and seizure	15
Harassment	21
Other	9
Multiple (not brutality) allegations	10
Totals	100*

* Includes 181 cases for which no police investigation was conducted.

Perhaps the most serious allegation a citizen can bring against a policeman is brutality. Since the police have been given the legitimate use of violence in our society, indiscretion in that respect is a damaging charge—one to which the police are rightly sensitive. Yet brutality, or its more euphemistic label—excessive use of force—is very difficult to prove; indeed, no clear definition of brutality exists. The charge has been raised when the police used racial or ethnic slurs against members of minority groups as well as in cases where policemen have beaten citizens or even shot at them.

As was noted earlier, the Disciplinary Code of the Philadelphia Police Department does not include an allegation of brutality or excessive use of force. The police, of course, are disturbed by this term because of its

emotional overtones. If the allegation is made by a citizen, a more bureaucratically neutral charge is employed. The PAB felt no necessity to neutralize the term because its creation stemmed, in part, from the failure of citizens to obtain redress in cases where brutality had been charged. And since the PAB's allegation categories were based upon the language citizens used, its inclusion was only natural.

CONCLUSIONS

The data from Philadelphia strongly suggest that something more than a jurisdictional rearrangement resulted when citizens were offered a mode of redress other than police jurisdiction over all citizen-initiated complaints. Differences in mandate, staffing, organization environment, and ideology resulted in two distinct types of review agencies. The conceptualization of the problem, the ways in which altercations were settled, and the other functions served were markedly different. These distinctions can be summarized as follows:

The PBI is an internal, administrative-judicial body close to the center of a paramilitary bureaucratic organization. Its primary task is to assist the commissioner in formally maintaining discipline within the department. As a consequence, the PBI never receives some citizen complaints—those with insufficient grounds for charges against a specific officer and those settled by other means at the precinct level or through the intervention of the Community Relations Office. When the PBI does receive a case based on a citizen's complaint, its organizational focus remains fixed upon the officer charged with violation of the Disciplinary Code. It has no mandate or staff to pursue alternative resolutions to a police-citizen dispute, even if a finding against the policeman is not the main purpose of the citizen who registered a complaint.

The PAB was an appointed board of citizens whose mandate was broadly interpreted to include advice to the mayor on improving police-community relations on the basis of citizen complaints and, more narrowly, to assist the citizen in a resolution of this problem whenever the board, through public hearings or other means, was satisfied that the complaint had substance. The board or its executive secretary reviewed every complaint in detail, and the choice of a public hearing was available to any complainant, regardless of the evidence available prior to the hearing. In many cases the complaint amounted to a specific charge against a police officer, and the board recommended disciplinary measures whenever it found such charges warranted. But in many other cases the complaint involved no charge against a particular officer but rather a desire for other measures of redress, restitution, or changes in department or precinct practices.

The analysis presented here does not permit one to include whether one or the other is the better method of resolving police-citizen altercations, but it does indicate some of the problems in developing a satisfactory redress agency. It is hoped that this investigation will throw some light on what continues to be a very sensitive problem in police-community relations.

NOTES

1 See, for example, *The National Advisory Commission on Civil Disorders* (The Kerner Commission), 1968; The President's Commission on Law Enforcement and Administration of Justice, *Task Force Report: The Police,* 1967; *Police Review Boards,* prepared by National F.O.P. Committee on Human Rights and Law Enforcement, Cincinnati; Open letter by J. Edgar Hoover, *FBI Law Enforcement Bulletin,* January 1965.

2 A rather extensive report of the Philadelphia Police Advisory Board prepared by the author appears in the *Police and the Community: The Dynamics of Their Relationship in a Changing Society* by Joseph D. Lohman and Gordon E. Misner (1966), pp. 205–284, also published as *Field Survey IV,* Volume 2, by The President's Commission on Law Enforcement and Administration of Justice (1966). A more condensed version is found in James R. Hudson, "The Civilian Review Board Issue as Illuminated by the Philadelphia Experience," *Criminologica* **6** (1968): 16–29.

3 See in the matter of *Harrington, et al.,* v. *City of Philadelphia,* Court of Common Pleas, June Term, 1965.

4 *The First Annual Report of the Police Advisory Board of the City of Philadelphia* (1959), p. 1.

5 Spencer Coxe, "Police Advisory Board," *Connecticut Bar Journal* **35** (1961): 139.

6 The concept "breach in technical competence" was suggested by Harvey Farberman.

7 *The Fourth Annual Report of the Police Advisory Board of the City of Philadelphia* (1962), p. 4.

8 In the *Police Board of Inquiry Annual Report 1970* this outcome was stated as follows: "There have been occasions when even though the civilian complainant failed to appear [for a hearing], disciplinary action was taken based on violations of departmental regulations."

Neighborhood Police

JEROME H. SKOLNICK

Decentralization is increasingly prescribed as a remedy for the urban ills of America. Even President Nixon picked up the theme in one of his State of the Union addresses, and even he immediately ran into the problems of dislodging entrenched institutions that have grown with years of centralized officialdom.

If "revenue sharing" represents a Republican Administration's idea of decentralization at the national level, "community control" of such public services as schools and police is emerging as its local counterpart, particularly where urban residential patterns and styles of life can be readily distinguished from those of the officials who occupy positions of formal power.

One of the most interesting and controversial efforts to implement a program of community control is one that was considered in Berkeley, California. It proposed that the City Charter be amended to establish police departments serving the so-called "Black Area" of West Berkeley; the "Campus Area" of South Central Berkeley, which would include both the university and the major downtown shopping area; and the "White Area" of Thousand Oaks, Claremont, and the North Berkeley Hills. These would be further divided into five neighborhoods (two in the "Black Area," two in the "White," and one in the "Campus"), each governed by a police council of fifteen, elected by neighborhood precincts. Each council would select a

From *The Nation* (March 22, 1971): 372–373. Reprinted by permission.

police commissioner, who would run his police department subject to the review and instructions of his council.

The impetus for the proposal came from the Black Panther Party, especially from Bobby Seale, who urged a radical coalition to work for community control of the police. Some, including the Progressive Labor Party and the Weathermen, considered the proposal too moderate and unrealistic. Only a general revolution, they felt, would end police oppression in America. But a proposal by the Panthers to work within the system is hardly vulnerable to criticism from the Left.

Both initial support and initial opposition to the Charter Amendment seemed to correspond with affinity or hostility toward the Panthers and the closely associated National Committee to Combat Fascism. Local newspaper editorials denounced the proposal as anarchic and outlandish, really quite beyond serious consideration. A vote for the proposal was made to appear a vote for the kind of people who go around screaming "Off the Pigs." Several events, together with the public stance of certain supporters, helped solidify this conception of what was in fact a complex charter amendment. After the Marin County shoot-out, the Panthers hailed Jonathan Jackson as a hero and willy-nilly associated violent revolution with community control of the police. Second, in the wake of the "Off the Pig" rhetoric, a Berkeley policeman was shot to death in the street early one morning, in cold blood and for no apparent reason. He turned out to have spent his childhood during World War II in an internment camp for Japanese. Finally, a rash of bombings and bomb threats during the fall gave an increasingly violent image to such groups as the Red Family, who were conspicuous in supporting the community police proposal. Many liberals, even those in Berkeley, found it hard to take seriously a proposal so closely associated with these groups. That other Berkeley radicals and Left liberals with solid professional credentials in law and criminology also supported the proposal seemed, at first, less evident. But with time, the materials issued by proponents began to sound more and more analytic and responsible; they even backed the idea with quotes from former Attorney General Ramsey Clark and the President's Commission on Crime and the Administration of Justice. Public support also broadened to include newly elected Representative Ron Dellums. It became clear that to win or even to garner a respectable vote, the proposal would have to appeal to a Berkeley constituency beyond radicals, street people, and a few scattered hill liberals.

When considered on its merits, the proposal made more sense than the early rhetoric suggested. The polemical title, "Community Control of the Police," helped mobilize anti-police activists to obtain ballot signatures. Yet it might have fared better as "A proposal for the Establishment of Neighborhood Police Forces." Actually, that was the heart of the amendment. It was based upon the theory that police planning and policy should be concentrated in smaller neighborhood units, particularly where these are associated with existing racial or cultural patterns. It also presupposed the belief that community residents should participate heavily in their own policing. Opponents of the proposal gave the impression that a vote for it meant a vote for such groups as the Black Panthers

and the Red Family, but that was not at all implicit in the proposal.

Other objections to the proposal were more telling. First, there was the question of the size of Berkeley. Although no longer the middle-class white suburb of San Francisco it was twenty-five years ago, Berkeley is still a relatively small community both in size (15.75 square miles) and in population (113,165). The entire population of Berkeley—black and white—could be swallowed up by a segment of New York's East Harlem. Moreover, although the breakdown into neighborhoods itself makes some sense, most neighborhoods lack homogeneity and even a sense of identity. For instance, the area to be covered by Police Department 3, Division A, is heavily populated by students, lightly by blacks, and by whites of varying social class. When pressed, proponents of the proposal said that Berkeley's small size was an advantage, because it would force the five police boards to develop policies together. But then, one wonders, why the breakdown at all?

A related criticism concerns the economics of the proposal. Under the plan, the police budget for the city would be set by the Berkeley City Council and divided—along with existing files and equipment—among the new departments. Funds would automatically be apportioned on the basis of population. Accordingly, only about a third of the total police budget would go to the "Black Area," while nearly half would fall to the "White." It seems questionable that government funds ought to be distributed on the basis of population, particularly where urban services are concerned. If the proposal had been passed, Berkeley might have found itself saddled with a radical proposal that enriched the well-to-do by taking money from the poor.

Another controversial provision was the proposal's requirement that all police live in the area governed by the local board. This is inconsistent on its face—if neighborhoods are to decide what their police should be like, then neighborhood boards should be allowed to decide where local police may live. There are two final and related major objections to the proposal. One is whether the whole conception isn't too unwieldy. Does a city the size of Berkeley really require five police boards consisting of seventy-five people, and will these ever be able to agree on anything? The proponents assumed that people, especially poor people, have all kinds of free time and public interest. In fact, it may well turn out that those who control the community boards will be precisely the sort of people who presently control the City Council. Middle-class people are responded to in Berkeley (and elsewhere) because they know how to say and do the things that get response. Would poor blacks, for example, do any better under the bureaucracy of a local board?

Finally, the proposal was at times badly drafted. For example, police commissioners could be recalled "by a petition bearing the signatures of 20 percent of the number of people voting in the precincts comprising the neighborhood to which the commissioner is responsible." Does "number of people voting" mean registered voters, or does it mean those who voted in the last election? Since a significant percentage of registered voters normally do not vote, it might mean that a police commissioner could be recalled by obtaining signatures of only 15 percent of the voters in any district. One wonders who would take the job.

Considered in these terms, the proposal was obviously problematic. The interest it generated in Berkeley was more an expression of dissatisfaction with police policies and actions than a response to a careful study of its provisions. Part of the problem is that the Berkeley Police Department is judged against its own history. Some years ago, for instance, Albert Deutsch, in *The Trouble with Cops,* singled out Berkeley's Police Department as a model for the rest of the country to emulate. Even in those days, however, Berkeley was not the rest of the country. Under Chief August Vollmer, the Berkeley Police Department was able to recruit a force of well-educated young men who were trained to be polite and courteous. To one coming from the East, as Deutsch did, the Berkeley Police Department must really have seemed miraculous. There was only one hitch in the beautiful dream. At the time, Berkeley had little crime. It was a nice, respectable, white middle-class suburb and university town not at all comparable to New York or even Jersey City.

In 1974, Berkeley is still small, but it has a growing black population, a sizable concentration of itinerant street people, a politically active student body, a menacing drug problem, lots of political demonstrations, and a history of riots. Those supporting community control charge that police have been largely responsible for the riots, and there is some substance to their charge. Moreover, there is no doubt that Berkeley is not easily understood by the average white suburban cop, even if he should happen to hold a degree from a junior or state college. The philosophy of J. Edgar Hoover dominates the police departments of America, and Berkeley's cannot escape the dominant assumptions of contemporary law enforcement. Thus like every other police department, it has zealously guarded its complaint system against any civilian incursions. It is heavily engaged in preparing for counterinsurgency tactics and gets along quite well with other policing agencies—all while the crime rate rises. Without doubt, the views of the average Berkeley policeman do not represent the politics of a city that sent a black "radic-lib" to the U.S. Congress.

The proposal was defeated, but despite its defeat, it made an important statement about police and the community. It was a significant step in the direction of change, and the challenges it made to traditional police organization and control remain to be met.

ABA Standards for Criminal Justice
Relating to the Urban Police Function

AMERICAN BAR ASSOCIATION

INTERNAL PROCEDURES

In the view of the President's Commission on Law Enforcement and Administration of Justice, the best means for ensuring that personnel are complying with departmental policies and general notions of fairness is through effective internal police procedures:

> Internal discipline can be swifter and, because imposed by the officers' own superiors, more effective. If properly carried out, internal discipline can assure the public that the department's policies . . . are fully meant and enforced. This is particularly true when the department's own investigation discovers misconduct without any citizen complaint.
>
> Strong discipline shows the public that misconduct is merely the action of individ-

ual officers—the few who violate the rules in any organization—and not action which is customarily tolerated in the department.[1]

While recognizing this as an ideal, the Commission went on to find that internal controls and sanctions within most police departments were not effective. For example, the Commission found that: (1) internal investigations against individual or widespread misconduct are rarely effective on a continuous basis; (2) there is generally unwillingness among officers to complain about or testify as to the misconduct of other officers; (3) few departments have adequate procedures for receiving and investigating citizen complaints; (4) few departments have adequate hearing procedures or disciplinary policies which ensure fairness for all parties; and (5) most departments handle internal disciplinary matters in secrecy, thus creating community concern about whether complaints are handled fairly.[2]

There are other and possibly more serious deficiencies in internal police control procedures as well. The police rarely have written administrative policies and, therefore, lack clear standards by which to judge the practices of police officers. Most internal police regulations relate to matters of dress and bureaucratic formalities; few relate to norms governing the discretionary process of handling sensitive problems involved in peacekeeping and crime control.[3]

Police administrators are reluctant to articulate proper standards of police conduct which may be controversial among the rank and file and which may affect the outcome of criminal cases and potential civil and criminal actions against individual officers. Further, many police administrators are caught up in the bureaucratic requirements of civil service which restrict their right to discipline officers for misconduct.[4]

For these reasons, police administrators often abdicate their responsibilities for controlling their personnel, leaving this to the courts. Unfortunately, the courts are ill equipped to control police conduct. The need is for more effective administrative control.

EXTERNAL REVIEW

Civilian Review Boards

There are only a few ways, other than through the courts and internal procedures, in which attempts have been made to control police misconduct. Prominent among them—and most controversial—has been the civilian review board. Impetus for its creation came from a general feeling on the part of many members of the public, particularly the members of minority groups or inner-city residents, that they had no opportunities to have their complaints heard. Written documentation of police illegality,[5] as well as the visual documentation on television of the brutal treatment of civil rights demonstrators, brought to the surface problems which most Americans had never known existed.

The independent police review board, which seemed to many to provide a potential means of handling grievances and clearing the air of tensions between the police and the public, giving the public greater confidence in its police and the police a certain amount of protection from malicious and unfounded complaints,[6] never was able to achieve its purpose.[7]

Although the police themselves played a major role in defeating civilian review boards in many cities, inherent defects in the idea of the review board also contributed to its lack of success. Primary among these was the fact that the review board focused solely on the misdeeds of policemen while ignoring the potential for abuse of discretion and impact on minority groups of other administrative agencies: the welfare department, the board of education, the Immigration Service, among others. Second, the procedures for determining the truth of any complaint in order to protect the rights of both parties require many procedural safeguards. Informal settlements, used in Philadelphia,[8] avoid these problems (a typical settlement procedure might be a meeting of the complainant and the immediate superior of the officer involved, followed by an apology by the department or a withdrawal of the complaint by the citizen) and often result in an adjustment of the dispute which is quite satisfactory to the complainant. Yet many members of the community are not satisfied without a formal finding of guilt or innocence. Finally, the creation of civilian review boards tended to make police administrators defensive and often caused the administrator and his department to close ranks against the outside instead of taking aggressive action against obvious individual or pervasive abuses.

Investigation by Ad Hoc Groups

In the absence of an institutionalized system of civilian review, some communities have authorized investigative commissions on an ad hoc basis to respond to a particular incident of police-community tension or to charges of inefficiency, corruption, and illegality in the police department.[9] In some cases these are groups specially constituted for the investigation; in other instances, an existing group or a committee of the city council handles the study. In a few cases, as in the famous study of criminal justice in Cleveland,[10] outside experts are utilized. The disadvantages of such an approach to the continuing supervision of community policing policies are obvious. The investigation, in response to a large-scale controversy, must be carried on in an atmosphere of recrimination and defensiveness. It is necessarily focused on one primary cause of concern to the exclusion of other potential problems. Generally there is no follow-up on the recommendations over any period of time—in fact, the recommendations are usually forgotten, once the purpose of the study, which is to divert responsibility for the resolution of the conflict from those who do not wish to assume it, is achieved.

THE FAILURE OF EXISTING METHODS OF REVIEW AND CONTROL OF ACTIVITIES

Existing methods of review of and control over police conduct are inadequate. The reasons are numerous. Failure on the part of the courts and the public to understand the actual nature of police work or to acknowledge the amount of discretion exercised at the lowest levels of the department; failure to recognize the factors which influence change in any organization; and failure to appreciate the opportunities for abuse in the vagueness of the criminal statutes, so that what appears to be the legal nondiscretional enforcement of the law can be a tool for selective discrimination and harassment, are only a few of the obstacles in the path to an effective system of review and control.

There are other reasons as well. The search for one single, completely effective method, such as the exclusionary rule, is bound to fail. Experience in the regulation of administrative agencies generally indicates that there is no single method which will protect the rights of all citizens and ensure the commitment of all administrators to democratic principles and public service. There is need for the development of a variety of methods which are carefully designed to complement each other.

There has been a failure to think of the police department as an administrative agency with policy- and rule-making potential. This has meant that little attention has been paid to an analysis of an individual policeman's behavior in the context of departmental policy. Most of the controls have been in the form of sanctions against actions of a particular policeman, leaving departmental policies and practices unaffected.[11]

While sanctions against the illegal acts of individual policemen are important, they are of limited effectiveness in bringing about changes in attitudes or actions of the whole department. Nor do they even touch the problem of actions which are not illegal but may be unwise or improper under particular circumstances.

Because the police department is an administrative agency having multiple and complicated responsibilities, the problem of control is not easy. Making administrative agencies adequately responsive to proper standards remains a vexing problem for government, in spite of the amount of attention it has received.[12]

There are aspects of police work and police organization which make it particularly difficult to administer the kinds of external controls which have been tried on other agencies. First, there is a great amount of discretion exercised by the beat policeman in contrast to most agencies in which only the narrowest amount of discretion is exercised by the line workers. Second, most of a policeman's work is done out in the field and often in an adversary situation, which makes it particularly difficult to make controls work.[13]

It is evident that the policing of the police cannot be left entirely to the courts because judicial review cannot be sufficiently consistent nor can it influence the greater part of police work which never comes up for review in the courtroom. There is, thus, great need for strengthening the police administrator's contribution to the adequate guidance and control over police conduct.

Section 5.4 of the Task Force Report reads as follows:

> 5.4 Need for administrative sanctions and procedures.
>
> In order to strengthen administrative review and control, responsibility should formally be delegated to the police for developing comprehensive administrative policies and rules governing the duties and responsibilities of police officers together with procedures and sanctions for ensuring that these duties and responsibilities are met. Police administrative rules and procedures should establish effective investigative, hearing, and internal review procedures for alleged violations. Such procedures should include provisions for handling, monitoring, and reviewing citizen complaints in such a way as to ensure diligence, fairness, and public confidence. In developing such rules and procedures, rec-

ognition must be given to the need to conform procedures to administrative due process requirements, to develop means for ensuring impartial investigations, and to keep the public informed of all administrative actions as they are taken.

Section 5.4 deals with some approaches that can be taken to strengthen administrative review and control of police conduct. It is not possible to develop an effective system of accountability without strong internal procedures which provide a police administrator with appropriate controls over his personnel.[14] Although the exclusionary rule, criminal and civil actions against police officers, and other external remedies may well provide important additional checks, there is need for the police administrator to accept primary responsibility for controlling the vast discretionary power of police officers. Few police administrators have yet accepted this challenge, and this is the primary reason why there has been constant pressure for civilian review boards, ombudsmen, and other external review agencies. But police administrators cannot validly reject pressures for broadened external review without demonstrating their willingness to assume responsibility for ensuring that their personnel comply with the requirements of law and the needs of a democratic society:

> [T]he police administrator is typically ambivalent over the responsibility he has for controlling the activities of his force in the exercise of discretionary power in dealing with crime or potential crime situations. While he views the physical appearance of his men as his concern, he often sees the methods by which the law is enforced as involving matters which are the primary responsibility of others outside the police establishment. This deference may, in part, be attributable to the sharing of responsibilities with other agencies—particularly

the courts. Unlike internal matters over which the police administrator has complete control, much of what the police do relating to crime and criminals is dependent for approval upon the decisions of nonpolice agencies.

Strengthening of administrative control requires the creation of the same sense of personal responsibility on the part of the police administrator for the implementation of proper law enforcement policies as he presently has for implementing policies relating to internal matters.[15]

The mere adoption of administrative policies will not ensure compliance with them. This will require: (1) a commitment by the police administrator and his superior officers to the objectives and priorities set forth in the administrative policies and the development of training programs which concentrate considerable attention on the implementation of these policies; (2) the establishment of systems of accountability; (3) the designing of procedures for checking and reporting on performance; (4) the careful definition of appropriate and inappropriate conduct and penalties for inappropriate conduct; and (5) the establishment of effective investigative, hearing, and review procedures for alleged violations.[16]

All of these areas are of considerable importance, but the careful delineation of appropriate and inappropriate conduct and penalties for inappropriate conduct and the establishment of effective and fair procedures for handling alleged violations, particularly, require additional comment. The President's Commission on Law Enforcement and Administration of Justice found in its studies that there were gross deficiencies nationally in: (1) internal investigations relating to individual or widespread misconduct; (2) the investigation and processing of citizen complaints; (3) the procedures for hearing and

reviewing alleged violations; (4) the policies relating to disciplinary actions taken against officers guilty of misconduct; and (5) the procedures for publicizing whatever actions are taken.[17] The Task Force Report on the Police made several recommendations for improving such procedures:

1. Urban police departments should have an internal investigation unit responsible to the chief administrator. The unit should have both an investigative and preventive role in controlling actions by police officers.
2. Departments should make clear that they welcome complaints.
3. Departments should reassess their hearing procedures to determine whether they meet appropriate standards of fairness.
4. Departments should examine penalties to determine whether they are effective in deterring future misconduct and whether they are justified when the nature of the offense is considered.
5. The complainant should be notified of the decision and of the basis for it. And the public should have access to the facts of the case and the nature of the decision.
6. When an incident has raised tension in an area, it is desirable for the decision to be explained directly to the residents of the area through either the community relations unit, a neighborhood advisory meeting, or some other similar procedure.[18]

Whether these or other procedures are adopted,[19] every effort must be made by a police administrator to include provisions for handling, monitoring, and reviewing citizen complaints in a way which is thorough and which commands the respect of the community as being both careful and fair. This will be enormously difficult. There is considerable distrust of the police in many communities and particularly in our black ghettos. Historically, much of this distrust is warranted. Therefore, in order to establish that a new commitment is being made to ensure that internal procedures are fair and that complaints are diligently pursued, it may well be necessary to make substantial changes in existing procedures. These changes might include more openness in the complaint process, use of impartial citizens in investigation and adjudication, and better provisions for review of the disposition of complaints. Such involvement might reassure not only the public but the police administrator as well that impartial and fair actions will be taken.

In summary, the process of administrative rule-making and strong internal procedures hold the greatest promise of being the basis for effective review and control of police conduct.[20]

Section 5.5 of the Task Force Report deals with municipal tort liability:

> 5.5 Municipal tort liability.
>
> In order to strengthen the effectiveness of the tort remedy for improper police activities, municipal tort immunity, where it still exists, should be repealed, and municipalities should be fully liable for the actions of police officers who are acting within the scope of their employment as municipal employees.

Government liability for the misconduct of police officers acting within the scope of their employment is crucial if a tort remedy is to become a significant deterrent to police abuse:

> Government liability is important not only to provide financially responsible defendants but primarily so that the deterrent will be effective where it is needed—at the level where police policy is made. If cities are responsible for torts committed by officers who are known to be vicious and ill-tempered or dangerously insane or chronically alcoholic, the liability is likely to discourage the retention of such officers and compel a better police force. Most illegal arrests and searches probably arise within the scope of everyday police activity, a fact recognized by cities which allow the city attorney to defend officers sued for false imprisonment. Where the officer makes an illegal arrest under the orders of his superiors, while this may not excuse him, evidence of the fact will be admissible in mitigation of damages. However justifiable this may be as an act of justice to the defendant, it should be irrelevant to the plaintiff's cause of action and illustrates the desirability of enforcing the sanction at the policy-making level. Furthermore, some police illegality is an inevitable concomitant of law enforcement. The expense should be borne by the state, which can spread the loss where actual monetary damage results and which is in the position to control and minimize the risk.[21]

The doctrine of governmental immunity has been extensively modified in many states and almost completely abolished in several states in the last fifteen years by judicial decision.[22] There seems to be no reason why the abrogation of sovereign immunity should not be carried out by the courts.[23]

Governmental responsibility for the improper conduct of police will hopefully be a greater incentive for police administrators, mayors, and city councils to institute the kinds of policies and practices which will guard against tort liability.[24]

It is discouraging to note that, in some of the states which have abolished the doctrine, there are instances of backing away from full tort liability. In Wisconsin, for example, the legislature has enacted a provision excepting governmental units from liability for the intentional torts[25] of their employees. In New York, municipalities have been held not to be liable for their failure to act in situations where their duty runs, not to a particular person or group of persons, but to the general public.[26] Many jurisdictions retain governmental freedom from liability for "actions or decisions of a legislative, executive, or judicial character which are performed within the scope of authority of the governmental body." [27]

The District of Columbia has recently proposed legislation, with the support of the Metropolitan Police Department, which could lead to effective use of the tort remedy.[28] Chief Justice Warren Burger has suggested the creation of an administrative or quasi-judicial remedy against government to afford compensation and restitution for persons whose Fourth Amendment rights have been violated:

A simple structure would suffice. For example, Congress could enact a statute along the following lines:

(a) a waiver of sovereign immunity as to the illegal acts of law enforcement officials committed in the performance of assigned duties;

(b) the creation of a cause of action for damages sustained by any person aggrieved by conduct of governmental agents in violation of the Fourth Amendment or statutes regulating official conduct;

(c) the creation of a tribunal, quasi-judicial in nature or perhaps patterned after the United States Court of Claims, to adjudicate all claims under the statute;

(d) a provision that this statutory remedy is in lieu of the exclusion of evidence secured for use in criminal cases in violation of the Fourth Amendment; and

(e) a provision directing that no evidence, otherwise admissible, shall be excluded from any criminal proceeding because of violation of the Fourth Amendment.[29]

These and other proposals merit serious and immediate attention, since improvements in tort remedies offer considerable hope for achieving increased deterrence against police illegality.

In summary, the identification and implementation of effective systems of control will require considerable analysis and development.[30] But the need for further study should not be interpreted to mean further delay. The continuing failure to devise and implement necessary procedures and sanctions to deal with police abuses is one of the most critical problems now confronting our society. Thus, the highest priority must be given by the legal profession, state legislatures, the courts, police administrators, city officials, and the public to identifying and testing new and more effective approaches to control the use of police authority. Innovation and experimentation are clearly needed. To stimulate these, financial and research support should be provided to assist in the research, development, demonstration, and implementation of model systems of control over and sanctions against improper police activity.

NOTES

1 The President's Commission on Law Enforcement and Administration of Justice, *Task Force Report: The Police* (Washington, D.C.: U.S. Government Printing Office, 1967), pp. 193–194.

2 Ibid., pp. 193–197.

3 Egon Bittner, *The Functions of the Police in Modern Society* **42** (National Institute of Mental Health, Public Health Service Publication No. 2059, November 1970), p. 61. For

a striking example of this, examine the data in Cohen, The Police Internal Administration of Justice in New York City 39 (The New York City Rand Institute, November 1970).

4   Ibid., p. 133.

5   See, for example, Note, "Philadelphia Police and the Law of Arrest," *U. Pa. L. Rev.* **100** (1952): 1182.

6   See Burger, "Who Will Watch the Watchman?" *Am. U. L. Rev.* **14** (1964): 1.

7   See *Task Force Report: The Police*, 200–202. Philadelphia, one of only a few cities actually to establish a working independent review board, probably came closest to fulfilling the expectations of the proponents of review boards. See Note, "The Administration of Complaints by Civilians Against the Police," *Harv. L. Rev.* **77** (1964): 499; Comment, "Police–Philadephia's Police Advisory Board," *Vill. L. Rev.* **7** (1962): 656.

8   Comment, "Police–Philadephia's Police."

9   One recent example of this approach was the formation of the Commission to Investigate Alleged Police Corruption (the Knapp Commission) in April 1970 by Mayor John Lindsay in New York City. This commission was formed following the publication of charges in the *New York Times* of widespread police corruption and charges that high officials in the Lindsay Administration and the police department had not acted when informed of specific acts of corruption. See Burnham, "City Opens Study of Policing Police," *New York Times,* April 24, 1970, p. 1, col. 1.

10   F. Frankfurter and R. Pound, eds., *Criminal Justice in Cleveland* (1922).

11   This is also a product of course, of the doctrine of governmental immunity, but it could be argued that the doctrine might not have had such a long existence, in this field at least, if the courts had examined the extent of departmental condonation—or even approval—of the tortious acts of their officers which involve an abuse of police authority.

12   See, for example, W. Gellhorn, *When Americans Complain: Governmental Grievance Procedures* (1966).

13   For a more complete discussion of this point, see H. Goldstein, "Administrative Problems in Controlling the Exercise of Police Authority," *J. Crim. L., C. & P.S.* **58** (1967): 160.

14   *Task Force Report: The Police,* at 193.

15   Ibid., p. 29.

16   Ibid., pp. 29–30, 193–197.

17   Ibid., pp. 193–197.

18   Ibid.

19   For another example of proposed procedures, see Office of the Massachusetts Attorney General, Uniform Procedures Recommended for the Investigation and Disposition of Citizens' Complaints Concerning Police Officers in the Commonwealth of Massachusetts (April 1971).

20   Amsterdam, *The Supreme Court and the Rights of Suspects in Criminal Cases,* 45 N.Y.U.L. Rev. 785, 812 (1970), p. 83.

21   Foote, *Tort Remedies for Police Violations of Individual Rights,* 39 Minn. L. Rev. 493 (1955), pp. 514–515.

22   See, for example, *Hargrove* v. *Cocoa Beach,* 96 So.2d 130 (Fla. 1957); *Molitor* v. *Kaneland Community Unit District No. 302,* 18 Ill.2d 11, 163 N.E.2d 89 (1959); *McAndrew* v. *Mularchuk,* 33 N.J. 172, 162 A.2d 820 (1960); *Holytz* v. *City of Milwaukee,* 17 Wis.2d 26, 115 N.W.2d 618 (1962). (California and New York abolished sovereign immunity by legislation.)

23   "[T]he limitation on the normal operation of *respondeat superior* was originally placed there by the Judiciary. Surely it cannot be urged successfully that an outmoded, inequitable, and artificial curtailment of a general rule of action created by the judicial branch of the government cannot or should not be removed by its creator" (*McAndrew* v. *Mularchuk*).

24   "The responsibility of the master or principal for the negligent acts of a servant or agent, committed while performing his delegated tasks, has always existed in [New Jersey] as a matter of public policy. One basis for the doctrine is that it creates an incentive to be careful in the selection, instruction and supervision of such persons" (*McAndrew* v. *Mularchuk*).

25   *Strong* v. *City of Milwaukee,* 38 Wis.2d 564, 157 N.W.2d 619 (1968)—(including false imprisonment).

26   For example, *Motyka* v. *City of Amsterdam,* 15 N.Y.2d 134, 256 N.Y.S.2d 595, 204 N.E.2d 635 (1965); *Riss* v. *City of New York,* 22 N.Y.2d 579, 240 N.E.2d 860, 293 N.Y.S.2d 897 (1968).

27   *Williams* v. *City of Detroit,* 364 Mich. 231, 111 N.W.2d 1 (1961). Note that the same court held in *Sherbutte* v. *Marine City,* 374 Mich. 48, 130 N.W.2d 920 (1964), that the

action of a police officer in making an arrest could not be considered to be within the broad scope of discretionary activity enjoying immunity.

28 District of Columbia Law Enforcement Liability and Legal Assistance Act of 1971. Among other things, the bill provides for civil liability of a police officer not to exceed $500 compensatory damages and $1,000 punitive damages and District liability not to exceed $25,000 for wrongful death actions, $50,000 to any claimant in any other case, and $300,000 for any number of claims arising out of a single occurrence. Costs are allowed to a successful litigant and attorneys' fees are limited to 25 percent of a judgment. The Commissioner is authorized to settle cases provided an award not exceed $10,000, of which the police officer would be liable for the first $500 of such award and up to $1,000 in punitive damages. The police officer must consent to such award. Finally, judgments against the District or a police officer would constitute a complete bar to any further action by the claimant by reason of the same subject matter.

29 See dissenting opinion in *Bivens* v. *Six Unknown Named Agents of Federal Bureau of Narcotics,* 403 U.S. 388, 422–423 (1971).

30 For example, the American Law Institute is considering recommending a state certification procedure which gives certification only to those departments which develop effective procedures for ensuring compliance with proper police practices. See ALI, A Model Code of Pre-Arraignment Procedure, Sanctions and Means for Procuring Compliance with the Code (Discussion Memorandum, May 3, 1971). In addition, Professor Joseph Goldstein proposed that legislatures should create Policy Appraisal and Review Boards to facilitate coordination of municipal police policies with those of other key criminal law administrators and to constantly review how police discretion is being utilized. See J. Goldstein, "Police Discretion Not to Invoke the Criminal Process: Low-Visibility Decisions in the Administration of Justice," *Yale L.J.* **69** (1960): 543.

About the Editors

Jerome H. Skolnick is Chairman, Center for the Study of Law and Society, and Professor of Criminology, University of California, Berkeley. He has taught at Yale Law School, the University of Chicago, and the University of California, San Diego. He has also lectured to police groups throughout the country and consulted with various government commissions and agencies. Among his many books and articles is *Justice Without Trial: Law Enforcement in Democratic Society* (Wiley, 1966). In 1972 he received the August Vollmer Award of the American Society of Criminology "for distinguished research in Criminal Justice and Law Enforcement."

Thomas C. Gray is Associate Professor of Criminology at Golden Gate University, San Francisco. He was formerly Chairman of Law Enforcement Management at the University of Texas of the Permian Basin. For seven years he was a Deputy Sheriff in Los Angeles County. He holds a bachelor's degree from Pomona College, a master's degree from the School of Criminology, University of California, Berkeley, and is currently completing a study of police socialization for a Doctorate in Criminology. He has also been a consultant to several police departments in the area of recruitment, training, and management and has served as a liaison officer between the University of California, Berkeley, and police departments throughout California. He has taught Police Science to police officers and administrators and has lectured extensively before police academies and civic groups.